A Reader's Companion to Augustine's *Confessions*

Edited by
Kim Paffenroth
   and
Robert P. Kennedy

Westminster John Knox Press
LOUISVILLE • LONDON

Scripture quotations marked RSV are from the Revised Standard Version of the Bible, copyright © 1946, 1952, 1971, and 1973 by the Division of Christian Education of the National Council of the Churches of Christ in the U.S.A., and are used by permission.

Confessions (Oxford World Classics) by Saint Augustine, translated and edited by Henry Chadwick (1991). Reprinted by permission of Oxford University Press.

The Confessions of Saint Augustine (The Works of Saint Augustine: A Translation for the 21st Century), translated by Maria Boulding, O.S.B. (1997). Used with permission of New City Press.

Book design by Sharon Adams
Cover design by Pam Poll Graphic Design
Cover art: Ornate initial with Saint Augustine teaching. © *Archivo Iconografico, S.A./ CORBIS*

First edition
Published by Westminster John Knox Press
Louisville, Kentucky

This book is printed on acid-free paper that meets the American National Standards Institute Z39.48 standard. ∞

PRINTED IN THE UNITED STATES OF AMERICA

03 04 05 06 07 08 09 10 11 12—10 9 8 7 6 5 4 3 2 1

Library of Congress Cataloging-in-Publication Data

A reader's companion to Augustine's Confessions / Kim Paffenroth and Robert P. Kennedy, editors.—1st ed.
    p. cm.
   Includes bibliographical references and index.
   ISBN 0-664-22619-1 (alk. paper)
    1. Augustine, Saint, Bishop of Hippo. Confessiones.   I. Paffenroth, Kim, 1966–
   II. Kennedy, Robert Peter.

  BR65.A62 R42 2003
  270.2'092—dc21   2002193393

Dedicated to the memories of
Gloria Mae Paffenroth (1930–1980), Gregory George Willis (1966–1986),
Ella Kennedy Cormack (2001), and Alison Lidstad (1963–1999)

"But blessed is the man who loves you, and his friend
in you. . . . For he alone loses no dear one to whom
all are dear in him who is not lost." (Conf. 4.9.14)

Contents

Introduction

Kim Paffenroth and Robert P. Kennedy

Part of what makes Augustine's thoughts so fascinating and frustrating is that in every part of his *Confessions*, the reader is presented with another revelatory moment, another turning point in his life, in his thought, or in his depiction of them. How can one settle on just one reading of his greatest work? Or should one? It would seem that a sensitive and intelligent reader could reasonably argue that any one of the thirteen books of *Confessions* is, in fact, the interpretive key to the whole, in one of several possible senses. Perhaps a particular book presents a summary or epitome of the ideas expressed throughout the work, and the part reflects the whole; or perhaps one book presents ideas that are found nowhere else in the work, but which can be argued are the crucial ones for understanding it, in which case the part does not reflect the whole, but rather undercuts or exceeds it in some revealing way; perhaps one book is the turning point in the narrative, and the books that follow it turn in a direction different from those that precede it, and the part has determined the shape or path of the whole; or perhaps one book contains an exegetical key or lens—whether it is a concept or an image or a hermeneutics—with which or through which to read the other twelve books, and the part is the window or doorway to the whole. To have just one person present so many different readings of Augustine would be frustrating, perhaps even disingenuous, for it is part of the personal, affective, subjective dimension of Augustine that he affects each of us differently. A commentary written by one person therefore necessarily gives preeminence to one view, and makes the rest of the work subservient to that view: each of us finds the one jewel that fascinates us, and then makes everything else into a setting to accentuate that jewel's beauty. But our collection of thirteen essays by thirteen different readers instead presents thirteen jewels—each one beautiful and independent. We now have a useful and challenging introduction to Augustine's most famous work, as well as a unique contribution to scholarship on the *Confessions*. For both students and scholars, our volume shows the richness and ambiguity of Augustine's work, as well as the ambiguity and multiplicity of our thoughts on him. Rather than finding (or imposing) some overarching view on the thirteen individual books, we have let each individual book project its vision onto the whole. It is this variety and depth of insights into Augustine's thought that set this volume apart from other works on the *Confessions*, letting readers appreciate each individual book as an integral and integrating part of the whole.

Part of this multiplicity of interpretations of the books of the *Confessions* has to do with how one answers a fundamental but elusive question: Who was Augustine, *really?* The question is relevant and suggestive, even if one does not mean it historically or biographically, nor even as an inquiry into the author's intent, but merely as a probing of the author's effect on the reader. Augustine has filled a great many roles for his readers over the centuries, some of which he himself must have felt were distinguishable, if not in conflict. Saint, sinner, bishop, son, father, theologian, philosopher, Platonist, Christian, Manichee, rhetorician, autobiographer, polemicist, apologist, exegete, mystic, misogynist, ascetic, sensualist: Augustine was definitely several of these at any one time, and arguably all of them, and which of these one regards as the author of the *Confessions* would greatly influence how one reads the books individually or together. As we individually argue for the centrality of each book of the *Confessions*, we are implicitly arguing for the centrality of one particular role for Augustine, or for the centrality of one dimension of his personality, or one idea in his thought. Although this surely says much more about us than about Augustine, these arguments taken together should finally form a more accurate and nuanced picture of Augustine, as well as of his greatest work. Which of us would want to be known only as a spouse, or parent, or teacher, or North American, or Christian? Our lives and the meaning of our lives are finally composed of some rich and confusing combination of such elements. We are therefore not merely confused, but fortunate that Augustine left us a literary record of his own ambiguity and complexity as a person.

On the other hand, our multiple readings of the *Confessions* may not only be our own subjectivity, nor the multifaceted complexity of Augustine's own person, but differing interpretations of what is the most important part of a text. If it is the point at which the text finishes saying what it meant to say, and thereby reaches its goal (this is one of the definitions of priority given by Augustine in *Conf.* 12.29.40), then Book Thirteen is clearly the most important. But although the final hole in a golf match is the end and goal of the game, any of the previous holes may have been the most exciting part of the game, the real turning point, the really decisive moment that determined the end. But literary works are much more ambiguous than golf: to continue the sports analogy, they are more like boxing, which itself relies on judges to interpret what has happened in the ring in order to determine the winner, because most of the time it is not unambiguously clear at the end who exactly won, and even less so which of the hundreds of punches thrown was the decisive blow. It is with this sense of centrality or decisiveness that we each can begin to argue for the primary importance of each of the thirteen books, based on differing criteria of how each book affected or produced the outcome or meaning of the whole.

Beginning our investigation, Charles T. Mathewes alerts us to how Augustine is fully aware of the presumptuousness inherent in any attempt to write one's own life story. One may understand the *Confessions* as the story of Augustine growing in the knowledge of that presumptuousness, and as the story of Augustine finally surrendering his sinful desire to be his own author. Book One confronts this issue immediately, by exploring what may be called "the paradoxes of beginning"— paradoxes contained in the fact that one can never fully begin, though one is always begun. This realization is fundamentally retrospective: it is only by remembering in the right way—and avoiding remembering in the wrong ones— that we can come to inhabit our state as "being begun." This lesson is also the primordial form of grace. Therefore, Augustine's exploration of the paradoxes of beginning in Book One of the *Confessions* foreshadows the logic of grace in later books, and when properly understood as such, it casts a crucially illuminating light on them.

John C. Cavadini shows how in Book Two Augustine invokes the biblical narrative of the fall, by his use of imagery and allusion, to provide a coherent account of what is otherwise incoherent—the descent into sin and self-destruction. Just as this descent has no rationale or logic, and just as sin has no substance, Augustine's narrative would have no possibility of coherence—it could not be a narrative— without the coherence offered by the biblical narrative. From a complementary point of view, the biblical narrative is interpreted by Augustine's account of his adolescent sin, as we get an image of a culture so bent on seeking praise that it obliterates even a memory of the one who ought ultimately to be praised. We don't understand the biblical text, nor what it might mean to reject God, until we see as its reference the genesis of a culture bent on seeking praise at all costs, effacing the very memory of the Creator with the "drunkenness" of the world.

Todd Breyfogle next traces the progression from infantile and unruly bodily willfulness (Book One), and the social pressures of acceptance (Book Two), to the misplaced desire for intellectual goods in Book Three. In Book Three, Augustine struggles to find the permanence of truth, "in whom there is no changing nor shadow caused by any revolving" (*Conf.* 3.6.10). Partly, his struggle is a process of elimination: physical or aesthetic satisfaction, self-satisfaction, philosophy, and Manicheism are all tried and found wanting. It is also a matter of foreshadowing developments later in the work: suffering, friendship, creation, time, and eternity are all treated in Book Three in ways that dispose the reader to a more refined understanding of their subsequent developments. In contrast to what has gone before, Monica's dream that ends Book Three has its origin in truth. It is a reminder that providence sustains all things, and an invitation to join in the exultation of a truth that knows no shadows.

In his analysis of Book Four, James Wetzel shows how Augustine's grief is empty and self-entombing, a partner to fear and arrogance, and how its redemption lies in genuine mourning. Augustine will piously confess that no one dies in the true God, hence the friend's death in God offers the fullest consolation possible for the friend's death. But Augustine also comes to realize that the answer cannot be a merely intellectual acceptance of the idea of immortality, but rather a change of heart that still allows (even demands) real grief, at the same time as it makes both life and death hopeful and meaningful, not hateful and empty. To lose a loved one is both to lose life and to regain it, by losing a false sense of self-control and self-sufficiency in exchange for a real sense of one's dependency and trust of God.

In his essay on Book Five, Frederick J. Crosson analyzes the *Confessions* as a retrospective meditation on the way in which Augustine distanced himself from God and the way in which God drew him into the path of return. He discloses a carefully structured journey with its center in the fifth book, the middle of the narrative, "autobiographical" books of the *Confessions*. Although the dramatic climax of the path of return is the famous garden scene, Augustine, in looking back over the course of his life, discovers God's "merciful dealings" with him long before he became aware of them. Examining the text from this perspective, one discovers a number of artfully traced components that support such a reading, some of which clearly differentiate the first half (Books One to Five) from the second (Books Five to Nine), some of which form chiasmic series that converge on and diverge from Book Five. The increment in meaning that comes about through covert structure in the telling reflects the hidden dealings of God with the path of Augustine's life, and he writes the *Confessions* to give glory and thanks to God for such hidden dealings.

In his chapter, Eric Plumer examines Augustine's use of a variety of persons and events in Book Six to illustrate such central themes of the *Confessions* as faith and reason, grace and free will, concupiscence and original sin. Having seen through the pseudo-rationality of the Manichees, Augustine resolved to be more cautious thereafter in his search for truth, adopting a skeptical position. Thus, even though Ambrose's preaching dispelled many of his prejudices against Catholic biblical interpretation and enabled him to see how reasonable the Catholic faith was, Augustine would not commit himself to that faith unless he knew for certain that it was true. By contrast, Monica's simple faith gave her the power to reassure others, knowledge of the future, and a love that willingly yielded to authority. Unable to go further in his pursuit of truth, Augustine turned to goods within his grasp—honors, wealth, and marriage. But the closer he came to attaining them, the more unattractive they appeared, as their inability to bring true happiness became clearer. It is only when God used the manifestations of grace working in the lives of Monica, Ambrose, and Alypius as signs that Augustine was led back to the one true way of Jesus Christ.

In his analysis, Phillip Cary shows how Platonism is central to Augustine's thought, so that Book Seven is central to the *Confessions*, and perhaps to the whole of Augustine's career as well. From the other direction, he provides a reading that convincingly puts Book Seven at the center of the meaning of the *Confessions*, and therefore goes far toward putting Platonism at the center of Augustine's understanding of his own life. In both these ways, the philosophical issues resolved in Book Seven rise in importance and become the lens through which to see the rest of the *Confessions*, including the famous garden scene of Book Eight.

In his essay, Professor Emeritus Leo C. Ferrari describes how a long series of discoveries about the *Confessions*, spanning three dozen years and presented in over fifty articles, culminated in the proof that Augustine's account of his conversion through reading Romans 13:13–14 in the garden of Milan is fundamentally fictional in nature. The story of his research reveals how his scientific background enabled him to illuminate both specific incidents and important themes in the *Confessions*. These many years of patient labor in a spirit of scientific inquiry came to fruition in a conclusive proof that has, once and for all, settled decades of controversy over the conversion scene.

To allow Book Nine out of the shadow of the preceding book, Kim Paffenroth examines its rhetoric and psychology, rather than trying to see how it completes Augustine's "conversion." He shows how rhetorically the book provides the crucial turning point in Augustine's presentation of Scripture, philosophy, and time, determining the direction that the whole work takes in relation to these central concepts. Psychologically, Book Nine shows us the real climax of the book, with Augustine resolving all his interpersonal and intrapersonal issues, as he finally understands his relationships and his feelings in ways that are not painful or sinful, but life-giving and fulfilling.

In her essay, Pamela Bright examines both the role of Book Ten in the structuring of the *Confessions* as a whole, as well as the inner structuring of Book Ten itself. She provides an integration of the elements of Book Ten: the introduction in which Augustine elaborates his understanding of the ecclesial purpose of "confession"; his profound meditation on the God-seeking self in the visible world of creation and then through the labyrinth of memory and beyond; and, finally, the unflinching exploration of the depth of woundedness of the self. The paradox of strength and frailty is kept in creative tension throughout Book Ten, which concludes with a ringing confession of trust in the Divine Physician, a confession that sums up the narrative of the earlier books and points toward the reflection on creation and re-creation in the books that follow.

As we turn to the less popular books of *Confessions*, Robert P. Kennedy argues that the *Confessions* are an eschatological reappropriation of the self as created by God, redeemed in Christ, and led to fulfillment in heaven by the Spirit. Book Eleven is therefore the center of this project, as it is here that Augustine brings together the problem of his own intelligibility with the problem of the intelligibility of Scripture, refuting all attempts to bypass the literal meaning of the text and all attempts to reduce or remove the paradox of the eternal relating to the temporal. Because the paradoxes of creation and revelation are the same, in resolving the mystery of God's autobiography Augustine will find the way to make his own autobiography truthfully.

Thomas F. Martin, O.S.A., next shows how Book Twelve and its exploration of the task of biblical interpretation (exegesis) tie together the overall biblical project that is the *Confessions*. What Augustine has been practicing throughout the entire work now becomes an explicit consideration, and he has definite audiences in mind as he addresses the task of biblical interpretation. Equally he has in mind clear principles that are essential for a true and correct execution of this task. This essay and Book Twelve itself remind us that the *Confessions* are not ultimately about Augustine, they are about God and God's Word, Scripture.

Bringing us to the end as well as the beginning, Robert McMahon identifies the allegory of Genesis in Book Thirteen as the paradigm for the narrative process of the entire volume and each of its parts. The allegory as a whole embodies the fundamental Christian-Platonist pattern of "return to the origin," and this pattern also governs Books Ten through Twelve, as well as Books One through Nine. Working on several levels, the allegory parallels Augustine's autobiography, at the same time as it uncovers in Scripture a microcosm for all of creation and history. In it Augustine finally expresses in worship, prayer, and sacrifice the dialectical relation between sinful, temporal humanity and its redemptive, eternal God.

As one can see, our analyses are literary, philosophical, theological, historical, psychological, structural, and rhetorical, for the *Confessions* require at least this many analytical methods to begin to grasp their meaning and beauty. And we ourselves are Catholic and Protestant, female and male, old and young, liberal and conservative, for the *Confessions* speak powerfully to every human being and through every human experience. So let us turn now to the *Confessions* with new enthusiasm and humility, as the greatness of Augustine's mind has offered us a literary treasure so rich and complex that it has taken thirteen lesser minds just to begin to uncover some of its meanings to a new generation of readers. Reading over these essays has been truly rewarding to us as editors, enriching and complicating our understanding of Augustine. A further reward will be when these essays prompt more discussion, debate, exploration, and elaboration of Augustine's thought: thirteen readings of the *Confessions* might be an improvement over only one, but with a work of such towering importance and brilliance, they are still not nearly enough.

Finally, we have dedicated this volume to the memory of two family members and two friends who are, for the time being, lost to us. Though not scholars themselves, their love and goodness have often inspired our teaching and scholarship more than any of our fellow word-peddlers. Since their lives and deaths resemble some of the events in the *Confessions*, which describe the deaths of Augustine's mother, child, and friends, and since our volume is intended to make that work more understandable and relevant to nonscholars, we hope this dedication will not seem out of place.

Chapter 1

Book One: The Presumptuousness of Autobiography and the Paradoxes of Beginning

Charles T. Mathewes

INTRODUCTION

Certainly one of the most remarkable facts about human beings is the resilience of our desire, perhaps even our need, to portray our lives, to ourselves even more than to others, as telling an intelligible story. This fact is made even more remarkable when one considers the awesome stubbornness we exhibit in refusing to recognize the regularity and rapidity with which we change these stories: our lives are not so much written as *re*written, constantly, as if we were characters in a Kafka parable—poor, harried copyeditors coping with an endless stream of revisions faxed in by a distant and infinitely fickle author. Autobiography is *orienting*: it gives us a place to stand, a way of making sense of ourselves. Perhaps some such orientation is necessary. Yet the slipperiness of our narratives, their evanescence, bespeaks the obvious problem we face in being our own narrators—the problem, that is, of being always *in medias res*, in the middle of the journey. We are *disoriented*: we do not know "where we are" in the broadest sense—at what moment of what story we are in the midst of. Think about how you would have told the story of your life ten years ago, and compare that story to the one you would tell today; most likely the two stories differ quite dramatically. Perhaps we would be more honest in our self-narrating if we were to assemble the whole ensemble of our autobiographies—all the various retellings we have told—and offer that as our "true" autobiography: not a person, but a series of versions, drafts of a self. Our longing for an "absolute" description, a "final vocabulary" for our lives that we do not make so much as find, is vexed by the fact that our lives are deeply plastic. Yet we curiously rarely recognize, let alone reflect upon, this plasticity.[1]

This revisionist behavior reveals the presumptuousness of autobiography, and the fact that we refuse to recognize this revisionism confirms our acknowledgment that autobiography *is* presumptuous. The danger of presumption is the danger of "knowing already" what I will ultimately be; it refuses to be open to the transforming presence of God's grace. This presumptuousness is, in Christian terms, perhaps the deepest and most pernicious form of sin that we possess—or that possesses *us*.

Augustine knew this. He knew that we presume we are our own authors, because we presume that we are the root cause of ourselves, our own explanations, our own creators. His work on grace is in part an extended diagnosis of this pathology, and a prescription for its cure.[2] But he also, and famously, wrote the *Confessions*, which many take to be the first great autobiography. So this leaves us with a question: what is the point of Augustine's book? It has become a scholarly commonplace to state that the work is not an autobiography in any exegetically useful sense.[3] But this statement's very character as a commonplace may make us believe prematurely that we understand what it means, and what it is meant to resist. One of this essay's aims is to suggest that we do not in fact know, and that we cannot know until we escape the will-to-autobiography, which still has us enchanted.[4] Not only do our expectations of autobiography as a genre mislead us about Augustine's aims in the *Confessions*; they positively obstruct our apprehension of its purposes. Recognizing this suggests that the urge to autobiography is symptomatic of a deep problem—namely, our presumption of beginning. And it is precisely this problem, this presumption, that is Augustine's target throughout the work.

He takes as his task not so much to help us directly to escape from the tendency so to narrate ourselves (such a task would be Pelagian, presuming that what we lack is some *technique* and not, as is in fact the case, grace), but rather to tell a story that is ultimately legible only from the perspective of salvation, from the perspective of one whose understanding has been redeemed from the ceaselessly futile task of trying to tell one's own story. In doing so, he urges on the reader a reconsideration of not just the propriety, but the very possibility of imagining that one can tell one's story from within it. The *Confessions* is the story of a life, but it is a life still *in via*, and until death or (better and more appropriately) the eschatological consummation of that life, its meaning remains, for us and for Augustine, unknown. The work is not in fact merely *not* autobiographical, it is properly speaking *anti*-autobiographical. Yet this, Augustine seems to be saying, is what any true "autobiography" should be: it is the story of a life from the inside, and from the inside, our lives are not yet narratable.

The aim of this anti-autobiography is pedagogical and psychological: it wants not directly to reshape our dispositions (it has no hope that a text alone can do that; such is the work of God alone), but rather to vex our comprehension until those dispositions begin to be reshaped. Rather than seeking to comprehend our lives better, Augustine hopes his readers will more appropriately *fail* to comprehend them; and insofar as one fails to fail to comprehend in the right way, one is blocked from understanding the deep character of what the *Confessions* is all about. This is a crucial exegetical fact about the *Confessions*, though one rarely noticed.

What do I mean by this? I mean that Augustine wants us to see our lives as much less intelligible than we usually think they are, both positively and negatively. Negatively, we are to come to see the absolute unintelligibility of our sinful lives *as* sinful: we must unlearn the false explanations we give of our corruption, and we must come to be shocked that we are as corrupted, as messed up, as we are—and we must come to be humbled and mournful about it. Positively, we should be bewildered by the sheer gratuitousness of our bare existence, by cultivating our recognition of our inability to explain our existence as "merited" by anything else: we must unlearn the false explanations of our existence, the stories we tell ourselves about how we got to be the way we are, and see our lives instead as a great gift to us, wholly unmerited by anything we have or could have done—and we must come to wonder in gratitude at the sheer gift of our existence. In undertaking this quest for greater self-understanding, we discover that instead we gain a deepened *in*comprehension of our lives.

Two things follow from this. First, in terms of genre, the *Confessions* may be the least apologetic text Augustine ever wrote, despite all those who try to read their way to faith through it; it is not meant for those outside of the church, but for those inside, to help them in their quest to become more fully Christians. Second, we can properly read the *Confessions* only if we fully accept the eschatological dimensions of human understanding; we must accept that our "beginnings" will only be comprehensible (insofar as they will be comprehensible) from the perspective of the end, and that therefore much more of our lives as currently lived must seem to us to be mysterious. Our lives are not our own, and not yet even fully given to us; we will be given to ourselves only eschatologically.

How does the work help us to see ourselves in this way? It suggests that we begin to reconceive our lives not so much as self-starting, but as "being begun," and begun by another—namely, God. The crucial move in the *Confessions*, as I said above, is to resist our presumption that we are our own beginnings. One may understand the work as the story of Augustine growing in the knowledge of that presumptuousness, and as the story of Augustine finally surrendering his sinful desire to be his own author. It is by trying to *be* "the beginning" that we sin; such is the lesson of the fall of the rebel angels. We must learn to see our lives, and the actions that constitute them, as reducible, without remainder, to response.

The *Confessions* is a series of deconstructions of our presumption of self-starting, and its disruption of our presumption of beginning begins just where you might think it will—in the beginning, in Book One. Book One immediately and profoundly explores this central theme by exploring the paradoxes of beginning, paradoxes contained in the fact that one can never fully begin, though one is always begun. By doing this it aims to encourage wonder and gratitude at God's grace in our lives, and repentance and bewilderment for the obvious incoherence of our deeds, in reflecting on the course of our lives. And this reflection is fundamentally retrospective: it is only by remembering in the right way, and avoiding remembering in the wrong ones, that we can come to inhabit our state as not so much beginning, but as creatures that have been begun by God. This inhabitation, and the recognition that enacts it, is *a*, and perhaps *the*, primordial form of grace. As such, Book One's exploration of the paradoxes of beginning foreshadows the logic of grace in later books, and when properly understood casts a crucially illuminating light on them.

The narrative flow of the book itself mirrors this argument. Augustine first undoes a series of apparent beginnings that we presume are under our control, showing that they all rely on the prior reality of God. Then he begins to explore the kind of "beginning" we in fact have, in the many false beginnings that define our sinful condition as seeking autonomy from God. In conclusion, I suggest that, through responding to the recognitions Augustine urges on us, we learn why the book is named the *Confessions*, and we glimpse what it would be to confess our gratitude for God's gifts to us and our mystified shock at what we have, in sin, done with them.

THE BEGINNING OF SELF

Augustine's most famous works are in a way about the opposite of what their titles may at first suggest. His *De civitate Dei* (*City of God*) spends a great deal of its time—all of the first ten books and fully half of the last twelve—talking about the *civitas terrena* (earthly city). His *De Trinitate* is dedicated to understanding the Trinity, to be sure, but its matter is more focused on theological anthropology than on philosophical theology. In a way that any academic can admire, the key for Augustine seems to have been the fundamental importance of getting your initial bearings rightly set; the solution to any project seems to be in the preparatory prolegomena.

A similar truth is to be found in Augustine's explorations of the self in the *Confessions*. We expect this work to be concerned with Augustine's life. But it turns out that the details of Augustine's life seem surprisingly replaced in the book by meditative reflections on the nature and providential plan of God. Think about how the book begins:

> Great are you, Lord, and exceedingly worthy of praise; your power is immense, and your wisdom is beyond reckoning. And so we humans, who are a due part of your creation, long to praise you—we who carry our mortality about with us, carry the evidence of our sin and with it the proof that you thwart the proud. Yet these humans, as a due part of your creation, do still long to praise you. You arouse us so that praising you may bring us joy, for you have made us for yourself, and our heart is unquiet until it rests in you. (1.1.1)[5]

As beginnings go, this is fascinating on several levels, for it begins by allowing another to go first, in at least three senses. First, it begins not with its own words, but with a citation of another work, the Psalms (specifically Ps. 48:1). Second, it begins not in Augustine's own voice, but in that of another—namely, David. Third and finally, it is not speaking of the self, but of someone else—namely,

God. In three ways, our assumptions about autobiography's egocentric *incipit*—our expectations of "what autobiographies are like"—are subverted. Something quite different is going on here.

What is going on is Augustine's exploration of what vexes our presumptuous claims to self-sufficiency—the always-prior presence of God. Insofar as Augustine investigates the mystery of the self, he finds the key to that mystery to be God. We can see this even on the surface of the text. What is fundamental in this opening, in the remainder of Book One, and in all the following books, is the absolute priority of God in all matters. God *is*, "before" the world begins; hence God is not so much temporally prior as prior to temporality. Yet God is not just prior in temporal terms, God equally possesses a "spatial" priority, prior to space itself, creating the conditions for space and all the objects therein. Indeed they would not exist were it not for God's constant preservation of them: "The vessels which are full of you do not lend you stability, because even if they break you will not be split. And when you pour yourself out over us, you do not lie there spilt but raise us up; you are not scattered, but gather us together" (1.3.3). God cannot be somewhere except as God is everywhere, and God cannot be contained, but God contains: "Are you not everywhere in your whole being, while there is nothing whatever that can hold you entirely?" (1.3.3). Here is the Augustinian critique of ontotheology: in trying to speak of God discretely, we find that we have no frame to use as a "backdrop" against which to "foreground" God. God is always "behind" and supporting every horizon "against" which we can imagine placing God.

The upshot of this, for Augustine, should be that our first words about ourselves—the first words of any confession we utter—should be words of thanks to our proper beginning, God. In coming to understand ourselves, we must understand that we are always secondary, an effect of God's gratuitous love. Here is one way that the work will be autobiographical: properly speaking, theology precedes autobiography, and the first word of theology is gratitude for God's grace. So Augustine's first task, in beginning to tell the story of his life, is to teach his readers to see his life (and by analogy their own) as gifted gratuitously by God. He wants to show us our true beginning so as to show us whom to praise.

The Beginning of Thinking

God is prior even to our thinking of God; indeed, God frames our thinking, by providing the categories for cognizing any reality at all. This is the epistemological implication that Augustine draws from God's absolute immanence and transcendence. People today mouth these words, but act in a way that suggests a failure to understand them. Our usual "folk" understanding of thinking goes something like this: we "think" by constructing a picture in our mind (which is conceived as something like an "inner space" accessible only to the self), and then we try to hold that image "up against" the "outer" world (how this imposition works is left vague). That is, thinking moves from inside to outside, from "subjective" to "objective." This is in no way a recently developed picture of the mind; its origins go back four centuries, to Descartes and Locke. And it has shaped the way we read the *Confessions* too, to the extent that many people think of Augustine as most basically exploring human subjectivity and interiority in a quasi-Cartesian way.[6]

Yet it is not actually the position that Augustine propounds; indeed his position is quite radically opposed to this vision, and he wastes no time in showing us this. The mind does not construct mental representations and then attempt to *paste* them onto reality; that would raise the question of how the mind could get the "sideways-on" view of the mind's attempt at pasting, to judge whether or not there is a good fit. Yet he does not think that the mind cannot know reality, or that such knowing does not rely implicitly on God; far from it. For him, the mind is "always already" in dialogue with reality; minds are created *subjoined* to creation.[7] Our minds are made to know the world; that's what we have minds for, in a sense. Furthermore, it is only *through* God that we can know anything at all. (I leave aside the tricky question of whether our knowledge is properly God's knowledge, or whether it is properly and in a way autonomously our own.) Ontology itself is organized in a conceptual structure borrowed from God's nature as triune: "From you derives all modes of being, O God most perfectly formed, who gives all things their form and ordains their order" (1.7.12).[8] The trio of barely subterranean concepts giving structure to this thought—*modus, species* (here, *forma*), and *ordo*—is famously the basic structuring field for reality as a whole; and it is also intimately bound up with God's nature as Triune. One cannot help but rely on God in knowing anything at all.

Yet this reliance on God does not mean that in our comprehensions of reality, however partial, we are also, even partially, comprehending God's own being. Our minds are unable to comprehend God, for as creator, God transcends all the possible categories of created being. Yet God's transcendence of them is not a transcendence that escapes any conceptualization in such categories, so that the categories return "unopened to the sender" (that is, us), as W. H. Auden once put it.[9] It is not that the categories fail to have any positive relation to God, but rather they fail fully to contain or comprehend God. God overflows them all, exceeds their capacity to capture reality, and indeed does so in a way that we may exhibit, by straining the capacity of language to make sense. At least, this is Augustine's belief in a passage that James O'Donnell argues presses language "beyond its own extremes":[10]

> You are most high, excellent, most powerful, omnipotent, supremely mer-
> ciful and supremely just, most hidden yet intimately present, infinitely
> beautiful and infinitely strong, steadfast yet elusive, unchanging yourself
> though you control the change in all things, never new, never old, renew-
> ing all things yet wearing down the proud though they know it not; ever
> active, ever at rest, gathering while knowing no need, supporting and filling
> and guarding, creating and nurturing and perfecting, seeking although you
> lack nothing. You love without frenzy, you are jealous yet secure, you regret
> without sadness, you grow angry yet remain tranquil, you alter your works
> but never your plan; you take back what you find although you never lost

it; you are never in need yet you rejoice in your gains, never avaricious yet you demand profits. You allow us to pay you more than you demand, and so you become our debtor, yet which of us possesses anything that does not already belong to you? You owe us nothing, yet you pay your debts; you write off our debts to you, yet you lose nothing thereby. (1.4.4)

This is a complex and richly contradictory set of ascriptions; and Augustine immediately follows this paragraph by saying, "After saying all that, what have we said?" (1.4.4). While we have said much, any attempt to summarize it will fail. Yet Augustine has *shown* something quite profound: when applied to God, metaphysical categories such as these cannot capture God. But it is not that they break down, reflecting merely our inability to gain any understanding of God: they *all* apply, supremely so. God does not so much foil our understanding as infinitely "gift" it, as if we were trying to drink from a fire hose. God's "transcendence" is not so much a negative transcendence, as a positive one. Divinity frames the mind, enables it to know, indeed, enables its very being.

Ironically enough, for Augustine it is precisely our failure to comprehend God that is the instigating spark for our reflection at all. For we come to think about thinking, by coming to think about thinking about God—or rather, by coming to realize that we have no idea of what it would mean to think about God in any adequate way, and by exploring the implications of our inability to comprehend God. And this realization of our failure to comprehend God arises when we reflect on our failure to find any language of praise that could do justice to God. As James O'Donnell says, inquiry arises "from a moment of unfulfilled intention," the intention to "praise" God: for "humans . . . do long to praise you" (1.1.1).[11] This reveals something important about thinking, a lesson Martin Heidegger retaught us in the twentieth century: intentional mental deliberation is itself parasitic on the breakdown of our ordinary comportment in the world— our ordinary maneuvering through the world's obstacles. Theory only "breaks out" when our usual, taken-for-granted ways of behaving are blocked, or our continuing involvement in them creates pressures to which it is impossible not to attend. But Augustine goes beyond Heidegger in suggesting that what we learn, theologically speaking, is our own failure to think theologically at all—the inability of the mind to conceive God.[12] We learn that thinking cannot encompass God by seeing how God always exceeds our understanding; we realize the futility of our attempts at comprehension only once we have confronted our perplexing inability to praise God. We do not gain any knowledge by this deliberation; in fact what we come to understand is our own failure to understand, our own inability to comprehend.

But *what* is it, strictly speaking, that we fail to comprehend? It is the priority of God's presence to all attempts at human understanding. We seek to invoke God, to ask God to illuminate our understanding; yet this very invocation suggests we already know what we seek. "But who calls on you who does not know you?" (1.1.1).[13] The mystery of God is that God is always already there before us, inspiring and framing and illuminating our questioning. The full extent of our inability to comprehend God, and the alternative routes for realizing a kind of ascetic and redemptive understanding of God, is pursued elsewhere, most notably in Augustine's *De Trinitate*. Yet it is essential to the project of the *Confessions* that "the mind's road to God" be a road that is not paved with propositions. Augustine's realization of this ends up being a crucial moment in the story of his conversion; and it has its first inklings here in Book One, in his "mature" (authorially mature, anyway) sense of the mind's failure to know God. Here he exhibits the proper mode of inquiry: not an attempt to *grasp* God, but rather a beseeching of God to *be grasped* by God, to be taken "out of oneself" and given some understanding of one's place in God's providential plan. Thus Augustine's attempt to understand is framed as a request for a gift from God: "Grant me to know and understand, Lord" (1.1.1). This sort of understanding is not finally that of a spectator, aiming to paint a picture which we can admire. (Here the metaphors of vision, especially the "vision of God," can misdirect our thinking about Augustine's picture of seeking knowledge of God.) It is an understanding of one's place in a larger drama, of one's role in the "script" of salvation.

Nonetheless, despite the fact that God's existence transcends our comprehension, we are yet called upon to praise God, to form thoughts in language that seeks, however feebly, to honor God for all the good works God prepares for us to walk in. We do this not because God in any way needs our praise, but because our lives' delight is found in praising God. We are created to rest in God, of course; but such "rest" takes the form of ecstatic and endless praise. Hence for Augustine a strict skeptical silence is not an option: "Yet woe betide those who fail to speak, while the chatterboxes go on saying nothing" (1.4.4). Furthermore, it is not only impossible *not* to speak, it is also *pointless* to seek to avoid it; any such desire to avoid speaking would seem to be based on the idea that it is pointless to speak about God without some possibility, however idealized, to praise God's being adequately. But this assumes some criterion of adequacy for speech, and any such criterion would presume that there is *some* way in which human speech, and human thought, could "do justice" to God, could adequately represent divinity, could enframe God's reality. No such enframing is possible, because God is the final frame that enframes all. We cannot "do justice" to the transcendent standard of all justice. And, as we will see next, our capacities for speech put us in no better position either.

The Beginning of Language

If God is the beginning of reflection, it may yet make sense to think that we might still be the ones who begin language, who begin the attempt to give the distinctly human form of speech to reality. And like his reputed Cartesianism as regards deliberation, Augustine has been commonly read as supporting this program. Most famously, Ludwig Wittgenstein believed something like this was Augustine's position. Indeed, he inaugurated his epoch-making *Philosophical Investigations* by citing Augustine in Book One on language. Here is the passage:

It was not that older people taught me by offering me words by way of formal instruction. . . . No, I taught myself, using the mind you gave me, O my God, because I was unable to express the thoughts of my heart by cries and inarticulate sounds and gestures in such a way as to gain what I wanted or make my entire meaning clear to everyone as I wished; so I grasped at words with my memory; when people called an object by some name, and while saying the word pointed to that thing, I watched and remembered that they used that sound when they wanted to indicate that thing. Their intention was clear, for they used bodily gestures, those natural words which are common to all races. . . . In this way I gradually built up a collection of words, observing them as they were used in their proper places in different sentences and hearing them frequently. I came to understand which things they signified, and by schooling my own mouth to utter them I declared my wishes by using the same signs. Thus I learned to express my needs to the people among whom I lived, and they made their wishes known to me; and I waded deeper into the stormy world of human life. (1.8.13)

While he admires Augustine immensely, Wittgenstein takes his account of language as representative of a common, comprehensive, and disastrously and radically wrong picture of language learning in particular, and more generally of what it is to be a human with a mind in the world. Wittgenstein takes this as a classic account of language learning as based fundamentally in ostensive definition, in the explicit identification of single objects and then attaching names to them. This picture, he believes, compels us to picture our minds as working to "represent" reality in some sort of neutral, pictorial way. His complaint about this is simple: "Augustine describes the learning of human language as if the child came into a strange country and did not understand the language of the country; that is, as if it already had a language, only not this one."[14] Wittgenstein's larger project is basically an attempt to help us escape this picture, not so much to put another in its place, but to make us rethink the value of such "picturings" altogether.

It is immaterial for our purposes to determine whether Wittgenstein is correct that such a picture is grounded on a deep philosophical misunderstanding of the human condition (though I believe that he is). But what is important to note here is that, were Augustine to hold the position Wittgenstein imputes to him, it would seriously subvert my argument. It would suggest that, far from resisting our desire to see ourselves as self-starting, *ex nihilo* creators, we should imagine ourselves entering the realm of language in an entirely voluntary, self-conscious, and intentional way, by *naming* things. (Think of Adam and the animals in Genesis; but even today the act of naming—a child, a yacht—has the air of sovereignty about it.) Had Augustine accepted such a picture of language, it would not bode well for the plausibility of my thesis.

Yet Wittgenstein is in fact wrong about Augustine's theory of language, and in fact Augustine's actual account of language agrees with Wittgenstein that the "naming" account of language is radically flawed philosophically, and theologically as well. As Wittgenstein's larger corpus is explored (particularly his work on rule following), and as his thought's anti-Cartesian impact on contemporary thinking (particularly contemporary thinking on Augustine) grows, his view seems less and less distant from that of Augustine. Indeed, they seem to share a basic appreciation for the way that language is not neutrally representational, but is an instrument we employ for our (diverse) purposes.[15] Where they differ, perhaps, is on the flexibility of the "purposes" people can have: Wittgenstein believes human nature, and human desires, can be quite dramatically mutable, while Augustine insists that human nature is significantly less plastic, and in some way inescapably goal oriented. But this divergence does not immediately apply to their technical accounts of language acquisition and language use, which are, in fact, interestingly similar.

Their similarity resides most basically in their mutual dismissal of the idea that humans begin with minds "fully furnished" with prelinguistic thought, and use language only as an outward expression of what is there naturally and necessarily "inside" their minds—that the mental thought patterns are the "basic code" and the concrete human languages are the various "superficial user-interface codes." In fact for Augustine, humans learn language through authority and love—through the need fundamentally to *accept* what is given as proper speech in a prereflective, prevoluntary way. Yet this authority is not tyrannically *imposed* on the infants; they actually seek it out, driven forward by the love of others and the craving for their love. (This underlies Augustine's criticism of the Platonic doctrine of *anamnesis* or "recollection" as well.) Examples of this riddle Augustine's discussion of language learning. He says he learned Latin simply "by paying attention, without any fear or pain at all, amid the cuddles of my nurses, and teasing, and playful, happy laughter" (1.14.23). In contrast, his study of Greek, motivated not by the needs and urgings of love, but rather by the fears of being beaten and shamed in front of his peers, never "caught" his mind; it was always cryptography, not language-speaking, a difficult and painful labor.

Like our reflection, language—even our capacity for language—is given to us. We accept what language is given to us, and only later come to see it as our own. Language is not its own autonomous sphere of human fabrication; it is no more our own, no more a consequence of some originating action on our part, than is the love that inaugurates it. Love is our greatest teacher, the true grammarian. Hence language is value-laden for Augustine from the beginning, and our learning of language is driven by our desires, not by our decision to name a world that we already, prelinguistically, fully cognize. We learn to speak, that is, out of the love which drives us. And love is not started by us; when we love, we are more basically responding to aspects of the world than bestowing value on the world *ex nihilo*. Love—that which is most intimate to us, what is most deeply ours—is not simply our own. It comes from beyond us, and reaches out before us, perforating the boundaries of self, or showing us that we have always been in part outside those boundaries, showing us, indeed, that the whole idea of rigorous "boundaries" of inner and outer, self and other, need rethinking. This is why our first word of confession must be God, and the first mode must be thanks.

Yet the confession of praise is only part of confession; there is also the confession of sin. This is where *we*, as disastrously "independent" actors, come in.

BEGINNING OF ACTION AND HABIT

If we are not our own beginning in terms of our thinking, or our speaking, perhaps we still are our own beginning in our deeds. This seems a safe assumption, doesn't it? Yet Augustine will dissent from this claim also. We may be the efficient cause of our wills, but this says nothing about the final or formal or material cause. Indeed we are formed into who we are—into the creatures with the particular desires we possess (or that possess us) and the particular life plans we affirm—in large part by others. This is precisely the way that Augustine makes sense here of the idea of original sin—an idea that sounds horrendous to many people today. For him, original sin simply points to the fact that we are corrupted by inheritance before we even have a chance to decide for ourselves whether we want to be corrupted. And by the time that we can choose, "after" we have been corrupted by our inheritance, we invariably are misoriented toward choosing the bad. Just as we discover that we must confess our thanks and praise to God for our ability to think and speak, we discover that we must confess our bewilderment and shame before God at what we have done with the gifts God has given us. Hence Book One is not just praise; it begins the "double confession" of our helplessness and God's grandeur that will occupy the remainder of the work. Along with training us to see our lives as graceful gifts, it teaches us to be bewildered at our sins.

Beginning in Infancy: The Mystery of Original Sin

Augustine can show infants to be prevoluntarily corrupted, and hence ruined before they have begun, relatively easily. Infants are not fundamentally their own creatures, but are shaped profoundly by those who have care over them. Indeed, Augustine would not be surprised at contemporary child psychology's emphasis on the severely underdeveloped character of infants at birth—their need of being surrounded by mature humans who will bring them into the human community, the absence of which, such psychologists believe studies of "feral children" show, will leave the human who that infant grows to be forever stunted, quite possibly trapped in a prelinguistic, mentally underdeveloped condition. Augustine would go even further. He thinks that infants are *already begun*—first by being created by God with the capacity to will and love (if we want ultimately to distinguish those two), and only then by being submerged, almost drowned, in the sinful habit of society's customs.

This gets us, of course, to Augustine's scandalous (to many of us, at any rate) doctrine of original sin. As he says, "the only innocent feature in babies is the weakness of their frames; the minds of infants are far from innocent" (1.7.11). This claim can sound shocking to many people today; how, after all, could Augustine speak so harshly of those cute little sweeties? Sure, they may get a little rambunctious now and then, but the poor dears can't help it. Their diaper is soiled or they need a nap or they're just confused. But positively malicious? No way.

Here we see the charge of a harsh, puritanical moralism that is so commonly attributed to Augustine: he didn't even like babies!

In truth, Augustine's view is more humane than the one just expressed, for it connects infants' condition with our attitudes toward more physically mature human beings. We mistake his position as suggesting that we treat babies the same way we treat criminals—with the rack and flame, with harsh and pitiless punishment. But he is arguing just the opposite: we ought to treat adult criminals more along the lines of how we treat infants—protecting others from their depredations, watching assiduously for their misdeeds, correcting them (in love) when they do ill. Adults are just larger children, and their sins are intelligible as expansions of childhood cruelties: "First it is offenses against pedagogues and teachers, or cheating over nuts and balls and sparrows; then later it is crimes against prefects and kings, and fraud in gold and estates and slaves, just as a schoolboy's canings are succeeded by heavier punishments" (1.19.30). (In his *Antimemoires*, André Malraux reports a conversation he had with an aged priest about what the priest had learned in his lifetime of hearing confessions; the priest replied, "One thing: there are no grownups." One imagines Augustine would agree.)[16] His humanity toward adult criminals (even Donatist terrorists) was real and effective, and his merciful behavior toward them is entirely of a piece with his vision of infant sin. We may accuse Augustine of a deep paternalism, but we cannot accuse him of lacking mercy.

Yet we should see that, for Augustine, even this paternalism is not his own, but rather God's. Adults are like small children, but Augustine includes himself in that category too. (Much of what was embarrassing about Book Ten to other late antique men, such as Pelagius, was the humiliations Augustine candidly confessed. Yet their scandal at such humiliations, as well as our titillations at them, both have their root in our failure to see what Augustine is trying to do from the beginning of the work.) Just because there are no exceptions, this paternalism is actually part of God's mercy: we are all subject to the same paternalism, just as we are all subject to original sin, and yet God seeks our redemption from our sin. This renders any attempt on the part of humans to judge one another both preposterous and hypocritical: to presume to be able to judge (let alone to presume to *want* to do it) bespeaks a fundamental failure to recognize one's own status "before the law," under the steady, condemning gaze of divine righteousness. Augustine's well-known distaste for his judicial obligations—as bishop of Hippo he often spent long wearying days listening to court cases—is not simply caused by his sense of valuable time squandered: there was, for Augustine, something impious in putting before a human court matters that are properly the affair of God alone. Augustine certainly did not flinch from such duties—he saw the meting out of justice as in a way the acme of social life in this world—yet he undertook them with a fear and trembling to which we should pay more attention than we typically do.[17] Augustine's recognition of original sin's profundity and universality is simply one more part of his insistence that God is sovereign, and that grace has the final word. It is a device to short-circuit another form of our presumptuousness of beginning, our presumption that we can speak from a position of anything like innocence.

Boyhood: Teaching and Habits

Paternalism shapes Augustine's view of human society quite dramatically, as is shown in his meditations on his post-infancy childhood. For him, our childhood is no more a matter of our self-will than is our infancy; indeed we suffer both in the same basic way, as different stages in the onflowing flood of time. As he says, it was not that he entered into childhood from infancy, but rather that the one ended and the other fell upon him, as if he were swamped in a flood: "My boyhood caught me and followed upon my infancy" (1.8.13). In childhood, our illusion of *ex nihilo* agency is wildly buffeted by the wills and whims of our elders. Most importantly, we are taught, both formally and informally, to become full participants in the "game" of human society. What is crucial here is the dynamic of habituation: we are habituated into a world of illusions, we play games and so learn to play "an uglier game later in life" (1.9.15). The language of "game" is crucial here too, for it suggests the fundamentally *unserious* character of most human life, what Pascal described as *divertissements* (diversions)—its essential pettiness and ability to distract us from attending to what matters, such as the health of our soul.

This teaching was not only many-headed, it was also importantly at odds with itself. Hypocrisy reigned supreme. Yet in another way the deep message of this education seemed fundamentally consonant with what he learned in the schoolyard and in the street, and so Augustine's depiction of school serves as a synecdoche of society as a whole. Most of his education came not explicitly, in schoolrooms, but on the playground and at home: forming cliques, taunting others out of fear that one will be taunted if one does not get the first hit in, watching mom and dad squabble, watching them be obsequious to some people and cruelly haughty to others. Training in school is fundamentally no better: most teaching was managed by violence and brutality, seemingly capricious beatings meted out for the slightest infraction. Yet the informal lessons—of domination and mastery—legitimated resisting the strictures of the formal ones. For the final content of his lessons was too often about trickery, and so they "seemed to invest the disgraceful deeds of human beings with an aura of divinity, so that depraved actions should be reckoned depraved no longer, since anyone who behaved so could pretend to be imitating not debauched humans but the gods above" (1.16.25). Cheating seems to be fine so long as one does not get caught. Augustine wasted himself on these things, and now deems them "all so much smoke and wind" (1.17.27). What strikes Augustine as most astonishing was the insane superficiality of this pedagogy, in which young boys were taught to hold to linguistic conventions fanatically, while ignoring "the eternal rules directed to unending salvation" (1.18.29). The consequences were, quite predictably, the deformation of Augustine's whole life, step-by-step:

I did not love you, and breaking my troth I stayed away from you. Even in this fornication the approval of people all around me rang in my ears: "Fine! Well done!" To pander to this world is to fornicate against you, but so loudly do they shout "Well done!" that one feels ashamed to fall short of their expectations. For these things I did not weep, yet I wept for Dido, "slain as she sought her last end by the sword." (1.13.21)[18]

Hence Augustine cannot claim to have begun his life as a series of events, either; he found himself thrown into an ongoing stream of life, and he was trained to live in that stream—to treat it as the truth about the world—by his elders and his peers, and finally by himself.

In light of this, we might perhaps be tempted here to suggest that, while we do not begin ourselves, our elders do; and hence perhaps our capacity to begin is simply indirect, our capacity for self-starting deferred from ourselves to our children, so that they are more fabrications of our will than we ourselves are. (Many parents act as if they think so.) But Augustine will have none of it; our children are no more objects of our making than anything else. This is most profoundly so in Augustine in terms of the dynamics of education—the very dynamics that suggested a way to imagine ourselves as having determinate power. But the truth is, for him, that we do not ultimately possess the power to "teach," if by teaching we mean the power to cram bits of information, or styles of thought, into the minds of other, presumably younger, humans. There is a gap between our "teaching" and students' actual learning that can never be traversed by human intention. As Stanley Cavell has argued, what we must realize about language acquisition—and what Wittgenstein's discussions of learning to follow rules tries to get us to see—is how much more infants *learn* than adults could ever *teach*.[19] Most basically, children are not taught by our intentions at all, but rather they are initiated by our love. It is love that drives teaching and learning. Yet while we recognize this insight sporadically, it fails to infect our typical systematic thinking about education in any significant way. We recognize on an empirical level what we fail to make room for on a theoretical level.

Yet despite Augustine's deemphasis on the teacher imparting his wisdom to his students, he also (and notoriously, for many) emphasizes the importance of authority for teaching and learning, and here again he is quite insightful, and strategically clever. Many people affirmed the importance of authorities in education. Indeed the study of pedagogy in the ancient world was little more than the legitimation of "authorities," whether in fleshly or bibliographic form. But Augustine cannily understood the fundamental way that this vision of authority, with its apparent confidence in the controlling hand of the master, was subverted by God's providence. Much of his discussion of his own education, especially in his justification of the right use of authority, takes place in a context where the education is doing things to the students that they do not fully comprehend, and, what's more surprising, planting seeds that the teachers cannot control. (Think of the later example of Alypius being warned away from the games by an offhand remark of Augustine's, an event that Augustine did not intend to apply to Alypius [6.7.12].)[20] This tells us something important about the real importance of authority, even though humans themselves only exercise it indirectly and "on loan" from God: authority is legitimate *only* on theological grounds, because sin disorders human society and human individuals, and because human authority is ultimately grounded on divine authority (1.12.19). Most basically, God exploits the opportunities offered by education to equip people to be redeemed from the very practices in which that education is immersing them. (Again, evil's status as essentially parasitic on God's goodwill means that it simply cannot win, that it is finally futile.) So just as education is used as a synecdoche for society in general, God's use of our miseducation comes to symbolize the divine providential governance of all reality, and it provides the paradigm for how we should inherit our own pasts.

The right response to our immersion in sin, Augustine suggests, is not the Manichean response of attempted renunciation (a response whose attractions, and ultimate inadequacy, are addressed later in the *Confessions*), but instead a response that attempts to use by converting—or better, *re*converting or *de*converting from sin, really—our misshapen instruments. Let me use the skills I learned as a child to serve you, he begs (1.15.24). But how is such use possible?

This moves us to the edge of the discussion of grace that occupies so much of the later books, and which we may happily defer here. Suffice it to say that the general story of Augustine's "autobiographical" recountings in Book One is the story of a victimization in which the victim participated. Most basically, Augustine is lured away from one love, the love of God (*amor Dei*), by another, the love of the world (*amor mundi*): "I was swept off helplessly after profitless things and borne away from you, my God" (1.18.28). And when he could, he cooperated fully in this folly, and so came to merit the incoherence and anarchy that inhabited his soul. The effect of this folly is disastrous: by seeking what is not already ours, we end in misery (1.20.31). The story of our lives, that is, is the story of sin. Augustine takes the story of the prodigal son as the deep structure of our fall away from God, though he allegorizes the distance between fallen humans and God in psychological terms, as a distance in loves: "to be estranged in a spirit of lust, and lost in its darkness, that is what it means to be far away from your face" (1.18.28).[21] Yet the capacity to tell the story is itself a kind of achievement, or rather, a foreshadowing, of his redemption; it is in our recognition of our sin, our slowly dawning realization that our lives are fundamentally insane, that we first begin to see the workings of God's grace.

CONCLUSION

If Book One recounts the failure properly to begin, and the failure rightly to tell the story of our lives, it is nonetheless a work of hope. While the story of Augustine's "start" in life is a story of growing chaos, and while he deems it unintelligible in the present, it will ultimately be intelligible at the eschaton. In telling us this story, he is suggesting that we come to see his life, and by analogy our own, as unintelligible by today's lights. And here is another way in which the work turns out to be profoundly anti-autobiographical, for insofar as autobiography presumes to tell *the* story of a life, Augustine offers us a story that dismantles a life's apparent though false intelligibility and replaces it with a constant practice of austere longing for an eschatological intelligibility.

The cure for presumption—the way we learn this practice of longing—is not, unsurprisingly, any sort of labor: "Not with our feet or by traversing great distances do we journey away from you or find our way back" (1.18.28). What we need is what is *already given* to us; the cure is grace. Indeed, insofar as *Confessions* is a book about grace (far more than it is about sin), its essence is contained, *in nuce*, in Book One. For grace is a pattern in our lives that, for Augustine, we directly and immediately know only very rarely, if ever. Grace is almost always retrospective. And yet if our very beginning is itself retrospective—if we cannot witness but only retrospect our origins—then our beginning is itself the primal grace. For what do we have that we have not received? Perhaps the deepest recognition of grace is that which sees its limitlessness, its endlessness and its beginninglessness in our lives—or rather, its function as the only end and beginning we have.

This goes back to the idea of autobiography discussed at the beginning of this essay. Autobiography is orienting, but it is flawed (in Augustine's eyes) by being fundamentally *self*-orienting; it describes us in ways that we finally impose on the chaos of our lives. This is why autobiography is fundamentally untrue to our lived experience, deemphasizing some things and actually forgetting others. Augustine's aim is to make this sort of spurious life story unintelligible to us, and hence to make us seek our orientation through another person's actions, God's providential governance, and through another time than the present, in the final eschatological revelation of the significance of history.

Hence we should be prepared, by the end of Book One, to "comprehend" our lives as in a crucial way ultimately *in*comprehensible, finally unintelligible. Augustine's general aim in the *Confessions* is to help us be prepared to relearn ourselves, and yet, and by doing so, truly to know our lives for the first time. Yet this is a curious "knowledge," composed mostly of the resolute *un*knowing of certain fables human society tells itself. It means living in a mode of openness to the future, a mode based fundamentally not on an attempt to make something of the future—to impose our will on it—but instead to accept what it will be, to receive it as a gift. This is first and foremost an affective change: as Augustine puts it later in the *Retractationes*, the *Confessions* were meant to "arouse the human mind and affections toward [God]. . . . they had this effect on me in my writing of them, and still do when I read them now" (*Retract.* 2.6.32).

Yet this affective change must have cognitive dimensions. If the confession of our lives is only really possible eschatologically, still the confession of God's grace can begin now, for every moment is equally a sacrament of God's love. Hence even though we cannot say anything yet about ourselves with full confidence, we have a "foretaste" (though that's too weak a word) of what we will one day enjoy in fullness, the gift of being itself. We can begin at least, then, to praise God in full sincerity (though not in full understanding of what we are doing), and join with Augustine both in the first line of Book One—"Great thou art, Lord, and exceedingly worthy of praise"—and in the last as well—"that I exist is your gift" (1.20.31).[22]

Chapter 2

Book Two: Augustine's Book of Shadows

John C. Cavadini

INTRODUCTION

What is Book Two about? As with many things in the *Confessions*, it depends on how you look at it. The *Confessions* is one of those texts whose beauties emerge gradually to the person willing to read and reread over time, to one who is willing, too, to see its various facets from different perspectives. Sometimes, if you are looking in just the right direction, one facet glimmers out and seems to illuminate all of the others, and it is a source of further enjoyment and understanding to share these discoveries with others.

Book Two contains, among other things, Augustine's depiction of his being carried away by the currents of youthful libido, some reminiscences of his father and mother, and the long, seemingly overscrupulous examination of conscience on the theft of pears he committed as a youth with a gang of other boys. Book Two is therefore one of the more "infamous" books in the eyes of the interpreters of Augustine, not so much for the content itself, but for the proportion, or lack thereof, that the book seems to exhibit between its content and the rhetoric used to describe it. This is the book most likely to be cited for evidence of Augustine's propensity to overstatement, adducing for example his extravagance in obsession over an adolescent prank,[1] or his habit of indulging the luxurious language of sexual excess without, it is suspected, very much of actual excess to show for it.[2] He seems to say as much himself.[3] Book Two is also, therefore, one of the prime loci for commentators who would deflate the rhetoric into the plainer terms of a more commonplace narrative readily seen, by the trained observer, to underlie the overstatement. For example, Augustine reserves some of his choicest words of filial contempt for his father to this book, while he treats Monica at one point as a virtual oracle, and this has proved irresistible to those looking for indications of the oedipal narrative as the underlying story.[4] The melodramatic language of overflowing

25

and of uncontrolled flux seems to others to mask little more than the narrowly male narrative of loss of control over seminal emissions.[5] Perhaps, on the other hand, the prominence of the allusions to the Catiline conspiracy shows that the underlying story is one of social transgression, of acting against the established social order in turning to sexual excess instead of marriage.[6]

Another, more promising way of looking at Book Two comes from scholars who would see in it the narrative of Augustine's fall into "concupiscence of the flesh," the first of the three sins given in a catalogue at 1 John 2:14 (the others being "concupiscence of the eyes" and *ambitio saeculi*, the vain ambition of the world).[7] Book Two begins the pattern of Augustine's declension through each of these three sins, one per book through Book Four, followed by a chiasmus of healing in Books Six through Eight in reverse order. The narrative of the fall in Genesis 2, mediated to the text through the allusive story of the theft of pears, stands as the master narrative of the fall into sexual concupiscence. Surely this reading of Book Two as the story of Augustine's fall into concupiscence of the flesh is correct, and yet this reading is far from rendering the rhetoric of Augustine invulnerable to the narrative-narrowing strategies mentioned above, especially if concupiscence of the flesh is taken as a kind of absolute. For one thing, as already noted, it still seems extravagantly overstated. Concupiscence of the flesh, if it stands on its own terms, seems unable to sustain the claims of the great magnitude of iniquity with which the lavish rhetoric of this book is weighted. If concupiscence of the flesh qua concupiscence of the flesh is the main reference of Book Two's lament, such that it is the literal referent of all the narratives in the book (including the theft of pears as a kind of parable for the fall into concupiscence of the flesh, and even the Genesis narrative of the fall as mainly a story of the fall into this sin), then the text is still vulnerable to the strategies of reduction mentioned above, because the interpreter will always want to know what is at the bottom of the seemingly exaggerated (both to antique and to modern ears) worry over the universal experience of adolescent turbulence.[8]

THE EMPTY SELF

A different tactic would be to try to find the story that, rather than being the one "underlying" the rhetoric, would be instead one larger than the rhetoric, as it were, something to which it can only point, but not in the end fully describe. After all, as a trained rhetor, Augustine had a good sense of how to match style with audience and subject.[9] Along these lines let us begin our search with an image, programmatically and strategically placed in the very last words of the book, the image of the self reduced to a *regio egestatis*, a land of want or lack, a land of famine or of emptiness. Perhaps it is the saddest confession in the whole work: "I had made of myself a land of empty lack."[10] Book Two is pervaded not only by fulsome rhetoric, but by sadness, the sadness of someone who has "emptied himself" not in the way Christ did, but in the sense of evacuating oneself of oneself in exchange for precisely nothing, of simply canceling the gift of selfhood in favor of nothing.[11] It is the sadness, or even pity,[12] for someone who has haplessly, if culpably, paid out his whole self to purchase nothing, and now has no leverage to get it back. The book is suffused with the sadness of the Prodigal at the moment he came to realize the extent and folly of his waste of his inheritance and his father's love,[13] and, in Augustine's case, the waste of his own precious self and of the love that had given it to him in the first place.

This sadness is therefore present in the text as evoked by an act of memory. Book Two begins with the words *Recordari volo,* "I want to call to mind," and so sets its sadness in a particular rhetorical structure, not as the memory of how he felt as he was experiencing lust, but of the memory of that time from the perspective of the one who realized finally what was happening and was accepted back in love. It is the sadness of narration created in the memory of someone who had squandered the joy of having a self, having learned to love emptiness instead, and contrasted with the joy of receiving oneself back only "late,"[14] and only as a complete gift out of the "ruin" or "want" he had made of it. It is the act of memory, pervading the narrative with a sadness that was not present at the time itself, that forms the poles of the rhetoric of this book, charging it with emotion and generating all of the striking rhetorical paradoxes of the book: "There was a time . . . when I was afire to take my fill of hell" (*Conf.* 2.1.1, *exarsi enim aliquando satiari inferis*); "I was in love with my own ruin" (*Conf.* 2.4.9, *amavi perire*). The rhetorical paradoxes arising out of the sadness of memory give expression to the larger rhetorical or narrative problem of Book Two. It is, in a way, a major rhetorical problem of the whole of the *Confessions*, namely, how do you give an account of something for which there is no accounting? Putting together the first and last phrases of the book demonstrates the problem: "I would like to call to mind" (*Conf.* 2.1.1) how "I made myself into an empty land of want" (*Conf.* 2.10.18). But how can you construct a narrative of the passage into incoherence, something the very essence of which is irrational, so that to try to account for it would be, in effect, to push it past its own inherent unintelligibility, to make it accessible to thought and reflection? The rhetorical paradoxes say it all: How can I account for my burning desire for the hellish? For my love of my own perishing? Apart from the paradoxes that evoke the problem, any attempt to reduce what they represent to narrative logic will have caused the incoherence to be lost in the coherence of the narrative. The narrative will have been narrowed to a "logical" account.

Why does Augustine tell his story? Not so much for God, but for fellow members of the human race, "So that I and whoever reads this might think together about how deep is that depth from which we cry to you."[15] It is the description or evocation of that depth, the depth from which the psalmist cries, that Augustine hopes to accomplish with his narration. But here is the narrative problem, once again. In order to render that depth, he has to collect himself from it: "recalling my most wicked ways (*recolens vias meas nequissimas*) and thinking over the past with bitterness . . . I will try now to give a coherent account of my disintegrated self (*conligens me a dispersione*), for when I turned away from you . . . and pursued a multitude of things, I went to pieces (*dum ab imo te aversus in multa evanui*)" (*Conf.* 2.1.1). The *conligens* here cannot refer to his actual reconstitution from dispersal, since that was God's doing and has already happened. Rather, the participle is parallel to *recolens*, so the "collecting" is to be done in the recalling, the remembering, the narrating: it is the narrative problem of "collecting" a self which has "disappeared" or "evaporated" (*evanui*) into incoherence. How can one remember or "re-cultivate" where there is only a void of dissipation, a wasteland, in a sense no subject to have a memory of, a scorched earth rendered sterile? The memory of such a depth of dereliction is the sadness or, as it is put more strongly in this passage, the "bitterness" (*amaritudo*) that pervades this book.

The key to Augustine's resolution of this problem is to see how in Book Two the fall into concupiscence of the flesh is, surely, to be taken literally, but not merely literally. Augustine's "unquiet adolescence" (*Conf.* 2.3.6) becomes the interpretation or presence of the "unquiet heart" (*Conf.* 1.1.1), the heart that has not rested in God but promiscuously tried to rest everywhere else instead. Augustine's illicit love affairs are described in a way that presents a veritable feast of restless motion: "I was tossed to and fro, I poured myself out, was made to flow away in all directions and boiled off" (*Conf.* 2.2.2; my translation). The result of this restless motion is expressed later in terms that keep with the metaphor of flowing and boiling: *evanui,* "I evaporated [into the nothingness of dispersion]."[16] Augustine's fornications are, though real fornications, precisely, as such, figures of the underlying evaporation and dispersal of the self. As literal fornications, they are themselves representations, they are *res* ("things, realities") that are *signa* ("signs"), to use the language of the contemporaneous *Christian Instruction,* Book Two. The very indeterminate character of the references to the sexual sins, far from serving a purpose of empty "titillation,"[17] serves to keep the language open rather than closed. It keeps the sin described open enough to mediate a sense of the spiritual state it reflects, the state of the wasting away of the self with all its beauty (*contabuit species mea*) in the pursuit of "shadowy loves." Here the very phrase *umbrosis amoribus* ("shadowy loves," *Conf.* 2.1.1, my translation) is just determinate enough to refer to furtive physical trysts, but indeterminate enough to make those trysts themselves stand for the deeper, darker loves, the sterile seed of which they are but the useless fruit.[18] As Augustine explains, "A soul that turns away from you therefore lapses into fornication when it seeks apart from you what it can never find in pure and limpid form except by returning to you."[19] Fornication itself is a kind of figure here for abandoning God, who is pictured as a Lover in whose embraces we find ourselves and can take joy in ourselves as God's.[20] Augustine in this sentence gives us the literary key to the book, effortlessly, since this use of the word *fornicatio* is common in his oeuvre.[21] The *umbra,* "shadows," of the "shadowy loves" are identified here, too: "Behold! Here is that servant who, fleeing from his Lord, went to hide in the shadows!"[22] unmistakably a reference to Adam, who fled from the Lord after his sin (Gen. 3:8, 10). But the only shadows Adam could find was the darkness of his sin itself, that pride (*superbia*) barely named in the narrative,[23] but evoked as the "shadowy similitude of omnipotence," the nowhere and nothing of perverse independence from God that is the only refuge of the dissipated, disfigured self, lost in its bitterness: *O monstrum vitae et mortis profunditas!* "What a parody of life in death's deep!" (*Conf.* 2.6.14; my translation). More than any other in the *Confessions*, Book Two is the Book of Shadows, of insubstantiality, of emptiness, of want.

THE PEAR TREE: EMPTY COMPANIONSHIP

This mention of the servant who fled from his Lord occurs in the middle of Augustine's recounting of his theft of pears with a gang of other youths,[24] and its presence there is enough to tie the story conclusively to the narrative of the fall in Genesis 3, if the parallels of forbidden fruit and the plucking of it were not already enough. What is the function of this evocation of the biblical narrative? It is nothing less than the solution of the narrative problem of Book Two. It is this narrative, in itself opaque in its declaration of a mystery, that renders all the other narratives of evil transparent, makes them windows to a deeper narrative, the one of the fall of Adam and Eve. Its opacity is the fruitful opacity characteristic of all authoritative biblical narrative for Augustine. The Bible in its simplicity, as Augustine will explain later, blunts the pride of the would-be interpreter and his or her easy assumptions that the divine letters will carry no more than the rhetorical products of the schools would. Scripture is a thing "veiled in mysteries," opaque to the proud whose sight cannot penetrate its interior parts or inner meaning, while for the humble these very narratives, as it were, grow up with them.[25] In Book Two, therefore, the allusion to the Genesis narrative of the fall does anything but return the narrative to the level of literal fornication (as though the story of the fall were simply itself a story of a fall into *concupiscentia carnis* ["concupiscence of the flesh"]). Instead, the presence of the Genesis narrative in the tale of the theft of pears and so in the surrounding story of Augustine's fall into *concupiscentia carnis,* serves to make these other narratives a conduit into the master narrative, which itself remains opaque, irreducibly veiled with mystery. All the other narratives become windows onto this mystery, partake of its irreducibility in the very process of becoming transparent to it. Augustine's physical fornication, as an image (and instance) of the fornication of the soul dissipating itself into the embrace of everything and anything besides its true, divine Lover, becomes a symbol of the irreducibly mysterious evil of fleeing from the Creator to hide in a self independent of the Creator, a self that evaporates in that very fleeing.

The story of the pear theft, linked as it is to the story in Genesis, is an especially clear instance of a narrative window onto the primal scene of the fall narrative, a particularly powerful evocation of the mystery at the heart of the fall narrative. Augustine will go on later to exegete the fall narrative without the aid of a parable drawn from his own life. In *City of God*, Book Fourteen, he tells the story of how Adam and Eve's sin, though merely the plucking of a fruit, was so heinous because there was no possible particular motivation for it. They had absolutely everything they wanted there—food, comfort, companionship, even sex if they had desired it—nor was there anything in Eden to provoke fear. Their sin was therefore a fully deliberate act of pride.[26] And, although Augustine only elaborates on this text in this way years after the writing of the *Confessions*, the pear tree story is meant to serve in the same way as this more discursive later exegesis. Augustine's rhetoric builds up the significance of the story of the pear theft precisely by emphasizing the trivial and motiveless character of the theft itself. The rhetorical minimization of the deed itself is a way of telling us that the story points beyond its own letter, almost erasing the letter of the story itself in favor of the Genesis narrative of the fall. That is another way of saying that it serves as a commentary or an exegesis of the Genesis narrative.

So, for example, as Augustine tries to analyze his motivation for the theft, he finds nothing in particular that could have motivated him. Like Adam and Eve in the garden, he was under no compulsion of need or lack, but lived in the midst of abundance, at least as far as pears were concerned: "I was under no compulsion of need. . . . I already had plenty of what I stole, and of much better quality too, and I had no desire to enjoy it when I resolved to steal it. . . . We took enormous quantities, not to feast on ourselves but perhaps to throw to the pigs. . . . We derived pleasure from the deed simply because it was forbidden" (*Conf.* 2.4.9). Augustine's rhetoric drives relentlessly toward the conclusion that there was no reason for him to have committed this act, as he goes over the kinds of specific motivations that usually prompt one to sin (*Conf.* 2.5.10): "Even Catiline did not love his criminal acts for their own sake, but only the advantages he had in view when committing them" (*Conf.* 2.6.12). Here we have come right to the deep, or in this case, more emphatically, "the depths of the abyss" (*Conf.* 2.4.9), from which we cry to God, "Look upon my heart, O God, look upon this heart of mine, on which you took pity in its abysmal depths (*in imo abyssi*). Enable my heart to tell you now what it was seeking in this action which made me bad for no reason, in which there was no motive for my malice except malice" (*Conf.* 2.4.9). This malice is irreducible to any further account, or accounting for it: "The malice was loathsome, and I loved it. I was in love with my own ruin, in love with decay: not with the thing for which I was falling into decay but with decay itself" (*Conf.* 2.4.9). How to explain this without explaining it away? It must be linked to the biblical narrative, which presents this mystery (of loving one's own decay) in an authoritative fashion and so ratifies its opacity, its irreducibility to any further narrative except as an exegesis of the Genesis text. The story of the pear tree, as a kind of window onto the biblical scene, must be taken finally as just such an exegesis. There is simply no accounting for such an irrational act except insofar as it can serve to illustrate the biblical narrative.[27]

Augustine peers closer and closer at his sin in an examination that, as already indicated, has seemed obsessive for such a trivial incident, but it is just its triviality that Augustine belabors: "What did I love in you, O my theft, what did I love in you, the nocturnal crime of my sixteenth year? There was nothing beautiful about you, for you were nothing but a theft. Are you really anything at all, for me to be speaking to you like this?" (*Conf.* 2.6.12). Augustine reiterates that he did not want the pears themselves: "I had plenty of better ones, and I plucked them only for the sake of stealing, for once picked I threw them away. I feasted on the sin, nothing else, and that I relished and enjoyed" (*Conf.* 2.6.12). He remarks that his theft did not even have the "sham, shadowy beauty with which even vice allures us" (*Conf.* 2.6.12), and he gives examples of these (*Conf.* 2.6.13). Augustine's relentless rhetorical examination makes the story of the sin efface its own "letter." The sin is rhetorically constructed into a direct window, unobstructed by the particularities of wants and desires, onto the essence of sin itself. But since there is in fact no essence to sin, it cannot be represented except by referral to the authoritative narrative that preserves the original sin in all its mysterious and irreducible emptiness. Not even the story of Catiline, oddly enough, can stand in as an adequate account of evil in its "essence," for Catiline was, after all, seeking money and power (*Conf.* 2.5.11). The story of the Catiline conspiracy may rank in Roman imagination as an archetypal tale of evil, but for Augustine the obvious and finally pedestrian nature of Catiline's motivation precludes one from seeing past it to a more profound, staggeringly abysmal depth. It must yield to the biblical account as the archetypal narrative of evil.

After considering all of the alternatives, Augustine comes to the short section, *Conf.* 2.6.14, from which we have already taken many passages, and which is in a way the key to the whole of Book Two. Here the governing themes of fornication, of turning away from God in the quest for a self-subsistent existence without God, the consequent lapse into the insubstantiality of shadow and death, and allusion to the Genesis text all come together. Every soul that commits fornication, turning away from its Creator and Lover to set itself up against him and apart from him, thereby tries to replace God, that is, "perversely imitates" God. But such a soul only achieves a "crippled liberty," which if it has any agency at all has it only in shadows, in darkness, furtively, like a thief. It is the liberty of a "prisoner" (*Conf.* 2.6.14). Augustine's theft is an image of Adam's fleeing the Lord because it demythologizes the attempt to replace the Omnipotent. Far from looking like something glorious, something terrifically evil like Catiline, or like a grandiose mythical rebellion such as that of Zeus against Kronos, the best image of pure or archetypal evil is something so unpoetic as an adolescent prank carried out in the dark whose uttermost success resulted "at best" (*vel, Conf.* 2.4.9) in a few more satisfied pigs. At bottom evil is unglamorous and irrational, the seeking out and enjoying of a radical constriction of the self, leaving the warmth of a lover's close embrace for the insubstantiality of a shadow. Why? "How like that servant of yours who fled from his Lord and hid in the shadows!" (*Conf.* 2.6.14). Here Augustine brings us rhetorically to the edge of the abyss out of which we cry to God in a passage we have already quoted once: *O putredo, O monstrum vitae et mortis profunditas!* "What rottenness! What a misshapen life! Rather a hideous pit of death!" (*Conf.* 2.6.14). And he got us here through a literary exegesis of the narrative in Genesis that presents the irreducible mystery of someone who did what was wrong simply because it was wrong.

In its poignant statement of gratitude to God, the next section (*Conf.* 2.7.15) serves to evoke this abyss in a different way, more explicitly from the perspective of having been rescued from it. Augustine asks God what he could repay God for being able to recall all of these things without fear.[28] "Without fear" because God forgave the sins and so there is no penalty, but also perhaps because he can call these things to mind without fear that he is slipping back into the abyss. He is clinging to God in the very confession of God's mercy and grace, which not only forgave him his past sins, but gave him the power to refrain from the sins he did not commit: "For what deed is there I could not do, I who loved a gratuitous, unprofitable crime?"[29] To remember the crime is to remember the abyss of the self which loved a crime without reason. To look on that abyss without fear is to have freedom in clinging to God in the act of confession: *ut amem te,* "let me love you," Augustine had told God at the outset. In this love, there is no fear of the fornication of the soul, the fornication of even the physically chaste soul, which would ascribe its bodily chastity to itself, and not to God, so that it might "love God less."[30] Such a soul, though physically chaste, is at the edge of the abyss, desperately trying to love God less as it ascribes more to its own power. We are all this close to the abyss, perhaps *especially* in our chastity; and yet, in acknowledging this closeness and God's mercy in keeping us from falling in, we have in this very vulnerability and dependence (even though it may seem like insubstantiality) the solid freedom of God's creatures when they cling to him in love. It is in this paragraph, it seems, where the confession of God's mercy is at once a memory of the joy of being rescued in the nick of time (*O tardum gaudium meum!* "O my joy, how long I took to find you!" *Conf.* 2.2.2), and a self-awareness of how we all still hover at the verge of self-destruction. This is made the most poignant moment in Book Two by the fact that this self-destruction is the irrational love of death instead of a Lover's embrace, in the awareness that we have absolutely nothing to repay God for all of this love and mercy, no leverage over God whatsoever, not even our virtues.

The book ends, though, with a return to the recollection of the theft of pears. Augustine reemphasizes that he received no benefit, no "fruit" literally or metaphorically, no "enjoyment" or "gratification" from his theft, but only more unhappiness.[31] Yet, as Augustine goes on to point out, he (like Adam)[32] would not have done it alone. This final pass over the inscrutable does resolve the love involved, irrational as it may have been, one degree of magnitude further. Augustine says he loved the *consortium,* the fellowship of those with whom he committed the sin. Augustine loved nothing but the crime, but would not have loved doing it alone, but only in the company of others. The pleasure was in the crime committed with others who were sinning at the same time: "it [my pleasure] must have been in the crime as committed in the company of others who shared the sin."[33] But what kind of love or emotion is this?[34] Why would it not have been thrilling to steal alone, but only together?[35] The only thing one cannot have alone is praise, and there is no worthy "similitude of omnipotence" unless there is praise: "When someone says, 'Let's go! Let's do it!' I feel shamed not to be shameless."[36] The little band of thieves is a kind of mutual admiration society,[37] praising each other for doing something that they did just because it was forbidden, for breaking the law just to break it. Pride is not something that can be enjoyed alone, for there must be others to praise you, even if present only by the social conventions that make something praiseworthy or prestigious, such as the orthographic and rhetorical conventions that mark praiseworthy speech.[38] Augustine's little band of young thieves becomes an image of the sinful fellowship of Adam and Eve, as well as an analytical image of the society depicted in Book One, a society bound together by conventions of speech that enable one to be praised without being virtuous, where it is easy to seem larger than life simply by one's pronunciation.

In fact this passage describing a fellowship or friendship based upon mutual admiration in breaking God's law is tied to other passages in this book and Book One. For example, Augustine notes that he was ashamed to follow the counsel of his mother, a woman, to be at least somewhat chaste. By contrast, he was part of a group of friends who boasted about their excesses, glorying in them and expecting to receive praise for their stories: "When I heard other youths of my own age bragging about their immoralities I was ashamed to be less depraved than they. The more disgraceful their deeds, the more credit they claimed; and so I too became as lustful for the plaudits as for the lechery itself."[39] He goes on to remark, in a passage already noted above, that he even made up vices so that he would not be caught without something about which to boast. Augustine is following the example of his teachers, who, he reports in Book One, would be embarrassed to commit a barbarism while narrating some blameless deed they committed, but would happily seek praise by narrating licentious deeds in perfect Latin.[40]

Lust is something that is against the Creator's law, but licensed by human custom: "The frenzy of lust imposed its rule on me . . . licensed by disgraceful human custom, but illicit before your laws."[41] To put it another way, lust is something forbidden that one can brag about. The deeds committed in lust are praiseworthy, but only to a fellowship bent on breaking the laws of the Creator. Not to try to curtail the lust of one's offspring is to participate in the underlying fellowship that sanctions lust in the first place. This is the position of both of Augustine's parents: "Yet none of my family made any attempt to avert my ruin by arranging a marriage for me; their only concern was that I should learn to excel in rhetoric and persuasive speech."[42] In their own desire to have their offspring become the most persuasive, and thus the most prestigious, speaker possible, they don't take care that he be married. It would thwart his career. Augustine's father is particularly guilty. His overweening ambition (*animositas*, *Conf.* 2.3.5) to get his son an education at all costs is praised by everyone, but he did not care that Augustine be chaste. He cared only that he got an education so that he might be skilled in speaking, *disertus*, and yet by these very actions his father was actually seeing to it that he became a void, an empty place, *desertus*, far from the cultivating (*cultura*) of God. Augustine's father sees to it that he becomes a member in good standing of the fellowship of the world, the *consortium* of those sinning together and praising each other for it. He is the author, in a way, of his son's emptiness. Augustine's father is a symbol of the culture at large and its lust to propagate its own sterility.[43] The parable of the Prodigal Son, as it is evoked in

Book Two, has the effect not only of indicating the distance Augustine travels away from God, but of indicating the distance between his own physical father and that of the father in the parable. Augustine's father is completely unsuited for that role. The "bitterness" of remembering that is infused into this book of the *Confessions* is in part bitterness at the shocking distance between the father of the parable and Augustine's own father, who not only did not rescue his own son from emptiness, but positively cultivated it in him.

CONCLUSION

Where in the *Confessions* is Book Two, as it were, completed? The spell it casts of sadness and bitterness is dissipated only slowly in the text, persisting unabated until Book Five, when Augustine finally meets someone else he is willing to refer to, even if briefly, as "fatherly," namely Ambrose.[44] As "father" to Augustine, Ambrose is the symbol of the exegetical culture of humility, which he propagates in Augustine. Later, amid tears, Augustine is comforted by the figure of Continence in Book Eight, and in joy he interprets Psalm 4 in Book Nine. But there is still plenty of sadness to go around in Book Nine, as we read of the deaths of his friends, his son, and his mother, and the same is lingeringly true for Book Ten as we listen to Augustine's struggles with temptations. His lament about the lateness of God as Joy to him is the most direct echo of Book Two in the latter part of the *Confessions*. It is not until the final book that the story of Book Two comes to a close and its sadness is finally dissipated. It is there that Augustine gives the praise of confession as he unfolds the narrative in Genesis, and uses the story of creation from nothing as a figure for God's re-creation of the self from the nothingness of sin. It is only with Book Thirteen that, in a sense, we complete our reflection, with Augustine, on the "depths out of which we cry" to God, for it is there that we recognize those depths as the primal nothingness out of which we came by God's gratuitous act. But having read Book Two, we can also recognize this nothingness better, as the nothingness to which by our own inscrutable choice we had burned to return. When we recognize how far we had retreated into this nothingness, and the gratuitous love by which God re-created us, we are in a renewed position to see the goodness of the original creation, which came equally gratuitously from God's love. Against the Manichees, we can, from the perspective of a narrative of redemption, see creation in its beauty for the first time, unencumbered by pride or bitterness, and so understand both ourselves as God's creation, and the narrative of Genesis, which declares that truth. We can offer the "sacrifice of praise" in which all bitterness and sadness has been forgotten in the joy of the fecundity of love, enriching all the earth with fruits of charity and vision, as we enjoy fellowship (*consortium*) in the witness to God's goodness, the culture of true praise. The story of Book Two is completed only when the narrative from Genesis, present in Book Two only by allusion, in shadow and figure, can be spoken explicitly, in the heartfelt voice of joyful praise that is confession.[45]

Chapter 3

Book Three: "No Changing Nor Shadow"

Todd Breyfogle

INTRODUCTION

"I came to Carthage and all around me hissed a cauldron of illicit loves."[1] These tantalizing opening references to "the sizzling and frying of unholy loves"[2] of Augustine's student days in fact introduce his reflections on his misplaced *intellectual* loves. Book Three is Augustine the bishop's account of his youthful awakening to the life of the mind and things of the spirit, and his analysis of those things which then impeded an adequate understanding of that awakening. At the same time, Augustine uses the chronological narrative as the structure for exploring an important philosophical-theological question: how are the changeable things of this world related to the world of permanence? In Book Three, the cloud has parted, if only briefly, and Augustine strives to find that truth "in whom there is no changing nor shadow caused by any revolving."[3]

BOOK THREE IN THE STRUCTURE OF THE *CONFESSIONS*

The discussion of the misplaced desire for intellectual goods in Book Three follows upon the account of the physical needs of the infantile body (Book One) and the soul's need for the love of one's fellows (Book Two). The vicissitudes of the realms of the body and of society are readily perceived; less easily discerned are the shadows that play across the field of intelligible truth. Augustine comes to see both the body's desire for bodies and the soul's desire for friendship as increasingly elevated species of a higher desire for the truth of the intelligible world. Physical needs and fellowship culminate in philosophical desire; the several misplacements of philosophical desire described in Book Three set the stage for subsequent books. Vicarious suffering in the theater points Augustine to his own suffering, which is resolved only in the decisive conversion of Book Eight. His lack of friendly intimacy renders more striking the close friendships described in Books Four and Six. The failures of Manichean doctrine and community are pursued further in Books Five and Seven and answered exegetically in Books Twelve and Thirteen, on creation and the church. The invocation of poetry as an analogy for understanding the relation between God's eternal command and differences of custom anticipates the discussions of memory and time in Books Ten and Eleven, and in Book Twelve Augustine takes up the relation of matter and form raised initially in Book Three.

Book Three advances the three fundamental questions that structure the philosophical engagements of subsequent books: From where does evil come? What is the nature of God's existence? What is the relation of change to permanence? These philosophical questions (answered over the course of Books Three through Nine) are ultimately seen to depend upon the theological accounts of time and creation advanced in Books Ten through Thirteen. Book Three also marks the first drawing together of the three lusts (of 1 John 2:16) that anchor Augustine's analysis of the human soul in the work: the lust of domination (pride), the lust of the eyes (curiosity), and the lust of sensuality (pleasure).[4]

If *Confessions* as a whole describes and enacts a movement from shadow into light, in Book Three the restless Augustine wrestles with the bright emergence of Truth only to place himself back into the shadow of deception. By the end of Book Three, Augustine has given us a coherent map of the intellectual territory of his narrative confession, and in so doing disposes the reader to a more refined understanding of his subsequent spiritual developments. Book Three, then, enacts a recurring pattern of advance and resistance as Augustine struggles to provide an account of permanence in a universe of change.[5] How are we to discern the light of truth in a world of shadows? The answer, Augustine suggests, lies in an analysis of the soul as it resists the light for the shadows it casts.

THE INTERNAL STRUCTURE OF BOOK THREE

Book Three is typically noted for its criticism of Roman theater, Augustine's encounter with philosophy, his tentative conversion to Manicheism, and his mother's dream foretelling his conversion to Christianity. The chapter divisions (introduced by Amerbach in his Basel edition of 1506) afford a rough recapitulation of the text.[6] The truth does not lie in physical satisfaction (Chapter One), in fictional and aesthetic delight (Chapter Two), or in a sense of self-satisfaction (Chapter Three). After Augustine does discover, in Cicero's *Hortensius* (Chapter Four), the mode and object of philosophical truth, he rejects its expression in the vulgarity of Scripture (Chapter Five), and his insight into permanence is shaded by his lengthy, if troubled, commitment to the Manichees' religious and philosophical doctrines (Chapters Six and Seven). What the Manichees cannot account for, Augustine tells us (Chapters Eight through Ten), is how variations in custom, law, and matter can be undergirded by something fixed and unchanging. Unlike the world of imaginative fiction (the stage plays of Chapter Two), Monica's dream (Chapter Eleven) is a product of imagination that has its origin in truth. The promise of Augustine's eventual conversion to Christianity (Chapter Twelve) is a salutary counterpoint to the unredeemed and disordered loves with which Book Three began and a reminder, against the revolutions of temporal existence, that providence sustains all things. Book Three clarifies the path of light by rendering more distinct the areas of shadow in the pursuit of intellectual goods.

The literary dynamic of this (or any other book in *Confessions*) lies in the complex interweaving of chronological and philosophical concerns against the backdrop of the author's engagement with his own history. The chronological structure does not by itself answer the questions why Augustine the author has emphasized one thing rather than another in his account, nor does it render intelligible how Augustine conceives of the relation between the themes he engages alongside his chronological narrative. Indeed, accustomed as we are to reading works as history, and especially personal history, we are unknowingly prone to be attentive to those elements which bear directly on the chronological narrative. To do so is mistakenly to assume that the *Confessions* itself is primarily a chronological skeleton with philosophical flesh attached. But no skeleton is linear or rectilinear; its beauty lies in the interconnection of structure, ligaments and flesh—in the intelligibility and coherence of the various directions in which it branches.

To identify a key to Book Three would oversimplify the text's complexity. Nonetheless, there are a number of discernible features from which the reader of Book Three may take his bearings in his own exploration of the text. Chronologically or historically, the book divides into three sections:

> Augustine's life as a student at Carthage (3.1.1–3.6);
>
> Augustine's quest for wisdom (3.4.7–10.18), both
> in reading Cicero's *Hortensius* (3.4.7–5.9) and
> in his affiliation with the Manichees (3.6.10–10.18);
>
> Augustine's account of his mother's dream (3.11.19–12.21).

Alongside the chronological structure, four thematic divisions emerge:

> the peculiar interplay of pleasure and pain (3.1.1–3.6);
>
> philosophical illumination and deception (3.4.7–7.14);
>
> the anatomy of sin and humane action (3.8.15–10.18);
>
> the stubborn love of self-created fiction (3.11.19–12.21).

Additionally, these overlapping chronological and thematic structures are developed in a twofold movement of narrative affirmation and negation. Augustine recounts both what he thought at the time of the events he is narrating (ca. 372) and what he thinks about those thoughts and events at the time of his writing (ca. 398); and he indicates how his intellectual encounters brought him both closer to and yet farther away from God. In conveying the dual motion of his appreciation of and resistance to intelligible reality—the movement of assent and dissent, ascent and descent—Augustine simultaneously gives an account of why it is that human beings generally resist what is good for them and embrace what is not, why we prefer that which is changing to that which does not change.

THE PECULIAR INTERPLAY OF PLEASURE AND PAIN

This first section of Book Three views the three lusts of 1 John 2:16 through the lens of the pleasure we take in suffering. Augustine is masterful at tantalizing without titillating the reader. Augustine must convey the force of his experiences in such a way as to involve his readers vicariously in the spiritual quest, but without exciting their emotions to feel the pleasures and pains themselves. Augustine's literary strategy may account for the fact that readers often are left cold reading passages about deep and emotional events (the death of his friend in Book Four, the sending away of his mistress in Book Six). When Augustine appeals to his reader's imagination, it is never to evoke sympathy or to titillate the fantasy. Augustine's art does not trade on cheap thrills. To move the reader with discussion of childhood, of suffering, of sex, of friendship, of love of the divine, but without inciting fictional emotions or stimulating lustful desires is a considerable artistic achievement. Were Augustine so to excite the reader, he would subject his own art to the criticism he levels against fictional portrayals in the theater.

The "sizzling and burning loves" with which Book Three opens promise, but do not deliver the illicit goods. From the opening line the reader desires to know about that which is not good for Augustine's or his own soul. Our souls want to ingest that which causes pain. Thus, this opening paragraph not only links Book Three to what has gone before, but elicits in the reader the experience Augustine will analyze for the next five paragraphs: Why do we take pleasure in pain? Why do we delight in, why do we love, things that nonetheless do not make us happy?

The "restless heart" of *Confessions'* opening lines (*Conf.* 1.1.1) takes pleasure in pain because it mistakenly conceives its inward hunger as an external hunger to be satisfied externally. "I was famished within, deprived of inner food" (*Conf.* 3.1.1). The cauldron of earthly loves derives from a failing of spiritual loves.[7] External food cannot nourish an internal hunger; what gives pleasure to the body may starve the soul. These illicit, disordered loves are attributed to a "hidden poverty,"[8] understood not merely as ignorance, but also as a willful "hatred of being less destitute of spirit."[9] Book Three is Augustine's chronological and philosophical attempt to discern his internal hunger accurately and so to understand why the soul perversely enjoys its hunger.

The physical imagery of Book Three is palpable. In addition to the hunger metaphor (which permeates the book), Augustine makes reference to ulcerous wounds, itches to be scratched, infection, physical torture, and sexual imagery of moisture and thrusting out. All of these images lend an especially corporeal texture to his account of spiritual destitution and evoke common physical appetites (or revulsions) whose permanent satiability is never within reach. If there are physical appetites that matter cannot satisfy, the reader is left to reflect, how much more difficult is it to expect matter to satisfy the spiritual appetite? The bodily metaphors encourage the reader to discern what Augustine himself struggled to discern—the soul that animates physical things: "physical things had no soul. Love lay outside their range."[10]

The hunger of being "in love with love" is a hunger that seeks to satisfy the soul with that which is not-soul. The very experience of our embodiment, Augustine suggests, discloses that we are more than bodies. Augustine's loves are illicit because he either loves things that have no soul, or in loving animate things he loves their matter, not their soul. Soul is the only proper object of love, the only locus of true pleasure. By the end of Book Three's opening paragraph, Augustine has identified the spiritual source and physical expression of human restlessness, as well as the impulse that resists its resolution. The sweetness he enjoys is mixed with vinegar; he mistakes vinegar for wine (though God has begun to turn vinegar into wine).[11] So it is that Augustine can speak of his delighting in a false joy, the "joy that enchains (*vinculum fruendi*)."

The exemplary delight of the "joy that enchains" is the theater, or fictional portrayals more generally, which "fuels the fire" of the soul's restless thirst. The pleasure of the theater is found in its pain—the soul suffers and is thankful for that suffering.[12] Augustine is enraptured, he is raped (*rapiebant me spectacula theatrica*), yet enjoys it. For the spectator, "The pain itself is his pleasure."[13] The soul undergoes an ordeal in the theater; it is the subject of a passion. In its poverty, the soul enchains itself further to the passions enacted and evoked by the theater and cultivates an emotional response that lacks true mercy because it is not directed at true suffering. Fiction produces a delight devoid of responsibility. The impoverished soul's curiosity for the sufferings of others ultimately has reference only to itself. The compassion evoked aims only at self-indulgence, not the love of another. Augustine identifies love's object and the mode in which love proceeds. The problem with fiction is not so much that we are deceived as that we deceive ourselves. In loving the theater, we love ourselves wrongly.[14]

Augustine is not primarily concerned here, significantly, with the fictional mendacity of the theater or entertainment as a distraction from the soul's spiritual hunger. Rather, he is disturbed by the perversity of "tears and agonies" being objects of love. "No one wishes to suffer, but there must first be pain for mercy to be shown. Is this the one reason we love suffering, that we may show mercy?" (*Conf.* 3.2.3). In responding to fictional suffering, we feel the urge to mercy, yet are deprived of the possibility of its performance. The spiritual problem is shown to have become a moral one. Do we love suffering that mercy may abound? Surely it is not right to love the suffering that makes the good possible, but are we not implicated in some love of suffering when we delight in acts of mercy? Theatrical delights are predicated on fictional suffering; true mercy prefers that there be "no cause for grief" (*Conf.* 3.2.3). Sufferings (*dolores*), Augustine writes, "may sometimes be loved," but more often than not, what begins as true mercy or compassion descends from a "heavenly serenity" to "something distorted and base," altered by its own consent.[15] Even the most noble actions and sentiments are subject to corruption.

At the root of Augustine's considerations is nothing less than an examination of what it means to suffer—in oneself, for oneself, and for another. At the heart of Augustine's discussion is the distinction between compassion (*compassio*) and mercy (*misericordia*). Human compassion is still a *passio*, a suffering, a partaking of what is changing and temporal rather than of what is eternal. Compassion always risks descent into tainted love, even in friendship.[16] Authentic *misericordia*, however, does not take pleasure in pain.[17] And if the love of tears and agonies is problematic, how are we to understand the salutary tears of Monica and the suffering of Christ crucified?[18] In quoting from 2 Corinthians 2:16 at the conclusion of his discussion of tears and agonies, Augustine implicitly contrasts Christ's suffering with our own self-indulgent sufferings; the freedom of Christ's suffering is contrasted with the bondage of our own. Christ does not love our suffering (or his, for that matter), but rather the souls that suffer. To be moved by suffering is pity (which is ultimately self-regarding); to be moved by another's soul without regard to their suffering is a supreme act of mercy. God's love is never injured by suffering. Our loves are diminished in proportion to the degree that they fail to love soul.

Properly speaking, Augustine concludes, we should not love suffering, though we may notice or acknowledge it.[19] We are, rather, to love souls. Fiction reinforces our propensity to love the feeling of compassion rather than the soul of the one who suffers. And if our "mixed emotions" are confused in baser things, how much more confused are we in higher things? "But, wretch that I was, I loved to feel pain and sought after opportunities to suffer" (*Conf.* 3.2.4). Augustine's love of fictional sufferings as superficial thus reveals the superficiality of all love of suffering as rooted in self-love rather than in love of another's soul.

Ultimately, Augustine sees the spiritual destitution of taking pleasure in pain as rooted in the sin of curiosity. "I wasted myself in so many iniquities and pursued them with a sacrilegious curiosity."[20] Here *curiositas* is more than an irreverent inquisitiveness; it is a deliberate quest for knowledge of the self-destructive. The Latin *sacrilegus* refers specifically to the robbing or profanation of temples. As he describes his flagrant rebellion against God, Augustine's actions and imagery fold back upon themselves—the temples he plunders are his own body and his soul. In delighting in iniquity for its own sake, he does not steal from God but robs himself, simply for the sake of stealing.

Augustine's analysis transposes the perverse pleasure of pain into the realm of worship and fidelity. Augustine's *curiositas* is not merely an intellectual failing, but one of volition also—an act of worship in which his quest "led me, in my desertion of you, down to the depths of infidelity and to the deceptive, ensnaring service of demons, to whom I offered my own evil deeds as sacrifice."[21] Augustine desecrates God's temple literally when, during the celebration of the Mass, he indulges his lusts and begins an affair. Instead of loving the church, the bride of Christ, as a setting of holy worship, Augustine nurtures a fornicating lust after a body. The misplaced love of self is false worship or idolatry, squandering of the riches of one's own soul and of God's blessings alike. In the infidelity of false worship, Augustine was "loving a fugitive liberty (*amans fugitivam liber-tatem*)."[22] Augustine's liberty is that of a "deserter"—precarious and lacking peace because pursued from within by God—like the liberty of a fugitive slave.[23] The liberty he enjoys, the object of his love, is fleeting—his soul is restless because it loves something that cannot last. Like the prodigal son who squanders his inheritance, Augustine sacrilegiously steals from himself and wallows in the mire of his fugitive liberty.[24] The unfaithful son, who has fled but not yet returned to his father, sacrifices himself for objects that are changeable and so can never be faithful to or nourish him.

Having explored the inner workings of the soul's prodigal love of inward destitution, Augustine returns to a practical example of taking pleasure in pain—rhetoric, his other great love in Carthage. In rhetoric, "one is praised more highly the more deceptive one is" (*Conf.* 3.3.6). A manifestation of *ambitio saeculi*, the third sin of 1 John 2:16, rhetoric is doubly dangerous, for it feeds a pride based on the deception of self as well as of others, and Augustine even boasts of crimes he has not committed. "Human beings are so blind that they boast about their blindness" (*Conf.* 3.3.6). Rhetoric, as an art of deception, is a form of fiction. The law courts and the stage converge as places where falsehood flourishes and one delights in and profits from the suffering of others.

Not content to wait for professional practice, Augustine's fellow students indulge in premature prosecutions of their own. Just as his adolescent friends plucked pears from the tree solely for the sake of stealing, Augustine's adult companions delight in looting the souls of their younger fellows solely for the pleasure of inflicting pain. Augustine is aloof but implicates himself in the fullness of the crimes by desiring his companions' approbation. The "Subverters" (as the Carthage gang called itself) strove to persecute new students by deception and mockery and "feasting upon their own malevolent amusement."[25] They are, in a word, in love with (others') suffering. The Subverters doubly invert the perversity of the theater because they become both actors and audience. As actors, their performance causes others to suffer. But unlike theatergoers, those who suffer take no pleasure in their suffering. As audience, the Subverters watch and take delight in the suffering they have caused. In both cases, while the deception is fictional, the suffering is very, very real. The mocking love of others' suffering folds back upon itself; *ambitio saeculi* and *sacrilega curiositas* entail a self-consuming prodigality. Those who mock others, Augustine notes, are themselves being mocked by the devils who ensnare them. The mockery and deception of others is rooted in self-mockery and self-deception, a fugitive and fictional domination of others by those who are themselves enslaved to evil spirits.

This first section of Book Three, then, explores the diversity and unity of the three sins as variations on taking pleasure in pain. The book begins with *concupiscentia carnis* and moves on to consider *sacrilega curiositas* before taking up *ambitio saeculi*. The loves which animate all three sins share a thirst for that which starves rather than nourishes the soul; all three trade on the double edge of fiction in which they willingly deceive both themselves and others. Augustine the spectator has come to see himself as an apprentice performer who enacts for himself and others a public, inward destitution that takes pleasure in pain. The readers of *Confessions*, Augustine's audience, are left to reflect upon our own participation in deceptive fictions, to measure the extent to which we ourselves are tempted to play and delight in imaginative theatrical roles animated by the love of suffering and the diminution of others' souls.

PHILOSOPHICAL ILLUMINATION AND DECEPTION

The young Augustine's inward destitution contained the seeds of hope of spiritual satiety, though it was only later that he came to recognize his pursuit of a career in rhetoric as "a damnable and conceited . . . delight in human vanity."[26] His soul was ripe for philosophy. Cicero's *Hortensius*, an exhortation to philosophy, impressed Augustine not for its style, but because of its content.[27] In this second section of Book Three, Augustine charts his fragmentary ascent to philosophical illumination and his descent into metaphysical and moral error. In turning from fiction and rhetoric to philosophy, Augustine momentarily transcends his indulgence in the pleasure of pain—he comes to seek the nourishing food of intelligible reality. At the same time, he finds that philosophy has the capacity both to elevate the soul and to deceive.

In contrast to the prodigal suffering of sin, in reading Cicero's *Hortensius* Augustine suffers a salutary *passio*—he is acted upon, he undergoes a change. The encounter with the *Hortensius* is, arguably, the first of several significant moments of conversion. "That book truly changed my disposition, it both redirected my prayers toward you, O Lord, and gave me different longings and desires."[28] His *affectus*—his whole being and set of inclinations—has a new direction of worship (*ad te*). His love has been dislodged—temporarily, yet decisively—from temporal to eternal things. "Suddenly every vain hope became worthless to me, and I longed for the immortality of wisdom with an incredible leap in my heart, and I eagerly began to rise up to return to you."[29] The recognition of his external hunger as an internal hunger transforms earthly *sacrilega curiositas* and *concupiscentia carnis* into a longing for the immortality of wisdom. His rising up (*surgere*) is directed not toward himself or other bodies, but toward God. This is nothing less than a fundamental transformation of Augustine's desire.

The profound turning of Augustine's soul occasioned by his reading of the *Hortensius* refocuses his gaze from form to content, style to substance.[30] All things are to be judged according the end—self or God—to which they refer. The burning scabs and itches of *sacrilega curiositas* and *concupiscentia carnis* are transformed into an ardor for returning to God. "How I burned, my God, to fly away from earthly things, to fly back to you."[31] Augustine has begun to reconceive his fugitive journey as a homeward pilgrimage. In language and imagery strikingly reminiscent of Plotinus, Augustine's flight is no longer from himself (a negative journey), but toward the fatherland.[32] He longs now to leave earthly things and fly back to God. Having passed through the fire of descent and dissent from God, we now have a fire of ascent and assent to God.

The emotional, philosophical, and literary intensity of this passage anticipates the abandoned Platonic ascents of Book Seven, the decisive conversion scene of Book Eight and the vision at Ostia of Book Nine. Though it lacks the extended development and artful depiction of the later scenes, the importance of this passage cannot be overestimated.[33] The punctuated brevity of the account is revealing: the moment of insight is fragmentary, narrated in two short bursts (and further fragmented by the introduction of the paragraph division), and interspersed among mundane details (rhetorical training, his mother's financial support, and the perfunctory notice of his father's death). Augustine had had the experience but missed the meaning. His disordered soul could not accommodate such an experience—he is not yet ready to learn, nor does he yet have at his disposal the philosophical grammar and vocabulary of "the books of the Platonists" (*Conf.* 7.9.14), with which he comes to understand and articulate such an experience. Augustine's narrative makes it clear that he recognizes the decisive significance of this experience, not only at the time of his youth, but also almost thirty years later when he chooses to write about it. If his experience is an interrupted ascent which ends in misconversion, it is a momentary ascent nonetheless. His soul has been awakened decisively to a discernment of the unchanging reality in which temporal things participate. But this tentative apprehension of the divine realm both is and is not lasting. Augustine returns—as he must, in narrative and in life—to the mundane voice of chronological narrative, and the fragmentary spell is broken.

Augustine's conversion to philosophy is from the "love of love" (in reality a masking of his direction of the love of self), to the "love of wisdom (*philosophia*)." The objects of his love are now permanent and unchanging, yet that love is still susceptible to deception and misdirection.[34] Philosophy is subject to change, manipulation, and misunderstanding stemming from human frailty and a propensity to confuse the right relation between spiritual and material reality. The highest things become the most dangerous when corrupted.

In commenting on his own misconversion, Augustine invokes St. Paul: "See that none deceives you by philosophy and vain seduction following human tradition; following the elements of this world and not following Christ; in him dwells all the fullness of divinity in bodily form" (Col. 2:8–9 RSV, Oxford Annotated). Only in the incarnation is the fullness of spiritual substance found in material form. In Christ, the Word made flesh, both Word and flesh are redeemed. Cicero's *Hortensius* lacks the name of Christ; and while it launches Augustine's soul upward, it does not adequately orient him for the journey that he now faces. Augustine's spiritual advance is simultaneously the occasion for a retreat.

The moment of philosophical illumination pulls Augustine in several different directions. On the one hand, the *Hortensius* persuades Augustine of the call of wisdom and the nonsectarian character of its pursuit: philosophy gives form and articulation to his heretofore aimless wandering. He is initially attracted to Cicero's advice not to join a particular sect, but "to love and seek and pursue and hold fast and strongly embrace wisdom itself however possible."[35] On the other hand, Augustine notes that he was dissatisfied with the absence of Christ's name from the philosophical text. Later in *Confessions*, Augustine will articulate a vision of philosophy as a mode of recollection, ideally directed toward (because satisfied by none other than) Christ.[36] But the young Augustine in Carthage had no such resources at hand. Moreover, he finds in Scripture a literary language so undignified as to be offensive to both his ear and his intellect. Can ugly words convey something beautiful?[37] Despite the attraction of nonsectarian philosophy, Augustine proudly and confidently seeks out an articulation of Scripture that has philosophical sophistication and joins a sect.[38] In his impatient philosophical conceit and his love of words, Augustine "fell in (*incidi*) with men delirious in their pride, too carnal-minded and full of empty words" (*Conf.* 3.6.10).

Metaphysics, like rhetoric, appeals to pride in an overabundance of words.[39] But Augustine was also attracted to Manichean metaphysics because it wrestled with questions of spiritual or intelligible reality (issues awakened in Augustine in his reading of the *Hortensius*) and answered those questions with reference to Christ and the Paraclete (names lodged in Augustine's memory from his childhood). But knowing words and names are not enough—the mere invocation of those names had no force without knowledge of the Truth to which those names referred.[40] Philosophy cannot remain at the level of the sign: it must penetrate to a proper knowledge and love of intelligible truth.

In becoming an auditor with the Manichees, Augustine takes a tentative misstep on the path to truth. He never entered into full membership, but his engagement with the sect lasted at least nine years. He has committed himself to philosophy and to *cultus*, but not wholeheartedly. In a recurring pattern of advance and resistance, Augustine implicitly asks that he be given true philosophy, but not yet. Despite the significance of his joining the sect, Augustine mentions the Manichees by name only once in Book Three and even then only in the last sentence of *Conf.* 3.10.18, just before the Psalm passages that introduce Monica's dream. In deferring his explicit engagement with the Manichees to Books Five and Seven, Augustine focuses attention on fundamental metaphysical questions (in the frame of historical narrative) on their own terms.[41] Yet, the answers the young Augustine adopts mislead him. Metaphysics, no less than the seductive powers of literary fiction, may be a deceptive enticement.[42]

Perplexity over three matters in particular shields Augustine from the truth at this stage of his journey: the nature of creation (how are material and spiritual things related?), the existence of intelligible reality (how do we know eternal and permanent things?), and the philosophical intelligibility of history (how is eternal justice discernible in the contingency of time?).[43]

The improper view of creation to which the young Augustine apparently subscribed correctly conceived a spiritual reality above material things, but did not go far enough in discerning God himself.[44] The worship of spiritual creation instead of the Creator is a metaphysical idolatry. "On these platters, in my hunger for you, they set before me the sun and moon, your beautiful works—but they gave me your works, not you yourself, nor the first of your creations."[45] There are echoes here of later passages in *Confessions*, notably when creation cries out not to love it, but rather the God who made it.[46] While spiritual creation has ontological and epistemological priority over material creation, the metaphysical dishes placed before Augustine were "splendid hallucinations" that satisfied his soul as much as food pictured in dreams satisfies the body. Nourishment of the soul becomes a criterion of truth. The truth for which Augustine sighs is God himself, "the life of souls, the life of lives, living in you yourself, and not changing, life of my soul" (*Conf.* 3.6.10). To perceive the spiritual reality behind material creation is not necessarily to see into its center.

But where are we to look to find the center of spiritual reality? Where is God? "Where then, at that time, where were you and how far away?" (*Conf.* 3.6.11). The answer to the question requires Augustine to acknowledge where *he* is in relation to God—on a prodigal and fugitive journey feeding on spiritual fantasies. Augustine was seduced by "that bold woman" of proud and curious cupidity because he was "living outside, and outside of myself, in the eye of the flesh, and chewing over in myself the cud of what I had devoured by means of that eye."[47] Augustine's quest was both in the wrong mode (one of pride in words) and misdirected outside himself.[48] The flight from God takes Augustine outside himself; the return to God requires that he return to himself.

Though he was far from God, Augustine tells us, God was more inward than his most inward part.[49] Yet Augustine sought God according to the fleshly sense of words rather than according to "the intelligence of mind."[50] His failure of vision is an ignorance "of that other reality, that which truly is."[51] Material and spiritual creation cannot be adequately conceived without the knowledge of intelligible reality. For Augustine to understand how he is related to God, he must understand how all created things are related to intelligible things. The issues that perplex him have been refined as follows: the origin of evil, the nature of God's being, and ethical contingency. Each is a feature of how fragmentary experience can be understood in terms of a unifying truth.

The groundwork for understanding the metaphysical problems has already been laid, and the elements of their later resolution are only summarized at this point in the narrative. Evil, Augustine comes to realize, is a privation of being: the spiritual world is not the realm of the clash of equal and opposite positive and negative principles, but rather a continuum of fullness and lack. But to understand this, Augustine had, additionally, to overcome his philosophical imagination of the restrictions of mass and physical diffusion in space.[52] That is, he had first to come to understand God as spirit, not subject to the same limitations governing the extension of mass in space. Spirit is characterized by an extension impossible for bodies.[53] Coming to understand that God could be conceived as not having a body was nothing less than coming to understand matter and spirit as both distinct and in relation to one another. A body may participate fully in being, yet our knowledge of it is incomplete unless we discern the spirit that animates it and judge the degree to which it participates in being. Evil is not a deficiency of body, but a disorder of the soul in relation to itself, to the body, and to eternal things.[54]

Spirit may have continuity across the fragmentation of space. But what of continuity of spirit over time? How is the unchanging God present in history? Having discerned the intelligible reality which animates material creation, how is it that intelligible reality is compatible with contingency in human history? The problem of continuity in ethics occupies Augustine at this stage of his narrative, and is treated at much greater length than the metaphysical problems whose resolutions are deferred to later in the work. Philosophical questions, for Augustine, are not merely academic, but bear directly on how one lives one's life.[55] Augustine shifts (in *Conf.* 3.7.13) from metaphysics to ethics, focusing on the relation between diverse customs and God's unchanging law. The relation between unity and multiplicity is now complicated by the introduction of *time:* How are we to discern what is unchanging in the realm of moral action when diverse customs, especially as depicted in Old Testament revelation, cannot be reconciled with one another? How is eternal justice to be reconciled with the mosaic of contingent practices?

True inward justice judges not according to custom but according to divine law.[56] "By this law, the moral customs of different regions and periods were adapted to their places and times, while that law itself remains unaltered everywhere and always" (*Conf.* 3.7.13). He who takes it upon himself to judge the past must discern both the congruity of custom with time, and the right relation of the part to the whole.[57] To understand justice—rendering unto each its due—requires an understanding of what is fitting and appropriate in each circumstance.

Those criticisms of the morals of past ages—and particularly of the patriarchs—are unjust precisely because they do not give the age its due. One must, as a matter of justice, view past actions according to the time, not according to the prejudices of one's age.[58] (In this, the principle of justice is also one of charity and humility.) To do otherwise is to misconceive the relation of parts to the whole, as when (the examples are Augustine's own) one tries to put a helmet on one's leg, or when one complains that, because of a public holiday, one cannot sell in the afternoon something that he was permitted to sell in the morning. What is allowed behind the stable is not proper in the dining room; the same liberties, Augustine continues, are not permitted to all members of the family. All ages submit to the same justice though God's precepts may vary according to historical contingency. Justice depends on appropriateness of time, place, and person. What is appropriate or fitting (*congruo, propria*) thus mediates between eternal principle and historical circumstance.

Justice presides or rules over times (*tempora, saecula*), but rules differently because times are always different. The congruity of justice to an age entails incongruity over time; what is permitted to the patriarchs is forbidden to us, and vice versa. Augustine advises a cautious skepticism: "human beings, 'whose life on earth is short' [Wis. 15:9], are not able, by using their senses, to reconcile the relations of cause and effect that obtained in previous ages and in other nations, of which they have no experience, with those of the times and peoples of whom they have direct knowledge" (*Conf.* 3.7.13). One age cannot judge other ages or nations of which they have no direct experience. It is difficult enough, Augustine implies, to discern and judge the spirit of one's own age.[59] To ignore the limitations of our own self-knowledge and to judge the patriarchs unjustly risks succumbing to the sins of pride and envy.

Far from quarreling with these philosophical insights, poetry confirms and exemplifies fittingness and appropriateness as criteria of moral action.[60] Just as in poetry, discrete elements in ethics must be considered in the context of the larger whole: "And even in the same verse one could not put the same foot at just any place in the line. Yet, the art of poetry did not have different rules for different occasions, but contained all the rules simultaneously" (*Conf.* 3.7.14). There is one justice but many forms. In Augustine's presentation, difference is affirmed as difference because it is acknowledged and recognized as a function of *arrangement in time*. Justice embraces time in an instant; custom cannot escape contingency and the linear flow of time. Instead of prescribing its principles all at once, justice at various times prescribes principles "appropriate to the occasion." And this, Augustine says, is "a much more excellent and sublime way" (*Conf.* 3.7.14). So, the Old Testament fathers were not immoral, despite the fact that many of their actions are impermissible in Augustine's own age.[61] Just as God's presence as spirit extends throughout space, so too it extends in time.[62]

Yet, at Carthage, the young Augustine had not yet come to conceive of God's spiritual extension in time and space. Awakened to the vision of intelligible reality, he lacked the philosophical vocabulary and humble disposition to appropriate that vision and so slipped further into deception. His seduction by corrupt metaphysics derives from a mistake he would not have made reading imaginative literature, for literature may nourish the soul. Literature, Augustine notes, is less susceptible to being believed as truth and, if believed, is less deadly than corrupt metaphysics.[63] So, Augustine's progress in Book Three is both an ascent (from literature to philosophy) and a descent (from philosophy to corrupt metaphysics). And wallowing now in philosophical fictions, the young Augustine suffers from a failure of not only philosophical but also moral imagination.

THE ANATOMY OF SIN AND HUMANE ACTION

If fiction prompts too great an indulgence in the pain of others, philosophy risks an inhumane lack of interest in human suffering. Bad metaphysics leads to a deformation of disinterest, corrupting consideration of humane action toward fellows. One's attention to spiritual things must never compromise humane earthly relationships. Ethical contingency does not entail, for Augustine, moral relativism; his skepticism is epistemological, not moral. Further, Augustine's sense of justice is animated not by a mild aestheticism as much as by a humble skepticism mindful of an inscrutable providential order.

In this third section of Book Three, Augustine moves from the ethics of the patriarchs to ethics in general. In so doing, he sketches—again within the chronological narrative of his intellectual struggles in Carthage—three bonds of sociability to which we are rightly bound in any age: fidelity to God, conformity to nature, love of one's fellows. Each of these reflects and judges ethical contingency against the twofold injunction of charity: to love God and neighbor.

The injunction to love God and neighbor is immutable and Augustine sees little need to elaborate on the point. He devotes considerable space, however, to the ways in which we are bound to nature and nature's law, which proscribes sexual perversity in particular. Why sexual perversity, and homosexuality in particular, is exemplary of the violation of a bond with nature remains puzzling in the context of the argument of Book Three.[64]

Perversions of ordained nature (and especially sexual desire) are contrary to divine law and violate what Augustine calls the "fellowship (*societas*) which ought to exist between us and God" (*Conf.* 3.8.15). This portion of Augustine's argument (*Conf.* 3.8.15–16) is structured according to a distinction made in *De doctrina christiana* (3.10.16) between *flagitia* (sins against God and self) and *facinora* (sins against others).[65] That which does not fit into the pattern of the whole is unseemly or base (*turpis*).[66] The implication is that an offense to the pattern of the whole offends both natural law and the "law of nations (*ius gentium*)" (although the invocation of the latter is not explicit). Unseemly sexual desire, understood in terms of married love and so against the backdrop of the matrimonial relationship of Christ and his church, is a sin against God and self. As one of the highest ordained forms of human expression, sexual love is base in proportion to the degree it is corrupted. The law of nature may be disregarded only in response to divine command, which must be followed despite established custom. In the natural hierarchy of authority God's command is, of course, superior over all.[67] Obedience to divine command is always fitting and appropriate; not to obey would be to fail to give God his due.

Just as we ought not to violate the social bond with God, we must not violate the bond with our neighbor. Augustine singles out the lust to harm our neighbor by verbal insult or physical violence, which he treats as equivalents. Both impulses derive from an abandonment of God and spring from the three lusts of 1 John 2:16: the lust of domination (pride), the lust of the eyes (curiosity), and the lust of sensuality (pleasure). All three are manifestations of a failure to discern eternal things and result from a "self-centered pride which loves a part as a false unity."[68] Private pride has subverted the social bond with others: the partial is falsely conceived as the whole and is thereby made *turpis*, an offense to the whole.

While the sinful soul is the author of its own punishment, its correction lies in following the path of humility and abandoning the false liberty of *avaritia*, the desire to possess more and to love what is our own (*proprium nostrum*) more than God and the good of all.

In addition to deliberate sins against God (*flagitia*) and fellows (*facinora*), Augustine speaks of the inadvertent sins of "those who are making progress (*peccata proficientium*)," those who are learning, whose actions are still judged lacking according to the scale of perfection, but whose souls incline toward God.[69] Augustine pays relatively little attention to sins of this sort, for such is the condition of all in this life, insofar as none can achieve perfection. Instead, he turns to examine a second, more interesting category of actions and one that follows naturally on his discussion of custom—those acts which resemble injurious acts but which in fact are *not* sins, for they offend neither God nor fellows (*sociale consortium*). The first example of such actions Augustine gives is that of when the useful things of life are accumulated appropriate to the time (*congrua et tempori*), though it is uncertain whether they are accumulated out of the lust of possession. The second example is that of when punishment is inflicted by an ordained power (*potestate ordinata*), but it is uncertain whether the act was done out of a lust to hurt.

It would appear that there is a category of actions which are in themselves neutral. While the moral valence of the category may be neutral, any specific action within the category is necessarily either praiseworthy or blameworthy (either the goods are accumulated out of lust or they are not). Just as Augustine exercised a humble skepticism of restraint in judging past ages, he maintains—with certain kinds of actions—a skepticism with respect to the secret loves of the heart. We cannot always discern from a particular act (i.e., within the category of neutral acts) the love that animates the person acting. There is a sphere of action (perhaps a large sphere) about whose justice we must be agnostic in the absence of other evidence, for we are unable to discern another's motive desire.[70] Congruity or appropriateness to the time emerges again as a criterion of moral judgment, though justice is solely subject to divine approval, for who can doubt, says Augustine, that a just society submits to God.[71]

In an apparent non sequitur, Augustine descends from these lofty philosophical heights to discuss the absurdity of the Manichean diet dictated by their metaphysical doctrines.[72] Yet, in juxtaposing the dietary with the metaphysical concerns, Augustine is keen to demonstrate that the vibrancy of the spiritual life is qualified by and reflected in the vibrancy of the ethical life. The Manichean diet emphasized the purity and spirit of vegetable life and held that vegetable matter contained parts of the divine. Yet, Augustine says, the food did not nourish the soul, but rather corrupted his social bonds with others: "And I in my pathetic state believed that more mercy should be shown to the fruits of the earth than to human beings for whose sake the fruits came to be."[73] The Manichees go too far in seeing and loving soul in everything. The ethical life may be corrupted by a concern for the spirit run amok no less than a wrongly directed love of the body. The fruits of the Manichean diet are bitter and inhumane.

Augustine's discussion of the Manichean diet leaves the reader with a developing sense of *humanitas*. Misplaced intellectual desire—whether in fiction, solitary philosophical inquiry, quirky metaphysics and cultic practice, or hyperspirituality—may all diminish rather than expand the soul's charitable directedness to God and others. Care for spiritual things is dramatically qualified, to Augustine's mind, by human flourishing, beginning with basic (rightly ordered) physical needs. The errors of sin are not simply errors of intellect, but failures of souls to live in charity. The reader has been instructed by a series of contrasts. One of the movements of Book Three has been to show the ascent of the soul in learning to see the spirit as well as the body, while revealing the descent of the soul by a wrongly ordered love of the spirit. Even the love of spiritual things can be primarily self-regarding; the absence of charity is revealed in the corresponding absence of humaneness. In this way, Book Three sets the stage for the even more painful driving home of this point in Book Four, where Augustine discloses that his love for his dear friend was really a love of himself and his own suffering.

THE STUBBORN LOVE OF SELF-CREATED FICTION

The final section of Book Three marks a decisive shift in tone and content, and stands as a coda to the rest of the book. In a dream, Monica stands on a wooden rule and is promised that where she is her son will be also. Monica's dream is a promise of hope for the wayward young Augustine's conversion, but it is also a thematic recapitulation of what has gone before. The words of promise are introduced by two quotations from the Psalms: "'You extended your hand from on high,' and from this deep darkness 'you rescued my soul.'"[74] The recapitulation displays the prodigal soul in its recurring pattern of spiritual advance and willful resistance to that which will nourish it—the persistent preference of shadow for light. While literature, philosophy, cultic metaphysics, ethics, and—with Monica's dream—prophetic revelation all contain the seeds of reformation, Augustine's response is to transform each of them into self-imposed fictions that blind him to the truth each discloses.

The immediate thematic links are mercy and purity: the promise of God's mercy for the spiritually malnourished Augustine stands in contrast to the false Manichean spirituality that would leave a hungry man to starve. But like the Manichees, who despised the non-elect, Monica herself has adopted a rigid purity: in shunning Augustine on account of his heresy, she neglects his well-being and sets herself apart in pride.[75] As a consequence of her dream, Monica comes to see that such behavior is uncharitable and unchristian. In her immoderate love of spiritual things, she has violated the principle of humane charity. Thus, in Augustine's first portrayal of Monica as a full human personality, as distinct from a stock figure,[76] Augustine demonstrates both the strengths and weaknesses of her fidelity, themselves reflections of his own. Both Monica and the young Augustine, in striving to do well, do poorly as a consequence of their respective stubborn attachments.

In prefiguring the eventual reunion of Monica and her son, the dream authorizes their reconciliation in the present, quite before Augustine's conversion. Monica learns charity, hope, as well as faith in providential arrangement. The dream suggests that things presently apart shall—at a fitting time and place—be brought together. The statement in Monica's dream, "Where you are, there will he be also," parallels the bride's statement in the ancient Roman marriage rite: "Where you are, there will I be."[77] The imagery is almost inexhaustible. Augustine, having shunned the Mother Church, is shunned by his mother. His mother is reconciled to him in a dream that promises Augustine's own reconciliation to the church, the faithful bride of Christ. Human events must always be viewed, so far as possible, both as they are and as they will be in the light of divine truth.

In her dream, Monica stands on a rule, a measure or standard that evokes earlier discussions of propriety, judgment, and appropriateness. It is possible that the wooden rule (*regula*) mentioned was a kind of level used in the construction of aqueducts,[78] signifying a smooth way, a deliberate direction of (once again) flowing water from its source to its end, implying a reservoir and perhaps the waters of the baptismal font.[79] Additionally, the wooden rule may be understood as a mediation between general standards and local customs, for many measures would have been local measures—equal and appropriate for a given community, but inadequate when judged by a definitive, authorized imperial measure.[80] The dream enjoins Monica, and Augustine's readers, to judge matters both according to a standard of perfection and according to the appropriateness of the time.

While Monica learns from the dream and acts accordingly, Augustine himself does not immediately learn from the dream. His inability to learn is not an intellectual failure, but a deliberate resistance to the movement of the divine. Augustine rejects the dream's prophetic sign and the corrective injunction of Monica's bishop. Augustine was struck less by the dream than by Monica's correction of his deliberate misinterpretation of it. Revelation remains subject to interpretation and misinterpretation, for it is always mediated through words; the young Augustine, despite all he has learned in the events recounted in Book Three, instinctively uses words to deceive himself of the dream's true import.[81] Yet, the rising orator turned philosopher is stung by the truth of simple Monica's correction of his deliberate misinterpretation. The young Augustine is determined to trade the light for the shadows it casts.

Monica's bishop (himself an ex-Manichee) tells Monica that Augustine is "unteachable (*indocilem*)"—he is not yet ready to learn. "Let him be," the bishop tells her, for Augustine must learn for himself when the time is right (*Conf.* 3.12.21). Learning to see in the spirit, it would seem, requires that we learn to discern the time. No disputations would have shaken Augustine from his errors; he must find by his own lights the error of his ways. So too, it is implied, the reader himself must learn to see into the spiritual center of things, to identify his own willful conceit, to discern (in a rightly ordered fashion) the spirit appropriate to time and place, and to work out his own salvation.

CONCLUSION

Book Three opens with the hissing cauldrons of lust and closes with quiet words of reassurance "as if they had sounded from heaven" (*Conf.* 3.12.21). Augustine and his reader are emboldened; the landscape has changed, there have been fresh advances—and yet, the rush for fugitive liberty has not yet become the devout walk of the pilgrim. In Monica's dream, she and Augustine stand together on a ruler. Later, in Book Nine, they stand together on a balcony in Ostia, enjoying the silent exultations of the chorus of eternity. Book Three, like *Confessions* as a whole, is Augustine's invitation to the reader to join him on the ruler and the balcony. With the promise of hope, Augustine commends his readers—coinitiates with him in confession—to reexamine their misplaced intellectual loves and to discern more accurately the appropriate pattern of that which partakes of no changing nor shadow.

Chapter 4

Book Four: The Trappings of Woe and Confession of Grief

James Wetzel

INTRODUCTION

Augustine announces at the beginning of Book Four that he spent a good nine years of his life, from age nineteen to twenty-eight, publicly teaching the liberal arts and privately binding himself to the false religion of Manicheism. As if to underscore that he was not bound alone, he uses the first-person plural to set the mood for the confession to follow: "During these same nine years . . . we were used to being seduced and to seducing, to being deceived and to deceiving, in a variety of excitements" (4.1.1).[1] When he lapses back into the first person and—grammatically speaking—extricates himself from his friends in seduction and deception, he more or less catalogues his life as a Manichee in Carthage.[2]

It is a catalogue of restrained vices. He versed students in the unprincipled art of rhetoric, greedy to enhance his own reputation for speaking, but he preferred the sort of student who was principled enough not to use rhetorical tricks to get an innocent person condemned. He took on a woman to be his sexual partner out of wedlock, hoping to have no more than the one unplanned child he had already parented with her, but he remained faithful to her during their fourteen years together. He looked to astrology to relieve him of the responsibilities of his tangled human freedom, but he refused the ministrations of soothsayers, who sacrificed animals to win the favor of spirits that cared about things like poetry contests and who won them. All things considered, the life he describes was not an especially bad one, but nor was it especially good.

"Badly consoling" is a phrase that more aptly captures the flavor of Augustine's years as a committed Manichee. Consolation is bad or false in cases where the need for consolation has been misperceived, and the need is either not there at all or of the sort that demands consolation of a different order. At the heart of Book Four—its moral center of gravity—Augustine recounts and anatomizes an

53

experience of howling grief. He is back in Thagaste, his hometown, having returned there from Carthage. A young man of about twenty at the time, he is full of enthusiasms. Carthage was the city where he fell in love with love, developed his taste for theater, dedicated his passion to philosophy, and converted to Manicheism—a religion from which he expected answers to his most burning questions. Shortly after his return home in the fall of 375, he reconnects with a childhood friend, whom he soon convinces to become a Manichee. Although Augustine refrains from retrospectively describing his relation to this man of like age, background, and interests as a "genuine friendship" (4.4.7), the bonds of affection between the two young men were obviously heartfelt. When the "friend" (for lack of a better word) dies of a fever, Augustine is inconsolable. He drags his "broken and bleeding soul" around town, visiting familiar haunts—where "all things were a horror, even light itself" (4.7.12)—until he decides to leave home again and return to Carthage. There he will seek repair in "causes of other sorrows" (4.8.13), friendships seeded in the soil of a false religion.

In his commentary on Book Four, James J. O'Donnell tells us that "this book is made up of reminiscences of Carthage (376/83) framing the Thagaste episode (375/6) in the mid-section of the book."[3] From a strictly chronological point of view (a view not always easy to apply to the *Confessions*), O'Donnell is surely right about the framing. When the imperatives of Book Four's confession are weighed in, however, I am inclined to invert the picture. It is the Thagaste episode that frames Augustine's memory of Carthage and not the reverse. After Thagaste, Carthage became to Augustine what fleshpots were to dispirited Israelites wandering in the desert: a falsely consoling memory. The Carthage that Augustine flees to in 376, fleeing from the familiarity of his grief-hued life, is not very different from the Carthage of 371, the "cauldron of dissolute loves" (3.1.1) that beckoned a seventeen-year-old boy to leave the house of his father. Admittedly he didn't know himself in 371 to be seeking solace for a wounded heart. His heart seemed restless, but not grief-stricken. But it would be premature to conclude that in 376 he came to Carthage knowing the grief that dogged his steps. His friend's death had turned his life into a "great question" (4.4.9), and it was the sort of question that his Manichean pieties had ill equipped him to entertain. Augustine had touched upon a grief in himself that defied limits and so defied chronology. It spoke to a loss in his heart that preceded all the losses of a finite reckoning, and to hear of this loss terrified him. He confesses that he ran from his heart rather than enter into the question of its grief: "My straying was my god" (4.7.12).

When I speak of the imperatives of Book Four's confession, I don't mean to set these imperatives apart from the confession that is the common concern of all the books. The basic imperative of confession holds constant throughout Augustine's thirteen tries at self-recollection and knowledge of God, and that is for him to face the great question of himself. Part of what it means for him to face this question is to suffer the death of his straying self; the other part is to surrender to the life that works through this death. These parts are as inseparable from one another as sin is from grace. Hence all of Augustine's confessions have a twofold aspect: they speak of not hearing God, and they speak of God's having made use of the "not hearing" to be heard.

I am not going to try to make better sense of confession in general beyond trying to fathom the particularities of Book Four's confession, which I have referred to in my essay's title as "a confession of grief." The suggestion in my title is not that grief is always some kind of sin—perhaps a lack of faith in God's keeping—but that grief is sometimes God-bereft and to confess it as such is to be called home. For Augustine the return of the soul to God is the heart's return to itself. His own suggestion, then, is that the human heart is always in God's keeping and so cannot express a God-bereft love that is not divinely claimable in the end. His view of love, it seems to me, limits the power of sin considerably (even to the point of making sin powerless), but not sin's misery. We are too rooted in God, in other words, really to have broken from God, but not so rooted that we can't feel like we have.

My main interest in this essay is Augustine's theology of grief, since it is this theology that underwrites Book Four's retrospective confession of a God-bereft grief. His theology of grief is also a psychology of grief. I would like to be as faithful as I can to Augustine's inspiration, and keep God and soul together, but this kind of fidelity is hard to come by. I am aware of two major difficulties that stand against me. These are in fact difficulties that stand against many readers of the *Confessions*, but against the scholarly ones most of all.

One I will call a difficulty of address. How is Augustine best addressed by his interpreter? He is writing in a confessional mode. I do not take myself to be writing about him in a confessional mode. Is it possible then for me to hear Augustine's posing of his "great question" about himself—the question that he is—and not be moved to enter into a great question of my own? I would like to say that it is possible, or if it is not, that at least I have the option of posing my question privately and not have it burden my exposition of his. Reading Book Four has troubled my hope about this, however. That book is largely about failed friendships, or the ways in which friends tacitly conspire with one another to keep great questions from being asked. When Augustine loses his one friend so painfully— the one who at a crucial moment had refused the conspiracy (as I will soon explain)—he abandons himself to all the virtual, not-quite-real friendships that were left to him. It is as if a whole world of affection had collapsed for him into a single death.

I have the uncomfortable feeling that if I try too hard to be the impartial observer, or to maintain too studied a detachment from his confessional mode of address, I risk perpetuating the very kind of conspiring that compelled Augustine at the beginning of Book Four to pluralize his confessional voice. Must he confess for me? My worry here is not that I will end up being a bad friend to Augustine, whatever that could mean, but that I will end up being a bad reader or bad guide to other readers, and perhaps that is all being a bad friend to him could mean in this context. To be a good reader of Augustine, I need to allow him the chance of addressing me and not restrict myself to erudite eavesdropping on his conversation with God. I give him this chance less by sharing his beliefs and empathizing with his experiences than by keeping an eye on the motive I have for reading him at all. What do I expect from Augustine?

That brings me to my other difficulty. I will call it a difficulty of expectation. Take the case of Book Four. I expect to be able to move from Augustine's episodic account of his dark bout with grief to a more general consideration of what makes his grief fit matter for a confession. The move to the more general issue raises the question of sin and grief: namely, where is the sin in grief? Here, it seems to me, comes the really hard part. How am I supposed to isolate, identify, and analyze the sin in Augustine's confession of grief? Let's assume for the moment I plan to do all this objectively—without concern, that is, for whether I share in the sin that Augustine confesses. I may not even believe that there is such a thing as sin. Let's assume I don't. I will want, given these assumptions, to treat sin as one of Augustine's constructs, as an artifact, that is, of his clime and culture, albeit a culture he has helped to shape. I will leave it to him to be one of the architects of his own distant world, but not of my world, the one near to hand. Were I to try to bring him into my world, presumably I would be compelled to take his influence on my own terms—according to the constructs, that is, that govern my own world of experience.

Now let's apply the logic of this line of reasoning to the identification and analysis of sin in Book Four's confession of grief. Sin there is what Augustine would have identified as a bad conceptualization of his experience of grief. Since he has been busy trying to discredit the Manichean beliefs of his young adulthood, it must be those beliefs—about God and the soul—that frame and misshape his grief. And yet there is no way to test this hypothesis directly. The line of reasoning I have been sketching works on the assumption that experiences are just conceptualizations of experience, and so there is nothing to compare to a conceptualization except a further conceptualization. The interpreter of Augustine is thus left with the task of determining whether his description of his troublesome grief is of a piece with his once Manichean conceptions of his own psyche. Simply put, are the conceptualizations consistent?

I don't think that the question of consistency is a useless one to pose. In his commentary on Book Four, Colin Starnes has done a brilliant job of helping readers see the consistency between Augustine's adherence to Manicheism and his descriptions of his life's miseries during that time.[4] One moral of this consistency is that Augustine, like most any one of us at one time or another, has been the prisoner of his own perceptions. When he perceives important matters badly, he is not likely to live much better than he perceives. But what else is consistency supposed to tell us here? That Augustine's Manichean beliefs were the *cause* of his sorrow?[5] We expect too little of him if we are apt to conclude this. He would want us to honor better his struggling love of the truth and ask what it is about *him* that has led him to seek his truth in a false religion. Of course it is a much safer, much neater proposition not to seek the truth when reading him and focus on words and their life-shaping possibilities. The results may be diverting, even alluring, but so restricted a focus will never reveal to us Augustine's basis for making his words and their life-shaping possibilities his own.

Not to care about Augustine's basis for selection is not to care about reading him. He is too alive as a writer to the difficulties of putting himself in his words to be read as if his words and their historical currencies automatically defined his much-desired sense of self. His words are hopeful gestures to selfhood or halting attempts to break his soul out of its infancy. We won't read these gestures well unless we can imagine like gestures in ourselves, and that requires not just a concern for the possibilities of words but for using words to speak the truth. I don't mean that we ought to bring some crude defensiveness about truth to reading Augustine and then join him in rejecting what he rejects. I mean that we ought to care enough about truth to notice *how* Augustine goes about seeking his. For all his talk about Manicheism as a false religion, he says precious little about why it is false. If we read him with that question in mind, we are left with a short list of things not to believe: that God is material, that evil is a substance, that God is passive in the face of active evil, that souls are either purely good or purely evil.[6] This listing, however accurate as a list of untruths, skirts the issue of what would move anyone to believe things of this sort in the first place. That is just the issue that Augustine refuses to skirt in his confession. It may be the case that Manichean doctrines are false, but the falsity that counts most for him—because it does the most damage—is falsity of the heart. If the words are true, but the heart is false, the words are of no avail.[7]

Augustine's concern for truth, when set in the register of the heart, comes across as a problem of articulation. To be truthful it is not enough for him to declare and believe true things; he must also be present in and through the truth he declares, otherwise there is a real sense in which *he* hasn't declared anything. The grief that Augustine confesses to in Book Four is false not so much because the beliefs that frame it are false, but because he uses those beliefs to keep his distance from himself. His grief was noisy, but inarticulate. His confessional mode of remembering his grief is his attempt to give it a better voice, a voice that says better what was lost and what there is left for which to hope.

When I think of Augustine's confession of grief in this way—a way that has some hope of meeting my difficulties of address and expectation—my mind tends to wander to *Hamlet*, Shakespeare's great drama of a man's belated self-conception. I think especially of the problem Prince Hamlet had in making his grief believable. Hamlet lost a father and clung to black mourning; his mother lost a husband and wed herself to her husband's brother. She wants to know from her son why his grief persists. He is not the first son to lose a father; he will not be the last. Death is the common lot of mortals. Why should one death seem so particular to him? He answers her as follows:

> "Seems," madam? Nay, it is. I know not "seems."
> 'Tis not alone my inky cloak, good mother,
> Nor customary suits of solemn black,
> Nor windy suspiration of forced breath,
> No, nor the fruitful river in the eye,
> Nor the dejected 'havior of the visage,

> Together with all forms, moods, shapes of grief,
> That can denote me truly. These indeed "seem";
> For they are actions that a man might play.
> But I have that within which passeth show—
> These but the trappings and the suits of woe.
> (*Hamlet* 1.2.76–86)

Hamlet tells Gertrude, in effect, that she has not seen the particularity of his grief for his father, but only its inadequate forms—"the trappings and the suits of woe." He knows in himself that he feels his father's loss uniquely, but also that he is powerless to convey that uniqueness to her or anyone else; he can only seem to. What he has within, he says, "passeth show." I take his point to be not that his grief is too much for sighs, tears, and a dejected visage, but that he is not play-acting. His grief isn't *for* show. Hamlet's curse, as he sees it, is that he was born into a world where men and women commonly play-act feelings for personal gain and so debase the common language of feeling. Have enough people show grief and not mean it, and it becomes hard, if not impossible, for a person to mean grief by showing it. "Denmark's a prison," Hamlet tells two of his uncle's spies (2.2.243). It is the sort of prison that keeps his heart confined to silence, a prescription for madness.

Augustine lost his father years before he lost his unnamed friend. He records the death of his father with all the affect of a necrology: "when I was eighteen and my father had already been dead for two years" (3.4.7). The thought of his father's death is tacked on to another thought (about receiving money from his mother for books); it doesn't even rate its own sentence. By contrast Augustine is eloquence itself when it comes to the death of his friend (4.4.9):

> My heart was wholly in grief's shade, and death was whatever I looked at. My native land was a punishment to me; my father's house a strange and luckless place. The things I had shared with him turned and tortured me cruelly in his absence. My eyes kept seeking him out everywhere, and he was gone. I hated everything because nothing had him; nor could anything still say to me, "Look, he is on his way," as when he was alive and just away. I had become a great question to myself.

If I could put to Augustine a form of the question that Gertrude put to Hamlet, I would want to know why the death of his friend should have seemed so particular to him. The difference between Augustine and Hamlet, aside from the difference in their respective occasions for grief, is that Augustine has anticipated my question and posed it of himself. Hamlet casts doubt on even the propriety of his mother's question. The barest suggestion from her that he may be unnaturally affected offends him. How could she, whom he takes to be false herself, possibly be in a position to tell?

The burden of Hamlet's knowledge is indeed heavy. Casting himself as the only true soul in a world of pretense and theater, he has no way to act in his world except as a pretender of pretense. The irony finally undoes him, and in the end he is left with no other resolution to his life's drama but death. Augustine is also aware that he was born into a world of pretense and falsity. Unlike Hamlet, however, Augustine acknowledges his human lot. The curse of his birth, as he sees it, is not the singular exception of his life, but his commonality with all the world's pretenders—the curse of original sin. So whereas Hamlet sets himself the impossible task of inventing a wholly original language of action and emotion (who would understand it?), Augustine works to redeem his use of familiar words and gestures.

I turn now to the particulars of Augustine's efforts in Book Four to recollect himself in grief and thereby redeem his language of grieving. The need for such redemption will show up in his peculiar failure to be in his grief. Augustine's description of this failure—which is anything but a *simple* failure of memory— takes in a psychology of self-escape. Augustine's return to himself and to his reluctantly human expressions of grief over loss is a possibility he vouchsafes to theology. Because I will proceed as he does and begin with the psychological complexities of his remembered grief, I need to issue this caveat at the outset: Augustine's transits from psychology to theology are misleading if we read him under the assumption that his theology takes up where his psychology leaves off.

The sense I get from the *Confessions* as a whole is that all of us have to begin a quest for knowledge with psychology, in that the human desire to know is everywhere twisted and hobbled by bad presumptions of self-knowledge. But it is not Augustine's view that we work at a question of self whose answer is then revealed to us from above—as if we were simply in need of further information. His perspective is more radical than that. It is the question of self that is the revelation. We take this question to God, the maker of selves, but God's answer is already implied in the continual opening of the question. Augustine's respect for the piety of faithful questioning—a respect that he shares with Plato's Socrates—runs throughout the *Confessions*, and Book Four is a paradigm case.

THE WORD FOR GRIEF

First I need to say a few more words about that friend of his. Augustine doesn't furnish us with many details about his friendship at Thagaste, beyond his saying that it was an "exceedingly sweet" affection, "cooked in the fervor of like enthusiasms" and snatched from him all too soon—scarcely past a year into it and well before he had had his fill (4.4.7). The most telling part of Augustine's recollection picks up the friendship at its end. Sometime over the course of a long fever, when the friend seemed to his family very likely to die, they had him baptized. The sick young man was quite out of his senses at the time, and for his part Augustine simply assumed that his friend would laugh off the baptism once he came back to consciousness and was told of it. Their friendship, after all, had been built on Augustine's success at turning his friend from the Catholic faith to the religion of the Manichees. (For Augustine at the time, barely into his twenties, this would have been a choice between a superstitious and authoritarian faith and a philosophical, if somewhat esoteric, quest for truth.) When he finds his friend temporarily revived and lucid, Augustine is surprised, stunned really, at his friend's response to his jests about baptism: "He was horrified at me, as if I were his enemy, and with an astonishing and sudden sense of independence, he warned me that if I wanted to be his friend, I would have to stop saying such things to him" (4.4.8). Augustine's immediate reaction to his friend's change of heart is one of disbelief and reserve. Because he can't quite believe that the change in his friend is other than illness-driven, he decides to wait for a better time to work on his friend and restore him to his more compliant disposition. That time never comes. The fever returns a few days later, while Augustine is away, and the friend dies.

Thinking back on his last encounter with his friend, now with the benefit of distance, Augustine is prepared to find some consolation in a death that had opened a black hole in his heart: "That one was taken abruptly from my madness, so that he might be safe with you and a consolation for me" (4.4.8). There are really two distinct offers of consolation acknowledged here in Augustine's confession: one is of being able to know that a beloved is safe with God, and the other is of being able to know that a beloved is safe from oneself. These consolations are intimately related in Augustine's confession, and ultimately they must be read to reflect a single consolation and a single source of redemption. The desired convergence of the consolations—the convergence that makes consolation consoling—is best approached, however, by way of distinction.

Consider first the consolation that Augustine would take from knowing that his friend is with God. This will be the hardest consolation for him (and his reader) to take in directly. The difficulty is that it is all too tempting here to confuse being with God with being dead, as if his friend or any friend were *better off* dead. The flip side of that confusion is to suppose that the living are not yet with God. Neither sentiment makes a bit of theological sense, but Augustine's alternative sentiment isn't easy to understand either: that we are always with God but not always or even usually with ourselves. A paradoxical psychology of self-escape needs to be confronted, it seems, before anyone can ever hope to take much consolation from God.

Augustine comes up against just such a psychology in himself when he tries to take the other kind of consolation from his friend's death. He thanks God for putting his friend out of reach of his madness and therefore for sparing Augustine the guilt of having corrupted his friend for a second time. And it would have been a far worse corruption than the first. The first time that Augustine had convinced his friend to reject the Catholic faith and share in his Manichean fixations, his friend was young and impressionable and "not deeply rooted" in "the true faith" (4.4.7). The second convincing, were there to have been one, would have worked against the forthright independence that Augustine was so startled and disturbed to see emerge from his friend. No longer would Augustine have been misleading an impressionable youth, whose principal failing up to then had been his uncritical desire to please his charismatic peer; he would have been turning a man against his own best conviction, robbing his love of its love of truth. But thankfully, recalls Augustine, the worst was not to be. His friend's death left Augustine alone with his madness, and under the guise of a bereft lover, he tried desperately to escape himself.

I am suggesting that there was a significant element of pretense in Augustine's grief over his friend's death, that his grief was not a reliable measure of how much he loved this person in life. In suggesting this, I am entering into an aspect of Augustine's own puzzlement over his motives and behavior. He would like to know, looking back at his days of weeping, what made him hold on so long and so tightly to his grief, as if something bitter could itself be a relief from bitterness. He wonders whether his grief might have harbored some hope of having his friend restored to him, so that in holding on to the grief he was holding on to the hope. He rejects the idea. Hope would have made his grief into a kind of prayer, and he had no God to pray to then, but only the phantom of his Manichean imagination—a divinity as helpless as he was. The closest he comes to answering his question is this further question, left poignantly unanswered: "Or is weeping really a bitter thing and pleasing only in place of the distaste we have for the things we formerly enjoyed but now shrink from in horror?" (4.5.10). If Augustine means to ask this question of himself, then he has to face the terrible prospect of getting this answer: that his grief had less to do with mourning his friend than with avoiding his own guilt. The prospect is terrible because his guilt may suggest to him that he never loved his friend at all.

In his confession, Augustine is sufficiently aware of the ambiguities in his grief back then not to want to return to it too precipitously. For confessional purposes, it would be good of course for him to face his guilt about the friendship and unearth his sin from there. But if grief was once his way not to face guilt, then recollecting grief may simply harden and renew his defenses. Augustine pauses to survey his motives for continuing: "Why do I talk about these things? Now isn't the time to be asking a lot of questions, but to be confessing to you" (4.6.11). He continues nevertheless to entertain the question of his grief. He has no choice but to continue with it, for his confession turns on the answer. So what does he think his grief was finally all about?

His first attempt at a definitive answer ends on a false note. He applies a poetic trope for the bond between two committed friends—two halves of one soul—to his own case, and then he uses this trope to suggest a reason for why he preferred a miserable life to joining his friend in death: "Perhaps I was afraid to die, because then the whole of him, whom I loved so much, would be dead" (4.6.11). In his *Retractationes*, a review of his life's writings written three years before his death, Augustine will look back on that sentence in Book Four and admit that it seemed to him more like a "trifling disclosure" than a "serious confession" (2.6.2). Actually, I find it hard to believe that Augustine's intent was ever other than serious while he was writing Book Four, the offending line included, but I think I get the old bishop's point. There is something theatrical or showy about Augustine's image of himself as half his dead friend's soul, and theatricality in his *confessional* self-image is wholly out of place. A "serious confession" would expose, not perpetuate, the theatricality of his friendship. It would expose, that is, what was false or affected in Augustine's love of his friend.

Augustine has already in fact supplied us with a means to take a more sober view of his friendship and begin to see through its pretense. He has said that death was God's way of removing his friend from Augustine's "madness" (*dementia*). Let's consider what manner of madness that might be. I don't think it can simply be the madness of wanting to reinduct his friend into a false religion. At the time Augustine doesn't believe that Manicheism is false, and it isn't especially mad behavior for him to want company in his convictions. It would be mad behavior on his part only if Manicheism were so wildly implausible a religion that it would have been crazy for him ever to have put any trust in it and crazier still for him to think he could have elicited a like trust from others. But it wasn't a wildly implausible religion. The aspects of Manicheism that came most to disturb Augustine—its materialism, its limited view of God, its us-and-them dualism, and its obsession with a God-given purity—have appeared in many different forms in the history of human consciousness and are likely to have a long future. And with his gift for persuasion and his rare intelligence, Augustine was more than capable of making just those very aspects seductive to others. He had good reason to believe that he would have won his friend back over to his side, had he been given the chance. He won others to his side in Carthage, and he was consoled by their attentions to him.

Seen from another angle, however, it is Augustine's very confidence about what would have happened with his friend that betrays his kind of madness. The thought never even occurs to Augustine that his friend, had he lived, might have been the one doing the convincing. I don't mean to suggest that his friend would have had a whole new arsenal of arguments to marshal against Augustine and a newly discovered ability to use them effectively. *He* had not been, after all, the man to master Aristotle's *Categories* at the tender age of twenty, and without benefit of instruction (4.16.28). That was Augustine. Nor had he been the man known to possess the "quickness of mind" and "sharpness of insight" that made him a natural for the study of the liberal arts (4.16.30). That was Augustine too. No, it was only out of "some unknown higher instinct" that Augustine's friend took his deathbed baptism to heart and refused Augustine's mockery of the sacrament.[8] Augustine did not of course owe his friend *belief* in the face of his friend's transfiguration, but he did owe it to the friendship not to dismiss out of hand what had elicited his friend's independence of heart and mind. It would have been enough had Augustine been willing to question his own self-certainties before his friend had to die. That is the sort of self-questioning we offer to someone, not out of respect for a superior argument, but out of love.

"Oh what madness it is," Augustine exclaims, "not to know how to love human beings humanly!" (4.7.12). He refers to the same madness that had distorted, if not falsified, his friendship. His mind could accept the basic truths about loving other human beings—that they were different from him, that they didn't live forever—but his heart could not. His heart preferred to have a friend who would be wholly the creature of his desires, specifically his desire not to have to face his own corruptibility. That was the same desire that drove him to embrace Manicheism. The madness in all this was that Augustine loved his friend on terms that made it impossible for him to have a friend. The consummation of his love would have been, spiritually considered, his friend's death.

But there is more to the story of Augustine's love than his fear of death, or he would have found a perfect consolation in the friends who were willing to recon-firm him in his Manichean fiction of himself—that the part of him that was right would never die. Instead he speaks of his love for these friends as having taken the place of his love for God, this being the continuation for him of "a tall tale and an old lie" (4.8.13). Once again Augustine was wedding himself to a bad pat-tern of loving and to the extravagant mythology he would need to justify it to himself, but he is not in retrospect entirely condemning of his heart. He doesn't think that he never loved his friends at all (that he was just pretending, in other words), but that he loved them only after he had rejected a profounder love.

The effect of this rejection on his or anyone else's love is to place an impossi-ble burden on the human desire to know the unity of love. "This unity is so loved," he observes, "that we feel guilty when we don't love the one returning love to us, or if we don't return love to the one loving us, seeking nothing from his body but signs of a good will" (4.9.14). Augustine's complex use here of the Ciceronian coinage *redamare*—"to return love for love"—suggests his belief that if we refuse God, whose love is always first in the order of loving, it becomes too late for us to return love to others, a belatedness that darkens and adds guilt to grief. Behind this belief lies the story that is his alternative to the Manichean mythology of human beginnings. In Augustine's version of Genesis, we were all somehow present in the choice of Adam and Eve to turn from the love of their heavenly father and seek an abundance of life by other means (the quest for divine knowledge). But as there is no way to secure immortality other than by respond-ing to the love of God, they bound themselves to seek immortality where it could not be found. Their original sin, thinks Augustine, has altered the disposition of the human heart. All of us are now disposed to substitute some other love for the love of God, but this is less the direct substitution of one love for another (we lack the imagination for that) than it is the terrible impoverishment of the love we have always had.

Original human love, as Augustine conceives of it, is love that has what love most wants, at least until the day that love decides it wants something else. It is a paradoxical notion, to be sure, to be moved to want less than what you want most, but I won't enter here into Augustine's intricate and (as I far as I can tell) not always coherent reflections on the psychology of original sin.[9] I invoke his notion of original love in this context to help frame what he thinks human love is like on the *other* side of the paradoxical choice to seek life's fruition "in the land of death" (4.12.18). It is like knowing that your best chances at love are always behind you. When Augustine tells us of how his dying friend set new terms for their friendship, he also tells us of how he felt threatened by this—as if he had been made out to be an enemy—and of how he resolved in himself to reject those terms. From his confessional perspective, Augustine casts himself then as having rejected God's offer of love, at that very moment when his friend, in the deepest sense of the words, had come to his senses. Augustine's friend had not rejected him, nor had God. It was Augustine who was doing all the rejecting. But he came to understand this long after his friend had died, when it was too late to respond to the love he most wanted.

Most reflective people will know something about the pathos of Augustine's kind of hindsight. His readers may be forgiven for wondering, however, what good it does to cast the follies of missed opportunities in love in the form of a rejection of God. There is no easy or quick answer to that question, I think, but we would do well to remember that Augustine's God is a God of both judgment and forgiveness. The judging side of God commends us to our responsibilities. We are not free to consign all our failures at love to the waste bin of bad luck; we will be found wanting for the love we have overlooked and trampled upon in the name of some other value. The forgiving side of God commends us to the judgment that is not our own and so releases us from the hell of self-torment. We are not free to absent ourselves from God, despite our best efforts, and so we are not the final arbiters of our love's imperfections. That is why confession of sin is for Augustine a hopeful act.

These two sides of God—punishing and forgiving—come together in Augustine's description of Christ. His description is worth citing at some length (4.12.19):

> He who is our life came down to us, took up our death, and killed it with his own life's abundance: and like thunder, he called us to return to him from here and into that hidden place from which he first came forth to us— the virgin womb. It was there that humanity was wedded to him, mortal flesh, not to be mortal forever. And like a bridegroom from the bridal bed he leapt with joy from there, a giant to run his course. For he did not delay, but ran calling out with his words, actions, death, life, descent, ascent—calling out for us to return to him. He left our sight, so that we might return to our heart and find him there. He went away, and look: here he is.

Augustine's imagery here, especially his use of Psalm 18:6 (RSV 19:5), conveys the idea that human life, from birth to death, is a love affair with God. It would be a depressingly unrequited love were we the ones to determine the terms of God's absence. Those terms would dictate a life lived in God's absence, free of the heart's responsibilities, but bound to the demands of the flesh and mortgaged to death. Augustine's God has preempted this humanly willed absence and willed an absence of his own. The place where either out of despair or pride we hope to be rid of God is the place he awaits our return.

Consider once more the consolation that Augustine hopes to take from knowing that his friend is with God. His pride would tell him that his friend, as a creature bound to follow Augustine's madness, could never have been with God in life. His pride would be wrong. It is not the friend's death that informs Augustine's confession, but his living voice, speaking against irreverence. It has become

Augustine's voice too. His despair would tell him that he has heard the voice of his friend too late, well past the time for responding. His despair would be wrong. The friend's death conveys to Augustine God's absence. This absence calls Augustine to return to himself and be in his love for others. Were he to think that loving others would not also be to love the one departed from view, he would still be looking with his eyes and not with his heart. Perhaps he would still be caring too much for his old madness, as if it were ever his madness alone.

Augustine finds something consoling in the thought that his friend, by dying, had moved beyond his love's madness. But this is a thought that is more about Augustine or his friend than about his friend's absence, and so it has nothing directly to do with what need there is for consolation. Augustine passes through this thought in his confession in order to get to what turns out to be the only kind of consolation possible for him: the hope that life is (still) in God's keeping. Getting to that hope is partly, if not wholly, a matter of taking the true measure of a beloved's loss.

THE AESTHETICS OF SIN

"Back then I didn't know about these things; I loved lesser beauties, and I was sinking into an abyss" (4.13.20). Augustine describes here, near to the end of Book Four, the quality of love that would animate his friendships in Carthage. "I used to say to my friends," he continues, "'For what else do we love if not beauty? What is a beautiful thing? What is beauty? What is it that attracts and unites us to the things we love? If it weren't for the grace and beauty in them, they would move us not at all.'" The fascination that he had for beauty in the years immediately following his friend's death had a telling blind spot. His thoughts did not give him a way to comprehend his love of the dead.

Around the age of twenty-six, Augustine began to pull together some of those thoughts, and the result was his first book, a study of the difference between absolute and relative beauty. Something relatively beautiful needs the right context to set it off: as part of a body, for instance, a foot can be pleasing, but when met detached, it tends to horrify. Absolute beauty isn't like that. It is "as though whole" of itself (4.13.20). Augustine called his study *On Beauty and Aptness*, a title that signaled his inclination to think of relative beauty not as a kind of beauty but as something of a different category: not as "beautiful" (*pulchrum*), but "apt, fitting" (*aptum*). We don't know all the details of how he worked out this distinction. His work was lost some years later, and thinking back on it from the vantage of the *Confessions*, he can't remember when it got lost or even whether it was originally divided into two books or three. What he does remember of his first work, however, is sufficient for his confessional aims in Book Four. In particular he is able to use his piecemeal recollection to frame better what he was forgetting back then, when he didn't know the things he needed to know to be a good friend and to mourn a good friend well.

In one respect it is not hard to identify what Augustine didn't know at the time. The things to be known make up a list of big truths: that God is spirit, not matter; that God's spirit became incarnate in Jesus of Nazareth; that Jesus was the Christ; that souls are redeemed through Christ's death, resurrection, and ascension into heaven. The list could be emended or its items elaborated, but the list would still be a list—and there's the rub. Augustine is very aware of his education in the concluding sections of Book Four, of the years he spent reading every book he could on the liberal arts and feeling that he had grasped them all. He wonders what he really learned from all that. Let's stipulate, for present purposes, that the items on my list of big truths are all true, and that these truths are often encountered in traditions of liberal study. But to bring the example closer to home, let's just say that some tradition of liberal study includes the works of Augustine, and that this tradition takes Augustine to be an authority, a reliable teacher, that is, of the truth. Would a reader in this tradition, reading Book Four of the *Confessions*, have the benefit of the truths that Augustine names there but sees as having been absent from his understanding during his student years?

Even were the reader a "believer" (as we now tend to use the term), Augustine's answer to my question would still have to be this: that it's not for him to say. Sure, he may have presented some big truth persuasively enough to convince his reader to consent to it; still, he suggests, the benefit to the reader may yet be lacking. I take that suggestion from his summary assessment of his own years of greedy reading and study: "I had my back to the light and my face to the matters illuminated, and as a result my face, my means for looking at these matters, was not itself illuminated" (4.16.31). The big truths either take in the truth of the person trying to grasp them, or they are diminished truths and therefore dangerous (in that they may continue, though diminished, to be believed big).

This brings me back to the "great question" that Augustine's grief had made of him. It was clearly not a question he was ready to have posed. Perhaps no one is ever ready for this kind of question at the time of its posing, but few have been as eloquent or as insightful as Augustine about their lack of readiness. In one of the more lyrical passages of the *Confessions*, he speaks of the belatedness of his love for God. His words recapitulate the psychology that had turned his grief into a wasteland: "Late have I loved you, beauty so ancient and so new, late have I loved you! And look you were within me and I outside; there I looked for you, and into the beauties you made I rushed, misshapen myself" (10.27.38). The beauties of his misshapen affection and the "lesser beauties" of his Carthage years are one and the same. His trouble then and later would lie not with beauties that pale in comparison to God's beauty (there is no scale of comparison here), but with his inclination to use beauty as a venue for self-exit. He hoped, in effect, not to have to be included in his knowledge of the whole.

This is not to say that he was directly seeking the "abyss" of nonbeing. Quite to the contrary, he was seeking a self that seemed to him better, more beautiful, than the one he was fleeing. His youthful reflection *On Beauty and Aptness* suggests his terms for success. He offers two key disclosures about that text in Book

Four. One concerns his motive for writing it. Augustine had been moved to dedicate his work to the orator at Rome, a man named Hierius. Although he had no personal knowledge of Hierius, he loved and admired the image of the man in cultured circles—an unusually gifted speaker of both Greek and Latin, well versed in the subtleties of philosophy. Augustine had been used to getting recognition from those who craved his (his friends): now he was the one craving to be recognized. He was after his ideal self, whose beauty would be confirmed or denied for him in a word from an important man.

Although that word never came to him in either form, Augustine tells us that he continued to think well of what he had written. His other important disclosure about *On Beauty and Aptness* speaks directly to its content. Augustine's conception there of a supremely good soul, one good enough to be called divine, was that of a "monad," a mind free and clear of erotic disturbances and conflicting desires ("a sexless mind"); its contrary he called a "dyad," a soul at odds with itself and so constantly prey to lust and anger (4.15.24). The basic idea seems to be that it is good to be single-minded, bad to be diversely driven—not the easiest of ideals for a spirited personality, such as Augustine's, to attain. But he wasn't envisioning himself as having to move from dyadic to monadic life. His exotic Pythagorean categories spoke to wholly distinct genealogies. Either he was carnal or spiritual in essence; if spiritual (the only sane possibility) then the carnal "part" of him was there to be excised, not redeemed. His judgment in Book Four upon this way of thinking was succinct: "I didn't know what I was talking about" (4.15.24).

I take Augustine at this word, but why then does he spend time in his confession rehearsing thoughts from a lost book of nonsense? The answer has to do, I think, with the seductiveness of the nonsense at issue. Suppose you are a reader who brings to your reading of the *Confessions* an aesthetic sensibility akin to Augustine's in *On Beauty and Aptness*. You are not likely to find the grief that he describes in Book Four any prettier than did the author of the *Confessions*. There is too much evidence in that description of a soul torn between conflicting impulses—to live or to die. But what then would be your ideal expression of grief? I don't think that you can have one. Even the expression "ideal of grief" is an inept one. Grief is at best appropriate, but never ideal. It is not properly part of the beautiful.

There are two broadly metaphysical intuitions that can underwrite such an aesthetic sensibility, and I wonder whether Augustine would have been all that careful to distinguish between them in his earliest work. In one the wholeness that is absolute beauty has no involvement with vulnerable beauties, and in the other that wholeness takes in vulnerable beauties and gives them their ultimate significance. The first intuition suggests that we ought to be indifferent to goods that we can lose; they are to be held as of no account. The second intuition allows us to value these goods as good, but it calls us to value them from the perspective of the whole, where loss drops from view.

Augustine's sense of God discounts both intuitions. His God is neither the whole that is indifferent to the divisible wholes, nor is he the whole that is the sum of all the parts. That leaves human beings searching for a wholeness that they can never fairly hope to comprehend. Although this lack of comprehension is meant to be a liberation for the spirit and not a depressing feature of finitude, human resentment of finitude is usually potent enough to suggest otherwise. As he gets older, Augustine gets less tempted to heap contempt directly upon the vulnerable beauties of this life, but he never quite gets over his desire for a world-disdaining faith. In Book Nine, where he describes his intense grief over the loss of Monica, the vulnerable beauty who was his mother in life, Augustine is unapologetic but defensive. He sends God this note to pass along to a judgmental reader: "Let him read and interpret as he wants; if he should see sin in my having wept for my mother a small portion of an hour, the mother who died before my eyes and wept for me many a year that I might live before yours, let him not deride me, but rather—if he is someone of great charity—let him weep to you for my sins" (9.12.33). Part of what stands against Augustine's grief is his faith that his mother died in God's grace and so lives without want. Does he think, then, that were his faith perfect, there would be nothing for him to grieve? Does the reader "of great charity" weep for his lack of faith?

A perfect faith—or the closest that human beings ever get to *knowing* that all life is in God's keeping—does not, in fact, rule out grief. On the contrary, it is what allows grief its truest expression: sorrow, pure and simple, over the loss of a beloved. We will miss the person who continues to be with God but who is no longer with us. In a less than perfect faith, we get distracted by other claims on grief, most of them coming from guilt, resentment, and fear. Those claims are ignored at one's peril, though they are the hijackers of grief and not its natural ally. Augustine is probably wise to confess that his most faithful grieving may yet have an element of falsity to it, some mere trapping of woe.

SUMMARY REFLECTIONS

Book Four's theology of grief is a confession of loss and of the heart's confusion over the magnitude of loss. This confusion, for Augustine, has to do with sin and so with the prospect of ultimate and irredeemable loss. Not long into his *Confessions*, he comes up with this concise characterization of his sinful disposition: "My sin was this, that I was seeking pleasures, sublimities, truths not in God but in his creatures—me and the rest—and in this way I was heading into pains, disorders, errors" (1.20.31). It is easy to notice Augustine's apparent antithesis here between God and creatures without paying too much attention to the work that the preposition "in" does to define a branching of human desire: for good things *in* God, or for good things *in* creatures. (This is an "in" of origination and could be happily translated as "from.") It is generally easy, when reading Augustine, to turn God and the created world into competing objects of desire. The ease and temptation of this reading, which is in fact a disastrous misreading of Augustine, is due not to his concision or carelessness as a writer, but to the disposition he would have identified as sinful.

Book Four is the greatest check in the *Confessions* against one potent form of the sinful disposition: the craving for an absolute antithesis between God and humanity. As sin in this form obviously entails a denial of a divine incarnation—either its possibility or its importance—it is no accident that Book Four is one of the most explicitly christological of the *Confessions'* thirteen books. The God who calls Augustine home walked the earth as a human being, tried to teach other human beings how to love humanly, and suffered a human death. The christological emphasis in Book Four on the absence of Christ from human eyes—on the passing, that is, of Jesus of Nazareth into history—figures into Augustine's attempt to reassess his own human losses. He was not alive to see Christ die; he did live to see others die: both of his parents, his son Adeodatus, the unnamed friend of Book Four, still others. Somehow Augustine hopes to find in Christ's death the measure of all his palpable human losses. That is the hope of his confession in Book Four. How is a reader to conceive of it?

In making his way to a connection between Christ's death and the deaths of his own experience, Augustine is having his heart freed from having to choose between loving God and loving a human being. In Book Four he describes having done his level best to love a mortal human being as if he were immortal and presumably divine. The result was not that Augustine loved something of lesser value in place of something greater, but that he lost touch with the man he was loving and so had no way to take in the magnitude of his loss. Augustine's grief was painful, disorderly, erroneous. If the sin in his grief had been a matter of his loving his friend in place of God, then he would have been guilty of loving his friend too much. The idea of loving someone too much strikes me as confused, but even if it makes some kind of sense, it's not the idea that Augustine's confession conveys to us. He failed to love his friend *in* God, and this left his friend to be the creature of Augustine's fears and desires—or it did, at least, from the point of view of the prodigal Augustine, who had abandoned his father's house.

The terrifying prospect of Augustine's confessional logic is that love is an all-or-nothing affair. Either we love someone well and therefore in God, or we love a fiction of our interior poverty, a desperate projection of sin. Apart from God, in other words, we never get outside the fiction we take to be the self. It is only the vision of God as a redeemer who passes through death that diverts Augustine's logic from its all-or-nothing disjunction. If it is possible to love Christ after the death of Jesus, not abstractly but in the palpable form of love of neighbor, then it is possible to redeem a lost love by loving the ones who come after. This speaks to the solidarity in love that goes along with and even presupposes solidarity in sin. The redemption of love from sin allows us the consolation of love that admits of degrees. More profoundly but infinitely harder to grasp, it releases us into a greater-than-human perfection.

Chapter 5

Book Five: The Disclosure of Hidden Providence

Frederick J. Crosson

INTRODUCTION: COMPOSITION AND HERMENEUTICS

It has been a commonplace for some scholars to say that the *Confessions* is not carefully composed. It is "a badly composed book," Augustine "was not able to plan a book," he "composes badly. . . . the ancients generally did not give to composition the attention that we do."[1] If one has such views, it is unlikely that subtler indications of meaningful structure in the text being read will be noted. And if those structures are not attended to, it is likely that the text may seem to lack design, to lack unity. But as Ovid said, "It is art to conceal art," and some of Augustine's art is easy to overlook.

Perhaps part of the reason for some modern inattention to such factors is the decline of a tradition that considers the possible intention of an author to speak differently to different kinds of readers by the same words. Augustine was familiar with such a tradition from his long and careful study of the classical rhetorical and philosophical authors, even before he first came to learn how to read the Scriptures from Ambrose. So, for example, he comments in the *City of God* on the practice of philosophers of communicating on two levels: Socrates and Plato, Cicero, Varro, and Apuleius.[2] But already much earlier he speaks of the Scriptures and of the practice of Jesus as exemplifying the method of "all rational disciplines"; such a practice, he says, "teaches partly quite openly and partly by similitudes," and he adds, "If there was nothing that could not be understood with perfect ease, there would be no studious search for truth and no pleasure in finding it."[3]

It is the understanding of Scripture that is paradigmatic for Augustine in the *Confessions*. Thus, he speaks of how he came to think of the authority of the Scriptures:

> scripture was easily accessible to every reader, while yet guarding a mysterious dignity in its deeper sense. In plain words and very humble modes of

71

speech it offered itself to everyone, yet stretched the understanding of those who were not shallow-minded. It welcomed all comers to its hospitable embrace, yet through narrow openings attracted a few to you.[4]

Indeed he speaks of his own desire to be so read:

Of this I am certain . . . that if I had to write something to which the highest authority would be attributed, I would rather write it in such a way that my words would reinforce for each reader whatever truth he was able to grasp about these matters, than express a single idea so unambiguously as to exclude others, provided these did not offend me by their falsehood.[5]

This hermeneutical attitude stands in a mean between the position that thinks the words of a teacher need not be moderated in this way—and so everything is on the same depth level, so to speak—and the position of someone who believes that what is to be taught is not determined by what is so, but by what the student/reader should hear.

Augustine's view that these two attitudes may sometimes need to be blended is explicitly stated in a slightly different context in *Christian Instruction*.

Where certain truths are, by reason of their own character, not comprehensible, or scarcely so, even when explained with every effort on the part of the speaker to make them clear, these one rarely dwells on with a general audience, or never mentions at all: but in writing, the same distinction cannot be adhered to, because a book, once published, can fall into the hands of any one at all, and therefore some truths should be shielded by obscuring words, so that they may profit those who will understand them and be hidden from the simple who will not comprehend them. (4.9.23)

This view is reaffirmed by Thomas Aquinas in his commentary on Boethius's *On the Trinity*. There he maintains that

the words of a teacher ought to be so moderated that they result to the profit and not to the detriment of the one hearing him. Now there are certain things which on being heard harm no one, as are the truths which all are responsible to know; and such ought not to be hidden but openly proposed to all. But there are others which, if openly presented, cause harm in those hearing them.

Citing the text from *Christian Instruction* just quoted, he adds, "by this procedure no harm is done to anyone, because those who understand are held by that which they read, but those who do not understand are not compelled to continue reading."[6] Clearly this is a different basis for writing with two levels of address than the one suggested above for Augustine writing the *Confessions*. But it makes clear Augustine's understanding of such writing, and Aquinas's confirmation of it.

Granting for the moment that Augustine was aware of a way of writing (and reading) that permits a structure, a dimension of meaning in a text to remain latent, why would he want to do that in a work intended "to give you glory that [my soul] may love you the more, and let it confess to you your own merciful dealings" (5.1.1)? Why would he do that in a work addressed to "the ears of believing men and women . . . my fellow citizens still on pilgrimage with me" (10.4.6)? Because Augustine wants to show the hidden character of that providence: "I must not omit to confess to you the reasons why I was so persuaded [to move to Rome], because in them your deep, secret providence was at work, and your ever-present mercy, and these are to be pondered and proclaimed" (5.8.14). Augustine wants to present that hidden providence for the reader not only by asserting it, but by leaving partially hidden what he has discovered about God's providence in the events of his life through the process of thinking back on that life and writing the story of his confessions, by indicating to the alert reader the latent dimensions of his story. In such a case, part of the confession of God's secret providence will be explicit, but part will remain implicit.

THE CENTER AS STRUCTURING PRINCIPLE

So what would be an example of structure that might help to guide the reading of a work? Well, a simple one might be the center of the text, in either (or both) the sense of halfway through, or the sense of where the argument turns, where the course of the first part gives way to a different course for the second part. For instance, Augustine's work *The Usefulness of Believing* (*De utilitate credendi*) is divided into two parts exactly in the middle of the text. That locus marks the place where the issue of the first half is dropped (the need to find teachers from whom to learn how to read texts appropriately, and to be taught wisdom), and the issue of the second half is introduced (how to seek and find a preceptor, a preacher of true religiousness in whom to believe). Between these two topics (one about seeing, the other about believing), Augustine inserts an autobiographical section, recounting in brief compass the intellectual and spiritual journey of what is related (ten years later) in the first five books of the *Confessions*, just the point in the latter work where he begins to reflect about the indispensability of believing some things, as opposed to the Manichean ridicule of the Christian requirement to believe.

Of course, the axial or transition point of a text need not lie at its physical center. It might lie at the climax, for example at the moment of recognition and reversal in a Greek tragedy like *Oedipus Rex*, where the climax comes three-quarters of the way through the play. If we were to follow that analogy, the central point or event of the *Confessions* could seem to lie in Book Eight, the scene in the garden where Augustine recognizes God speaking to him and turns his life around.[7] That scene may well be the dramatic center of the story Augustine is telling, the moment when his long quest for wisdom and for true religiousness are at once fulfilled and metamorphosed by a fervent and moving experience of faith.

But is it that dramatic narrative that is the object of Augustine's writing? Is it to tell the story of his life, of his childhood, education, teaching, affiliation with

Manicheism, the quest for wisdom, of its *peripeteia* in the garden, of the new life that began to open to him? What is the purpose of his confession? At the beginning of Book Five he writes, "Accept the sacrifice of my confessions . . . to confess to you your own merciful dealings, that it may give you glory."[8] The perspective that has been disclosed to Augustine as he meditated on the course of his life up to his conversion is a dimension that he had not been aware of during those years. One *could* describe those years by saying that the desire and quest for wisdom, aroused in him by reading Cicero, led to the Manichees, then to the Platonists, then to the Scriptures he had learned to read from Ambrose, and finally to the fulfillment of his quest in the encounter with God, the hearing of God's word, in the garden.

But that description would put the initiative for the searching on Augustine, whereas what he came to see, reflecting on those years with the eyes of faith, was that it was God who had brought it all about. "You acted on me that I might be persuaded to go to Rome,"[9] he writes in the middle of Book Five, but the motive that moved *him* at the time was what he heard about students in Rome, and *his* motive for leaving Rome to become master of rhetoric in Milan, in turn, was to advance his career. Looking back, he discerns the providential hand of God as the reason for the journey to Milan, but he little knew it at the time: "Unknowingly I was led by you to [Ambrose], so that through him I might be led, knowingly, to you."[10]

Indeed, when one thinks about it, the conception of a providential, loving God, who created us to come to him, who made us so that our hearts would be restless until they rest in him, who—unlike the One of Plotinus and the Platonists—comes seeking us, calling us,[11] such a conception entails that God will have been working to bring us to him long before we become aware of it.[12] Such are the "merciful dealings" referred to above, which Augustine wants to confess in order to give glory to God's love and providential care.

If we think of the *Confessions* from this perspective, it becomes apparent why it is not an autobiography, why the scene in the garden is not the center of the narrative, and why the axis of the narrative is in Book Five, when God brings it about that Augustine is turned away from the Manichees and (although he does not know it yet) toward Ambrose. Book Five is in fact also the middle book of the historical narrative, Books One through Nine. Book Ten is not part of the historical narrative, but deals with the philosophical questions about memory, and with Augustine's spiritual situation at the time of writing. It mentions nothing of the years that have intervened between that time and the end of Book Nine, the waiting in Ostia for a ship to Africa, or the death of Monica.

We have been using spatial metaphors, of turning, of going toward, and so forth. In doing so, we are, of course, only following the lead of the author himself, who regularly introduces the basic image of journeying away from and toward God: "Small wonder, then, that I was swept off helplessly . . . and borne away from you, my God" (1.18.28); "I was wandering away from you, yet you let me go my way. . . . I continued to wander far from you" (2.2.2). After reading Cicero, "I began to rise up, in order to return to you" (3.4.7). But he encounters the Manichees and, becoming a hearer in their sect, he "supposed that I was approaching the truth when I was in fact moving away from it"(3.7.12). These few examples are among many uses of this fundamental spatial metaphor, which is complemented by matching it with a literal spatial journey to Italy.

So let us think about Book Five, about the center.

The Center of Book Five

First of all, Book Five itself has a center, a midpoint. And it happens that that middle of the book is the point where the narrator, looking back, first attributes to God's acting on him, to God's guiding him, something he had decided to do for what seemed at the time purely his own reasons—to go to Rome.[13] God uses the motives of Augustine's moving (primarily, to find better behaved students), for his own ends, namely the good of his prodigal son, the return of his son. The passage from Carthage to Rome not only divides Book Five in the middle, it divides the narrative Books One to Nine in the middle of the middle book, so that the narrative is neatly divided between Africa and Italy. Although the *Confessions* is written a decade later in Africa, we are not told anything of his return there or of the events of the intervening years.

Second, immediately preceding his decision to go to Rome (in "God's secret providence," 5.8.14), he tells us that because of his encounters with Faustus, he had become disillusioned with the teachings of Mani,[14] so that Faustus unintentionally began his emancipation from the Manichees—"thanks to your hidden providence, O my God" (5.7.13). It is interesting and worth noting that the encounters with the two bishops, Faustus and Ambrose, are placed symmetrically around the center of Book Five. Three paragraphs from the beginning of this book we meet Faustus, three paragraphs from the end of the book we meet Ambrose, the two critical figures in the reorientation of Augustine's journey, a journey before Book Five away from God, and now turning toward him.[15] Without committing himself to either Manicheism or Catholic Christianity, he at first decides to remain loosely attached to the Manichean teaching: "since I had found nothing better than this sect [Manichees] into which I had more or less blundered, I resolved to be content with it for the time being, unless some preferable option presented itself" (5.7.13). Then at the end of the book, he decides to return to the status of a catechumen in the Catholic Church: "I resolved therefore to live as a catechumen in the Catholic Church, which was what my parents had wished for me, until some kind of certainty dawned by which I might direct my steps aright" (5.12.25).[16]

Third, this indecision is reflected in another facet that also marks Five as the center book, as a point of equilibrium between two balanced alternatives, two directions of motion, namely his opting in the final chapter for the Academic philosophy. "Accordingly I adopted what is popularly thought[17] to be the Academic position, doubting everything and wavering" (5.12.25). The inability to be sure, to know, was a consequence of his discussions with Faustus. He had had many problems about the teachings of Mani, and had been told to wait until Faustus came, who would answer his questions. The Manichees he had spoken with over the years had ridiculed the Christian requirement for belief, and promised to provide reasons for the teachings of Mani. But after Faustus, he gave up hope of *knowing*, being shown, why those teachings were true. He began to think that the skeptical philosophers (i.e., the Academics) were wiser than the self-styled teachers of wisdom (5.10.19). So Book Five ends with Augustine's deciding that it was best to remain uncommitted until something certain enlightened him.

Book Five and Books Three through Seven

This third aspect of Book Five as a midpoint can lead us out to a different and broader way in which it functions as an axial book. The last chapter of the book, as noted, deals with Augustine's being drawn to the teachings of the Academic philosophers. But if we look at the endings of the surrounding books, we discover that all of the books from Three to Eight conclude with the reading or discussion of different philosophers or teachers of wisdom. Not only is it remarkable that these books all close on this note, but the teachings discussed mark off stages in Augustine's journey away from and toward truth. The import of the end of Book Five has already been indicated: the Academic counsel to remain uncommitted, since the truth cannot be known, aptly fitted Augustine's mind at that time.

Book Three deals with his being inspired by Cicero with the love of wisdom (the literal meaning of "philosophy," as Augustine notes), and to search for wisdom as a guide to life, and how this in turn led him to the Manichean sect, in which he became a hearer. In addition to listening to their teaching he read their "huge copious tomes" (3.6.10).[18] In the last chapter of Book Three his mother, concerned at his increasing affiliation with the sect, goes to visit a bishop who had formerly been a Manichee and had "read nearly all their books" (3.12.21), to ask him to speak with her son and show him the error of his ways. But Augustine was not yet ready to listen, as the bishop rightly judged, and he replied that her son would discover, through further reading, how wrong his present ideas were.

In Book Four, he reflects on the beginning of his (nine) Manichean years, on (as he now sees it) the false conception of God and the world that Mani taught. At the base of the Manichean teaching was a story of God as light, a kingdom of light, having been long ago attacked and scattered by the forces of darkness, so that the scattered divine particles of light constituted (and were dispersed through) the universe, mixed and jumbled with the particles of darkness. This mixture explained, among other things, why creatures (who were mixtures of such particles), and especially human beings, had impulses toward evil as well as toward good. Apparently this doctrine appealed to Augustine's own experience of not only doing wrong but doing gratuitous wrong (the pear tree of 2.6.12).

After some reflections on these ideas, he tells us the story of a boyhood friend (of the same age as Augustine) who died during an illness. Deeply moved by the death, Augustine meditates on the transience not only of life, but of all creaturely existence. All creatures "belong to a society of things that do not exist all at once, but in their passing away and succession together form a whole" (4.10.15), just as our speaking requires that one word die away to be replaced by another, in order that a whole sentence (the unity of a thought) can be. Just so, what we were in the past must die away in order that what we are now can come into being.

In the last chapter of Book Four, he says that when he was about twenty, a copy of Aristotle's book on the *Categories* had been handed to him. It is striking that he relates this now, since he has been telling about his departure from Thagaste (where his friend dies) to go to Carthage in order to resume his teaching career, and—just at the end of the next-to-last chapter—how he wrote his first book during his years there, at the age of "twenty-six or twenty-seven." Why, having narrated the story of his life up to that age would he go back six or seven years to tell of reading Aristotle?

Perhaps because that book—highly praised as it was by his teachers and rightly understood by Augustine—was of no more help in freeing him from the erroneous conception of God he had acquired from reading Mani than the bishop of Book Three had been. For the *Categories* is an exposition of the ten ways in which things can be said to exist—either as substance or as one of the nine kinds of accidental attributes or qualities of a substance. In logical terms, in the most fundamental sense the substance is indicated by the subject of a sentence and the attributes or accidents by the respective predicates asserted of or ascribed to the subject.

As has been noted just above, the accidental qualities of a creature, of a substance, naturally change over time, so that for example what I once weighed (say 6 pounds at birth or 170 pounds some years ago) I no longer do. Now I weigh 150 pounds. Indeed, Aristotle says in chapter five of the work, "The most distinctive mark of substance appears to be that, while remaining numerically one and the same, it is capable of having contrary qualities," i.e., at different times.[19]

If we try to understand God in terms of such categories, misconceptions of the divine nature follow. One is that we can tell a narrative about what status or qualities the divine substance once had and what it subsequently became and what it is now, just as we can about my life. And of course that is just what Mani did, tell the story of how the divine light was attacked and dispersed and is being re-collected, stage by stage. Aristotle's metaphysical analysis of subjects and predicates supported such a telling of a story. But God is simple. There is in him no distinction of substance and accidental qualities: "I mistakenly attempted to understand even you, my God, in terms of [these ten categories], you who are wonderfully simple and changeless, imagining that you were the subject of your greatness and beauty, and that these attributes inhered in you as their subject."[20] So while reading Aristotle's work and understanding it without any help was a tribute to Augustine's intelligence, it not only left him with the Manichean misunderstandings of God, but actually provided support for them.

Book Five, as we have noted, ends appropriately with him being drawn toward the Academic skeptics (as they were popularly understood), who recommended suspending judgment as long as there was no certainty to be found.[21]

Book Six deals with Augustine's increasing dissatisfaction with the busyness that his post as master of rhetoric in Milan required—not only teaching, but cultivating contacts with officeholders and influential persons in government. Thirsting for wisdom and the time to think about its pursuit as he was, his time was taken up not with study, but with making a successful career. Coming across a drunken beggar in the streets, he comments to his companions on the contrast between the beggar's temporary happiness and his unhappiness. For the moment at least, the beggar is carefree and tranquil, and his pleasure seems preferable to the stress and strain associated with Augustine's pursuit of worldly success (6.9.10).

In a vivid dialogue with himself, Augustine presents the stressful demands that keep him from his real desire (6.6.9–10). He was living with his closest friends at the time, Alypius and Nebridius, all of them seeking some free hours for the same pursuit of wisdom and truth, and they talked about a life in community where responsibilities would be shared in turn, allowing some leisure to the others. But marriage plans and liaisons kept getting in the way, and nothing came of it.

So it is no surprise that, in the last chapter of Book Six where Augustine relates discussing these philosophical questions with his friends, he decides that Epicurus would win the debate among the philosophers about the way of life one should seek, if it were not for the soul and what would happen to it after death: "If we were immortal, and lived in a state of perpetual bodily pleasure without any fear of losing it, why should we not be happy?" (6.16.26). For Epicurus had taught the need for withdrawal from the worldly competitive and acquisitive life, and the pursuit of a state of undisturbed tranquillity, or pleasure (the absence of discomfort or dissatisfaction, which absence Epicurus identified with pleasure). He also insisted that friendship was basic to such pleasure or happiness, so that friends should share a common life.[22] One can see why, at this point in his life, Augustine could have found that position persuasive.

Book Seven is the culmination of this journey through the tutors of wisdom. Like the first of the series, Book Three, it goes from a philosophical wisdom that turns Augustine toward God to a disclosure of a religious path, a Tao. In Book Three the philosopher is Cicero (3.4.7), who first inspires the love of wisdom in Augustine, and the religious path he comes across is the teachings of Mani. In Book Seven, it is the "books of the Platonists" that set him on the final ascent toward the conception of God's nature that overthrows the Manichean doctrine of God's spatiality and mutability, and the religious path is laid out by reading the letters of St. Paul.

Perhaps the most crucial insight he derives from the books of the Platonists is the conception of God as spirit, as immaterial, and so not present everywhere by occupying space, but rather by not being in any place at all. Before he reads those books, he could not imagine a nonmaterial thing: "anything to which I must deny these spatial dimensions seemed to me to be nothing at all, absolutely nothing, not even a void [empty place in space]" (7.1.1).[23] Now he comes to see that God is immaterial and immutable, a transcendent, unchangeable, and timeless Truth, and so eternal, an infinite Being who is the source of all finite beings. The question of the Manichees to Christianity, "Where did evil come from if it were not eternal?" which had plagued him earlier (3.7.12), he now resolves. Moreover, he feels confident in borrowing the language of the Scriptures to describe what the Platonists taught. Seizing the writings of St. Paul, "I began to read and discovered that every truth I had read in those other books was taught here also" (7.21.27).

But there were problems in the other direction: there were things in St. Paul's writings that were not in those of the Platonists. Two were crucial, and related. One was the incarnation of the Logos. Augustine (and Alypius) had difficulty in conceiving how the transcendent, immaterial, immutable divinity of the Platonists and Christians could be this human being, who lived in space and time and like other humans ate and drank and slept. So he thought of Christ as a human person, excellent and wise, but human (7.18.24–19.25).

The second problem is not unrelated to the first. It is that in the Platonist teaching, as Augustine says, "no one there hears a voice calling 'Come to me'" (7.21.27). It is, as Plotinus taught, the task of the individual soul to make its way of ascent toward a return to the One, the ultimate eternal principle of all things. But Christianity taught that God came seeking us, came to call us to turn and come together to share God's life. How could a timeless, immutable, transcendent Being act in the world of space and time?

It is, of course, that question that is responded to not by philosophy, but by a personal experience in Book Eight, in the garden where Augustine hears a voice uttering what he takes to be a divine command, a call to open the book of Paul's writings and read. But here at the end of Book Eight it is not the reading of a book of wisdom that moves him, it is the experience of being called, spoken to by the words of the Eternal Word.

Book Five and Books Two through Eight

What has been primarily intended here is not the exposition of the stages of the philosophical encounters that close each of the books from three to seven, but rather the symmetrical structuring of those around a center, Book Five. This is exemplified by this symmetry and by the centricity of Book Five for the whole division of the journey into African and Italian phases, but also by the philosophy (skepticism) that marks his in-between state.

There is another structuring around this center book that reinforces the analysis thus far, and indeed advances it. There is a symmetrical gathering of the themes of his progressive alienation from God around that center. The stages of this alienation and return are those of the triad that runs through the text, as well as in other books of Augustine from the early *True Religion* to the late *Enchiridion*. This triad is the one discussed at length in the second half of Book Ten: concupiscence of the flesh, of the eyes, and of the pride of life (as St. John calls it).[24] It derives from Scripture, but it correlates with the three parts of the human soul that Plato had delineated in the *Republic*,[25] where the three sources of human action, the three principles for explaining why people do things, are identified as desire, reason, and aspiration. Desire is the appetite for what will please or satisfy us physically, whether it be food or sex or sleep; reason is thinking about what we ought to seek and why, and what we should do to achieve that end (whether it be contrary to our desires or not); aspiration is what moves us when we seek to rise above others, above a lower status, whether that be economic or political or educational or moral (e.g., doing something because it would be dishonorable or demeaning not to do it). In the view that Socrates puts forth in the *Republic*, disorder in one's behavior or conduct is the result of conflict in us between these three sources of action. So, for example, the sexual appetite can overpower reason's judgment that this behavior is morally wrong, or is shameful.

Augustine does not deny that wrongful behavior results from such disorder and conflict among these parts of the soul, but following St. John and the teaching of Catholic Christianity he also thinks that those three sources of action can be—and are, as a result of original sin—individually disordered or corrupted, so that they acquire an unnatural power in our behavior. Even reason has weaknesses that can lead us astray, for example, an inordinate curiosity about things not deserving our attention and study.

The three books before Book Five each record Augustine's succumbing to one of these three types of concupiscence, so that his increasing distance from God is traced by his alienation through sin in three stages: in Book Two, concupiscence of the flesh; in Book Three, concupiscence of the eyes or mind; and in Book Four, concupiscence of worldly ambition. He regains his freedom from these states of alienation in the three books following Five: ambition in Book Six, the mind in Book Seven, and his bondage to the flesh in Book Eight. Thus the symmetry around Five in this case is chiasmic, i.e., the liberation occurs step-by-step but in reverse order, and the stages mark his ascent toward God, culminating in the scene in the garden at the end of Book Eight.

Book Two opens, in fact, with the explicit statement of its theme: "Now I want to call to mind the foul deeds I committed, those sins of the flesh that corrupted my soul" (2.1.1), and how in this sixteenth year of his age "the frenzy of lust imposed its rule on me" (2.2.4). And for sixteen years he remained under the scepter of this concupiscence.

The second concupiscence (of "the eyes") is the compelling desire to see and to know. The desire to see, in the literal sense, produced Augustine's passion for theatrical shows in Carthage, where he went to continue his studies (3.2.2). But Augustine found the metaphorical sense of "to see," i.e., to know or understand, an even more consuming passion:

> There is still another temptation, one more fraught with danger. In addition to all the concupiscence of the flesh, which lures us to indulge in all the pleasures of the senses, and brings disaster on its slaves who flee far from

you, there is also concupiscence of the mind, a frivolous, avid curiosity. . . .
it masquerades as a zeal for knowledge and learning. Since it is rooted in a
thirst for firsthand information about everything, and since the eyes are
paramount among the senses in acquiring information, this inquisitive tendency is called in holy scripture concupiscence of the eyes. (10.35.54)

Book Three, as has already been noted, tells of his reading of Cicero's *Hortensius*
in the course of his studies in rhetoric, and tells how it inspired in him the desire
for wisdom, for knowledge of how one should live to be happy. He turned at first
to the Scriptures, but was put off by their lowly and unpretentious prose style,
and so did not perceive their "inner meaning": "I disdained to be a little child
and in my high and mighty arrogance regarded myself as grown up"(3.5.9). He
was an apt candidate for the "proud madmen" who proclaimed the wisdom of
Mani, with their pretentious trappings of pseudoscientific astronomy and biol-
ogy. Looking back, he now calls the Manichean teachings "chimera," "figments
of my imagination," "inanities" (3.6.10). But they posed questions about Christian doctrine that were problems for him, for example, whether humanity's being
made in the image of God meant that God had a body like a human, or (as mentioned earlier) how evil could emerge in a world made by a perfect creator, if it
were not as eternal as God.

Book Four opens with relating how through his nine years with the Manichees, while teaching the liberal arts, he pursued empty popular acclaim and "the
contest for ephemeral wreaths" (4.1.1), entering dramatic poetry contests and
similar attempts to win renown (4.1.3). He "admired people simply because they
were judged praiseworthy by others." He wrote a book on the nature of beauty,
dedicating it to a man of "splendid reputation" who found favor with others, an
eminent orator in Rome:

> This orator, however, was the sort of man I loved in the sense of wanting to
> be like him. I was driven off course by my pride and tossed about by every
> wind. . . . I had come to love him more for the love he aroused in those who
> sang his praises than for the achievements by which he won them. . . .
> Accordingly I set great store by bringing my oratory and my research to this
> man's notice. (4.14.21–23)

But by Book Six, although still "hankering after honors," the race is beginning
to pale. Augustine describes himself as "preparing to deliver a eulogy upon the
emperor in which I would tell plenty of lies with the object of winning favor with
the well-informed by my lying. . . . my heart was panting with anxiety and seething
with feverish, corruptive thoughts" (6.6.9). It is at this point that he encounters
the drunken beggar, mentioned above, and wonders which of them is the happier.
He re-creates the dialogue with himself that these thoughts engender:

> when are we to pay court to our important friends, whose patronage we need?
> When prepare the lessons we sell to our students? When refresh ourselves and
> relax our minds from concentrating on these problems? . . . Why are we so
> slow to abandon worldly ambition and apply ourselves singlemindedly to the

search for God and a life of happiness? Wait a little, for those things are very pleasant, too; they hold no slight sweetness. . . . Consider what a fine thing it is for a person to win a reputation. What prize could be more desirable? We have plenty of influential friends: without setting our sights unduly high, one may expect at least a governorship to come one's way. (6.11.18–19)

Alypius plays a role in this debate in Book Six about worldly ambition. He has become Assessor to the Chancellor of the Italian Treasury, and refuses a bribe from a very powerful senator. He thus exemplifies the choice of doing the right thing at the cost of gaining help from influential figures in advancing his career (6.10.16). By the end of the book, as we have seen, Augustine is ready to side with the Epicureans in their counsel of withdrawal from public life in the pursuit of happiness. Although he continues his career, it no longer has attraction for him: "I was irked by the secular business I was conducting, for no longer was I fired by ambition, and prepared on that account to endure such heavy servitude in the hope of reputation and wealth, as had formerly been the case" (8.1.2). So the events and reflections of Book Six undermine the desires described in Book Four for praise and reputation, and lead to the abandonment of those aspirations. The busyness involved in advancing his success has become a burden and the goal itself ephemeral.[26]

Book Seven is striking in that in it there is not a word about his sexual concupiscence (which is the theme of Books Three and Eight), or about the concupiscence of worldly fame that is now fading away (the theme of Books Four and Six). Every other book between Three and Eight touches on or deals with more than one of the three concupiscences.[27] Book Seven is wholly focused on the philosophical inquiry that guides Augustine toward God, that frees him from astrology and the Manichean "figments of imagination." Book Seven explicitly takes up the Manichean questions that had motivated his joining the sect (e.g., the question of the origin of evil—whence comes evil—and of whether God's body is like a human's—the Christian doctrine that humanity is made in God's image, 3.7.12), and resolves them. Being and goodness are correlative realities, and evil is not some infinite substantial being, but precisely the lack of being, the privation of what ought to exist in things (7.13.19). And it is the human soul, the animating principle of the body, not the human body, that bears the image of God (7.9.15). Not only do the writings of the Platonists resolve those puzzles for him, but they bring him to conceive rightly the nature of God as immaterial spirit, as Truth that is transcendent, immutable, eternal.

By the beginning of Book Eight, Augustine has been freed from the two concupiscences that had held him captive since Books Three and Four. The concupiscence of the mind, "a frivolous, avid curiosity," has been replaced by the vision of the Truth, and he is no longer "fired by ambition," though he still reluctantly treads the path.[28] His spirit no longer magnetized by the desire for worldly fame and fortune, and his mind no longer clouded by the teachings of Mani, he rejoices: "Concerning your eternal life I was now quite certain. . . . What I now longed for was not greater certainty about you, but a more steadfast abiding in you. . . . I was attracted to the Way, which is our Savior himself, but the narrowness of the path daunted me, and I still could not walk in it" (8.1.1). He is still held tightly—and has been since Book Two—by the concupiscence of the flesh, by the power of his sexual appetite. He refers to this in the opening sentence of Book Eight, speaking of his intention to give thanks to God for breaking the chains that bound him. And he returns to the same image later: "Now I will relate how you set me free from a craving for sexual gratification which fettered me like a tight-drawn chain, and from my enslavement to worldly affairs" (8.6.13). It is not reading philosophers or listening to Ambrose that finally turns his way of life around, or even reading St. Paul, but the experience of hearing God speak directly to his situation, to his heart's dilemma. Perhaps one could borrow John Henry Newman's terminology and say that by the end of Book Seven he has a notional assent to Christianity but not a real assent.[29] By the end of Book Eight the last of the bonds, of the concupiscences that chained him, is gone, and he can open Book Nine with a prayer of thanksgiving: "You burst my bonds asunder" (9.1.1).

The stages of Augustine's sequential bondage and liberation are told in books thus symmetrically centered around Book Five: Two corresponds to Eight, Three corresponds to Seven, Four corresponds to Six. This chiasmic narrative structure not only reinforces the perception of Five as the center of the narrative books, but displays it as the center of a descent into sin and isolation (he sails, apparently alone, for Rome in the center of the center book), and an ascent into graced freedom and community with God and his friends.[30]

Book Five and Books One through Nine

There is one more sign of the partition of the narrative around Book Five that is simple and evident, but easy to overlook. It is that in the earlier books, Augustine does not mention the names of any of the people he knows personally (with one exception). He uses the names of such figures as Virgil and Cicero and Aristotle, of Dido and Aeneas, of Christ and Adam and Abraham, and of the contemporary orator Hierius, to whom he dedicates his book on beauty (and carefully adds, "I did not know him personally," 4.14.21).

But in Books One to Four, he does not name his mother or father, or the boyhood friend who dies, or his common-law wife or son, or his friend and student Alypius, or Vindicianus (the physician who tried to disenchant him from astrology), all of whom are named in the books after Five. Only in Book Five do we begin to learn the names of people he encountered: Faustus the Manichean bishop and Ambrose the Catholic bishop, Elpidius who disputed with the Manichees (Augustine heard him back in Carthage, but only mentions him by name now), and Symmachus, who recommends Augustine for the post as orator in Milan. Each of the succeeding narrative books adds more names, but it is not until the last lines of Book Nine that his mother and father are named, just as he finishes his story.[31]

What do those named have in common, considering that some others are never named, e.g., his common-law wife of fifteen years, or any of his Manichean companions in Carthage and Rome? It would appear that all of those who are named were instrumental in assisting Augustine's turning and journey toward the true God, whether unintentionally (e.g., Faustus and Symmachus), or intentionally (e.g., Ambrose and Simplicianus). Faustus disillusions him with the teaching of Mani and so begins to turn him around, while Symmachus unknowingly sends him on his way to Ambrose. In contrast, his unnamed common-law wife and Manichean friends were obstacles on that path.

It was noted above that there is one exception to this partition in the naming: it occurs in Book Four when the there-unnamed Vindicianus (recalled and named in 7.6.8) and Nebridius (also recalled there) are trying to dissuade Augustine from consulting astrologers (4.6.5–6). After having described the criticism of Vindicianus, Augustine writes: "Yet at the time neither he nor my very dear friend, Nebridius, a fine and extremely sensible young man who ridiculed the whole business of divination, was able to persuade me." Why this singular instance in Books One to Four of naming someone Augustine knew personally?

Perhaps the first thing to say in response to that question, before trying to answer it, is to remark that its singularity implies that there is a deliberate pattern. As the saying goes, the exception proves the rule, shows that there is a rule. (Perhaps the saying should be that the [apparent] exception presses us either to reformulate the rule to include the exception or to explain why the apparent exception does not fit under it.) And the pattern seems too consistent not to be intentional. So why name only Nebridius in the first half and not, for example, Alypius, also close to Augustine's heart and converted with him in the garden?

Assuming that it was not a slip or oversight—unlikely, given the consistency— one can only speculate on why Augustine would have made an exception. Of various conceivable reasons, perhaps the likeliest is that by the time the *Confessions* is written, his "dear" friend (as he always refers to him) had died seven years earlier, and that naming him before all of the others is a commemoration of his friend and companion (who may, indeed, have been the comrade with whom he sailed to Rome).

CONCLUSION

Although it is certainly fair to say that the scene in the garden is the dramatic climax of his story, we have argued that telling that long dramatic story of the journey away from and returning to God is not the primary purpose of the *Confessions*. Anyone who is converted, turned about, toward faith in the God of the Bible, even if that conversion is dramatic and memorable, if they reflect on the nature of the God they have come to have faith in, will be led to recognize God's hand in the earlier course of the journey. And frequently, if not always, they will notice the hitherto unnoticed events, decisions, encounters, etc., that now show themselves to have been important steps on the way.

Already in his early treatise *The Usefulness of Believing*, written six years or so before the *Confessions*, Augustine had commented on this dimension of the search for true wisdom or true religiousness:

> When religion is the object of our quest, God alone can provide a solution. . . . We ought not to be seeking true religion unless we believe that God is, and that he brings help to human minds. . . . If the providence of God does not preside over human affairs, there is no need to worry about religion.[32]

The passage just cited contrasts with teachings about how the individual can make his own way toward the absolute, the unchanging and abiding—for example, the teachings of Plotinus and the "Platonists," and also those of Buddhism. In these teachings, it is up to the individual to realize the situation he is in and take measures to escape from or free one's self from this situation. The soul can, through coming to know the way, through right conduct and meditation, arise to union with the One (Plotinus) or with what is "Unborn, Unbecome, Uncreated" (Buddha). One can be told about the situation and the path, but one must act for one's self. As the famous last line of the *Enneads* of Plotinus puts it, it is "the flight of the alone to the Alone." But Augustine, like Cicero, thinks of religion as the offering of prayers and sacrifices to a superior being called divine, and the seeking of his help in making one's way. Prayers and sacrifices imply our need for assistance in that journey.

If the providence of God does preside over human affairs, and God cares about whether we come to him or not, then events that perhaps did not appear important to us at the time may now show evidence of that hidden providence. If the God we seek does not know of our seeking or is unable to help us, then that is not the God we should seek.

An important philosophical and theological issue arises here. It is the issue of whether there is a meaning in the sequence of events in our lives—or, more broadly, also in the lives of nations and empires. The *Confessions*, from this point of view, deals with the same issue as the *City of God* that Augustine will write toward the end of his life. For classical philosophy, the course of events could indeed be partially intelligible, could be something for our reason to understand in part, but only as illustrating or instantiating universal laws or tendencies in a particular context. So, for example, Plato outlines in the *Republic* a sequence of political constitutions, arguing that one form of constitution (e.g., oligarchy) naturally evolves into another (e.g., democracy), and that naturally into another and so on. Analogously, the "lifestyle" of a typical oligarchic citizen naturally evolves toward the way of life of a typical democratic citizen. These law-like progressions are the patterns through which contemporary Athens, for example, could be understood. Thucydides, writing about the war between Athens and Sparta, says that his history will be instructive for later generations, because such encounters between dominant opposing states as he is describing tend to repeat themselves in later eras.

But Augustine thinks of individuals (and nations) as singular, as having a life history that may indeed exhibit typical kinds of patterns of development, but which has a comprehensive, linear, noncyclic history, a history under God's providence. It is the *Confessions* that articulates that vision for his own life, and implicitly for the life of every individual. He wants all of his readers to understand his life not as unique in this regard, but to be able to think about the role of God's hidden providence in their lives.

Of course, all individuals (and nations) can look back at their past and see, in retrospect, an additional dimension of meaning in those past events, a meaning of which they were unconscious at the time. This is true simply because when, looking back, and now being aware of the then-unknown consequences of those events, the events take on a different significance for us. We now see, in retrospect, an importance (or unimportance) in what happened then of which we were unsuspecting at the time. The ever-widening horizon of subsequent events, of history, constantly changes—enlarges or diminishes—the significance of those anterior happenings. And that changing is in principle never-ending.

Augustine's perspective in the *Confessions* is fundamentally different, for at least two reasons. The first is that looking back he now sees some earlier events as intentionally aimed (although not by him) at bringing about the later events that give those earlier events their new dimension of meaning—intentionally planned by God's "hidden providence." (For example, his going from Rome to Milan.) And the second reason is that the perspective he is now endowed with will not itself fundamentally change with the passing of time, because he now shares, to some tiny extent, God's understanding of those occurrences. The viewpoint from which he writes the *Confessions* is that attained by the climax of the narrative, the understanding sown in the garden. For that event is not a chance event whose significance may be changed by what occurs later in his life.

This can be clarified perhaps by reflecting on the experience he has in the garden of picking up the Scriptures, God's Word, and reading those words addressed exactly to his life situation. But he has earlier been told by Vindicianus (4.3.5) that the common practice of picking up and opening some standard text and randomly reading the first excerpt one's eye falls upon will indeed sometimes find a relevant passage, but that will be due to chance. In that time it was usual to employ Virgil's poetry in this way (in our day perhaps Nostradamus). How is Augustine's experience different? Couldn't his relevant passage found by simply picking up the letters of St. Paul and opening them at random also be a matter of chance?

What makes the difference in the two readings is the understanding of the universe and all that is in it and all that happens in it as under God's providence, as his creation. God not only brought the world into being long ago, but continues to preserve it in existence along with all of its coming-and-going creatures. This conception of creation is the ontological context for the affirmation of God's providential design for us. So it is very different if I, on my own initiative, pick up a book and open it at random and find a meaningful text, or, on the other hand, if God moves me to pick up a book that describes itself as presenting the

Word of God and, opening it, find God speaking to me. Only the foundation of the doctrine of creation allows apparently random events to take on the status of being integrated into God's foresighted plan for all things. If God were not the creator of all events as well as of creatures, then what happens to me could be simply a chance event. It would be a chance event that I happened randomly to open, say, Virgil's *Aeneid* to just this page. And as Vindicianus tells Augustine, it would then only be by chance, coincidence, that I found some passage significant for my situation at the moment I did that. No one intended that significance. But as he writes at the end of Books Eleven to Thirteen, where he reflects deeply on God's relation to creation, "We therefore, see these things you have made, because they exist, but for you it is different: they exist because you see them" (13.38.53). What God foresees comes about in his timelessly creating the world, moment by moment, to put it paradoxically.

This conception of how meaning can be found in one's life is exemplified for the reader of the *Confessions* by the way in which Augustine describes how he discovered that providence in his own life. It is another example of the fruitfulness of the maxim that guides Augustine's theological reflection from the beginning to the end of his life as a Catholic Christian: unless you believe, you will not understand. Unless you believe in God, the creator and sustainer who calls to each of us, you will not understand those crucial aspects of your life that are part of God's "hidden providence."

Our argument has been that there are many indications, when you take note of them, that the central axis of the "autobiographical" narrative of Books One to Nine is in the center of those books, in fact in the center of the center book, Book Five. Many of those indications are easy to pass over, not to notice, but that is part of Augustine's intention. He wants us to discover the hidden signs of God's providence, just as those were hidden to Augustine himself until he recalled, with the eyes of faith, what led up to the moment in the garden. So writing, he will give glory to God for his farsighted mercy (5.1.1).

That argument does not claim exclusivity for Book Five as a central book. There is yet another problem, another dimension of the *Confessions* that first begins to come into view at the end of Book Seven. There he arrives, thanks to reading the Platonists, at a correct conception of God as transcendent Truth, as pure spirit, as immutable, infinite Being. But there he is also reading the New Testament, especially St. Paul, and he finds things in the latter which have no counterpart in the Platonists. He finds that that pure spirit, that immutable, infinite, transcendent Being calls to us, acts in time, can have a narrative told about him—just what Augustine had come to think impossible for the Platonist God/One. This problem needs to be addressed, but not in terms of the narrative of what happened ten years ago. It needs to be addressed by Augustine's reflections in the interim and now at the time of writing. So more books are needed. And that is why Books Eleven to Thirteen were included along with the narrative books, to address the question of the relation between God's eternity and our temporality, and how a narrative like the opening of Genesis can be told about the immutable God.

Chapter 6

Book Six: Major Characters and Memorable Incidents

Eric Plumer

INTRODUCTION

At first glance Book Six would seem to be a most unlikely "key" to the *Confessions* as a whole or even to the first nine books, dealing with Augustine's past. In fact, of those first nine books, Book Six comes nearest to losing sight of Augustine altogether, first by dwelling upon his mother Monica and her special relationship with Bishop Ambrose (6.1.1–2.2), then by including a series of anecdotes about Alypius (6.7.11–10.16) that seem more suitable for a volume of Alypius's *Confessions* than for a volume of Augustine's. Apart from these internal difficulties, the very position of Book Six in the overall structure of the work militates against our using it as the key to the whole, since it is neither the first nor the last nor the central book of the *Confessions*, any of which would be in a natural position to serve as the key.

If these criticisms are taken seriously (and they should be), then the question naturally arises whether there is any standpoint whatsoever from which Book Six may be viewed as the key to the *Confessions* as a whole. In the following pages I will argue that there is, and that it is one of crucial importance. For it is the standpoint of the vast majority of readers of the *Confessions* in the twenty-first century, and it takes into account more fully than any other the actual setting in which those readers first encounter the *Confessions*. That setting is, of course, the classroom or seminar room of a college or university. As a teacher of such students I will argue that of the thirteen books of Augustine's *Confessions*, Book Six provides the single most helpful introduction to the entire work.

Now it must be admitted at once that our choice of Book Six goes directly against what is undoubtedly the author's original intention—that the reader should begin at the beginning with Book One. But if we take the author's original intention as an absolute standard by which we must proceed, then we will quickly find ourselves in an impossible situation. For the author originally intended—indeed, presumed—that his readers would have Latin as their first language, that they would appreciate the innumerable ways in which he makes the very sounds of the Latin words and phrases enrich the meaning of his sentences, that they would find his careful deployment of a vast array of rhetorical devices intensely stimulating, and that they would find satisfaction and delight in recognizing the most subtle allusions to Virgil and the other standard authors of classical antiquity. All this is just the beginning of the long list of things that are presupposed by the notion of strict adherence to Augustine's original intentions. We are in fact so far removed from him in time and space that we cannot even imagine all the things that belong on that list, let alone fulfill them.

At this point it would be natural for readers of this chapter to experience a pang of despair and wish they could play the part of the noble Roman of old by running upon their swords. But they need not despair. They need only acknowledge that they are like the Corinthians in relation to the gospel that Paul preached: they can only be fed with milk, not solid food. And we perhaps have better reasons than the Corinthians for our limitations, since we are separated by more than 1,600 years from the original audience for whom Augustine wrote. When we consider how great a barrier a mere 400 years creates for native English readers approaching Shakespeare for the first time, we should be gentle with ourselves as we approach Augustine and willing to grant ourselves large concessions so long as they help us to reach a deeper appreciation of the *Confessions*.

Let me explain why I regard Book Six as the key to the *Confessions*, as the book that provides the most helpful introduction to that work for readers in the twenty-first century. By "readers in the twenty-first century" I am thinking primarily of American undergraduates, the vast majority of whom have little or no Latin and so would be unable to profit from a learned commentary on the *Confessions* such as J. J. O'Donnell's. Moreover, I presume that a book dominated by philosophical analysis, such as Book Seven, will be less appealing to American undergraduates than one dominated by character and incident. To put it more plainly, I am sure that on any American campus where the experiment can be conducted, a showing of Kenneth Branagh's screen version of *Much Ado about Nothing* will attract more undergraduates than a meeting of the Hegel Society (even one promising a dramatic reading from *The Phenomenology of Mind*). For similar reasons, I am sure that a book of the *Confessions* dominated by allegorical exegesis of the Bible, such as Book Thirteen, will be just as unappealing to American undergraduates as one dominated by philosophical analysis. By now it should be evident that we must begin with one of the books of the *Confessions* that is dominated by character and incident—in other words, by story. Of those books, none offers a wider range of important characters or memorable incidents than Book Six. The characters in Book Six include his mother Monica, his spiritual father Ambrose, his lifelong friend Alypius, and the woman who was his common-law wife for some fifteen years and the mother of his son. The memorable incidents include his mother's consolation of the sailors when their ship was in danger on the Mediterranean Sea, Augustine's repeated but unsuccessful attempts to speak in private and at length with Ambrose, Augustine's encounter with the drunken beggar on the streets of Milan, and Alypius's experience while at the gladiatorial combats in the Colosseum. By offering such a variety of vivid perspectives on God's providential activity in human life, Book Six enables the reader to attain a degree of insight into Augustine's understanding of divine grace and human freedom that is unmatched by any of the other twelve books of the *Confessions*.

It might be argued, however, that Book Five rivals Book Six in its presentation of personalities and events. Monica and Ambrose make notable appearances in Book Five, as does the Manichean guru Faustus. But the mere mention of Faustus raises a red flag. While Faustus himself is a colorful character, the Manicheism he represents and Augustine's fascination with it are largely unintelligible to contemporary readers. Readers beginning with Book Five rather than Book Six could easily lose confidence in their author for having been duped by such obvious absurdity (Augustine himself calls it "infantile nonsense," 6.4.5), not just for a few days or weeks, but for a full nine years of his adult life. Now it would be gross negligence on the part of a teacher to choose readings so carelessly as to cause students to feel alienated from Augustine before they have given him a fair hearing. It is one thing if they feel alienated after reading most of the *Confessions* (say, Books One through Nine), but if they feel alienated after reading only one book, then the teacher has not chosen wisely. For this reason it would be unsafe to choose Book Five.

A further reason for choosing Book Six over Book Five and indeed over any other single book as the point of departure for the reader is that even though it is not the central book, it is the beginning of the central part of the *Confessions*, comprising Books Six, Seven, and Eight. In Book Six we find Augustine fast approaching what was traditionally regarded as the beginning of maturity at age thirty and what he personally regarded as a momentous turning point in his life. In Books Six, Seven, and Eight Augustine will experience deliverance from that triple bondage which had come to dominate his life—bondage to ambition, to falsehood, and to sex. Book Nine then offers a kind of denouement in which Augustine renounces his worldly career, prepares for baptism, and finally is received into the church. Not only the period of his life, but also the place where it unfolded is worth noting. Book Six is the first full book set in Milan. In Milan Augustine will reach the pinnacle of his career when he speaks before the imperial court, and at the same moment experience a hollowness within unlike any he has known before. In Milan he will reach an intellectual dead end, but later meet a group of Christian Platonists who will show him a way out. And in a Milanese garden he will experience the healing power of God's grace in a way that will enable him at last to go forward for baptism, which he will receive at the hands of Bishop Ambrose in Milan. Thus in terms of both chronology and geography Book Six marks the beginning of the end of Augustine's narrative of his conversion to Christianity.

So let us begin to examine Book Six in greater detail and see how its presentation of character and incident illustrates and exemplifies the main themes of the *Confessions*. The preface to Book Six is brief but telling. Augustine begins by mentioning his "youth" (*iuuentus*), a term referring to the period of life between the ages of thirty and forty-five. It was the fourth of the traditional six ages of life, and marked the beginning of maturity. Augustine was now rapidly approaching this age. He was also entering a new stage in his spiritual development. In his long search for wisdom, which had begun twelve years earlier,[1] he had reached a crucial point: even though he had been "delivered from falsehood," namely, that of Manicheism, he "lost all faith and despaired of ever finding the truth" (6.1.1).[2] That is, although he had come to see that the teaching of the Manichees was false, his new skeptical position brought him no real consolation. These points, which recapitulate points made briefly in Book Five, will be explained at length in Book Six, as we shall see.

MONICA (6.1.1–2.2)

After these prefatory remarks, Augustine turns to a discussion of his mother, and there is a particular thematic reason why he reintroduces her at this point: if the young Augustine had "lost all faith and despaired of ever finding the truth" (6.1.1), his mother was an example of one who had found it and held on to it, and the way she had done so contrasts sharply with that of her son. Whereas Augustine relied upon his own unaided reason, Monica relied upon her faith, and her faith proved powerful. Thus when she sailed from Africa to Italy in pursuit of Augustine and her ship was in danger, her faith enabled her to comfort the sailors, just as Paul's faith had done when his ship was in danger in Acts 27. And just as Paul had based his confidence on a vision he had been granted, so Monica based hers on a dream. Later, when she was reunited with her son in Italy and learned that he had abandoned Manicheism, it was on the basis of a much earlier dream that she was able to gauge the real significance of the fact.[3] She knew that Augustine still had far to go before he would be received into the church, so she "redoubled her prayers and tears." Thus the knowledge she obtained from dreams did not supplant the need for faith and prayer, but depended on it. She knew that God would save her son, even though she did not know precisely how. The point to note is that she had knowledge of the truth, the very thing Augustine despaired of ever having. Monica's faith seemed to defy all logic. She believed in miracles so strongly that she was able to comfort the sailors in the midst of danger and to be convinced that her son was slowly but surely being converted to the Christian religion. By so doing she demonstrates the divinely ordained way to wisdom: by faith seeking understanding.

Later in Book Six (6.13.23) Augustine will provide another illustration of Monica's faith when he describes her search for divine assurance that her son should marry. Once again she consulted her own dreams, and her method of discerning whether or not they were from God is striking if not alarming: "She claimed that by something akin to the sense of taste, a faculty she could not explain in words, she was able to distinguish between your revelations to her and the fantasies of her own dreaming soul." It is hard not to feel a rising skepticism when reading this description. One is tempted to conclude that Monica was ensnared by her own delusions. Yet the truth is that she was not ensnared. By trusting in God to send her a sign if it was God's will that her son should marry, and acknowledging that no such sign had been given to her, she avoided becoming ensnared. Specifically, we see that she was not attempting to bring magical powers to bear on the situation, nor was she attempting to force the hand of God. She knew that she did not know God's will and that she must hope for further enlightenment. She knew, in other words, that her faith must continue to seek understanding. Here the author may well want any skeptical readers to recognize that however irrational it may seem for Monica to rely on a faculty "akin to the sense of taste," it is at least as irrational for them to dismiss her efforts out of hand as mere superstition.

But to return to the material on Monica at the beginning of Book Six, just as Monica's faith provides her with assurance of God's protection and care, and thus gives her a kind of knowledge, so it also enables her to perform acts of Christian love, and thus gives her a kind of power. Augustine illustrates this by telling the story of how Monica's devotional practices changed after she arrived in Milan. In Africa it had been customary to make offerings at the tombs of the martyrs, and Monica loved to do this. When she tried to follow the same practice in Milan, however, she was informed that Bishop Ambrose forbade it (6.2.2). Instead of balking at the prohibition as an unwarranted infringement upon her private devotions, she accepted it without objection and with such willing obedience that Augustine marveled. Part of the reason she accepted it was her recognition that it was for the good of others in the church who might want to partake of her offerings more from a love of wine than from a love of God. Monica thus gave up what was for her own benefit in order to benefit other Christians who might suffer harm. This power of surrendering something that is dear for the sake of others is a source of wonder to Augustine, who can hardly give up self-destructive practices for his own benefit.

Augustine adds that had anyone else forbidden it, Monica might not have complied so readily, but since it was Ambrose, who was helping her son to find the truth, she was happy to do so. For this and for the good works she did for the church she was warmly praised by Ambrose. Thus we as readers are made aware that Monica's motives were not entirely selfless: she wanted Ambrose to help her son and to think highly of her. Nevertheless, this should not blind us to the fact that her faith had power—the power to do extraordinary acts of love. Despite her sinfulness, Monica was bearing witness to the faith of Mother Church and indeed incarnating it. Even her excessive love for her son, which Augustine earlier calls "her too-carnal desire,"[4] is a sign, however imperfect, of that divine love that desires the salvation of all. It is true that for the young Augustine what probably impressed him most about Monica was her unyielding desire to control him emotionally. But in retrospect Augustine the author sees that her pursuit was at least partly motivated by the desire for his salvation and thus partly reflected God's will. Though a sinner, she sought God's will and was humble enough to receive correction from Ambrose. Her selfishness was not therefore an all-consuming and enslaving selfishness, but one that she was continually in the process of outgrowing under the influence of God's grace. So Monica's faith, hope, and love were able to serve as signs and instruments by which God guided Augustine to his destiny.

AMBROSE (6.3.3–4)

Just as Monica was Augustine's spiritual mother, so Bishop Ambrose would become Augustine's spiritual father.[5] Both symbolize the church. Ambrose appears to Augustine as a man of superhuman self-discipline; Augustine can only wonder at it—especially at his ability to lead a celibate life (6.3.3). Augustine would have liked to speak in private to Ambrose and pour out all his problems, but when he went to call on him in his office he was put off by seeing Ambrose reading silently to himself. Augustine was anxious to get his attention but hesitated and then withdrew in order not to disturb him. Another reason he hesitated was that he feared Ambrose would see through his mask and detect his Manicheism, just as he had seen through the mask of fantasy that envelops the Old Testament narratives when taken literally. But Augustine's abortive attempt to converse with Ambrose symbolizes more than this. Ambrose as bishop is the representative of the official church, and Augustine's attitude toward Ambrose epitomizes his attitude toward the church as a whole. In one of the Gospel phrases that is heard most often in the *Confessions*, Augustine was afraid to "knock at the door" (6.4.5.; cf. Matt. 7:7), to ask in order that he might receive. What if, for example, Ambrose shared with him the secret source of the strength whereby he remained celibate? Augustine was afraid to ask because he was unwilling to receive anything that might place restraints on his self-indulgent way of life.

Failing to obtain a suitable opportunity to speak with Ambrose confidentially, Augustine was compelled to join the rest of the congregation and pay attention to Ambrose's preaching. The contrast with the private teachings of the Manichee Faustus is striking. Indeed, Ambrose may have been avoiding private conversation with Augustine deliberately, in order to make him see that the Catholic Church does not reserve secret truths for a spiritual or intellectual elite, but proclaims the gospel publicly to all who are willing to listen. Augustine went to hear Ambrose preach every Sunday, but his motives were worldly: he wanted to know whether Ambrose could speak as eloquently as Faustus. Augustine the orator was still interested in the pomp and glamour of this world, and in his eyes Ambrose was inferior to Faustus. But God used this opportunity to correct Augustine in spite of his worldly motives. For by listening to Ambrose, Augustine discovered that certain Catholic doctrines were not what the Manichees claimed. Thus he found that the teaching of the Old Testament that human beings are made in the image of God does not mean that God has a physical body. These and other absurdities dissolved as Ambrose explained that in such cases the Bible must be understood spiritually, not literally.

FAITH AND REASON (6.4.5–5.8)

Although the light of Ambrose's preaching was beginning to dispel the darkness of Augustine's mind, indoctrinated as it had been by the counterfeit teachings of the Manichees, Augustine was still operating on the level of reason rather than faith.[6] "I longed," he says, "to become as certain of those things I could not see as I was that seven and three make ten" (6.4.6). That is why he continued to waver. Although he acknowledged that the Manichean claims about Catholic doctrine were false, he was not convinced beyond all doubt that Catholic doctrine itself was true.

Nevertheless, he was slowly moving forward. He began to see that even judged by strict standards of rationality, the Catholic Church was the more trustworthy of the two, acknowledging as it did that many of its teachings could not be proved, but had to be taken on the basis of authority. When Augustine reflected on his own life, he saw how many things he had necessarily to take for granted if he was to advance at all in either thought or action: he had to assume facts of world history, facts of world geography, even the fact that Monica and Patricius were his biological parents. Not to assume such things without ironclad proofs would have been absurd. As he recognized how many facts must be accepted on the authority of others if life is to proceed at all, he began to see that authority can be a help in the attainment of knowledge and not the inveterate obstacle he had long imagined it to be. It now appeared reasonable and indeed necessary that the Catholic Church should have authority to make up for the things that could not be explained, either because of the weakness of the human mind, or the brevity of human life, or the turmoil and confusion caused by human sin. Human finitude and human sinfulness hindered the ability to attain the knowledge that leads to life. The Bible as proclaimed in the church was a help to us in our predicament. Here was a supremely authoritative source, designed to give instruction to the entire church, and confirming its divine origin by its intrinsic capacity to accommodate its meaning to all levels of hearers. It was both simple enough for the simple and deep enough to satisfy the needs of the most subtle (6.5.8).

Through such arduous intellectual struggles Augustine made painful progress. Ironically, he could have made the same progress swiftly and easily if only he had relied on faith rather than reason. But having once trusted the Manichees and been betrayed, he was reluctant to accept anything that he had not first weighed in the balance of reason. "Just as someone who has suffered under a bad physician may often be afraid to entrust himself to a good one, so it was in my soul's case. It could be healed only by believing, yet it shirked the cure for fear of believing what was false" (6.4.6). It is worth noting how Augustine expresses the problem of faith and reason in terms of personal trust. He writes as one who knows what labyrinths the human mind can unwittingly build for itself and then become lost in, and he knows that when reason despairs of finding a way out, faith can clear a way. Thus the simplicity with which he speaks is not the simplicity of condescension or a subterfuge to avoid epistemological analysis, but a genuine conclusion that he has reached through experience. And to find this incalculably important principle of the primacy of faith over reason expressed so simply and so clearly is a further reason why Book Six commends itself as a key to the *Confessions* as a whole.

THE INCIDENT OF THE DRUNKEN BEGGAR (6.6.9)

Before we consider this incident, it will be helpful to recall that one unifying theme of the *Confessions*, running through the first eight books and the second half of Book Ten, is that of deliverance from the three overmastering desires spoken of in 1 John 2:16: the lust (or concupiscence) of the flesh, the lust of the eyes, and worldly ambition. An example of the lust of the flesh would be the overpowering sexual desire that Augustine experienced; this will be discussed later on in Book Six (6.11.20–15.25). An example of the lust of the eyes (curiosity that leads one into grave moral danger) would be Augustine's fascination with the secret knowledge of the Manichees; an even clearer example is that of Alypius's fascination with the gladiatorial games (6.8.13). An example of worldly ambition is presented to us now in the incident of the drunken beggar.

Since Augustine was struggling in his quest for knowledge and wisdom—indeed, was mired in skepticism—it was natural that he should have sought satisfaction in one of the other principal drives that had governed his life thus far. And so he turned to worldly ambition. "I was hankering after honors, wealth and marriage." He already had the high honor of being orator to the imperial court in Milan, and it happened that on the very day when he was to bask in the sunshine of his imperial post and deliver a speech in praise of the emperor, an incident occurred that exposed the vanity of his pretensions. While walking through the streets of Milan, he came across a drunken beggar and was suddenly struck by the fact that this man had already reached the goal—happiness and peace—that Augustine had hardly even glimpsed in a dozen years of frantic searching and was now doubtful that he would ever reach. It is one of the most vivid of the many instances in the *Confessions* where a seemingly trivial incident becomes for Augustine a moment of divine revelation, an epiphany. Suddenly Augustine saw that even though he stood at the pinnacle of his profession, it had brought him no nearer to happiness and peace than he was at the outset of his career. In fact, he was further from them, since he knew that all his eloquence was in the service of a lie and that it was recognized as such by everyone at court. It was a painful realization for Augustine, but at the same time a salutary one, for by seeing the vanity of his ambition, he was being freed from its allure. God was making Augustine's wanderings away from the truth so painful that he would eventually acknowledge the need to stop and turn back. This is how Augustine's freedom and God's grace interact throughout the story of Augustine's life: Augustine's freely chosen misery becomes the opportunity for God's freely given mercy.

ALYPIUS (6.7.11–10.16)

In Book Six we meet Alypius for the first time in the *Confessions*. Alypius was Augustine's friend from boyhood and the closest of his many friends. He was indeed "Augustine's alter ego."[7] Several years younger than Augustine, Alypius admired Augustine for the goodness and learning he saw in him, and Augustine admired him for the integrity of character that was evident from his youth. Alypius would follow Augustine, influencing him and being influenced by him, up to the moment in the garden of Milan when they both were converted (Book Eight). They would also be baptized together, along with Augustine's son Adeodatus, by Bishop Ambrose in Milan. In the company of other friends and family, Augustine and Alypius returned to Africa in 388, where they followed a monastic life until Alypius was called to be bishop of Thagaste, not long before Augustine himself became bishop of Hippo (ca. 396).

Four incidents involving Alypius as a young man are presented that throw light on his character. The fact that the young Augustine passes into a partial eclipse in these pages has led Pierre Courcelle to conjecture that they originated earlier and independently of the *Confessions* as the fulfillment of a request from the famous Christian ascetic Paulinus of Nola to be told how Alypius came to take up the ascetic life.[8] This conjecture has some support in the extant letters of Paulinus and Augustine. Nevertheless, by focusing on the historical circumstances that may or may not have provided the occasion for Augustine to write about Alypius, there is a danger that we may overlook the fact that the material on Alypius is thematically well integrated into the *Confessions*. The four narratives of Alypius praise God for Alypius's evil and good deeds in much the same way as the *Confessions* as a whole praise God for Augustine's evil and good deeds.[9] In terms of themes, these four narratives deal with grace and freedom, sin and liberation, in ways that illuminate the work as a whole, and without which it would be incalculably poorer.

The first incident occurred while Augustine was teaching in Carthage. He had been sad to see Alypius getting caught up in an obsession with the chariot races, regarding them as a complete waste of time. But since he was unable to do anything about it, Augustine put it out of his mind. Now Alypius was also in the habit of popping in and out of Augustine's classes to listen to what Augustine had to say. On this occasion Augustine was expounding a text for his students when the thought came to him that an analogy with the chariot races might shed light on the text, so he made the analogy in a very sarcastic manner. Although Augustine was not thinking of Alypius's obsession with the races when he spoke, Alypius took his words as a rebuke directed at him personally. But instead of taking offense, Alypius was grateful for the insight he had gained. "With a strong resolve of temperance (*temperantia*) he shook his mind free, and all the filth of the [chariot races] dropped away from him. Never again did he go there" (6.7.12). Alypius thus displayed an openness and an honesty that made him capable of being taught by God, and we see God working in a way that neither Augustine nor Alypius had been aware of at the time.

The second story shows that while Alypius had gained an insight, he had not understood it fully because he had not realized that it was God's gift and not his own achievement. Thinking that he had overcome his addiction to chariot races by the force of his own will, he made himself vulnerable to the temptation posed by another blood sport—the gladiatorial games.[10] Augustine continues his narrative by telling how Alypius, then in his early twenties, was eager to add the finishing touches to his education and embark upon a career in law. So he set out from Carthage to complete his education in Rome. The passage is worth quoting in full:

> He had been drawn toward a worldly course by his parents' siren song, and he was unwilling to abandon it, so he had gone to Rome ahead of me to study law, and there he was assailed by an entirely unexpected craving for gladiatorial entertainments. This came about in a way no one could have foreseen. He shunned such displays and loathed them; but some of his friends and fellow-students, returning from their midday meal, happened to find the stadium open to them and, as is the way with close friends, drew him in by force, despite his vehement protests and struggles. It was one of the days for cruel and murderous sport, and he kept telling them, "You may drag my body into that place and fix me there, but can you direct my mind and my eyes to the show? I will be there, and yet be absent, and so get the better both of you and of the performance." They heard what he said but took him along with them all the same, wishing perhaps to know if he could make good his claim. When they arrived and settled themselves in what seats they could find, the whole place was heaving with thoroughly brutal pleasure. He kept the gateways of his eyes closed, forbidding his mind to go out that way to such evils. If only he could have stopped his ears too! At a certain tense moment in the fight a huge roar from the entire crowd beat upon him. He was overwhelmed by curiosity, and on the excuse that he would be prepared to condemn and rise above whatever was happening even if he saw it, he opened his eyes, and suffered a more grievous wound in his soul than the gladiator he wished to see had received in the body. He fell more dreadfully than the other man whose fall had evoked the shouting; for by entering his ears and persuading his eyes to open the noise effected a breach through which his mind—a mind rash rather than strong, and all the weaker for presuming to trust in itself rather than in you, as it should have done— was struck and brought down. As he saw the blood he gulped the brutality along with it; he did not turn away but fixed his gaze there and drank in the frenzy, not aware of what he was doing, reveling in the wicked contest and intoxicated on sanguinary pleasure. No longer was he the man who had joined the crowd; he was now one of the crowd he had joined, and a gen-

uine companion of those who had led him there. What more need be said? He watched, he shouted, he grew hot with excitement, he carried away with him a madness that lured him back again not only in the company of those by whom he had initially been dragged along but even before them, dragging others. Nonetheless you rescued him from his plight with your mighty and most merciful hand, and taught him to rely not on himself but on you; but this was long afterward. (6.8.13)

The story of how the future bishop of Thagaste, who would be renowned not only for his legal expertise but also for his smooth urbanity, had once been overcome by pure blood lust provides a striking glimpse into the dark recesses of human nature.

At Rome, Augustine says, Alypius is seized by a craving (*hiatus*) for the gladiatorial games. The word "craving" does not capture all the nuances of the Latin word *hiatus*, which evokes an image of jaws gaping wide with greedy desire—an image exquisitely appropriate in view of the insatiable thirst for blood that Alypius then exhibits. The craving that overtakes Alypius is "entirely unexpected" and comes about "in a way that no one could have foreseen." This is expressed more emphatically in the Latin when Augustine uses the words *incredibile et incredibiliter*—an example of emphatic repetition. In this way Augustine blocks the reader from reaching for any facile rationalization of Alypius's behavior. The games are "cruel and monstrous," and "the whole place was heaving with thoroughly brutal pleasure." Although Alypius is confident that he can remain aloof simply by closing his eyes, the reader's sense of foreboding builds until it reaches its peak when the narrator exclaims: "If only he could have stopped his ears too!" From this point on, the narrative proceeds at a pace that imitates the rush of Alypius's emotions. When the gladiator is wounded and falls, the sight of blood drives Alypius into a frenzy. The inexorable, uncontrollable surge of madness is conveyed even in the English translation: "As he saw the blood he gulped the brutality along with it; he did not turn away but fixed his gaze there and drank in the frenzy, not aware of what he was doing, reveling in the wicked contest and intoxicated on sanguinary pleasure." In the aftermath of this great wave of frenzy he is no longer the person he was when he came into the amphitheater, but utterly transformed. Augustine describes an emotion beyond the control of the will and, symbolically, human inadequacy in the face of the power of evil. Only grace— God's "most strong and merciful hand"—can deliver Alypius from that power.

Note that Augustine says that Alypius "suffered a more grievous wound in his soul than the gladiator he wished to see had received in the body. He fell more dreadfully." A wound in the soul is precisely what Adam suffered when he fell. And the Latin word Augustine uses to describe the cause of that wound and that subsequent fall is *concupiuit*, the same root as the word "concupiscence." The translation disconnects *concupiuit* from *ceciditque* and *miserabilius*, which is unfortunate because these three words taken together form a concise description of the fall: he lusted, he fell, he was in misery. We need not worry that we are reading the narrative too closely. The literary style of the *Confessions* presupposes a sophisticated readership that would be attentive to every word. What we are seeing here is a presentation of the themes of the fall, original sin, and concupiscence in the form of narrative, rather than in the form of speculative theology.

Note too that other people—not only Alypius's friends but also the entire crowd—are a causal factor in the incident. We may view this as symbolic of humanity's solidarity with sinful Adam. Augustine's teaching on human solidarity in evil is often regarded as irrelevant and indeed unintelligible when it is expressed in terms of being "in Adam."[11] But when it is portrayed in narrative form, it is given concreteness, particularity, and the power to move the sympathetic reader. In essence what we are being given in this passage is something close to poetry—an artistic vision of the contrast between outer manner and inner nature, between a surface image of rationality and self-control and the hidden depths of brutality that lurk beneath. Here, in this concrete illustration, we see how concupiscence manifests itself in fallen human nature. In its portrayal of addiction to pleasure and the emotional bondage that ensues, it foreshadows the account of Augustine's own addiction to sexual pleasure in Book Eight. Finally, it makes credible one of the repeated claims of Augustine that modern readers find most incredible: that we are all children of Adam,[12] unable to set ourselves free from "the chain of original sin" (5.9.16).

Alypius would eventually be led to see that he must rely not on himself, but on God alone for his safety and well-being. This insight is expressed simply and in its simplicity it is comparable to the famous phrase in the *City of God* about the two loves that characterize the earthly city and the Heavenly City respectively: the one centered on the self and leading to forgetfulness of God, the other centered on God and leading to forgetfulness of self.[13]

EXCURSUS: 6.11.13 AS CULTURAL CRITIQUE

But there is much more to this passage: it provides nothing less than a critique of an entire culture. As the great literary critic Erich Auerbach observed, "it is not merely a random Alypius whose pride, [indeed,] whose inmost being, is thus crushed; it is the entire rational individualistic culture of classical antiquity: Plato and Aristotle, the Stoa and Epicurus."[14] Such a brief, circumstantial passage can embody a critique of classical culture because these philosophical traditions, despite their wide divergences in many areas, had one central point in common: a belief in the rational powers of the human mind and the self-sufficiency that those powers made possible. In Plato's famous analogy, reason is likened to a skilled charioteer who steers the two horses of spirit and desire toward the goal of intellectual beauty. And indeed in all these traditions rational knowledge is the guide of life. Knowledge of choices combined with the will to withhold or grant assent to them is able to render an individual invulnerable to vice. As the Stoic philosopher Epictetus remarked in words that seem almost to be echoed by Alypius, "You may fetter my leg but not even Zeus himself can overpower my will."[15]

Let us pause for a moment with Stoicism, since it looms so large in Augustine's writings as an object of his criticism. With the rise of the Roman Empire, Stoicism had been seen as eminently suitable for rulers, who must be cool, rational, and above the brutality of the common mob. Marcus Aurelius especially prized the notion of the soul as an impregnable fortress, capable of withstanding the fiercest onslaughts of the external world. "Nowhere," he remarked, "can a mind find a retreat more full of peace or more free from care than his own soul."[16] His ability to rise above his circumstances was seen in his attendance at gladiatorial games, which he himself put on in fulfillment of a public duty. Although he was present, his attention was conspicuously elsewhere, since he spent his time receiving and replying to official letters.[17] Marcus Aurelius's ability to detach himself from violence is also evident, however, in the cool ordering of the massacre of Christians in Gaul, which is described in a famous letter preserved by St. Irenaeus.

Apart from the role of emperor, the Roman profession that most nearly embodied the Stoic ideal was that of the law. The lawyer's expertise made him fit to govern others, and we should recall that his field of expertise—the law—was popularly regarded as the apogee of Roman civilization. That Alypius had gone to Rome to study law makes him an embodiment of the noblest ambition known to that civilization.

Augustine's fullest assessment of Roman civilization appears in the *City of God*, written many years after the *Confessions*. But it is worth considering what he says about it there. Augustine calls Rome the capital of the earthly city, the antithesis to the heavenly City of God, and recounts how Rome was founded upon an act of murder when Remus was slain by his brother Romulus. This murder was a type of Abel's murder at the hands of Cain, the first founder of the earthly city. In the same passage, Augustine conjures up a lurid picture of Rome by citing the words of the poet Lucan: "Those walls were dripping with a brother's blood."[18] Thus the murderous gladiatorial games in the Colosseum are symbols of Roman civilization,[19] and it is in the context of this symbolic world that we may most usefully interpret what happens to Alypius after his arrival at Rome.

For Augustine, the ideal of the cool, rational Roman trained in law to rule the world is simply an illusion possible only to people who imagine they know themselves but in fact do not. But this illusion is more than mere foolishness. If it were only foolishness, then the corrective would be more knowledge, and the Stoic ideal would be intact.[20] But for Augustine the whole quest for self-sufficient knowledge is not only foolishness, it is the pride that precedes the fall. For Augustine, what can be known consciously is but the surface of one's personality. The depths are known only by God. Despite his penchant for introspective analysis, Augustine is adamant that we can never adequately know ourselves. Hence one of his most frequent prayers is "Cleanse me of my hidden sins" (Ps. 19:12b [13b Heb.]).[21] Wisdom is not to be found by ascending to a godlike eminence that enables one to look down on the rest of humanity as so many fools, but rather by humbly identifying oneself with the crucified Christ, the foolishness of God that is wiser than human wisdom.

To recognize 6.8.13 as a critique of Roman culture is obviously not something that general readers can be expected to do simply by reading the text more carefully. They need the guidance of a teacher. But I raise the topic in this chapter as further evidence of how rich in content Book Six is. Cultural critiques recur throughout the *Confessions*, but few if any approach that of Alypius's experience at the gladiatorial games for sheer narrative power and intensity.

MORE STORIES OF ALYPIUS

The third story of Alypius takes us back from Rome to Carthage and seems therefore to be out of order, but as Colin Starnes has shown, it is perfectly in order when considered thematically.[22] The first incident showed a potential strength in Alypius—his openness to correction. The second showed a real weakness—an uncontrollable curiosity. The third will show that curiosity from another angle, and the fourth will return to that strength of character which Augustine says was present in him from his youth. So there is in fact a clear pattern of the same kind we find throughout the rest of the *Confessions*—thematic rather than strictly chronological.

The third story presents Alypius's weakness in a form that even has a touch of slapstick comedy about it. Alypius was unknowingly present at the scene of an attempted robbery while it was taking place. As soon as the robber was heard, he threw down his ax and fled. Alypius stumbled upon the ax and out of curiosity picked it up to examine it, but as he did so those who had heard the robber came out, saw Alypius with the ax, and apprehended him. Providentially a powerful man who knew Alypius well happened to pass by at that very moment, spoke with Alypius, and was able to find the real robber. It was providential for Alypius not only at that time but also for later in his life, since he learned how important it is not to make hasty judgments.

The fourth anecdote returns to Rome at a time when Alypius was serving as an aide to a judge. Augustine relates how the cowardly judge, unwilling and afraid to deal with a case involving a very powerful and dangerous senator, turned the case over to Alypius. Unlike his superior, Alypius refused to let the offer of bribes or the threat of intimidation affect his judgment, but judged the case entirely on its merits.

Despite their apparent lack of chronological and geographical continuity, we are here presented with a rounded view of Alypius, exhibiting his strengths and his weaknesses, his good deeds and his evil deeds, in order that God's mercy may be shown and praised. Beginning with this set of anecdotes about Alypius, the reader is presented with another set of "Confessions," only this time in miniature: the "Confessions" of Alypius,[23] which will also culminate in conversion in the garden scene in Book Eight. Thus Alypius, more than any other personality in the *Confessions*, serves as a foil to Augustine. And since we first learn about Alypius in Book Six and indeed gain most of our information about him there, that book once again proves to be uniquely helpful to the reader. The kind of helpfulness will become even clearer when we consider the ongoing discussion of sex and marriage that Augustine was involved in with Alypius at this time.

ON SEX AND MARRIAGE (6.11.18–15.25)

In 6.11.18–19 Augustine conveys his agitated and exhausted state of mind by means of a soliloquy in which he recalls the tortuous paths he has been running down for so long, only to end up mired in the same place. It is worth pointing out how useful this soliloquy is, and was intended to be. In the first place it offers a convenient summary of his agonizing quest for happiness since his nineteenth year. In other words, it recapitulates what Augustine wants the reader to remember at this point not only from the earlier parts of Book Six, but also from Books Three, Four, and Five. The recapitulation thus relativizes the importance of those three books and strengthens the case for the sufficiency of Book Six for the reader. Secondly, by compressing a dozen years of mental turmoil into one frenetic soliloquy, Augustine brilliantly conveys to the reader the sense of anxiety, confusion, and exhaustion that he had been burdened with for so long. Finally, the fact that it is a recapitulation also signals the crucial importance of what is to follow. We are now at the turning point in the narrative of his conversion. Augustine explicitly states at the outset of this section that he was nearing the age of thirty—the age that marked the beginning of maturity. For Augustine it is a time of spiritual ripening as well. From this point on, the *Confessions* take on a note of greater urgency and intensity, as a series of decisive movements take place that lead ultimately to the baptism of Augustine, Alypius, and Augustine's son.

One of the issues that had tormented Augustine was how he could ever live "deprived of a woman's embrace" (6.11.20). Yet it seemed to him that the pursuit of wisdom required nothing less, at least in his case. To him the pursuit of sexual gratification seemed to contradict the pursuit of that serene happiness which was the fruit of philosophical contemplation. For his part Alypius thought that marriage would complicate and eventually derail the life of leisure required by members of a philosophical community, such as he and Augustine and their other friends dreamed of (6.12.21). He could not understand how sex could have such a powerful hold over Augustine. Indeed, in terms of the strength of his sex drive, Alypius appears to have been at the opposite end of the spectrum from Augustine. Abstaining from sex was no struggle for him. Perhaps, Augustine speculates, it was because Alypius's sexual experience had been early, brief, and a source of shame and embarrassment to him. But as Augustine proclaimed his insatiable need for sex and for the inexpressible joy it brought him, Alypius began to grow curious. His besetting sin began to show itself again. In time, he began to think that his own brief experience of sexual intercourse so many years ago was not typical. Perhaps he had not experienced the real thing. He wanted to experience the ecstasy without which Augustine said he could not live. Thus Augustine unwittingly led Alypius into temptation, reawakening his curiosity and making him forgetful of where it had taken him in the past.

Amid such a confusion of thoughts and feelings on sex and marriage, it is no wonder that the dream Augustine, Alypius, and their friends shared of forming a philosophical community and devoting their entire lives to the pursuit of wisdom foundered. The entanglement of conflicting views was now hopeless. Yet it would find resolution in God. The idea of a philosophical community would surface again after Augustine and Alypius had their conversion experience in the garden. The friends later made a resolution to live together as servants of God (9.8.17). Thus their idea of a community had not been inherently wrong, it had simply not been founded and centered on God at this time.[24]

AUGUSTINE'S PLANS TO MARRY

Interleaved within the discussion of sex and marriage in 6.11.18–15.25 are two passages dealing with Augustine's own particular marriage plans (6.13.23 and 6.15.25). These two passages are among the most controversial of the entire work. Indeed, if resolving all the problems contained in them were necessary for an understanding of Book Six we might be forced to abandon that book as our key. Fortunately, however, what Augustine says in these passages is sufficiently clear to enable us to see how they fit thematically into Book Six, and once we have seen this we will be able to see also how they add further evidence in favor of using Book Six as our master key.

Augustine relates how he yielded to pressure to dismiss his common-law wife of fifteen years and become engaged to a girl two years below the legal age of marriage, which was twelve. Augustine says that Monica's motives were to see him baptized, since such a marriage would entail his baptism. (Presumably the girl's family was Catholic.) However, Augustine also notes that despite her prayers Monica never received the vision from God assuring her that Augustine would indeed one day be well married. All she had were her own dreams, which, as we have seen, she distinguished from genuine visions by a faculty "akin to the sense of taste" (6.13.23). Nevertheless she proceeded with her plans. Thus her motives for arranging Augustine's marriage were mixed. Although she wanted to see her son baptized into the Catholic Church, she was not willing to wait till she had received a clear sign of God's will. Moreover, the ostensible reason why Augustine could not continue living with his concubine but must marry an aristocratic heiress is essentially worldly: he cannot advance in his career without the right connections and the right amount of money. Finally, Augustine is less interested in marriage than in gratifying his lust, as he demonstrates by taking another sexual partner to fill the two-year gap until his fiancée reached the legal age for marriage. This taking of another partner was such a wanton act that it made Augustine realize that his sexuality was completely out of control—that he was now in the grip of what Margaret Miles has diagnosed as sexual addiction.[25] This is the third of the three lusts of 1 John 2:16 to manifest itself in Book Six. Augustine would remain hopelessly enslaved to it right up until he heard the voice in the garden telling him to pick up and read.

Augustine's behavior in taking a new sexual partner contrasts sharply with that of his common-law wife, who in leaving Augustine and their son vowed never to give herself to another man. Attempts have been made to cast Augustine's dismissal of her in a less offensive light, noting that common-law wives were normally dismissed in Roman society in order that socially acceptable marriages could be entered into. But while such arguments may be valid, they have left most modern readers dissatisfied. All we can do here is note that Augustine says his pain over her dismissal was very great and did not heal over time, but instead turned into "a cold despair."

AUGUSTINE'S MISERY THE SIGN AND INSTRUMENT OF GOD'S MERCY (6.16.26)

Augustine's despair was so unbearable that he would gladly have allowed himself to be "sucked still deeper into the whirlpool of carnal lusts" in order to escape it, but he could not. What prevented him was an equally oppressive fear of death and of God's future judgment. The turmoil caused by these emotions left Augustine unable to move forward. His pain seemed all-consuming and he could see no way out. Nevertheless, his growing sense of powerlessness and hopelessness was being used by God to prepare his heart to receive grace. Augustine was slowly coming to the realization that he faced utter loss unless he surrendered his life to God unconditionally.

CONCLUSION

Because readers are generally drawn more to portrayals of personalities and events than to analyses of abstract ideas, they are more likely to be engaged by Book Six than by any other book of the *Confessions*, for Book Six offers a greater range of major characters and memorable incidents than any other. Moreover, Book Six is the first of that decisive sequence of three books which forms the dramatic climax of the narrative running from Book One to Book Nine. These three books, all set in Milan, concentrate on the intense final phase of Augustine's conversion to Christianity, culminating in the garden scene at the end of Book Eight. Book Nine represents the denouement, in which the conflicts brought on by the demands of his career, his prospective marriage, and his desire to share a communal life with his friends are all resolved. But that denouement makes no sense unless the reader has first witnessed those conflicts in their fiercest form, which requires that he or she follow Augustine along the "dark and slippery path" (6.1.1) of Book Six.

Chapter 7

Book Seven: Inner Vision as the Goal of Augustine's Life

Phillip Cary

INTRODUCTION

In Book Seven of the *Confessions*, young Augustine reads some philosophy books, then turns inward to see God. This is exciting enough for anyone who loves a good book, longs for deep insights, wants to get in touch with the inner self or desires to know God. But to understand why it is central to the whole of the *Confessions,* we need to see precisely what problem it solved for Augustine and why this is the central problem of his life. Our author makes this easier for us by organizing Book Seven as the solution to a problem, and telling us up front what the problem is. (We must keep a sharp eye on the difference between young Augustine, the central character in the *Confessions*, and Augustine the author, who knows so much more than the character does about his own problems.) The fundamental problem is how to see God, when the only things we are used to seeing are of quite a different nature. Related to this are other, subsidiary problems, such as the nature and place of evil in the universe, which can be solved once there is a solution to this fundamental problem. And then, as always, the solution to one problem leads to further problems. Having caught sight of God, young Augustine longs to make his vision permanent, but cannot. That is why he needs Christ, the man who, as God incarnate, is humanity's road to the divine fatherland that Augustine has just glimpsed from afar.

Thus, Book Seven of the *Confessions*, after solving intellectual problems the author has been developing in the first six books, sets the agenda for the next six books, as well as for the rest of Augustine's life. Its own structure thereby reflects the structure of the *Confessions* as a whole, as the solutions at the center of Book Seven occupy the center of the *Confessions* as well: our author first gathers up a set of problems he has been introducing us to so far (7.1.1–8.12), then unfolds the solutions he saw after reading the books of the Platonists (7.9.13–17.23), and concludes by introducing us to the new agenda that results, based on Christ as the way back to the vision of God (7.18.24–21.27). To see the centrality of Book Seven to the *Confessions* and to Augustine's life, we can follow this three-fold progression from problems, to solutions, to more problems, then draw some conclusions, which will focus on the role of Platonism in Augustine's thought and in Christian theology generally. (Since in the course of this exposition I will say some things about Augustine's reliance on Platonism that not everyone will like, some readers may want to look first at the conclusion, where I put all my cards on the table.)

PROBLEMS

The big problem is how to see God. The conceptual structure of the problem, as our author explains it, is Platonist. To know God means to see something bodi-less or incorporeal (or as we would now say, "nonphysical"), and how can you see that? This is not how the Bible ever tackles the problem of knowing God. In fact it is so foreign to the Bible and to traditions outside of Platonism that Augustine the author needs to spend some time giving us a sense of what the problem is. We may think we can imagine a nonphysical thing, but the first lesson of Book Seven is that we cannot. We can see all sorts of things that have no solidity but are still bodies, like air and light. In ancient physics these are understood to be bodily things ("corporeal things" in Augustine's language), just as in modern physics they are treated as physically measurable phenomena. If you never get more nonphysical than that, then your thinking is as materialist as any philoso-phy can be: all you can think of is the material world of earth, water, air, and fire, the four elements of ancient physics. In fact young Augustine's problem is that he is accustomed to thinking of God as being nothing more than the light of the heavens, a physical element perceived by the eyes of the body.

This is how the Manichees conceived of God, our author tells us earlier: as a "huge bright body" of which the soul was part (4.16.31).[1] In fact according to his analysis, the Manichean heresy is thoroughly materialistic (5.10.20; cf. also 3.7.12). Manicheism is famed as a kind of dualism, of course, but Augustine traces this back logically to an underlying materialism. The Manichees' dualism consisted in their belief that the whole universe is made up of two radically opposed substances or natures, which we could call the Good Stuff and the Bad Stuff. Their underlying materialism consisted in conceiving of both the Good Stuff and the Evil Stuff as *stuff*, i.e., as material substances that take up space. The argument by which they had ensnared Augustine's mind could be paraphrased as follows: "Since there is such a substance as evil, we have to ask where it comes from. Whence is evil? You don't want to say it was created by the good God, do you? So it must not have been created at all. Therefore it has always existed and must be as eternal as God. Thus you must accept dualism: from the very begin-ning the universe has contained both good and evil, both God and what we

Manichees call the race of darkness" (cf. 7.5.7). Augustine the author thinks this conclusion is inevitable, unless one rejects the materialist premise that evil is a kind of substance. So the key to everything is overcoming materialist habits of thought, which our author describes as "the greatest and almost the only cause of my inevitable error" (5.10.19). After hearing the sermons of Ambrose, he tells us, he would have broken every hold the Manichees still had on his mind "if only I could have conceived of a spiritual substance" (5.14.25).

As Book Seven opens, he is no longer a member of the Manichean sect, but he has yet to overcome the materialist habits of thought he developed while he was still with them. His problem is that when he tries to conceive of God, he only *imagines* God. That is to say, his mind draws images from the world perceived by the five physical senses and then thinks that these mental images (which he calls "phantasms," related to the Greek word from which we get "fantasy") somehow represent God. Thus he still thinks of God as being a bodily thing: not like an old man with a beard sitting on a throne (as the Manichees had falsely accused Catholics of thinking), but rather as the very essence of light. What Augustine the author wants to show us at the beginning of Book Seven is that the latter is as materialist a way of conceiving God as the former. Both are based on the imagination, which is a function of the soul that is completely dependent on sense perception. For according to Augustine's theory of imagination, you can only imagine the sorts of things you can perceive with the five senses, and the senses can only perceive bodily things such as light. So if we only *imagine* God, we will conceive of him in material images drawn from the senses. We will be like the young Augustine, whose heart "ran through images of the sort of forms my eyes were used to running over" (7.1.2). This is an intellectual problem, but also a moral problem: he could only think of material things because his mind was "gross," i.e., heavy and weighed down by its attachment to things of this world. Hence the first thing he tells us about himself in Book Seven is that "the greater I got in age, the worse I got in emptiness, as I could not conceive of any substance except the kind I saw with these eyes" (7.1.1).

Because of this moral and intellectual failure, he can only conceive of God as taking up space. Our author spends a great deal of time trying to get this picture across to us and show what is wrong with it. God is present everywhere, young Augustine knows, but how? His materialistic heart can only imagine God as spread out through all the places in the universe, like water filling a sponge (7.5.7). But that means one part of God must be in one place, and another part in another place, and more of him in an elephant than in a sparrow (7.1.2). Augustine the author wants us to see that this is absurd. Clearly we need a better conception of God's omnipresence than that. Above all, we need a deeper understanding of the nature of being than that, an ontology that will provide an alternative to materialist conceptions of being. For as long as we are gross in heart, we will be in the same position as young Augustine, who was forced to think of God as "a corporeal something in space, poured into the world or even spread out infinitely beyond it . . . since whatever I took space away from, seemed to me to be nothing—nothing at all, not even a void" (7.1.1). We will know when we have a solution to this problem when we no longer have to say with young Augustine, "whatever was not stretched through some amount of space or spread out or clumped together or swollen or containing such things or capable of containing them, I judged to be altogether nothing" (7.1.2).

We do have a clue to start with. "In my very marrow," Augustine says, "I believed that You were incorruptible, inviolable, and unchangeable" (7.1.1). For purposes of understanding Book Seven, the key term here is "incorruptible." Following both biblical and classical usage, Augustine uses the word in a very broad sense. Corruption is any process that makes something worse (7.12.18). Unlike most modern Christians, Augustine (like every Platonist and nearly all ancient Christians) believes it is good that God is unchangeable, because this means God cannot change for the worse. Because God is unchangeable, he is incorruptible. But once again, young Augustine didn't know how. He had no ontology to explain how a being or substance can be unchangeable, and therefore his conception of God's incorruptibility was as inadequate and ill-grounded as his conception of God's omnipresence and bodilessness. He tried to use his concept of incorruptibility as a clue to the nature of God—as if with this one principle he could wave away all the phantasms from his mind's eye—but they kept coming back like a cloud of gnats to block his vision (7.1.1).

Still, this principle of the incorruptibility of God was enough to show what was wrong with Manicheism. It explains the power of an argument his old friend Nebridius had used years before against the Manichees (7.2.3). According to the Manichees, good souls are made of the Good Stuff; they are literally a part of God, fragments of the divine light that have been imprisoned in filthy bodies made of the Evil Stuff. For in the beginning (so their mythology went) the Evil Stuff or "race of darkness" attacked the divine realm of the Good Stuff, which was forced to counterattack. In the cosmic battle that followed, our souls got trapped as it were behind enemy lines and caged in these dark, evil bodies.[2] Nebridius's argument against this myth took the logical form technically known as "dilemma," where a critic offers his opponent two equally unpalatable alternatives.[3] According to the Manichean view of things, Nebridius asked, what would have happened if the divine Good Stuff had chosen not to fight back? Would it have been harmed somehow? If so, then God must be corruptible, capable of changing for the worse. No one (certainly not the Manichees) wanted to admit that this was possible. So look at the other alternative. Suppose God is incorruptible. If so, then why would he bother to fight back? If he is incorruptible, then by definition he cannot be harmed. So why bother getting into a battle with forces that cannot possibly do him any harm? The whole story of cosmic battle makes no sense if he is incorruptible.

So if the Manichees want to stand by their mythology, logic requires them to face the unpalatable consequence that God *can* be corrupted. Our own souls are fragments of the divine light that have suffered a change for the worse by being imprisoned in evil bodies. Since our souls are literally part of God, their corruption rubs off on him and he cannot be regarded any longer as incorruptible (cf. 4.15.26). This is the exact opposite of the religious consequences the Manichees wanted, but our author is convinced they have no logical way (short of abandoning Manicheism) to escape the conclusion: our souls are corrupted by our bodies, which means our corruption affects God. Augustine is convinced, of course, that the universe ought to work in exactly the opposite way. For our author, God, soul, and bodies are arranged in a hierarchy of being, from higher to lower.[4] Located between God and bodies in this hierarchy, the soul should be ruled by God above, but rule over bodily things below. Living thus we would dwell in a "middle region of safety or salvation (*salutis*)" (7.7.11), where our souls, though corruptible, are preserved from actual corruption by the incorruptible God. So we must understand the ontology of God—his immaterial, unchangeable and incorruptible being—before we can understand the nature of our salvation.

But we need another clue. The first clue was an explicit principle about the nature of God. The second is a subtle hint about the nature of the soul, an attempt to get us seeing what is so hard for us to see. The gross of heart, our author tells us at the beginning of the second paragraph, are not even clear to themselves: "My heart ran through images of the sort of forms my eyes were used to running over, and I didn't see that the very attention by which I formed these images was not something of that sort—and yet it could not form them if it were not something great" (7.1.2). If we would only look carefully at the very mind we are using to imagine material things, we would have the clue to what is not itself a material thing, something that is not spread out in space but is not just nothing either. It is indeed something very great, but not large in bulk or in physically measurable terms. It is the greatness of our own souls.[5]

Why is it that our souls have such a hard time seeing themselves? It is our fault, for we are used to looking outward at the world of bodily things, rather than inward within our souls. That is why, Augustine tells us, "the light of my eyes was not with me. For it was within, but I was outside" (7.7.11). This is the light of the *mind's* eye, which we can only see when we "awaken a different kind of vision," as Augustine's favorite passage from the books of the Platonists puts it.[6] We must become acquainted with a kind of seeing that frequently goes on in our souls unnoticed. The light by which we inwardly see comes not from the sun but from Truth itself, which is God. So long as we do not see this light or notice we are seeing it, we are far from God and even far from ourselves.

That is why these ontological problems about the nature of God and of evil tear his soul apart. Perhaps the deepest way we could misunderstand Augustine is to think that for him an intellectual problem is cold and abstract, having nothing to do with his heart, his moral life, his identity, and his very existence. Augustine suffers his intellectual problems deep within, where God alone knows his torment: "What tortures of my heart in labor! What sighs, my God! And Your ears were there, though I didn't know it. And as I sought forcefully in silence, the unspoken griefs of my soul were loud calls to Your mercy. You knew what I suffered, and no man" (7.7.11). This is an Augustinian prayer for grace—the darkened intellect's inner pleading for a gift of divine insight. Augustine's soul is out of joint, turned away from the inner light for which it longs, and therefore alienated also from its own nature. It has lost its place in the universe, no longer safe in that middle region between God above and the material world below, so that "You are true joy to me when subjected to You, and You subjected to me what You created beneath me" (7.7.11). Rather, he finds himself captive to material things, his soul outside itself, its back turned on God within. How shall he ever see the light?

SOLUTIONS

The pivotal event in Book Seven takes place when Augustine reads "certain books of the Platonists" (7.9.13). The most striking thing about these books is how little Augustine tells us about them. He describes their content by saying three times, "there I read . . ." and then quoting from the Bible (7.9.13, 14, 15)! For the key point about these books, our author wants us to know, is that they taught some of the same things as Scripture, but in different words. The pagan Platonists may not have known the Gospel of John, but they knew that "In the beginning was the Word, and the Word was with God and the Word was God" (7.9.13, quoting John 1:1). They knew that this eternal divine Word is the inner light, "the true light that enlightens every human being coming into this world" (7.9.13, quoting John 1:9). Unlike the Manichees, they knew that the human soul "is not that light"—i.e., that the soul is not a part of God—but rather "bears witness to that light" (1.9.13, quoting John 1:8, but predicating of the soul what the Scripture says of John the Baptist). Thus they knew of the key point of Trinitarian doctrine, that "before all time and above all time Your only-begotten Son remains unchangeably co-eternal with You" (7.9.14) and they understood its key soteriological implication: that souls are blessed only by receiving from his fullness, participating in his wisdom (ibid.).

This last point links the Platonist books with that earlier pagan philosophy book, the *Hortensius* of Cicero, which had initiated Augustine's search for wisdom when he was nineteen (3.4.7–8). What he did not understand then, but clearly has in mind as he writes now, is that Christ is the wisdom of God (1 Cor. 1:14). For when he first discovered philosophy, which as he reminds us is Greek for "love of wisdom" (3.4.8), he was stirred "to love, seek, pursue and possess or strongly embrace Wisdom itself, whatever that might be" (ibid.). And the only thing holding him back was that "the name of Christ was not there" (ibid.). So he evidently did not yet understand what was to become for him the key connection between Christianity and philosophy: namely, that Christ is the eternal wisdom that the philosophers seek. Hence "although I did not know what You were doing with me" (ibid.), this philosophical reading marked the moment when, like the Prodigal Son, "I began to rise and return to You" (3.4.7).[7]

In identifying Christ with divine Wisdom, Augustine follows the patristic doctrine of the Trinity, which turns on the identification of Christ as divine Word (in John 1) and wisdom (in Proverbs 8). The latter passage refers to a personified wisdom that was with God from the beginning and by which he created the world, which the church fathers saw as none other than the divine Word or reason (*logos*) referred to in the prologue to the Gospel of John as being "with God in the beginning" (John 1:2). Augustine's reading of these Platonist books was thus his initiation into the central point at which the church fathers forged an alliance between Christian doctrine and classical philosophy, identifying Christ as the eternal reason and wisdom by which God created the world. So what young Augustine learned from these pagans (according to Augustine the author) is the doctrine of the Trinity, but not the incarnation. They understood the key Trinitarian point that "the Word was God" (John 1:1) but not the key christological point that "the Word became flesh and dwelt among us" (7.9.14, quoting John 1:14). Like Cicero, they glimpsed the eternal wisdom of God, but did not realize that it bore the human name "Christ." Augustine proceeds to make an analogous division of the Trinitarian and christological portions of the Christ-hymn in Philippians 2, saying that the books of the Platonists taught the one (Phil. 2:6) but not the other (Phil. 2:7–11).

Since later Christian theology insisted that the doctrine of the Trinity was beyond the understanding of human reason,[8] one might wonder what books these were that Augustine is telling us so little about. Cicero's *Hortensius* is no longer extant,[9] but we know from ancient sources that it drew heavily on Aristotle's *Protrepticus*, an exhortation to philosophy written (most modern scholars think) when Aristotle was still a student of Plato.[10] Hence the continuity between what Augustine learned from Cicero and what he read in the Platonists is not so surprising. But what about these "books of the Platonists"? Scholarly opinion is divided on exactly which texts Augustine read, but there is broad agreement on several key points about their authors: he was reading little or none of Plato's dialogues, but rather the works of more recent writers, most probably Plotinus, the founder of what we now call Neoplatonism, and his student Porphyry—the two Platonist authors who play the most important role in Augustine's writings. But since the texts of Porphyry referred to in Augustine's writings are no longer extant, we must turn to Plotinus if we want to get an idea of the kind of Platonism that shaped Augustine's thought.

What we find in the books of Plotinus is of more direct relevance to the intellectual problems of Book Seven than anything in the Scripture passages Augustine quotes. For it was not the doctrine of the Trinity that solved his problems about the nature of God, but the Platonist notions of incorporeality, incorruptibility, unchangeability, and omnipresence, which are worked out by Plotinus with an intellectual depth and poetic beauty that Augustine would never have encountered before. Moreover, these ontological concepts are connected with soteriological issues, via the Platonist notion of a participation or sharing in the divine light that does not (in contrast to the Manichean view) make us literally part of God.[11] Especially important in this regard is a description of the inner vision of God toward the end of Plotinus's essay "On Beauty," which must count as our author's favorite passage from the books of the Platonists, because he quotes or alludes to it more than any other:

> What is the way? And what is the means? How can one behold this extraordinary beauty which remains in the inner sanctum and will not come outside to be seen by the profane? Let him who can arise and come into the inside, leaving the sight of his eyes outside and not turning back to corporeal beauties.[12]

It is as if the soul is a temple and God is found within it, so we must turn inward to see him, looking away from all external things. So when the Prodigal Son "comes to himself" (Luke 15:17) and decides he must "arise and go to my father" (Luke 15:18), Augustine thinks of this Plotinian call to "arise and come into the inside," where God is found.[13] The Prodigal's return to his father is not a physical journey through space, "not by feet or change of place . . . nor horses, chariots or ships," as Augustine says (1.18.28), picking up imagery from further on in the same chapter of Plotinus:

> Our fatherland is that from whence we came, and the Father is there. What then is our journey, our flight? Not by feet is it accomplished; for feet carry you from here to there all over the earth. Nor should you procure horse-chariot or ship; you should leave all such things behind and not look, but close your eyes and awaken a different kind of vision instead—a sort of vision which everyone possesses but few make use of.[14]

This is really a point about divine omnipresence. One of the recurrent paradoxes of the *Confessions* is that we somehow manage to flee from the omnipresent God (e.g., 2.6.14, 4.9.14, and 5.2.2). How can we be far from God, who is everywhere? Plotinus is deeply aware of the possibility of a nonspatial separation between God and the soul, as Augustine explains in a later work where he quotes this same passage and expounds it:

> Plotinus said, "So let us flee to the beloved fatherland. There is the Father, and there is everything. But what," he says, "are our ships, what is our flight? Becoming like God." For the more you are like God, the closer you are. There is no distance from Him except unlikeness to Him. And the human soul is unlike the incorporeal, eternal and unchangeable to the extent that it desires changeable temporal things.[15]

The only way we can put distance between ourselves and God is by a movement of the soul rather than the body, a turning of our attention and desire toward changing things, which causes us to become unlike the unchanging God. Hence the lesson Augustine draws from his reference to the Prodigal Son is: "in lustful and darkened emotion is distance from Your face" (1.18.28). We are far from God only when we turn outward and attach ourselves to external things, for then he is (as always) within us, but we are wandering outside ourselves (10.27.38).

The solution to all Augustine's problems begins, then, when he comes to himself and turns inward, just like this Plotinian Prodigal Son. Admonished by the books of the Platonists "to return to myself," and led by God's inward help, he "entered my inmost place" (7.10.16), and finds the light of eternal Truth:

> I entered and saw, with the eye of my soul, such as it was, above that same eye of my soul, above my mind, the unchangeable light—not the common light obvious to all flesh, nor as it were something greater of the same kind, shining more brightly . . . but other, quite other than all these things; nor was it above my mind as oil is above water or heaven above the earth, but it was above because it made me, and I was below because made by it. Whoever knows Truth, knows it, and whoever knows it, knows Eternity. (7.10.16)

The soul must turn inward and then look upward, shifting its attention from the bottom of the ontological hierarchy to the top: Augustine thus turns away from the external world of bodily things, enters the inner world of his own soul, and finally gazes above his soul at the light of Truth, which is his unchanging Creator.

This vision of the mind's eye gives him the solution to his problem of conceiving the nature of God. It teaches him how to think of what is literally unimaginable: something that takes up no space, yet is not nothing: "Now is Truth nothing, just because it is not spread out through finite or infinite space?" (7.10.16). According to Plotinus's conception of integral omnipresence, the divine is not spread out part-by-part in space like water in a sponge, but is present everywhere *as a whole*.[16] This concept plays a prominent role in Augustine's opening meditation on the nature of God at the beginning of *Confessions* (1.2.2–4.4), but perhaps the clearest explanation of it for our purposes is in one of his letters:

> God is not stretched out or poured out through space, whether finite or infinite (as if there could be more of Him in one part than in another) but is present as a whole everywhere—just like Truth, which no one in their right mind would say is partly in this place and partly in that; for after all, Truth is God.[17]

If you compare this with the language of Augustine's problem about divine omnipresence earlier in the book (7.1.1–2 and 7.7.11), you will see that this understanding of the omnipresence of Truth is the answer to his ontological problem of how to conceive of the incorporeal being of God.

This does not mean that one moment of insight instantaneously solved all Augustine's intellectual problems. It is clear from his early writings that it was not as simple as that. Augustine worked on the concept of the presence of divine Truth within the soul for years, taking several wrong turns, until he came up with the notion of a private inner world that we see in the *Confessions*.[18] This has important implications for how we read Book Seven, and especially the two accounts given there of his turning inward and looking upward to see God (7.10.16 and 7.17.23). I do not think these should be taken as narratives of Augustine's experiences at that time—in the summer of 386 C.E., shortly before the events recounted in Book Eight.[19] Rather, they are accounts of the psychological and epistemological structure of a certain kind of insight, which Augustine at that time did not fully understand and which he surely would not have described then in the same terms he is using now. For in 386 he had yet not mastered the Plotinian conceptuality that he uses so skillfully in the *Confessions*. So what we have here is a summary of Platonist insights that it took him years to develop. This means we should beware of familiar scholarly phrases like "Augustine's early Platonism," as if Platonism were a youthful phase that he soon got over. The *Confessions* is a far more Platonist work than Augustine's early philosophical writings, just as it is far more deeply Christian. For in the intervening years he has been learning both Platonist philosophy and Christian doctrine, in the course of developing the most powerful and influential form of Christian Platonism in history.

However, Augustine does mean to say that the solutions to his other intellectual problems follow logically from this key insight, as he proceeds to explain. Unchanging Truth is not the sort of thing that can be invaded or corrupted by forces of darkness. This is true Being, because it is unchangeable and "what truly is remains unchangeably" (7.11.17). Unchangeable Being is most truly being because it has always been and will never cease to be.[20] The reality of all other being is therefore measured by its relation to the incorruptible Being of God (ibid.). Now Augustine is ready to put the concept of corruption to work in explaining the nature of evil (7.12.18). True being is the supreme Good, incapable of changing for the worse. Other things have being to the extent that they share in the goodness of God, the supreme Good. But precisely because they are created rather than the Creator, they are not eternal and therefore not incorruptibly good. They are corruptible, for they are good but not unchangeable—and hence they are capable of changing for the worse. Modern usage of the word "perfect" misleads us here: God creates all things perfect in the sense of wholly good, but cannot create anything as perfect and incorruptible as himself, because that would be the same as creating God, which is impossible. So when God created the world it was perfect in the sense of uncorrupted, but not in the sense of incorruptible. It was not corrupted but it was capable of being corrupted.

This shows us how to answer the Manichean argument about where evil came from. As we saw above, they argued that evil must be an eternal substance that has forever existed independent of God, or else it must be that God created it. Augustine, on the contrary, can affirm that God created all things without admitting that he created evil. This logically implies that evil is not a thing at all (or in Augustine's language, it is not a substance or nature). Still more striking, it implies that "whatever is, is good," an implication Augustine accepts and insists upon (7.12.18). This may seem like an outrageously optimistic view of the world, or else like a denial of the reality of evil. But it is neither. It is an account of the peculiarly negative reality of evil. For Augustine evil is a corruption or defect in some-thing good, a lack or absence or deprivation of what ought to be. It has the real-ity of a particular kind of nonbeing, like (say) a hole in a shirt. The hole is certainly real in one sense (it makes a real difference in the way things are and how they work) but it is not a real thing, with a substance and nature of its own. For Augustine the presence of evil in the universe is like that, which is why he can say in effect: God created the shirt, but not the hole. For God created all things that have being, but he did not create evil, which is a kind of nonbeing. This is a view he shares with Eastern church fathers and bequeathed to the West-ern theological tradition, and it remains the fundamental alternative to dualist theologies like Manicheism.

If this approach seems overly abstract, bear in mind that Latin has only one word for both "evil" and "bad." So unlike most modern philosophers dealing with "the problem of evil," Augustine's concerns are not restricted to specifically human suffering, trouble, and evil. According to Augustine's Latin a hole in a shirt is an evil (*malum*), in the simple sense that it is bad for the shirt. Thus for Augustine to explain where evil came from is to explain any sort of badness: bad apples and bad shirts, as well as bad people. The first and fundamental point to make here, Augustine thinks, is that God doesn't create anything bad.

On the other hand, this does not mean he creates everything equally good. For Augustine all things are good but some are better than others. A shirt is not as good and noble a thing as the living body it clothes, which is not as good and noble as the soul that gives it life.[21] But the fact that some things are inferior in goodness does not make them evil (7.13.19). There is a hierarchy of value asso-ciated with the hierarchy of being, but everything in the hierarchy is good, from top to bottom, and the whole of the hierarchy is better off because the lower things are there along with the higher. In the good order of things established by God, everything is good in its place. It is as if to say: mud and mosquitoes are good things in themselves, but they should stay where they belong. We don't want them in the house or under our skin, but whoever studies their intrinsic being and truth with disinterested care (under a microscope, say, the way an ecologist or an entomologist does) will find them good and even beautiful. For "there is no soundness in those who are displeased with any of Your creations" (7.14.20).

The concept of order (one of the deepest and most elusive concepts in phi-losophy) affords an important enrichment of Augustine's account of the nature of evil: good things can bring badness into the universe not just by being cor-rupted in their own substance, but by being out of place, contrary to the divine order that places them where they belong. The hierarchical nature of goodness is especially important for understanding moral evil, which is rooted in our free will and its ability to choose things in the wrong order. I have found that American students (who typically do not quite grasp the point that free choice is an inher-ent power of the soul, not a set of options spread out before them like consumer items on a shelf) will often quite spontaneously construct an argument to the effect that God must create evil "in order to give us a choice." For how could God give us free choice, which includes the freedom to choose evil, unless he created something evil for us to choose? Augustine has an answer to this question: evil choices do not mean we choose evil things, but rather that we choose in an evil way. In effect, moral evil is best described with an adverb rather than a noun: it means choosing evilly rather than choosing an evil.

Augustine's approach to the problem of evil in Book Seven thus concludes with an account of moral evil as "not a substance, but a perversion of the will, twisting away from You, the highest substance, and towards these lower things" (7.16.22). Perversion of will here means the opposite of conversion: a turning away from God rather than toward him (both "perversion" and "conversion" being based on the Latin *vertere*, the verb for "turning"). Thus moral evil means that we use our free will to choose some good thing that God created in preference to God, as if this rather than God were our highest good. We make money our god, for instance, or wine or fame or even our friends—as if any of these could make us eternally happy. Augustine has been leading up to this definition of moral evil from the beginning, ever since he wrote "our hearts are restless until they find rest in You" (1.1.1). Sin means looking for lasting happiness where it cannot be found, and the punishment of sin is that we cannot find what we are looking for (4.12.18). We think money or fame or even friends will make us happy, but they ultimately bring us misery, the grief of loss that inevitably follows when we love what is mortal as if it were immortal and incorruptible and could not be lost (4.6.11).

MORE PROBLEMS

In the center of Book Seven Augustine catches a vision of God, which is the ultimate end or goal of human life. He finds himself amazed that "now I loved You, not some phantasm instead of You" (7.17.23). But his life has not yet reached its end, for he cannot keep his eye long on what he loves. His old habits still weigh him down, and he finds that he cannot continue to gaze at the light within. In both accounts of his vision of God, he describes himself as falling back down to his usual self, repulsed and dazzled by the brightness of the divine light (7.10.16 and 7.17.23). It is like looking at the sun: you can't do it for long. But like Plato, from whom this metaphor of dazzlement ultimately derives, Augustine thinks that with healing and exercise, our mind's eye will eventually be strong enough to gaze straight at the sun.[22] For this is what the mind's eye is all about, as the second account of his vision of God makes clear (7.17.23). Here our author summarizes an investigation he had undertaken years before,[23] following a path he will elaborate in more detail in the first half of Book Ten and use again (in quite a different form) in the second half of his great treatise *The Trinity* (Books Eight through Fifteen). He turns to examine the epistemic functions of the soul, ascending from the lowest functions to the highest, from those concerned with outward things to those concerned with inner things. This is what he means by saying "through my soul itself I will ascend to Him" (10.7.11). In Book Seven the ascent is specifically from the senses (concerned with bodily things), to the "inward sense" (the mind's ability to compare the deliverances of the five different outward senses), to his reasoning ability, and finally to the intellect, which is the mind's ability to see the light of Truth. The culmination of this ascent is a vision that is not mystical, but epistemological: an insight into the fact that all the mind's knowledge is dependent on its intellectual ability to judge things by the light of unchanging Truth (7.17.23).

Augustine's vision of God is cut short by dazzlement precisely because his mind is still diseased as a result of that perversion of will by which it attaches itself to temporal rather than eternal things. The mind attracted to external things cannot bear to gaze long at the divine light within. The need to overcome this perversion, to undo these earthly attachments and find his way back home to the fatherland he has glimpsed from afar, sets the agenda for the rest of his life, as well as setting up the key problems to be dealt with in Book Eight. The concluding paragraphs of Book Seven focus on one particular kind of this perversion, though it is the deepest and most important kind for Augustine. It is the turning of the will away from God to love not bodies, but the mind itself. This is the sin of pride, which Augustine finds particularly prominent in Satan, the pagan Platonists, and himself. He describes it using a favorite metaphor, itself derived in part from Plotinus.[24] Pride, in Augustine's recurrent imagery, is like a tumor or swelling of soul, a kind of outward greatness that is inwardly foul and unhealthy, and which actually makes the soul more captive to external things (as in the idolatrous polytheism that pagan Platonists took part in, though they ought to have known better).[25] Although pagan Platonists have caught a glimpse of the eternal light (which is why their books can admonish Augustine to turn inward and see God),[26] yet their pride, like Augustine's, resembles a swelling of the face that closes up the eye of the mind (7.7.11). They have a knowledge beyond that of ordinary, uneducated people ("the many" or "the crowd" as the Platonists contemptuously call them), but this does not ultimately help them, for "they are puffed up with knowledge" (7.20.26, alluding to 1 Cor. 8:1).

The pride of the pagan Platonists prevented them from recognizing the need to confess their sins with broken and contrite heart (7.21.27, quoting Ps. 51:17), to seek the grace of inner healing taught by the Scriptures and especially in Paul (7.21.27), and above all to recognize that the eternal Word whose divine nature they have glimpsed has descended to help us in our infirmity by taking on our own human nature (7.18.24). The man Jesus Christ is "the mediator between God and man" (ibid., quoting 1 Tim. 2:5), not by virtue of his divine nature (for he is not some intermediary god, such as the Neoplatonists or the Arian heretics supposed),[27] but rather by virtue of his human nature, through which he enacts a divine humility that is the cure for human pride. In his humility the Word of God, which is the goal of our vision, came down to become the road we take to reach this goal. As God he is the goal, but as man he is the way.[28] The Platonists have seen this goal from a distance, like Moses gazing at the faraway promised land from a mountaintop (an allusion Augustine makes near the end of 7.21.27), but they are too proud to descend from the mountain and set foot on the humble way of Christ. It is not the divinity of Christ so much as the humanity of God that offends them. But the result is the same: a refusal to see the man Christ as the Word made flesh, which leaves the human race with no mediator, no road (*via*) by which to return to the fatherland (*patria*).

This explains why God let young Augustine come upon these books before becoming a student of the books of Scripture. Having caught sight of the fatherland before he understood the way to return there, he can now appreciate the difference between Platonist presumption and Christian confession, which is "the difference between those who saw where to go but did not know the way, and the way which leads not only to see but to dwell in the blessed fatherland" (7.20.26). So it is no surprise that he received his copy of the books of the Platonists from an unnamed person who was "puffed up with the most monstrous pride" (7.9.13). This was all part of God's plan to show him "how You resist the proud, but give grace to the humble" (ibid.).[29]

Augustine confesses that he suffered from the sin of pride both in the past (7.7.11) and in the present (10.36.58–39.64). What he does not do is confess that this kept him from believing in Christ. In fact he never suggests that anything about Platonism kept him from believing in Christ.[30] He does spend a paragraph describing his failure to understand the incarnation, as it was some time before he learned that Christ was anything more than a great and virtuous wise man (7.19.25). But although this paragraph is stuck right in the middle of his long discussion of the pride of the Platonists, it mentions neither Platonists nor pride. In contrast to Augustine's misconception of the divine nature, his misunderstanding of the incarnation is not attributed here to any moral failing.

The reason is clear from earlier in Book Seven. In the estimation of Augustine the author, young Augustine was already a believer in Christ at this time, but one who had more to learn about orthodox Christology: "Stuck fast in my heart in the Catholic Church was the faith of Your Christ, our Lord and Savior, though as yet uninformed on many points and floating free of the norm of doctrine" (7.5.7). Lest there be any doubt on this, Augustine tells us a little further on that even in the midst of his agonized questioning,

> You did not allow me to be removed by any of the back-and-forth of thought
> from the faith by which I believed in Your existence, Your immutable sub-
> stance, Your care for human beings and Your judgment, and that in Christ
> Your Son our Lord and in the holy Scriptures which the authority of Your
> Catholic Church commends, You established for human salvation a road to
> that life which is to come after this death. (7.7.11)

In short, when Augustine comes upon the books of the Platonists he is already a Catholic believer, though unbaptized and largely ignorant of the Bible and Christian doctrine. Whatever the relation between Augustine's Christianity and his Platonism, it cannot be accurately expressed by saying that in Book Seven he becomes a Platonist and in Book Eight a Christian. Contrary to centuries of mis-reading that assimilates Book Eight to Protestant narratives of conversion to Christ, Augustine wants us to know that he already had faith in Christ in Book Seven. Nothing in Book Eight changes that, or even corrects his misunderstand-ings of the incarnation. What Book Eight does is get him inside the walls of the institutional church where he may learn better.

The point of Book Eight, like that of the rest of *Confessions*, can only be under-stood in light of Book Seven. For it is Book Seven that defines the goal of the journey, which is finally begun in earnest in Book Eight. The latter book is con-cerned not with coming to faith in Christ, but with Augustine's need to free his will from earthly attachments before he is ready to be baptized and wholeheart-edly pursue a life of Christian philosophy, the love of true Wisdom, as he has longed to do ever since reading the *Hortensius* (6.11.18 and 8.7.17). This requires of him the humility of a deeper submission to the authority of the church than he has ever ventured before. His pride did not allow him to "humbly hold on to my humble God Jesus" (7.18.24) by entering the body of Christ. Until the deci-sive change of heart recorded in Book Eight, he was like Victorinus, the convert from a previous generation who had thought at first that it ought to be enough just to believe in his heart. When a priest confronts Victorinus with the impor-tance of actually entering the church, he jokes, "So is it the walls that make Chris-tians?" (8.2.4). Augustine's subsequent narrative answers, in effect, yes. If one really wants to walk the way of Christ, one must enter within the walls of the church to receive the visible sacrament of baptism, and thereby be joined to that invisible communion of souls called the body of Christ.[31] The humble submis-sion to the authority of such outward signs bears fruit in Augustine's own life when he is united with his mother in the vision of God: he living a life of philo-sophical reason and she living by the authority of Mother Church are joined in a single vision, both catching sight of the same eternal Wisdom (9.10.24).

With this shared vision of reason and authority at Ostia, Augustine's narrative reaches its climax. The autobiographical portion of the *Confessions* is soon com-pleted, but the *Confessions* itself is not. For the *Confessions* is not an autobiogra-phy, but an account of how the soul wanders from God and returns to him, illustrated in part by the story of one particular soul.[32] So Augustine proceeds to analyze the present life of his soul in Book Ten, founded on the memory of lost blessedness (in the first half) and journeying along a road beset with temptations (in the second half). Then he devotes the final three books to an exegesis of Gen-esis, the scriptural account of beginnings that is also an account of the end to which we return, our eternal rest (as becomes clear in Book Thirteen). The rec-ollection of lost happiness that motivates our seeking (10.18.27) is the loving memory that remains after we fall, dazzled, from the vision of God (7.17.23).

This same vision must inform our reading of Scripture. For what we are look-ing for in Genesis is not what Moses meant, but what Moses saw. If we see inwardly the same Truth Moses saw, then it does no harm if we happen to inter-pret a passage differently from Moses' original intent in writing it, for the real origin of the passage is not Moses, but Truth itself (11.3.5 and 12.14.33–15.35). The hermeneutical principle here goes back to Augustine's early treatise *De magistro*. All words are signs we use to teach things,[33] but paradoxically we do not really learn things from signs: rather, we must understand the thing signified before we can know the meaning of the sign.[34] That is why Bishop Ambrose understands Scripture so much better than young Augustine: Ambrose teaches the spirit rather than the letter of Scripture, because he knows the incorporeal realities Scripture teaches, while Augustine at first knows only the words (5.14.24–25). This is the legacy of the Manichees, who had all the right words (Christ, Holy Spirit, Truth, and so on) but did not see the incorporeal things they signified (3.6.10). The words of Scripture reveal nothing to someone who has not already seen the Truth.

Thus the whole *Confessions* works toward the vision of God described in Book Seven. Augustine's Platonist account of the ontology of the divine nature (God's incorporeality, incorruptibility, unchangeability, and omnipresence) defines for him what the journey of our souls is all about. The distinctive feature of Christian religion, that God takes on human nature in the person of Christ, does not define what we are ultimately seeking, but rather the way we are to seek it. Our goal is not flesh and blood—not even Christ's flesh and blood—but inward vision. As Augustine's dazzled mind falls back into the region of unlikeness to God, he hears (metaphorically, of course) a voice from on high, saying: "I am the food of grown men; grow and you shall feed on Me. But you shall not change Me into yourself, as with the food of your flesh; rather, you shall be changed into Me" (7.10.16). A lasting vision of God, when it finally comes, will metaphorically change us into God in the sense of causing us to participate in the incorruptibility of the divine nature. We shall be kept safe from all changes for the worse by our union with him. This is ultimate happiness and eternal rest, for once found it can never be lost.

But we are not there yet. We are not yet ready to eat the food of eternal life, which is for grown men, and we must therefore feed on Christ's humanity, in which the food we are not yet capable of is mixed with the flesh taken on by the Word so that "Your Wisdom may nurse our infancy with milk" (7.18.24). The milk of Christ's flesh sustains us in our journey, but it is not the very food of immortality that changes us into what God is. In other words, Augustine is not in a position to affirm with later church tradition that Christ's humanity is "life-giving flesh."[35] Another way to put this is that Augustine does not associate the vision of God with the human face of Christ (like Paul),[36] or with the light of the deified flesh of Christ on the mount of transfiguration (like Eastern Orthodoxy).[37] His aim is ultimately to direct our attention inward to a vision of incorporeal Truth. Christ himself, he argues, intends this, for he ran his earthly race in a hurry, calling us to return to him and then departing from our bodily sight, "that we might return to our heart and there find Him" (4.12.19). Christ in the heart is not Christ in the flesh, but the eternal Wisdom who is our inner Teacher,[38] revealing Truth that must be seen with the eye of the mind, not the eye of the body.[39] The power of Augustine's distinctive brand of Christian Platonism is that it is the only form of orthodox theology after Nicaea that offers a powerful alternative to finding the glory of God in the flesh of Jesus Christ. For Augustine the humanity of Christ is indispensable, but it is only the road, not the destination. The destination is defined in Platonist terms, and it is the destination that is the point of the road, not the other way round.[40]

CONCLUSION: ON AUGUSTINE
AND CHRISTIAN PLATONISM

In what may be the most un-insightful remark ever made by a great philosopher, Martin Heidegger suggested that the god of philosophy is one to which "man can neither pray nor sacrifice . . . man can neither fall to his knees in awe nor can he play music and dance before this god."[41] Either Heidegger was forgetting about medieval philosophy or he just wasn't thinking. Augustine clearly prays and worships and sings to the god of the Platonists, believing that this is no different from the Truth signified by Holy Scripture, to which Jesus Christ is the way. *Our* problem with Book Seven of the *Confessions*, I suggest, is what to make of this. Augustine wants us to worship and pray to the god of philosophy in the name of Jesus Christ. Shall we follow him in this? Heidegger himself would lead us down another path, as he initiated a tradition critical of what he called ontotheology, a term covering roughly the same ground as that designated in the Anglo-American philosophical tradition by the term "classical theism." Roughly put, this is the attempt to combine a philosophical concept of eternal Being with a religious apprehension of God—an attempt whose roots can be found in Plato and Aristotle, but which grows most heartily in the Christian theological tradition, beginning with the church fathers, flourishing in the Middle Ages, and still alive and well in the Reformation.

Augustine must be on anyone's short list of candidates for the most creative, poetic, profound, and influential "ontotheologian" of all time. That doesn't mean we must agree with him. But neither should we be too hasty to reject his guid-.ance, as if it were so obvious that pagan philosophers knew nothing at all about God. I think Plato and Plotinus were right about a few things. Despite some dualist tendencies of its own, for instance, the Platonist tradition provided Augustine with the key to overcoming Manichean dualism, as we have seen. Or to use a much later example, when Martin Luther (no friend to pagan philosophers!) describes how Christ's body can be present both in heaven and in the bread of the Eucharist, he uses a conception of divine omnipresence that he gets from Augustine, who got it from Plotinus.[42] And I would say that Plotinus, as well as Augustine and Luther after him, are simply right about this: the divine is indeed present as a whole at every place in the universe. But one has no business accepting this Platonist conception of God's presence in all places without also considering the Platonist conception of God's eternity as a simultaneous presence to all times.[43] The strength of both conceptions is that they think of God's transcendence as his perfect presence rather than his absence from creation: because he is not bound by space and time, he is more fully and wholly present at every place and time than any creature can be, not spread out part-by-part from one place to another or different at one time than at another.

Nonetheless, such conceptions of God's transcendence are getting rather unpopular nowadays, because (not to put too fine a point on it) most of us want God to suffer, and that requires him to be subject to time and change. "Only a suffering God can help," Bonhoeffer famously says,[44] expressing the exact opposite of Augustine's fundamental conviction about soteriology—that only participation in an incorruptible God can rescue us from corruption and evil. The Christian tradition has a way of saying "both/and" here (the divine nature is immune from suffering, but the second person of the Trinity suffers in his human nature). Yet the one side of this paradox is so popular among us today and seems so obviously necessary to our modern obsession with theodicy, that we need some instruction on the other side from the likes of Augustine before we can even begin to understand what is involved in affirming both.

The philosophical tradition stemming from Plato (including his student Aristotle) has provided a conceptual vocabulary that Christian theology has found valuable in saying what it has to say, to the point where that vocabulary is now inseparable from the native discourse of Western theology (obviously so in figures like Aquinas, less obviously but no less truly in figures like Luther). It is useful, and for some theological purposes indispensable, to have available to us concepts like Plotinus's notions of omnipresence and eternity, which articulate the sense in which the Creator is free from the conditions that limit his creatures. Such concepts are extremely useful for dealing with rather abstract questions about what God is like (i.e., what are the attributes of the divine nature), but I am among those who think they do not show us *who* God is (i.e., what particular person it is we love when we love God), and therefore they should not be the terms in which we define the ultimate goal of human life or the proper focus of worship and desire.

This is not because they *cannot* do so, as Heidegger so misleadingly suggests. On the contrary, the Platonist tradition clearly offered Augustine (and through Augustine, offers us) a powerful spirituality, including a conception of the divine that calls for our devotion and worship. It is this Platonist call to worship that we should be most critical of, I suggest, when we think critically about Augustine's use of Platonist philosophy. And we must think critically about it precisely because its profound religious attractiveness ultimately draws our attention away from the flesh of Christ. Of course, Augustine affirms in the most emphatic way the incarnation of Christ and its necessity for our salvation. But as we have seen in Book Seven, he also gives us another place to look to find God, an inward space of vision that sees Christ as eternal Wisdom and Truth, but not Christ in the flesh (for there is nothing more external than flesh). Thus he inaugurates a tradition of Christian inwardness that would direct our attention differently from Catholic sacraments or Orthodox icons or Protestant preaching of the gospel, all of which are rooted in the bodily life of Christ, including his crucifixion and resurrection.

The pastoral issue—the key issue for Christian spirituality—is where we are to direct our attention. The inward turn is nothing if not an attempt to direct our attention, to turn our minds away from outward things to things we can only see within. My philosophical objection to this is that in turning away from the external, it turns away from the other. A spirituality of inwardness must attempt the paradoxical project of finding the other within the self. For my part, I do not think we can do without externality as the essential mark of otherness: if God is other than me then he is external to me. To seek God within, it seems to me, is to find only myself. The theological consequence of this philosophical point can be put like this. All religions have holy places, temples or shrines in which they seek to encounter their deity. The holy place of the Christian religion is called the body of Christ, which replaces the ruined temple of Jerusalem as the earthly place of God's presence (cf. John 2:19–21). What is wrong with Augustine's inwardness and its many spiritual descendants is that they offer us another place to find God than this particular human flesh.

But embracing a spirituality of inwardness is not the only way to be a descendant of Augustine, the great spiritual father of Western theology. It is not even the only way to appropriate his philosophy. Consider in this light the aftermath of the bitter mid-twentieth-century struggle in the Roman Catholic Church around the work of Henri de Lubac on the concept of the supernatural.[45] After Vatican II the kind of moderate Augustinianism de Lubac was championing not only survived the assaults of its Neothomist critics but was given expression in John Paul II's profoundly Augustinian view of the nature of the human person.[46] What drops out of this revived Catholic Augustinianism are three Platonist themes that have been with us throughout Book Seven: the notion that the body is a fundamentally different kind of being from the soul, that the soul is a kind of inner space one can enter to find God, and that finding God is a kind of intellectual seeing that is the natural function of the mind's eye.

The last point is the foundation of the other two, and thus the foundation of Augustine's spirituality of inwardness. Correcting it is fundamental to the Thomist tradition, which has always insisted that seeing God is necessarily supernatural, beyond the natural power of the mind's eye.[47] For Augustine, by contrast, the human intellect is an eye created to see eternal Truth, and this natural capacity for intellectual vision is precisely what opens up the soul's inner space, the new holy place in which to find God. But Augustine's Platonist notion that intellectual vision of God is natural to us has long since dropped out of Catholic theology in favor of the Thomist conviction that the vision of God is supernatural, requiring a gift of grace over and above the gifts of healing and helping that Augustine stressed in his own theology of grace. (Augustine never spoke of a supernatural grace elevating us above the capacities of our own nature: for him seeing God is a natural capacity limited only by sin, which will be restored to us once our mind's eye is restored to its natural health and strength.)[48]

What remains of Augustinian spirituality, for de Lubac as for John Paul, is the restless heart that cannot find rest apart from knowing God, a longing that remains built into our humanity. The result is the distinctively Catholic notion of a natural desire that can have only a supernatural fulfillment. This notion does not sit easily with Augustine's conception of the inner vision of God in *Confessions* Book Seven, which Catholic scholars tend to read as mystical rather than Platonist: i.e., as special supernatural occurrences rather than an inherent episte-mological power of the intellect. (This I take to be a typically Catholic misread-ing of Book Seven driven by the same motivation as the typically Protestant misreading of Book Eight as a conversion to Christ: an unwillingness to see how Augustine's Platonist philosophy defines the goal of his life.) Shorn of its dis-tinctive inwardness, Augustine's philosophical pursuit of Truth must play itself out not in an inner world, but in the shared inquiry of reason, which John Paul sees as essential to the dignity of the human person, one of "the two wings on which the human spirit rises to the contemplation of truth," as he puts it in the opening of his encylical *On Faith and Reason*. Thus, instead of the inward turn of *Confessions* Book Seven, we have a different, though equally Augustinian, appropriation of ancient philosophy: a spirituality of the love of Truth in which philosophical inquiry driven by a longing for wisdom becomes a task insepara-ble from the life of religious devotion.[49] Protestants like myself cannot be entirely happy with John Paul's teaching that faith and reason are the two (apparently equal) wings of the ascent to Truth (which John Paul, like Augustine and Aquinas, identifies ultimately with God). But if this, rather than a turn to find God within, is the future of Augustinian philosophy, then we should all be listening.

Chapter 8

Book Eight: Science and the Fictional Conversion Scene

Leo C. Ferrari

INTRODUCTION

As a student, the very first time I came upon the autobiographical *Confessions* of Saint Augustine, I found it incredible that the book had been written as long ago as 397–401. I immediately became spellbound by its many adventures, beginning with Augustine's first schooling, and his early sexual explorations (2.1.1–2.4), followed by the youthful theft of pears (2.4.9).[1] His later school days were brightened by the discovery of Cicero's book *Hortensius* (3.4.7) when he was inspired and enlightened by its exhortation to philosophy, but subsequently darkened (so to speak) by his joining the heretical Manichees (3.6.10). However, a dream by his mother, Monica, foretold his eventual salvation through his conversion back to Christianity (3.11.19).

After many other adventures, the flight from his North African homeland led him to Rome, then to Milan, where his mother later joined him (6.1.1). The eighth book of the *Confessions* sees him converted in the unforgettable climax of his conversion scene (8.12.28–29). Finally, in the ninth book his adventurous autobiography concludes tragically with the death of his mother, Monica (9.11.27–28).

Despite its actual antiquity, even today the *Confessions* sounds refreshingly modern to someone reading it for the first time. Indeed, the narrative was so compelling for me that soon after the first few pages I was "hooked" and read the story of Augustine's life from beginning to end. This was something that I was fated to do times beyond number in the succeeding years when I began repeatedly studying the book increasingly in depth and publishing critical articles about various aspects of the *Confessions* and its ingredients. While engaged in these investigations I always seemed to be opening new doorways upon each rereading, whence my retrospective article "Doorways of Discovery in Augustine's *Confessions*."[2]

In the present chapter, I will summarize my principal discoveries about Augustine's *Confessions* made over some thirty years. Along with this summary, I will briefly outline here the relevant details of my own story while researching that of Augustine. This procedure will entail concentrating not only on the "what" of Augustine's story but also on the "how" of my discoveries. Eventually my break came with some sixteen hundred years of tradition by proving the essentially fictional character of his famous conversion scene in the climactic eighth book of the work (8.12.28–30), of which more later.

Involving the relevant experiences of myself, the author of this article, will also mean getting more frank in trying to explain *why* long ago I left the once well-trodden path of scholars' opinions, particularly about the reality of Augustine's famous conversion scene. Much of my research encouraged me to strike out into what initially seemed to be the proverbial wilderness. I feel a certain embarrassment about admitting here that this is what has been done. But such was the truth of my new approach to Augustine's *Confessions*; an approach which was soon justified by startling results.

Looking back on these pioneering articles, I am struck by how many of my successes in analyzing the *Confessions* owe a great deal to my first career devoted to experimental science.[3] Basically, unlike most Augustine scholars, I had thereby become well practiced in the scientific procedures of collecting and organizing data. I had also learned to hypothesize, which involved looking for the *best explanation of data* and so, by careful analysis, producing surprising results.

These skills, I soon realized, were also admirably transferable to the challenge of reading between the lines of the *Confessions*, sometimes with new and even shocking results. As mentioned earlier, the ultimate climax of this kind of research was to be the first-ever scientific demonstration of the basically fictional nature of Augustine's climactic conversion scene in the eighth book of the work (8.12.28–30). But many other discoveries were to lead up to this achievement, the most important of which are featured below.

Along the way, I found it necessary to develop instruments that would bring scientific exactitude to the study of Augustine. Early in my researches I was amazed to discover that despite its popularity down through the ages, no concordance existed to expedite researches on Augustine's famous *Confessions*. Eventually, with the help of Professor Rodney H. Cooper of the Faculty of Computer Science of the University of New Brunswick, after mountains of work, the first-ever concordance to the Latin text of Augustine's *Confessions*—the *Concordantia in libros XIII Confessionum Sancti Aurelii Augustini* (in two volumes)—was finally published in 1991.[4]

Meanwhile, the addictive quality of the *Confessions* derived from many intriguing details in the author's story, which on deeper, scientific examination also revealed other items worthy of investigation, whence more articles. In this regenerative process the above *Concordantia* was to play an unprecedented key role by coordinating identical or similar data for analysis. Consequently, the investigative process came to feed upon itself, often revealing new insights that invited deeper and more detailed examination. As a result, today I am now quite surprised to find that over the intervening years I have published almost fifty articles on various topics in the *Confessions*. And (I hope) there are still many more to come!

As I stated earlier, the present chapter will outline (mostly in order of the story of the *Confessions*) my various principal relevant discoveries. Step-by-step, they eventually brought me closer and closer to the most amazing discovery of all, namely *irrefutable proof* of the fictional nature of the description of Augustine's own famous conversion scene. Thanks to my scientific background and patient plodding, after almost a quarter-century of research, and at a target distance of some sixteen hundred years, my efforts eventually bridged both space and time with the above conclusion, the most climactic one I have made, so far.

Finally therefore, despite many centuries of supposed certitude to the contrary, I was able to prove beyond a shadow of a doubt that the famous climax of the *Confessions,* namely the unforgettable "conversion scene" of 386 in the garden of Milan (8.8.19–12.30) as described by Augustine himself, never in fact occurred! It was born of the fertile imagination and ingenuity of the then forty-three-year-old Augustine.

Meanwhile, across the years, with patient detective work and the findings of other scholars, as well as by using the Bible, I did much repetitive plodding through the *Confessions* (always in relation to Augustine's other works), eventually making an accumulation of some very intriguing and sometimes explosive discoveries! The more discoveries I made, the more my successes lured me on. I have hoped to recapture some of the feeling of these adventures and discoveries in the succeeding pages of this chapter.

"THE STARS THAT SINK IN THE OCEAN"

To begin at the beginning, first to be recorded here is a detail that, with the help of a little science, for the very first time explains exactly *why* Augustine left the Christian faith of his childhood and joined the heretical sect of the light-worshiping Manichees (3.6.10). Of all possible reasons, he claims elsewhere that he did so because he "was terrified by a childish superstition," because his eyes were "fixed on the stars that sink in the ocean."[5]

This curious detail appealed very much to my science background as but one of the many allusions by Augustine to the nocturnal heavens. In particular, his reference in the same place to having been "terrified by a childish superstition" was a very curious detail indeed. It spurred me on to find some hypothesis, or tentative explanation. Regarding this reference to being terrified, much earlier, in 1948, R. Jolivet put it well with his observation: "We [scholars of Augustine's life] have much hesitated about the meaning of these words."[6] And lacking any scientific education, they just had to go on hesitating. On the other hand, with my background in science, it was my privilege to discover the actual cause of that "terror." My hypothesis was that some unusual coincidental event in the night sky could perhaps explain it all.

After much scientific investigation about the night sky around that time, my thesis was that it would seem that Augustine had in fact actually been first horrified, and subsequently converted to light-worshiping Manicheism, by the then-terrifying spectacle of what later became known as Halley's Comet. As I discovered with the help of a friendly astronomer, it blazed brilliantly in the night sky for almost a month and a half, from about 29 March till about May 10 of the year 374.[7] Also, its enormous blazing tail at its maximum stretched about a whole quarter of the greatest length of the night sky, measured from horizon to opposite horizon. That would be enough to scare anyone ignorant of the real cause of the enormous nocturnal apparition!

Not only could this awesome intrusion upon the night sky not be ignored, but it was also obviously a source of widespread horror and wild rumors, whence Augustine's apt use of the word "terror." The Manichees, as worshipers of the sun and of all physical light, offered the most optimistic explanation of this terrifying spectacle. They would have believed it to be an envoy from their fabled "Kingdom of Light," thus attracting the temporary allegiance of the terrified young Augustine.

Of this episode in his life, which persuaded him to join the light-worshiping Manichees, he was later to observe: "I fell among a set of proud madmen, exceedingly carnal and talkative people in whose mouths were diabolical snares" (3.6.10). But thanks to my own above discovery of the source of that terror, for the first time in some sixteen hundred years this coincidence also now gives us the precise date of around April 374 for Augustine's act of joining the Manichees.[8]

Concerning further relevance of the sky in effecting Augustine's alienation from the above sect of the Manichees some ten years later (hence about 384) is that this rupture seems to have begun even earlier with the spectacular solar eclipses of 378 and 381. At least these celestial phenomena (unlike the terrifying Halley's Comet of 374) were not without dated precedents and apparently were rationally explainable by the astronomers of Augustine's time.[9] These explanations probably counteracted the effect of Halley's Comet upon the life of Augustine and resulted in his return to the Catholicism of his youth.

Moreover, despite his repeated claims that he was a Manichee for "nine years," the evidence seems to show that his sojourn with that sect lasted at least ten years.[10] Meanwhile also, Augustine's Manichean period seems to have been favored by his passion for astrology, fired in part (as he himself admits) by his need to attribute his own sins to the influence of the stars.[11]

A CERTAIN ASTROLOGER IN HIS AUDIENCE

On the same general theme, much later in his life, in the appendage to one of Augustine's sermons he seems to be berating "a certain astrologer in his audience." He is accused of taking money from gullible persons in exchange for predicting their futures as written in the stars.[12] To the best of my knowledge, such an act of public accusation and humiliation, leveled at one single person in his audience, besides lacking in Christian charity, is without precedent in all of Augustine's sermons.

A far better explanation for his unique, publicly humiliating accusation supposedly directed at a member of his audience would appear to be that in this case Augustine was confessing to his audience his own former sinful life as a practicing astrologer.[13] This fact would have been obvious to his audience by his tone of voice and his manual gestures of self-accusation.

However, these qualities of tone and gestures, not being part of the verbal discourse, would have been routinely omitted by the transcriber of this sermon. Thereby, the modern reader would be led to conclude that Augustine was publicly condemning some member of his audience, as has hitherto been traditionally claimed, whereas it would seem that he was speaking of *himself*. It would therefore make much more sense to interpret the discourse as a self-condemnatory sermon on Augustine's own sinful past, when in his passion for astrology he once felt sufficiently skilled in that dark art to advertise his services for the gullible members of the public.[14]

A RETRO-CONVERSION

From the beginning of Augustine's Manichean sojourn in 374 (see above) a whole ten or even eleven years elapsed before his much better known conversion in 386 back to the Christian faith of his childhood. Furthermore, this reversed transition back to orthodox Christianity was not as uncomplicated as first appears. Despite the obvious modeling of his own conversion in his *Confessions* on that of Paul, this much earlier conversion of the apostle was undetectable[15] in Augustine's works prior to the date of the writing of his great masterpiece in 397–401.[16]

The young Augustine went through many adventures in the course of those earlier years, but despite worldly success, finally had to admit the futility of his life (6.16.26). In the eighth book of his *Confessions* (8.12.28) in ultimate desperation he throws himself on the ground under a certain fig tree (even this detail is significant, as will be seen below).[17] Meanwhile, his weeping is interrupted by a mysterious voice. His problems are not solved, but the way out of them is supposedly indicated by that voice telling him to take up the volume of Paul which was lying nearby, open it at random, and read the first passage upon which his eyes alighted.[18]

Regarding this scene, it is especially significant and here pointed out for the very first time in the history of the analysis of Augustine's conversion scene that in the above scene Augustine was using what was then "high technology," namely a book (*codex*) with pages,[19] in contrast to the then traditional scroll (*volumen*).[20] For the very first time in recorded history the book (*codex*) allowed *random accessing of the text*. This was distinct from the prior, laborious rolling and unrolling of the traditional scroll. The then recently invented book (*codex*) with pages (being at that time the equivalent of "high technology") was therefore a most important and novel element for Augustine's conversion scene. Doubtless, his audience was suitably impressed and even mystified.

This then-new, even magical convenience, unlike the traditional scroll, could be seen as providing a place anywhere in the text that was thereby chosen simply by opening the book *at random*. Amazing! Furthermore, for those so inclined, the chosen page with its singularly unique message could (hopefully) be really chosen by divine guidance. Accordingly, the very novelty of the process of the book-opening operation in this scene (8.12.29) was a convincing strategy to the audience of such divine guidance.

THE POLARITY OF THE TWO TREES

Again, regarding the above conversion scene, basic to the intrinsic dramatic structure of the *Confessions* is the fact that like the Bible[21] it is polarized between two trees—the tree of the pear theft in the second book (2.4.9) and the fig tree of the eighth book (8.12.28) under which Augustine casts himself, just prior to his conversion.[22]

Regarding the former case, the sixteen-year-old Augustine (2.3.5–6) in the dead of night, with the aid of some companions, stripped bare of its fruit a neighbor's pear tree, not to eat the pears, but merely to throw them to some pigs (2.4.9). The account of the theft is followed by a lengthy diagnosis of the motives behind such a vindictively wasteful and profitless action (2.5.10–10.18). The pointless nature of the action he instigated is expressed near the end of the second book: "I was greedy for another person's loss without any desire on my own part to gain anything, or to settle a score" (2.9.17).

Standing in obvious contrast to this seemingly pointless, sinful theft of the pears is the climactic moment of great grace in the eighth book of the *Confessions*, a scene dominated by another kind of tree, namely a fig tree (8.12.28–30). Augustine was weeping bitterly over his resistance to God's grace, when "a huge storm blew up within me and brought on a heavy rain of tears" (8.12.28). He describes his next reaction: "I flung myself down somehow *under a fig-tree* and gave free rein to the tears that burst from my eyes like rivers" (8.12.28, italics added). Next, he hears a mysterious voice telling him to open a nearby book of the apostle Paul.

ENLIGHTENMENT FROM PAUL'S TEXT

Supposedly then, by following the above divine instruction, Augustine opens the book of Paul (and again also, hopefully by divine guidance) at a randomly chosen page. So, as he says of the volume of Paul: "I snatched it up, opened it and read in silence the passage upon which my eyes first alighted" (8.12.29). He then quotes the passage of Paul (Rom. 13:13–14), which supposedly changed his entire life:

> Not in dissipation and drunkenness, nor in debauchery and lewdness, nor in arguing and jealousy; but put on the Lord Jesus Christ, and make no provision for the flesh or the satisfaction of your desires. (8.12.29)

Next, as Augustine puts it himself:

> I had no wish to read further, nor was there need. No sooner had I reached
> the end of the verse, than the light of certainty flooded my heart and all dark
> shades of doubt fled away. (8.12.29)

As he implies, Augustine was then supposedly immediately converted by an overwhelming feeling of confidence in God's guiding grace.

However, as noted above, this conversion scene, powerful as it is, has been
shown by myself (through some detective work) to be the climax of a whole series
of preceding conversions of Augustine in the *Confessions*, all artfully building one
upon the other with increasing, emotional insistence.[23]

Furthermore, regarding the sudden, prominent intrusion of Paul into the narrative, this intervention is vested with the appearance of being the very first casual
discovery of the apostle that occurred after Augustine's reading the "books of the
Platonists" (7.9.13). In actual fact, such was demonstrably *not* the case.

Long before his conversion back to Christianity as described in the eighth
book of the *Confessions*, while a closet Manichee Augustine would have become
very well acquainted with the writings of Paul the apostle, who was also a highly
favored author of that sect. Thus, instead of being a new and unprecedented
event, the espousal of Paul seems to have happened in distinguishable stages, as
already shown by myself.[24]

AUGUSTINE'S CONVERSION SCENE REEXAMINED

Like Paul's conversion on the road to Damascus, upon which it is demonstrably
modeled,[25] Augustine's above conversion scene has become one of the principal,
well-worn paradigms of Western Christianity. The reason for this is that it is so
vividly described by Augustine himself in the *Confessions* that his own conversion
seems possessed of an innate realism. Only in modern times has it acquired a
growing number of skeptics.[26]

Following the tradition initiated by Harnack[27] and encouraged by the much
more recent discoveries of Pierre Courcelle[28] among others, I was early persuaded
of the essentially fictional nature of the famous conversion scene in Augustine's
Confessions.[29] But the formidable question remained for me: how to prove conclusively the inherently fictional nature of the above famous conversion scene of
the *Confessions*, a scene that supposedly occurred just over sixteen hundred years
ago, in the year 386? After much thought about the matter, I eventually succeeded in doing just that! It turned out to be quite feasible, a hitherto novel and
unprecedented pioneering accomplishment, again achieved with the aid of my
background in experimental science.

First, it is necessary to recall that Augustine's "discovery" of Paul in the *Confessions* (7.21.27) carefully abstracts from the fact that Augustine had initially gotten to know the writings of Paul as an ardent young Manichee;[30] a sojourn that

(contrary to Augustine's repeated "nine years") lasted *at least* ten years.[31] With this in mind, the role of Paul in his conversion back to Catholicism is seen as the culmination of a drama, not a historical record.

A Mysterious Voice

Beginning with the well-known relevant facts, the famous conversion of Augustine back to orthodox Christianity is held to have occurred late in the year 386.[32] According to the dramatic description in the eighth book of his *Confessions*, the climactic event occurs after the weeping Augustine, in ultimate desperation, casts himself on the ground under a certain fig tree. Suddenly, as he says, he hears a mysterious voice chanting repeatedly: "Pick it up and read, pick it up and read" (8.12.29). Assuming that this instruction refers to a nearby book (*codex*) of Paul's epistles that he had been reading, he picks it up, supposedly opens the volume at random, and reads Romans 13:13–14, the very first section upon which his eyes alight, as described above:

> Not in dissipation and drunkenness, nor in debauchery and lewdness, nor in arguing and jealousy; but put on the Lord Jesus Christ, and make no provision for the flesh or the satisfaction of your desires. (8.12.29)

Supposedly Augustine is converted on the spot by the reading of this text. Following on the above conversion he is baptized in the succeeding year of 387. Some ten years later, in 397, Augustine began writing his famous *Confessions*, which he completed around 401.[33]

My Hypothesis

My hypothesis is that if the above conversion scene of 386, involving the divinely directed reading of Romans 13:13–14, were indeed a historical fact, then Augustine's subsequent works, especially those written soon after that date, must be stuffed full of references to the above-mentioned divinely directed reading of the extract from Paul's Epistle to the Romans. But how was one to prove, or disprove, this hypothesis?

Some years earlier (in 1964) I had been inordinately fortunate in having rescued the complete Latin works[34] of Augustine before they were shipped to the local rubbish dump (!) by an ignorant administrator, and had them consigned to my possession. These heaven-sent volumes later enabled me to address the above question in a preliminary manner by searching assiduously and visually through all the scriptural footnotes of Augustine's earlier works up to, and including, those of 401 C.E. I came up with nothing of significance in the way of references to Romans 13:13–14, which discovery formed the basis of an article on the question of the presence of these key verses in the earlier works of Augustine, especially those subsequent to the supposed conversion scene of 386.[35]

However, on later consideration, the question was of such momentous importance that a much more thorough search of Augustine's earlier works seemed to be eminently justified in order to settle, once and for all, the ancient question of the inherent reality of Augustine's conversion scene involving Romans 13:13–14. Accordingly, and not without some hesitation, I decided to enter upon that more thorough search of his earlier works.

After much thoughtful planning, the long labor was to enter into a computer file all the scriptural references in all those relevant earliest (i.e., from 386 to 401) works of Augustine, with complete records and data (meaning complete scriptural references and their precise locations in the texts) up to 401, and including the *Confessions* itself. In all, 8,378 records were thus collected by typing them individually into the computer.

This task occupied an entire summer, with myself as the patient laborer. The records were first computer-sorted alphabetically by books of the Bible, then by complete numerical order in each biblical book. The ultimate, sorted file contained 8,378 records. That no files had been lost in the process was verified by the fact that the final sorted file contained exactly the same number of records as the original unsorted file.

Next, the file that I had constructed did not contain all the possible scriptural references, as was shown by comparison with a more recent critical edition.[36] However, the main thing was that my edition sufficed for present purposes, namely the presence, or absence, *ut in pluribus*, of those above-mentioned verses of Paul (Rom. 13:13–14), which Augustine was supposed to have read spontaneously in response to an earlier divine command by that mysterious voice in the famous garden scene (8.12.28–29). If based upon a real experience they should have been scattered in appreciable quantities (especially throughout the earlier works) prior to Augustine's beginning the writing of the *Confessions* in 397.

According to one recent edition of the *Confessions*,[37] the conversion of Augustine occurred in the famous garden scene of late summer of the year 386:

> Hearing an unseen child say, "Take up and read. Take up and read," Augustine [randomly] opened the book of saint Paul, which he had been studying, to Romans 13, where he read: "Let us live honorably as in daylight; not in carousing and drunkenness, not in sexual excess and lust, not in quarreling and jealousy. Rather, put on the Lord Jesus Christ and make no provision for the desires of the flesh." (Rom. 13:13–14 in 8.12.29)[38]

But on examination of the above orderly file, *no* new significant references to either of these verses (Rom. 13:13–14) were found in the entire 8,378 scriptural references in all of Augustine's works up to, and including, the date of the completion of the *Confessions* in 401.[39] It remains then that, despite years of controversy, the reading of the above-mentioned verses (Rom. 13:13–14) in the well-known "conversion scene" of the *Confessions* was therefore *scientifically demonstrated* for the very first time in history as being obviously quite *fundamentally fictional in nature.*

The Day of Public Proclamation

After many years of disputes about the factuality or fictionality of Augustine's famous conversion scene at the climax of his *Confessions*, I had the privilege of reading a paper on the above question before an overflowing audience of scholars,[40] during the 1987 Tenth International Conference on Patristic Studies at Oxford University. My paper, explaining my solution (read before such a large and distinguished audience on August 28th, the very Feast of Saint Augustine himself, and during the year of the 1600th anniversary of his baptism in 387) was entitled "Augustine's Conversion Scene—the End of a Modern Debate?"[41]

All went well till the conclusion of the paper, whereupon to my astonishment a general uproar of my audience occurred, consisting of a loud cacophony of shoutings, accompanied by many violent gesticulations. I have never, anywhere, seen the likes of it, before or since! And there was I, the center of this rage. The possibility of a question period was not even mooted and I consider myself most fortunate to have escaped unharmed.

Subsequently, removed from this violent turmoil, I was granted the luxury of awaiting a massive onslaught of a plethora of literary attacks upon my paper in the learned journals. I patiently waited and waited. But some fifteen years later I am no longer waiting. I can only conclude that silence means consent, however begrudgingly conceded.

CONCLUSION

As for the factuality or fictionality of Augustine's once much-disputed conversion scene, we must begin by acknowledging two basic facts. First, it is necessary to realize that, in accord with his great passion for the theater,[42] his *Confessions* was not strictly a historic document, but was rather written basically as a romantic story to be read aloud before a live audience (cf. 10.3.3–5.7). And second, we must bear in mind that Augustine saw no contradiction between truthful history and figurative expression. Indeed, Augustine explicitly defends the use of figures in spiritual writings,[43] including even the Bible itself. What Augustine did not acknowledge is the crucially important fact that in the "real world" figurative language cannot but make factual truth a most elusive entity.

Chapter 9

Book Nine: The Emotional Heart of the *Confessions*

Kim Paffenroth

INTRODUCTION: BOOK NINE AS ANTICLIMAX

Many readers would consider Book Eight the climax of the *Confessions*: Augustine's pride, lust, and his doctrinal questions are all finally conquered and he can convert or return to the religion of his mother and his childhood. But he continues in Book Nine with incidents that seem hardly as dramatic or relevant:

> If Augustine's purpose in writing this autobiography was to provide a full explanation of the steps that led him to Christianity, why did he add the ninth book at the end of his first confession? Has he not already shown how he came to the church through the argument of the first eight books ending with his conversion? That was the point at which he freely willed to become a Christian. What more was there to add? Furthermore, the content of Book IX itself seems very arbitrary.[1]

Viewed with the presumption of Book Eight's priority, Book Nine tends to look anticlimactic at best, irrelevant and disconnected at worst. For those who attempt to make sense of Book Nine while still assuming Book Eight's priority, their usual attempt is to find what was lacking or insufficient in Augustine's "conversion," and then find that provided in Book Nine, with several different suggestions, all of which relate to Augustine's baptism: the church,[2] death and rebirth,[3] rest,[4] or Christian life in the world.[5] Never having shared the general interest in the garden scene in Book Eight, I am more free to examine Book Nine without necessarily connecting or comparing it to its prelude.

As noted in the introduction, how we read the individual books of *Confessions* has a great deal to do with what we think are the primary roles and values of the author. This finally has everything to do with us, the readers, but this does not mean that it has nothing to do with Augustine, the author. I am quite certain that my own personality, experiences, and interests have shaped what I now regard as the central points of Augustine's thought and personality. To be completely honest with the reader right from the beginning: with the death of my own mother being such an enormous event in my childhood and subsequent life, was there ever any doubt which book of *Confessions* I would regard as the most important? But this does not mean that the points we individually highlight were not waiting there to be discovered by someone who was predisposed to do so, one who was in tune with that aspect of Augustine's thought: my own subjectivity may help uncover real aspects of Augustine's subjective experience. As long as our readings are capable of being explained and defended to another person, they are not merely prejudices or fantasies, but our own interpretations of those parts of Augustine's thought to which we are each individually attuned or sympathetic.

My own unique background and mind-set draw me again and again to two aspects of any text: its rhetoric and its psychology. I am always fascinated by how an author builds his argument, and this curiosity is especially piqued by a work like *Confessions* where the plan or argument is not clearly laid out, and the text often flows in unexpected and surprising directions. This is the case for *Confessions* as a whole, and especially for Book Nine, which, as shown, does not immediately reveal its place or role in Augustine's argument. Therefore the first issue I will examine is how Book Nine fits into the overall plan of the work, showing how it provides the crucial transition or resolution in the entire work with regard to Scripture, philosophy, and time.

Second, I am always fascinated by the psychology portrayed or presupposed in a text. More than its final theory or analysis, I am most interested in what the text considers important and problematic in its characters' emotions, values, and relationships. Whether the text is theology or literature, it must first present us with characters and scenarios that are psychologically compelling, rather than plausible. Consider Sophocles's *Oedipus Rex:* totally implausible, but utterly true in its psychology (before or after Freud). It is in the process of deciding how and why these often implausible scenarios are nonetheless compelling that we begin to find out the author's meaning, and his or her unique insight into human nature. For a reader with such interests, the *Confessions* are fertile ground indeed, and Book Nine in particular, for it is here that Augustine resolves all his deep, personal issues—with father, mother, friends, love, guilt, mortality, and grief. The work is therapeutic in a deep and ancient sense—diagnosis and healing of a sick and broken human nature—and on this point at least I agree completely with the evaluation of Margaret Miles: "*Confessions* is primarily therapy in the Platonic sense of a methodical conversion from a 'misidentification of reality,' to . . . the construction of an articulated orientation to a final, authoritative, and implicit reality."[6] Examining the rhetoric and psychology of Book Nine will show how it is the central and unifying book of the *Confessions*: rhetorically, it provides unique transitions and resolutions in the argument and plan of the work, and psychologically, it shows us how Augustine makes sense of his life and finally finds happiness in it.

BOOK NINE IN THE RHETORIC OF THE *CONFESSIONS*

As he struggles to become and to be a Christian, an enormous conceptual problem constantly confronts Augustine: the unlikeliness and unappealing nature of Scripture, contrasted with the beauty and partial truth of philosophy. This problem plagues him repeatedly throughout the work after his introduction to Cicero in Book Three. We know from the beautiful beginning of the *Confessions* that Augustine longs for rest—"our heart is restless until it rests in you [God]" (*Conf.* 1.1.1)[7]—and he finds excitement and desire in philosophy, but no rest: "In such a fervor, the only thing that held me back was that Christ's name was not in it. . . . Anything that was without this name, no matter how learned and polished and truthful it was, could not hold me completely" (*Conf.* 3.4.8, my translation). But in the next paragraph, when he turns to the Scriptures that do contain Christ's name, they too fail to satisfy or bring rest: "For my swollen pride turned away from their style, and my keen insight did not penetrate to their inner meaning" (*Conf.* 3.5.9, my translation). Philosophy satisfies his mind, but brings no satisfaction to his restless heart, and exacerbates his sin of pride; Scripture appeals to his heart and promises rest, but fails to produce it, for it does not satisfy his probing, relentless reason, his "rational hunger."[8] He must maintain or achieve "intellectual integrity,"[9] and not just submission and obedience. The book of the *Confessions* that provides a resolution to Augustine's problems with Scripture and philosophy would surely have a significant claim to being its center.

As we readers struggle to understand Augustine's work, probably the most enormous rhetorical issue facing us is the abrupt and unexpected shift from autobiographical narrative in the first nine books to a discussion of time and Scripture in the last four. Although the shift may remain surprising to us, we will see that Book Nine in fact provides a foundation for the following books in its implicit treatment of Scripture and time, as well as a reevaluation of the preceding books. It therefore provides the largest and most important transition in the *Confessions,* giving structure and direction to the whole.

Scripture: From Disbelief to Confirmation

Although Augustine describes in the *Confessions* how he did not accept or appreciate Scripture at the time the events occurred, by the time of the writing he not only values the Bible, he clearly models his telling of his life after biblical stories and themes: how much less significant would the theft in Book Two be if he had stolen something from a market, or if he had sat under an awning in Book Eight? But although the two trees are the most overwhelming biblical images in *Confessions,* other biblical themes are woven throughout the narrative, one of the most notable and frequent being Augustine's identification of himself with the prodigal son (Luke 15:11–32).[10] His use of the parable includes many direct allusions,[11] as well as the overall structure of both stories around departure into sin and error, and joyful return to a loving and accepting parent. (Augustine's brother

Navigius may even have the unenviable honor of filling the role of the disapproving older brother.)[12] Although none of the direct allusions is in Book Nine, it is clear that the garden scene of Book Eight corresponds to the prodigal son's sorrowful decision to return to his father, while Augustine's baptism and the vision at Ostia in Book Nine correspond to the joyous return of the prodigal son and the ensuing celebration. The former is only the crisis that leads to the climax,[13] the problem that leads to the solution, the sorrow that leads to joy. Augustine's baptism is anticipated with his earlier description of the prodigal son, for it took place in God's house, and it included both joy and tears (*Conf.* 9.6.14): "The joy at the rites of your house calls forth our tears, when the story of your younger son is read in your house, how he was dead and made alive again, was lost and then found" (*Conf.* 8.3.6, my translation). Augustine has moved from regarding Scripture as irrelevant or uninteresting to seeing it as a paradigm or interpretive lens for viewing the events of his own life, and the paradigm he has intuited for his life puts the climax in Book Nine, not Book Eight.

But it is not just in how he interprets his life that Augustine sees the relevance of Scripture, but also in how he experiences it, as he eloquently shows in his description of how moved he was by the Psalms (*Conf.* 9.4.8–11) and by the singing of hymns (*Conf.* 9.6.14–7.16). Scripture and participation in the church that uses that Scripture in worship and belief no longer stand in the way of an experience of God; they are the best means for making God present in oneself: "Therefore, I wept the more at the singing of your hymns. For long had I sighed after you, and at length I breathed you in, as far as breath may enter into this house of grass" (*Conf.* 9.7.16). This experience of Scripture not only makes God present, it also incorporates and resolves earlier intellectual urges, for it finally succeeds at "transforming and elevating the long theme of rhetoric and empty language in the previous books."[14] Ironically and beautifully, the Scriptures that had previously been deemed inferior to philosophy now resolve the difficulties of philosophy and even provide a partial validation of it: "The unchanging One of Neoplatonism is the giver of rest in the Psalms. . . . The Psalms . . . catch up together his entire odyssey from the struggle with the Manichaeans to his grasp of Neoplatonism to his homecoming with the humble Christ."[15] The style of Scripture that had initially turned him away from it is now what draws him to it, for its humility provides an antidote to the pride toward which philosophy tends: "What cries did I send up to you, my God, when I read the psalms of David, those canticles of faith, those songs of devotion, which exclude a boastful mind" (*Conf.* 9.4.8).

Thus, Book Nine provides us with the final, climactic moment in Augustine's relation to Scripture. Not only has he moved from disbelief to acceptance (as though the Bible were a collection of doctrines to be intellectually accepted), but he has also moved to seeing Scripture and his own life as intimately related. This can be seen in his telling of his own story, as analogies to the events of his own life can be seen in Scripture, and scriptural images abound in his telling of his own life. But even at the time the events of Book Nine occurred, this joyful connection between his life and Scripture had begun to take hold of his life and imagination, as shown in his tearful joy at the singing of the Psalms or the reading of the parable of the Prodigal Son. Both in the events and in their telling, Augustine shows that it is here that his attitude toward Scripture fundamentally changed, at the same time as Scripture decisively changed him. The anguish and joy of his life now confirm the validity of Scripture, for it is in Scripture that these experiences are rendered meaningful and purposeful, rather than empty or painful.

Philosophy: Book Nine as Refutation of Platonism and Stoicism

Book Nine represents Augustine's unambiguous turn from Neoplatonism, the revival of Plato's thought in Augustine's time that often combined it with Christianity,[16] just as Book Seven included his decisive break from the Manichees, the gnostic-Christian group popular for its aesthetically pleasing dualism of light and dark matter.[17] This is shown first in his change of lifestyle: "I sent word to the citizens of Milan that they should arrange for another seller of words for their students. This was . . . because I had chosen to serve you" (*Conf.* 9.5.13). In many ways, the pride of the academic and philosophical life was much more likely to distance the ambitious Augustine from God than was his sensuality, so his deliberate resignation from the "chair of lies" (*Conf.* 9.2.4) here seems a more certain sign of his spiritual growth than the overwrought spontaneity of the garden scene of Book Eight.

Just as the vision in Book Seven shows the clear superiority of Platonism over Manicheism—"I wondered at how I now loved you, and not a phantom instead of you" (*Conf.* 7.17.23, my translation)—the vision at Ostia in Book Nine is intended to prove the superiority of Christianity over Platonism.[18] It does this not by rejecting Platonism, the way Manicheism is rejected in Book Seven, but by showing its incompleteness. The vision at Ostia is therefore thoroughly Platonist—rising above the created world to contemplate the Creator directly and ecstatically—but it is not only Platonist, and the added elements are clearly meant to show Platonism's inadequacy and the superiority of Christianity: "Augustine's purpose in his discussion of the vision at Ostia is to show the absolute difference between the vision of God as experienced by the philosopher on the one hand and by the Christian on the other. . . . the vision at Ostia . . . lies altogether beyond the province and possibilities of human philosophy."[19] At Ostia, Augustine sees the same God that he saw in Book Seven in Milan, but he has found a new and better way to see that God. He no longer regards physical conditions as irrelevant or distracting, but can gaze at a peaceful garden and find therein the peace and rest offered by God: the created world is embraced at the same time as it is surpassed, just as it is affirmed at the same time as it is reconstituted in the resurrection, to which Augustine refers (*Conf.* 9.10.25).[20] Augustine finally transcends his own pride, the real obstacle to vision, and which Platonism had only exacerbated in him by substituting intellectual pride for carnal distraction.[21] And most importantly, Monica can share this vision with her son: because the Word is not just the Creator, but is the Incarnate One, he has created, has experienced, and loves finitude and distinctions, and he can help anyone overcome them, even (or especially) someone without any philosophical training, such as Monica.[22] Here is a union with God that can be eternally shared with others: as such it goes far beyond anything the Platonists can offer, and is the true intellectual and spiritual climax of the book.

But Book Nine is not only or primarily intellectual, for it focuses consistently on the emotions, and in this it also anticipates Augustine's extended attack on the Stoics in the *City of God* some twenty years later.[23] It is striking how stoical Augustine attempts to be at the death of his mother, but it is more significant how he eventually repudiates this and finds real peace and wholeness by giving in to his emotions, not denying them. It is not that Augustine believes that human beings are incapable of controlling all our emotions all the time, it is just that to exercise such control would be to live a truly disordered life: "But since these feelings are the consequence of right reason when they are exhibited in the proper situation, who would then venture to call them morbid or disordered passions?" (*Civ.* 14.9).[24] Rather than having rightly ordered emotions, the Stoics offer us only a "ruthless insensibility" (*Civ.* 19.8)—numbing, cold, dead. Although Augustine would grant that God does not feel the same emotions as we, the Stoics' mistake is to try to make us more divine by denying our human weaknesses, when this only ends up making us less human: "if we felt none of those emotions at all, while we are subject to the weakness of this life, there would really be something wrong with our life" (*Civ.* 14.9). It is in Book Nine of the *Confessions* that Augustine finally sees that getting closer to God is not accomplished by imitating him in impossible ways, but by trusting him and laying our weaknesses before him. God does not deny our feelings, but listens to them and heals them. God's greatness is not shown by his imperturbability, but by his compassion, and our devotion to him is shown by our trust in his compassion: "I took comfort in weeping in your sight. . . . for at my heart were placed your ears, not the ears of a mere man" (*Conf.* 9.12.33).

Thus in both his experiences and in his analysis of them, Augustine shows that he can no longer be only a Platonist, nor can he be a Stoic. Like most of his educated contemporaries, Augustine would accept much of the metaphysics of Neoplatonism and the ethics of Stoicism, the dominant philosophical schools of his time: "Absorbing the principal doctrines of Stoic ethics and, in Porphyry's hands, much Aristotelian logic as well, Neoplatonism became altogether dominant over all other philosophical positions in late antiquity."[25] But he here shows the utter inadequacy of their anthropologies to explain how the human soul works, how it could be improved, or how it could unite with God or with others. Augustine undermines two of the greatest philosophical schools of antiquity with just two well-wrought vignettes—the vision at Ostia and his grief for his mother. And it does not seem insignificant that both of these crucial vignettes relate to Monica—the uneducated, unliterary, superstitious, overly emotional woman who would have had little value or importance in either of these philosophies. With a final flourish of irony, Augustine has made his pious, unphilosophical mother the symbol of the undoing of pagan philosophy. It would be hard to imagine a more unexpected or more moving "sacramental tribute to her memory."[26]

Time and Memory: Book Nine on Past and Future, Personal and Universal

Book Nine is the last of the autobiographical books of the *Confessions,* and it therefore must provide the crucial transition to the discussion of time and Scripture in the last four books. As confusing or disconnected as the last four books have seemed to generations of readers, if one considers an alternative scenario—turning from the garden scene at the end of Book Eight to the discussion of memory in Book Ten—one will appreciate that Book Nine provides a better, if still not wholly transparent, transition and preparation for what follows. I will show how it does this through its implicit treatment of the subject that will be treated explicitly in the following books—time.[27]

Throughout Book Nine, Augustine does two things that are rare in the preceding books. He frequently interrupts the chronological order of the narrated events, and he refers to many more deaths than anywhere else in his story: "The first eight books of the *Confessions* record but two deaths. . . . In book 9 alone, however, Augustine records five."[28] In the immediate context of Book Nine itself, both of these characteristics serve to illuminate Augustine's evolving attitudes toward death, grief, and love, and thereby to highlight the climactic instance of all three, the death of Monica. But in the context of transitioning from autobiography to abstracted discussion of time and Scripture, these characteristics of Book Nine disorient the reader's expectations about time and memory, and start the reader thinking not about a particular person's story, but about a universal story of humankind: "For now he had realized that the specific language of Christ, scriptures, and church was an entranceway into a language of universal philosophical truth, including academic rhetoric and dialectic, valid for all people."[29]

Augustine begins Book Nine quite typically with a praise of God,[30] in particular emphasizing Monica and himself as the servants of God.[31] He then describes his final weeks as a professor of rhetoric and his intention to resign from that post (*Conf.* 9.2.2–4). But the next chapter breaks the chronological order, narrating events that occur long after, events that in fact occur outside of the time frame of the autobiographical narrative of the *Confessions*: the conversions and deaths of Verecundus and Nebridius (*Conf.* 9.3.5–6). Augustine then resumes the proper chronological sequence of his story—the beginning of the vintage vacation (*Conf.* 9.4.7), Cassiciacum (*Conf.* 9.4.7–12), his formal resignation from his post (*Conf.* 9.5.13), and the baptisms of Alypius, Adeodatus, and himself (*Conf.* 9.6.14). But during the account of his baptism, Augustine again interrupts chronological order to recount briefly the subsequent life and death of Adeodatus, more events outside of the time frame of the *Confessions* (*Conf.* 9.6.14). Both of these events are interruptions of the narrative order, as well as accounts of deaths, doubly striking for their unusualness in *Confessions*. And both of these events serve as an introduction to the discussion of time and allegory in the rest of *Confessions*: "This violation of the 'natural order' of the narrative serves a program of correspondences between book 9 and the allegory. For Augustine dwells on the eternal rest that each of his friends now enjoys in God."[32] Augustine is subtly moving us from his personal story to a universal story by violating the order of his own story in order to make room for the conclusions to the stories of Verecundus, Nebridius, and Adeodatus. (As will be shown in the next section, this has the related effect of moving away from the narcissism of which Augustine is so often accused.) The climaxes to their own stories having been told, the three characters are dismissed from the narrative to make room for the similar climax to Monica's story.[33]

After a very brief return to the proper chronological order by narrating his baptism (*Conf.* 9.6.14), Augustine next departs on a long series of flashbacks (*Conf.* 9.7.15–9.22). First, he gives a description of the persecution under Justina and the rediscovery and translation of the relics of St. Gervasius and St. Protasius (*Conf.* 9.7.15–16) that is particularly awkward in this context.[34] As with the preceding breaks in chronological sequence, this story highlights the life of someone other than Augustine, possibly to use Justina as a contrast to the faithful Monica, or possibly as another example of the repentant sinner (though her conversion is only hinted at here). Focus is also brought on Monica, and on the universal "mother" and "handmaid," the church. This emphasis on worship and church is again universalizing Augustine's story to include others, and it is also moving from the discontinuity of solitary conversion to the continuity of community life and the continuity of that community's Scriptures:[35] both of these emphases anticipate the discussion of the later books.

Augustine next gives a lengthy flashback to Monica's earlier life (*Conf.* 9.8.17–9.22), much of which again would have occurred long before the time frame of the *Confessions*. The exact purpose of this little biography here is variously interpreted: "fond but highly selective memories of her" that eventually turn the story back to the real subject, Augustine himself;[36] a fitting final tribute to her;[37] or Monica as illustrative of the proper Christian life, either in contrast with Augustine's earlier sinfulness,[38] or as an example for him now to follow.[39] Each of these interpretations certainly gets at some of the significance of this flashback, but they all tend to emphasize the positive, praising aspects of Augustine's story of Monica—her meekness and patience with Patricius (*Conf.* 9.9.19) and his mother (*Conf.* 9.9.20), her calming influence over everyone (*Conf.* 9.9.21), and her devotion to others (*Conf.* 9.9.22). Such interpretations have therefore somewhat minimized the significance of Augustine's including here the story of her drinking as a child, the most unusual and therefore potentially significant part of it.

With Augustine's description of Monica's childhood drinking problem (*Conf.* 9.8.18), we have probably the only place in the *Confessions* in which we see Monica as deeply flawed and deliberately sinful (Augustine excusing the "bodily affection" she shows at *Conf.* 5.8.15 as being only that typical of all mothers). No longer the perfect mother and the perfect believer as she is uniformly presented in the rest of the *Confessions*,[40] she is seen here for the only time as someone exactly like Augustine himself, and by extension, exactly like all sinful humans. Although not precisely parallel (it is, after all, not theft, and intrinsically includes consumption, which the pear theft did not), Augustine deliberately describes Monica's youthful offense as similar to the pear tree incident (*Conf.* 2.4.9–10.18). It is most significant for Augustine that neither is motivated by desire for the lawful and permissible object obtained, but rather by sinful love of the sinful act of obtaining it: "Nor did I wish to enjoy the thing that I had gotten by theft, but only to enjoy the theft and sin itself" (*Conf.* 2.4.9, my translation); "She did this not out of a desire for drink, but from a sort of excess of those youthful spirits" (*Conf.* 9.8.18). Although Augustine says he himself was motivated by a perverse desire for sin itself, while Monica was only overcome by "youthful spirits," he has nonetheless made it clear that Monica, whom he so often contrasts to his own sinful self, was at least once exactly like him. Further, there is another point to consider with this story. Although he attributes the story to Monica's own telling of it to him (*Conf.* 9.8.18), the inclusion of this story seems so deliberate and unusual, and its parallelism to Augustine's childhood theft so contrived, that one should suspect some fabrication or at least embellishment on Augustine's part: he himself admits that his account is incomplete and leaves out many details (*Conf.* 9.8.17), so he has at least chosen this story for a reason. He has given us a very brief interpretation of Monica's life, not a chronicle of it, but this does not in any way thereby diminish its importance: quite the contrary, whether selectively chosen or even fabricated by the author for inclusion at this point, the story's unexpectedness and deliberateness make it seem especially revealing of Augustine's meaning and purpose here. Regardless of its origin, this is how Augustine remembers the story, and how he wants his readers to remember it, very much providing a prelude to the discussion of the power and problem of memory in Book Ten. The effect of the story of Monica's childhood on the reader is one of disorientation and reevaluation. This little vignette finally shows how this is not merely Augustine's own idiosyncratic story in which he neurotically exaggerates his own sinfulness, nor the equally unlikely and unappealing story of how he neurotically idealizes his mother, but a story of real people (who may well be neurotic, but not at all unappealing or unbelievable). One can finally admire or emulate Monica, for she only now emerges as a believable, rounded person, flawed as well as exemplary, and so does Augustine, as a sinner no worse than others, a son distraught over his mother's death and unable to restrain his tears by the "ruthless insensibility" (*Civ.* 19.8) expected by some of his contemporaries.[41] At the risk of some exaggeration, it is this episode, out of place chronologically and unexpected in its characterization, that saves the *Confessions* from being unrealistic, unbelievable, or merely neurotic. It gives to the story of Monica and Augustine the rough edges of real life (even if some of those edges are embellishments to the story), and therefore the relevance and universal applicability of a real, not an idealized story. As with the prodigal son, it gives Augustine's life story the power and challenge of a parable, rather than the sentimentality of an epitaph.

BOOK NINE IN AUGUSTINE'S LIFE AND THOUGHT

Viewed against the background of Greek and Roman antiquity, the uniqueness and innovativeness of Augustine's thought emerges as oddly and thoroughly modern for its deep and constant interest in psychology: "[H]e was far and away the best—if not the very first—psychologist of the ancient world,"[42] and his *Confessions* have a "towering significance for the history of the study and speculation about the relation between mind and will, between love and self-knowledge."[43] On the other hand, viewed prospectively against the subsequent legacy of his Christian descendants, Augustine reveals his own life and psychology to us in a way that other theologians do not, and he analyzes his experience with a theological and psychological profundity that few autobiographers could ever again reach: "[H]e narrates the history of his soul with a rare skill and exactitude, setting forth the most complicated and obscure processes in their native freshness and fragrance. It is a mirror in which we see ourselves and our own experience. . . . Among the great theologians, Augustine is pre-eminently the psychologist."[44] While I am not sure how much "fragrance" I can offer here ("native" or otherwise), I do think that Augustine more than any other ancient or Christian writer has presented us with a "history of his soul," a selective but nonetheless revealing "logos" of his "psyche." So now I would like to analyze how the events of Book Nine, and Augustine's analysis and shaping of them at the time of the writing, show the psychological factors at work in his life, and his understanding of the psychology of himself and others. I will look at both the interpersonal dynamics of the story—the relations between characters—and at the intrapersonal issues with which Augustine struggled at the time the events occurred, and again when he tried to understand and present them later.

The Personal Drama: Friends and Family, Love and Death, Grief and Guilt

For all the (partly deserved) accusations of narcissism against Augustine,[45] the remarkable prominence of the other characters in his life story has also often been noticed: "In the profundity of his heart Augustine held a story which was not only his own but that of Monica, of Adeodatus, of Alypius, of Simplicianus, of Ambrose, of Nebridius, of Romanianus, of the host of friends who had shared his experiences."[46] Certainly there is something thoroughly narcissistic in the very writing of an autobiography, but within this project, Augustine seems to have made a large amount of room for the other characters, and he treats them with concern and interest that goes beyond their effect on him or their place in his life. Augustine himself is the consistent and most frequent focus of the book, but he is not the only one. This is especially so in Book Nine, in which Augustine's acquaintances are more prominent than in any other book, other than perhaps Book Six, in which Monica, Ambrose, Alypius, and the mother of Adeodatus also figure prominently. I will examine how Augustine presents his friends, family, the Manichees, and his relations to all of them in this final autobiographical book, all of it to see the resolutions with them and within himself to which he has come in Book Nine.

It has often been observed how passionately devoted Augustine was to his friends throughout his life.[47] But at the same time as his passion remains the same, there are noticeable changes in his attitude through the course of events described in *Confessions*. Most noticeable in Book Nine is the change in his attitude toward the loss of a loved one: while it paralyzed him with grief and despair in Book Four, he recounts here the deaths of Verecundus and Nebridius with thanks for the love and faith they shared, and for the surety of their salvation (*Conf.* 9.3.5–6). Adeodatus's death is recounted with similar solemnity, and, most of all, peace and assurance: "I had experience of many still more wonderful things in him. . . . Quickly you took his life away from the earth, and now I remember him with a more peaceful mind" (*Conf.* 9.6.14).[48] Clearly Augustine has now learned how to love properly: "But blessed is the one who loves you, and his friend in you" (*Conf.* 4.9.14, my translation). He has learned how to have earthly loves that lead to and include God, rather than distract from knowledge or love of him. And it is with his friends at Cassiciacum that Augustine has some glimpse of the divine rest he has longed for throughout the work: "we found rest in you" (*Conf.* 9.3.5).[49] Book Nine is truly the climax and resolution to his crisis over friendship begun in Book Four, and the beginning of a new, more healthy, and more sanctifying conception of earthly attachments, one that will be even more profoundly felt for Monica. With the final mention of Adeodatus, this may even include some resolution of his feelings for his son's mother, though Augustine resolutely hides these feelings from us as too private and painful.[50]

I have already discussed Augustine's telling of the story of Monica's childhood, and the added dimension of believability and universality that it introduces into his *Confessions*. But following this, there is the equally problematic and revealing episode of his inability, unwillingness, and overwhelming need to weep at her death, all of which throw him into a lengthy description of his own confusion at his feelings, and a consideration of the psychology and morality of grief. Indeed, Augustine's own confusion here is certainly not confined to himself, but has understandably been shared by many of his readers, who have marveled at how inconsistent it seems with his earlier experience of grief in Book Four: "Is this the Augustine whose copious weeping, duly reported, had marked so many important moments in his life—the death of his unnamed friend (IV.4) and his conversion (VIII.12), to name only the most prominent?"[51] And although many express the same surprise, the explanations they offer for Augustine's confusion here are various: the epitome of Augustine as a divided, conflicted, alienated self;[52] Augustine turning his account of Monica's death back into a story about himself, the real topic of the story;[53] a story of Augustine struggling to see the event in its proper perspective, first ineffectively denying his temporal attachments, then coming to see them in their proper relation to the eternal;[54] or a wrestling of Augustine's emotional, humane side with an inhuman, coldly ascetic attitude toward grief, a "ruthless . . . indifference" believed to be noble at the time.[55] I would suggest that his confusion actually shows the development in his thoughts on grief, and the peace and rest he has found in his own life and relationships with his parents. This development includes three stages: his grief for the unnamed friend who died in 376 C.E.,[56] his grief for Monica as experienced in 387 C.E., and his description of both as written in 397 C.E.

In his description, Augustine makes clear the similarities and the differences between his relationships with the friend and with Monica. He uses the same image of the two as one single being: "For I felt that my soul and his soul were but one soul in two bodies" (*Conf.* 4.6.11, my translation); "For out of her life and mine one life had been made" (*Conf.* 9.12.30).[57] The attachment to each was profound and life-sustaining, and therefore the losses were shattering, potentially almost fatal. Augustine's copious weeping at the earlier death points to the difference in his outlook between 376 and 387. Earlier, he only felt despair, abandonment, hopelessness, annihilation, fear, loneliness: "For I wondered at how other mortals could live, while he, whom I had loved as if he would never die, was dead. . . . Perhaps this was why I was afraid to die, so that the one I had loved so much would not die completely" (*Conf.* 4.6.11, my translation). Augustine does not feel despair at Monica's death, but this leaves him wondering at how then to express grief, for the natural outlet of tears has been made suspect by its implication of despair or hopelessness: "We did not think it fitting to solemnize that funeral with tearful cries and groans, for it is often the custom to bewail by such means the wretched lot of those who die, or even their complete extinction. But she did not die in misery, nor did she meet with total death" (*Conf.* 9.12.29).[58]

But Augustine has given us many accounts in the *Confessions* of a far different kind of tears, the kind that Monica sheds for him (e.g., *Conf.* 3.11.19; 3.12.21; 5.8.15),[59] and Augustine specifically connects her tears with his in his description of his grief: "I wept for my mother . . . that mother now dead to my eyes who for so many years had wept for me so that I might live in your eyes" (*Conf.* 9.12.33). Monica weeps freely and piously throughout the book, and Augustine himself weeps in this way at his own baptism: "the tears ran down, and amid those tears all was well with me" (*Conf.* 9.6.14). Tears for another repentant sinner are tears of grief and joy—grief over the sin and pain of separation, joy at the repentance and eternal fellowship. But in 387, could Augustine have been immediately ready to shed such tears for her? The answer would clearly seem to be no, given the consistently idealized portrayal of her in the *Confessions* up until this point, for she has been "the idealized figure that had haunted Augustine's youth like an oracle of God."[60] How could he weep for Monica as she had wept for him, when he has only just turned from a life of sin, while she has lived her entire life as the perfect daughter, wife, mother, and Christian?

The difference in Augustine's experience of events and his subsequent understanding of them when he wrote them down is glaring at this point. At the time of Monica's death, Augustine was deeply confused because he felt a deep, carnal, and wholly appropriate need to weep for her, but the only kind of tears he deemed appropriate were those shed for another repentant sinner like oneself, and he could hardly have conceived of his saintly mother as anything like his sinful self. It is only ten years later when he is writing the *Confessions* that Augustine can see Monica as another flawed human being in need of God's grace, and he shows this particularly by the inclusion of the story of her childhood drinking problem, an episode that surely did not occur to him at the actual time of Monica's death. We have noted how this story renders Monica and the *Confessions* in general more believable and applicable to the reader, but it also seems to have impressed itself on Augustine's memory for the more manageable and meaningful depiction it offered to him of his mother, and the more humane and uplifting understanding it gave him of grief: "Monica . . . is subtly transformed, by Augustine's analysis of his present feelings on remembering her death, into an ordinary human being, an object of concern, a sinner like himself, equally in need of mercy."[61] It is only when he can understand his mother in this way that he can experience his tears as comforting and not painful: "I gave way to the tears that I had held back, so that they poured forth as much as they wished. I spread them beneath my heart, and it rested upon them" (*Conf.* 9.12.33). Here Augustine has achieved—at least briefly—the place where his heart can rest, the place he had longed for since the very beginning of the *Confessions* (*Conf.* 1.1.1).[62] But unlike the beginning of the *Confessions,* this place of rest is not just God (although it includes God), but is a bed of tears shed for an earthly love. Augustine here finds God's healing presence at precisely the place where he makes room for the affirmation and renewal of earthly loves and attachments, not the rejection of them: "Augustine's description of his mourning achieves a paradoxical affirmation of *eros*—of the love of that which cannot last—within a context of *agape.*"[63] Earthly loves need not be unhealthy (as the one for the friend in Book Four apparently was), for they can lead to joy as well as grief, self-fulfillment instead of selfishness.[64] And earthly loves, joys, and griefs need not be sinful: they can be proper expressions of a love that includes, presupposes, and leads to God. Whether one puts this development in psychological or theological terms, the change is profound and vital.

But as important as a reappraisal and renewal of his earthly love for Monica might be, perhaps more important (and much more surprising) is Augustine's partial but nonetheless enormous reconciliation with Patricius. The father who everywhere else in *Confessions* is "negatively represented"[65] finally emerges positively in Book Nine: "After Patricius' baptism, acceptance of Patricius replaces condemnation."[66] Patricius converts to Catholicism, and simultaneously stops his acts of adultery that had so long humiliated the long-suffering Monica: "After he became one of the faithful, she did not have to complain of what she had endured from him when he was not yet a believer" (*Conf.* 9.9.22). Before God, Augustine can finally acknowledge Patricius as his earthly father, even as a brother in Christ, and a fellow citizen of God's kingdom: "[R]emember Monica, your handmaid, together with Patricius . . . my parents in this passing light, my brethren under you our Father in our Catholic Mother, and my fellow citizens in that eternal Jerusalem" (*Conf.* 9.13.37). The turnaround is as sudden, unexpected, and significant as the simultaneous transformation of Monica from saint to reformed sinner: "With Patricius the move is from rejection to acceptance; with Monica it is from idealization to ordinariness."[67] But his feelings for his parents move in complementary, not opposite, directions, for the preceding quotation could just as accurately be rephrased as this: With Patricius the move is from rejection of him because of his ordinariness to acceptance of it; with Monica it is from an idealized denial of her ordinariness to an acceptance of it. In Book Nine, Augustine's feelings move from unhealthy to healthy in both cases: one need not be a psychologist to know that it is neither good nor healthy to idealize or resent either of one's parents, and at the end of Book Nine, Augustine no longer does so. And this reappraisal of both his parents leads Augustine to a deeper reappraisal of his whole past: "New and loving regard for his parents resulted from his disengagement from the training of his early years so that now, although he can accurately evaluate this training, he is not resentful but finds that it was both inevitable *and* the particular route by which he was led to the moment of conversion."[68] Here is an enormous step in "the conscious step-by-step appropriation of different spheres of meaning in the process of becoming an adult, human, ethical self."[69] Augustine no longer blames his parents for their failings or excesses, nor denies their shortcomings, for he now sees them and their actions for what they finally are—inevitable, unchangeable parts of who he now is.

Augustine is not finally a narcissist, for he concludes and climaxes the autobiographical part of *Confessions* not with a story about himself, but with a story about someone else, as indeed all of Book Nine has been guided by stories about others: "It is strangely appropriate that the autobiographical section of the *Confessions* should conclude not with Augustine's *crisis* conversion of book 8—his own spiritual death and rebirth—but with his account of the death of Monica, and the accompanying biographical elegy to her."[70] All of this represents a final integration and redemption of Augustine and his family by his right conception of himself as child—dependent and vulnerable, at the same time as he is caring and responsible (when all along he had tried to avoid all these signs of weakness or attachment). It is to be a child of God in a way that is empowering at the same time as it is humbling, and it "provides the final link to his conversion, and effects a reconstitution and redemption of the earthly family within the divine family: Monica and Patricius, Augustine and his sibling friends are transformed into Jerusalem the Mother, God the Father, and the children of the City of God."[71]

Finally, let us consider Augustine's final evaluation of the Manichees and his relationship with them:

> With what strong and bitter sorrow did I wax angry at the Manicheans, yet
> I had pity on them again, because they did not know of those sacraments,
> those medicines, and raged madly against the antidote by which they could
> become sane! I wish that they had been somewhere near me at that time,
> while I did not know that they were there, so that they could see my face
> and hear my voice as I read Psalm 4 at that time of rest, and perceive what
> that psalm wrought within me. (*Conf.* 9.4.8)

On the one hand, the passage clearly sets up a strong *contrast* between how Augustine is now, and how he used to be: it is "marked at every turn by measure of the distance separating his converted self from his old Manichean self."[72] But at the same time, there is a strong sense of continuity with the past, not in the sense that Augustine is still a Manichee,[73] but that there is a sense of identity and responsibility for what has gone before: "Augustine . . . saw his conversion as, in significant ways, a conversion *to* continuity."[74] (Indeed, it would be the height of Manichean folly completely to reject and repudiate the former self, as though by achieving a higher level of enlightenment the old self was fully discarded and there was simply a new self in its place.) And again, if the work is just an extended exercise in grandiosity and narcissism, there would be no point in hoping for reconciliation with the Manichees, or for their spiritual well-being or improvement. No stranger himself to polemic, Augustine could easily and quite reasonably have given a much harsher final analysis of the Manichees, but instead, exactly like his final evaluation of Monica and Patricius, there is a sense of peace and reconciliation with the Manichees. And as rhetorical as the whole passage is,[75] it seems to express a sincere connection and concern for his former co-religionists, for people he now sees as terribly misguided theological opponents. But this is not commanded love of enemies, this is "pity" (*misereor*) for what he sees as their plight, and hope that it could improve. Indeed, given Augustine's passion for and devotion to his friends described above, it is quite reasonable to assume that he had friends among the Manichees, and not all of them would have become Catholic.[76] For all of us who avoid or despise ex-lovers or former friends (even if such have not actually hurt us, but merely do not "fit" with our new friends or our new image), it is clear that such reconciliation is not easy: it is a difficult part of a deep, transformative, ongoing reconciliation with one's past, the "progressive ideal"[77] of the child archetype mentioned above, or the "self-knowledge [that] is never complete."[78] Parts of this past may now be considered mistaken, but even the "right" parts of it are problematic, for although they are irrevocably connected to the present, they are not identical to it: the past has created the present, but it has not simply duplicated or continued itself into the present. The final and integrative part of such a transformation is to see the sinful past as contributing (however imperfectly or painfully) to one's happiness and well-being, and not just as an obstacle that had to be overcome. This goes far beyond the already difficult task of reconciliation with one's parents described above. In lines I have quoted many times in class and in writings, Dante describes such a transformation the most beautifully when he has the blessed in Paradise speak of their attitude toward their past sinful lives and selves:

> But we do not repent, we smile instead:
>   not at the sin—this does not come to mind—
>   but at the Power that orders and provides.
> From here we gaze upon that art which works
>   with such effective love; we see the Good
>   by which the world below returns above.[79]

Such an attitude may well finally be the province of poets like Dante, for it is as mysterious and hard to achieve as love or forgiveness: denial, petrification in one's old ways, or constant reinvention of oneself would all be easier but ultimately more self-destructive ways of coping with a painful past, or with the realization that every past is, to some extent, painful. Final peace with one's past goes beyond a rational analysis or reaction and imagines a benevolent Providence (or a providential Benevolence), which mysteriously guides all our actions, and in which we put our trust and hope.[80] Augustine's attachment and loyalty to his friends, his appreciation and love for his parents, and finally this even more difficult attitude of forgiveness and hope toward the Manichees together go a long way toward such a reconciliation, and I think they clearly show that Book Nine is the real climax of *Confessions*. Conversion is not the climactic, most difficult, or most important step: reconciling one's postconversion self with one's preconversion self is the real challenge, and the real measure of personal success, psychological integration, and new spiritual health.

CONCLUSION: BOOK NINE AS RESOLUTION, TRANSITION, AND RECONCILIATION

The above examination shows how Book Nine of *Confessions* provides a resolution to Augustine's problems with Scripture and philosophy, a transition between the autobiographical books and the later books, and a reconciliation between Augustine's past and future. For all these reasons, I will continue to consider it the central, unifying, and climactic book of the *Confessions*. But another important point to consider when attempting to understand one of Augustine's writings is to remember both the change and continuity that we constantly see in his thought: "And yet beneath and behind these discontinuities there lay deeper continuities—or, ultimately perhaps, a single deeper continuity."[81] Always a Platonist, always a Christian, always a rationalist, always a mystic: practically any pair of labels we might seek to put on Augustine would best be connected by "both/and," rather than "either/or." Augustine never stayed put or rested content that he had achieved some final, authoritative point of view that would always satisfy him, nor did he reinvent himself in a way that would repudiate or deny all that had gone before. Rather, as Pascal would describe the mysterious dynamic between faith and reason thirteen centuries later, Augustine appreciated all the confusing, alternating aspects that go into experiencing God and happiness: "It is necessary to know when one ought to doubt, when one ought to affirm, when one ought to submit."[82] Thus it is well to remind ourselves again of the differences and similarities between Augustine's ideas as expressed in his dialogues, written at the time that the events of Book Nine occurred, and in the *Confessions* themselves, written ten years later. In his *Soliloquies*, Augustine makes his first attempt at an introspective journey, which he summarizes in a simple prayer: "God, who is always the same, may I know myself, may I know you. That is my prayer."[83] Augustine first wishes to know himself and know God. By the time of the *Confessions*, in the line immediately following the book upon which we have fixed our gaze so steadily, this has changed or been amplified somewhat: "I shall know you, my knower, I shall know you, even as I am known" (*Conf.* 10.1.1; cf. 1 Cor. 13:12). Augustine now wishes to know God and be known by God. On the one hand, one can easily highlight the differences between the two formulations, that the latter seems much more God-centered than the former, and clearly less Platonist (one would not normally express a wish to be known by the Platonic Good or the Plotinian One, but only to know It). At the same time, one could quite legitimately combine the two into a fuller account of introspection and faith: one strives to know oneself, know God, and be known by God. But a different sense of continuity besides combination would be to note that both prayers rely on the construction or retrieval of a self: one must have an integrated, unified, functioning self either to apprehend or love God, or to offer oneself as an object to God's knowledge and love. Part of this challenge is to understand oneself as both subject and object: one longs to know oneself (the self is therefore both subject and object), to know God (the self is subject), and to be known (the self is object). None of this can be done as long as the self is still fractured and dissipated by sin, pride, or despair, or as long as one still perceives oneself as a being split and at war between flesh and spirit (the mistake of the Manichees), reason and faith (the mistake of the philosophers), past and future (Augustine's own mistake until he could come to terms with his past): "A change from metaphysical 'discontinuity' to metaphysical 'continuity,' he insisted against the Manicheans, was not 'perversion' but 'conversion.'"[84] Such intellectual and spiritual barriers do not merely keep us from turning back to God, they keep us from being able even to conceive of a turning back to God.

It is in Book Nine that Augustine overcomes all these blinding, falsifying dichotomies that prevent self-knowledge, knowledge of God, and the giving of oneself to God. Augustine finally acknowledges that he is a reformed Manichee and a converted Platonist, but those years of his life were not wasted, they were a necessary part of the journey, and he can appreciate them for the partial truths they held, and the fuller truth to which they led him. He knows now that he was the ungrateful son of an overly possessive mother and a too-worldly father, but he knows and loves them for who they are. He has been passionately devoted to his friends, and although he is not nearly so close to Patricius, Adeodatus, or Adeodatus's mother, they are all a part of his life and journey, as he is of theirs, "fellow citizens in that eternal Jerusalem" (*Conf.* 9.13.37), and they are all beloved by a God who accepts them and longs for them. Except for those who are not "of large charity" (*Conf.* 9.12.33) and who think they are better adjusted, more faithful, or more normal than Augustine, the personal, intellectual, and spiritual integrity that he achieves in Book Nine must surely shine forth for the sincerity, power, and truth that it holds for all of us.

Chapter 10

Book Ten: The Self Seeking the God Who Creates and Heals

Pamela Bright

INTRODUCTION: BOOK TEN AND THE LITERARY STRUCTURE OF THE *CONFESSIONS*

> When I have adhered (Ps 72:28) to you with the whole of myself, I shall never have "pain and toil" (Ps 89:10), and my entire life will be full of you. You lift up the person whom you fill. But for the present, because I am not full of you, I am a burden to myself. . . . See I do not hide my wounds. You are the physician, I am the patient. (10.28.39)[1]

Augustine here contrasts an imperfect, sick, wounded "present" with the fervent hope of blessedness and health. What is the literary context of the "present woundedness" to which Augustine refers in Book Ten? Even more pointedly, where does Book Ten fit into the literary and thematic development of the *Confessions*? Is it a summation of the narrative sections from Books One to Nine, or does it fit more properly with the last Books Eleven to Thirteen? A third possibility is to argue that Book Ten is a somewhat awkward (even if brilliantly inspired) transition between the first nine and the last three books of the *Confessions*.[2]

There is a certain logic in arguing that Book Ten is a natural conclusion to the intensely personal narrative of his conversion from Book One to Book Nine; after all, Augustine himself in the *Retractationes* announces: "The first ten books were written about myself (*de me*); the last three about Holy Scripture (*de scripturis sanctis*)."[3] Following on the heels of the dramatic narratives of conversion culminating in his baptism in which he publicly "adheres" to Christ and forswears all that is not Christ, "We were baptized and disquiet about our past life vanished from us" (9.6.14), and following the poignant description of the death of his mother (9.8.17), which rounds off the account of the labyrinthine return of the prodigal to his Father's home,[4] it may be argued that Book Ten is a kind of existential reflection summing up the first nine books of the *Confessions*. In many ways Book Ten is the logical and literary conclusion of the search for God that Augustine announces in Book One—a search that ends when the God he has been seeking is nearer to him than his very self (10.16.25), but he cannot "adhere" to God while there is a fundamental "untruth" at the core of his very being. But the cure for this untruth is also uncovered:

> With good reason my firm hope is in him. For you will cure all my diseases (Ps 102:3) through him who sits at your right hand and intercedes with you for us (Rom 8: 34). Otherwise I would be in despair. Many and great are those diseases, many and great indeed. But your medicine is still more potent. We might have thought your Word was far removed from being united to mankind and have despaired of our lot unless he had become flesh and dwelt among us (Jn 1:14). (10.43.69)

The acknowledgment, the "confession," of his profound and continuing woundedness leads to the further "confession" of his need to "adhere" to the only physician who can heal his condition—the Mediator between God and man.

The argument that Book Ten is a kind of interiorized summation of Books One to Nine is strengthened when one considers how the concluding section of Book Ten echoes the themes and the very scriptural citation of seeking the Lord (Ps 21:27) of the introductory section of Book One: "'They will praise the Lord who seek for him' (Ps 21:27). In seeking him they will find him, and in finding they will praise him. Lord, I would seek you, calling upon you—and calling upon you is an act of praising you" (1.1.1). In calling upon God in the opening sections of Book One, Augustine asks, "What place is there where God can enter into me?" and concludes, "Why do I request you to come to me when, unless you were within me, I would have no being at all?" (1.2.2). Book Ten repeats this theme of calling upon God and seeking for God in a magnificently sustained meditation on the "ascent" into interiority through the "vast palaces of memory" (10.8.12): "Through my soul I will ascend to him. I will arise above the force by which I am bonded to the body and fill its frame with vitality. . . . I will therefore arise above that natural capacity in a step by step ascent to him who made me, in whom is true happiness" (10.7.11; 10.8.12). The theme of the God-seeking self continues through Book Ten: "How then am I to seek for you, Lord? When I seek for you, my God, my quest is for the happy life. . . . This is the authentic happy life, to set one's joy on you, grounded in you and caused by you. That is the real thing and there is no other" (10.22.29; 10.22.32). This meditation culminates in the famous cry: "Late have I loved you, beauty so old and so new: late have I loved you" (10.27.38). Immediately this confession of the "lateness," the delay and tardiness of the homecoming of the prodigal is suffused with the consciousness of his "present" woundedness: "But for the present, because I am not full of you, I am a burden to myself. . . . See I do not hide my wounds" (10.28.39). Indeed he does not hide his wounds, even as he continues his confession of praise, even as he ministers to others:

You know my inexperience and weakness (Ps 68:6). "Teach me and heal me" (Ps 6:3; 142:10). Your only Son "in whom are hid all treasures of wisdom and knowledge" (Col 2:3) had "redeemed me by his blood" (Rev 5:9). "Let not the proud speak evil of me" (Ps 118:22), for I think upon the price of my redemption, and I eat and drink it, and distribute it. In my poverty I desire to be satisfied from it altogether with those who "eat and are satisfied" (Ps 61:5). "And they shall praise the Lord who seek him" (Ps 21:27). (10.43.70)

Little wonder that the uncompromising radicality of such a description of the human condition roused the worst suspicions in Pelagius,[5] leading to the inevitable clash of opposing spiritual and theological perspectives in the early decades of the fifth century.

However, the argument that Book Ten is the logical conclusion of the *Confessions* is not without its problems. Books One to Nine are much more obviously a literary unity. One has only to consider the record of the publications of the English translations of the *Confessions* since the seventeenth century to see that the unity of the *Confessions* has long been questioned.[6] The seemingly abrupt change of style from the earlier narrative accounts of Books One to Nine, together with the appropriateness of the dedicatory prayer for his parents at the end of Book Nine as a fitting conclusion to the narrative of his conversion, was justification enough for a number of truncated versions of the *Confessions* that excluded the last three or four books.

The question about the relationship of Book Ten to the rest of the books of the *Confessions* can be examined from a number of different perspectives. Book Ten may be viewed as an integral part of the first ten books of the *Confessions,* as Augustine explicitly notes that the first ten books are "about me." The second perspective sees Book Ten as a kind of microcosm of the *Confessions.*[7] This would argue that Book Ten is an elaborate summation and commentary on the principal themes of the *Confessions*: the seeking for God, the woundedness of the human condition, and, above and beyond all, the overwhelming reality of the grace of God. Book Ten is a microcosm of the whole in the sense that the interior journey through the "fields and vast palaces of memory" (10.8.12) encapsulates the pilgrim journey that he had traced through Books One to Nine. But this is no triumphalist recollection. Book Ten asserts unambiguously before his readers that the profound woundedness of the God-seeking self remains long after the life-giving waters of baptism. The history of conversion is ongoing, just as the confession of praise is ongoing. It is from the consciousness of this woundedness deep within the abyss of self (10.2.2) that we confess our need to adhere to the Physician, the Mediator who is the way and truth and life.

A third perspective of Book Ten that I will present here is that it exhibits a kind of Janus-like character in the overall structure of the work. It looks back to Books One to Nine and forward to Books Eleven, Twelve, and Thirteen. The graced "restlessness" (1.1.1) that sets him out on the journey toward God also has a negative aspect. It is an existential "instability," an agonized inner "distension" (11.29.39) that militates against the firm "adherence" to the good, an instability that Augustine laments in Book Ten (10.28.39). At the same time, Book Ten points forward to the exploration of the need for a resolution between "restlessness" and "rest" in the exegetical framework of a Hexameron,[8] a spiritual reflection on the "six days of creation" in Books Eleven, Twelve, and Thirteen.

THE STRUCTURE AND UNITY OF BOOK TEN

Just as the relationship of Book Ten to the rest of the *Confessions* has long been a question to scholars, so too has there been considerable scholarly debate concerning the structural unity of Book Ten.[9] Augustine himself points to the dubiety and fractiousness of his life and work: "There is a struggle between my regrets at my evil past and my memories of good joys, and which side has the victory I do not know" (10.28.39). It is not just a question of the dichotomy between the poignant confession of "present woundedness" (10.28.39), on the one hand, and the ringing confession of Augustine's hope and trust in the Mediator Jesus Christ (10.43.68). That dichotomy is well incorporated into the understanding of the doubleness of "confession," deliberately explored in the introductory sections of Book Ten (10.2.2–5.7), and indeed throughout Books One to Nine. "The thirteen books of my *Confessions* praise the just and good God for my evil and good acts, and lift up the understanding and affection of men to Him" (*Retract.* 32.1). What is problematic in an analysis of Book Ten is the hermeneutical question of the structural unity of the book.[10] Even if one is skeptical of an obvious literary unity in the book, what sometimes happens is that either the first part on memory or the second part on the concupiscences receives a disproportionate degree of attention, ignoring the need for contextualization in interpreting the text. The need for a unified reading of Book Ten is underlined by Augustine himself toward the end of the book when he summarizes the seeking for God in the first part of the book (10.40.65), and then in the following section, with clear deliberation, Augustine juxtaposes a brief commentary on the concupiscences (10.41.66)—the subject of the long and careful analysis in the second half of Book Ten.

I would argue that there is a structural and logical unity in Book Ten. Following a prologue (10.2.2–5.7), the discourse on memory and the discourse on the concupiscences form the left and right hand "panels" of a literary triptych with the "true happiness"[11] as the central panel: the first panel (10.6.8–19.28) being the *ascent* of the God-seeking self, "a step by step ascent to him who made me" (10.8.12) through "the broad plains and caves and caverns of my memory" (10.17.26). This "ascent" through a deliberate turn to interiority (10.6.10) is paralleled by the third "panel" of the triptych (10.28.39–43.70), the *descent* of the wounded self into the mystery of the abasement of the incarnate Word, an abasement that is the paradoxical glorious ascent (Phil. 2:9–11) of the Servant/Son.

And in the central "panel" (10.20.29–27.38), at the very heart of Book Ten, Augustine sets a luminous exposition on "true happiness."

The intricate fusing of the biblical images of the departure and return of the prodigal and the more philosophical theme of the ascent of the soul throughout Books One to Nine of the *Confessions* finds its culmination in the ascent/descent motif so central to Book Ten. The *ascent* into interiority (a paradoxical *descent* into the recesses of consciousness and even into the regions beyond recallable memory [10.17.26, 28]) of the first half of Book Ten is paralleled by another vertiginous ascent/descent in the second part of the book. There, in an unflinching exposition of his continued vulnerability to the concupiscences (1 John 2:16), Augustine declares that the *ascent* to God has already been modeled by the Mediator in the paradox of his *descent* into flesh in the incarnation: "The true Mediator you showed to humanity in your secret mercy. You sent him so that from his example they should learn humility. He is 'the mediator between God and men, the man Jesus Christ'" (1 Tim. 2:5; *Conf.* 10.43.68).

Prologue: The Confession (10.2.2–5.7)

The first seven sections of Book Ten are devoted to a painstaking elaboration of the purpose of the *Confessions*. The "confessions" in their true nature are an intensely personal conversation with God:

> Why then should I be concerned for human readers to hear my confessions? (10.3.3) . . . Nevertheless, make it clear to me, physician of my intimate self, that good results from my present undertaking. Stir up the heart when people read and hear the confession of my past wickedness, which you have forgiven and covered up to grant me happiness in yourself, transforming my soul by faith and your sacrament. Prevent their heart from sinking into the sleep of despair and saying "It is beyond my power." (10.3.4) . . . When I am confessing not what I was but what I am now, the benefit lies in this: I am making this confession not only before you with a secret exaltation and fear and with a secret grief touched by hope, but also in the ears of believing sons of men, sharers of my joy, conjoined with me in mortality, my fellow citizens and pilgrims. (10.4.6)

But although the conversation partner is God, the audience is Augustine's fellow Christians. For when Augustine shares both his "secret exaltation" and his "secret grief" through these "confessions," he is exercising his ministry to all those "fellow citizens and pilgrims" to whose service "I dedicate my heart, voice, and writings," as he stated at the end of Book Nine (9.13.37). By grieving over his past sins and exalting God for his transformation, Augustine invites his audience to participation and community, not judgment: "So to those whom you command me to serve, I will reveal not who I was, but what I have now come to be. 'But I do not sit in judgment on myself' (1 Cor 4:3). It is, therefore, in this spirit that I ask to be listened to" (10.4.6). The beginning of Book Ten wonderfully unfolds the personal, theological, and communal dimensions of this "confession."

The First Panel: The God-Seeking Self (10.6.8–19.28)

The long narrative of his conversion related in Books One to Nine was never a monologue. It was a constant dialogue. The *Confessions,* as a literary genre, takes the form of written prayer. As a reader, one "overhears" this intimate conversation: "Truth, when did you ever fail to walk with me, teaching me what to avoid and what to seek after when I reported to you what, in my inferior position, I could see and asked your counsel?" (10.40.65). As he summarizes the first part of Book Ten and looks back at Books One to Nine, Augustine sees the joy and frustration of his search for God:

> To the best of my powers of sense perception, I traveled through the external world. Starting with myself I gave attention to the life of my own body, and examined my own senses. From there into the recesses of my memory, manifold vastnesses full of innumerable riches in wonderful ways, and I "considered and was afraid" (Hab 3:2). Without you I could discern none of these things, and I found that none of these was you. Neither was I you, though I had made these discoveries. . . . But in all the investigations which I pursue while consulting you, I can find no safe place for my soul except in you. And sometimes you cause me to enter into an extraordinary depth of feeling marked by a strange sweetness. If it were brought to perfection in me, it would be an experience quite beyond anything in this life. But I fall back into my usual ways under my miserable burdens. I am reabsorbed by my habitual practices. I am held in their grip. I weep profusely, but still I am held. (10.40.65)

All of creation, memory, and experience can point to God, but all can also be a "miserable burden" that hinders the quest. Everything is love, but not every love is good.

Typically, then, Augustine introduces this part of Book Ten with a confession of love, followed by an insistent question as to the object or direction of this love: "My love for you, Lord, is not an uncertain feeling but a matter of conscious certainty. With your word you have pierced my heart, and I loved you. . . . But when I love you, what do I love?" (10.6.8); "I asked the earth and it said 'It is not I'" (10.6.9); "Then what do I love when I love my God?" (10.7.11). With these questions, Augustine moves from the consideration of all the world of sense and enters that most intimate world of self, there to seek God: "Who is he who is higher than the highest element in my soul? Through my soul I will ascend to him" (10.7.11). Augustine then embarks upon the inner journey through the three great storehouses of memory: the impressions laid up through sense perceptions (10.8.13–15); skills, notions, and principles acquired through the liberal arts and the principles of numbers and dimensions (10.9.16–13.20); and memory of affections (10.14.21–22). "Memory preserves in distinct particulars and general categories all the perceptions which have penetrated, each by its own route of entry" (10.8.13).

In analyzing the structure of Book Ten, it has been argued that the first part, "the God-seeking self" (10.6.8–19.28), and the long discussion about the concupiscences in the second half of Book Ten (10.28.39–43.70) form two complementary "panels" of ascent/descent. The complementarity between these two is intensified if one looks closely at the triadic structure of the third "panel" of the literary triptych, "the wounded self."[12] The three concupiscences of 1 John 2:16, "of the flesh," "of the eyes," and "of the pride of life" (10.30.41), are the distorted mirror images of the positive faculties of memories: sense perception (10.8.13–15) later overwhelms us with the unruliness of sense images "of the flesh" (10.30.41–33.53); the capacity for acquiring knowledge (10.9.16–13.20) can turn into the unbridled curiosity "of the eyes"—"a vain inquisitiveness dignified with the title of knowledge and science" (10.35.54–57); the range of human emotions (10.14.21–22) can be twisted into the manifestations of pride and ambition, "the pride of life" (10.36.58–39.64). Even in the puzzling realm of "forgetfulness" (10.16.24–19.28) Augustine does not lose the thread of his question "As I rise above memory, where am I to find you?" (10.17.26), and finally "How then am I to seek for you, Lord? When I seek for you, my God, my quest is for the happy life" (10.20.29).

Through his examination of memory in the unfolding triptych, Augustine gives us a glimpse of its value and power in the search for God, as well as anticipating its perversions and frustrations by the three concupiscences.

The Central Panel: True Happiness (10.20.29–27.38)

Throughout Book Ten, the themes of seeking, finding, and striving to adhere to God are constantly uppermost in Augustine's thought. This is specially true for what I have called the central "panel" of the tripartite structure of Book Ten:

> How then am I to seek for you, Lord? When I seek for you, my God, my quest is for the happy life. (10.20.29) . . . That is the authentic happy life, to set one's joy on you, grounded in you and caused by you. That is the real thing, and there is no other. Those who think that the happy life is found elsewhere, pursue another joy and not the true one. (10.22.32) . . . It [the human mind] will be happy if it comes to find joy only in that truth by which all things are true—without any distraction interfering. (10.23.34)

"To set one's joy on you" (10.22.32) is the indispensable condition for seeking and finding the authentically happy life: "You were within and I was in the external world and sought you there, and in my unlovely state I plunged into those lovely created things which you made. You were with me and I was not with you" (10.27.38). The lyricism of the prose conveys the sweetness of the moment of finding, but it is also a moment more than tinged with ruefulness: "Late I have loved you, beauty so old and so new: late have I loved you" (10.27.38). It is also a moment filled with profound disquiet. "To set one's joy on you" is no sooner confessed than, in the presence of Truth, the truth of his wounded condition is manifest: "You lift up the person you fill. But for the present, because I am not full of you, I am a burden to myself" (10.28.39).

It is not the first time that Augustine had written on the happy life. Before his baptism, to mark his birthday celebration in November 386, he had written *De beata vita,* and at the end he quotes approvingly his mother's words: "This is unmistakably the happy life, a life which is perfect, towards which it must be presumed that hastening we can be led by a well-founded faith, joyful hope and ardent love."[13] Another work, *True Religion,* written before his ordination to the priesthood, also contains his reflections on this topic. What is significant in the second work is that not only is it much more scripturally based, but that the treatise establishes a link between the "happy life" and the concupiscences:

> The way of the good and blessed life is to be found entirely in the true religion wherein one God is worshiped and acknowledged with purest piety to be the beginning of all existing things, originating, perfecting and containing the universe. . . . In Christian times there can be no doubt at all as to which religion is to be received and held fast, and as to where is the way that leads to truth and beatitude. . . . From one particular region of the earth in which alone the one God was worshiped in order that men may receive the Word, love him and enjoy him so that the soul may be healed and the eye of the mind receive power to use the light, to the greedy it is declared: "Lay not up treasures upon earth" (Matt 6:19); to the wanton: "He who sows in the flesh, from the flesh shall receive corruption" (Gal 6:8); to the proud: "whosoever exalts himself" (Luke 14:11); to the wrathful: "turn the other cheek" (Matt 5:39); to those who strive (Matt 5:44); to the superstitious: "The kingdom of God is within you" (Luke 17:21); to the curious: "Look not on the things that are seen, but the things that are unseen" (2 Cor 4:18). . . . Finally to all it is said: "Love not the world nor the things which are in the world. For everything that is in the world is the lust of the flesh, the lust of the eyes and the ambition of this world" (1 Jn 2:16).[14]

It is this linking of the "happy life" and the concupiscences that Augustine repeats in Book Ten nearly a decade later.

In his commentary on Books Eight to Thirteen of the *Confessions,* James J. O'Donnell notes that if the *Confessions* "were merely the story of Augustine's ascent to God, the work could well end with 10.27.38; that it does not is a sign that the work is more ambiguously constructed, reflecting the continuing search for God and the continuing failure of that search to achieve perfect fruition."[15] The glimpse of the happy life in God that Augustine achieves here is still framed by the last part of the book, an examination of the wounds of concupiscence that God is still in the process of healing.

The Third Panel: The Wounded Self (10.28.39–43.70)

The final development of Book Ten has been well prepared, especially in the preceding discussion of the conditions for true happiness, which will come "[w]hen I shall have adhered to you," but "for the present" there is no sure adherence. Rather, there is an ongoing process of healing, unfolding the way the whole dialogue of the *Confessions* has unfolded, between Augustine and his God: "See I do not hide my wounds. You are the physician, I am the patient" (10.28.39). The woundedness is explored in the frame of the three concupiscences of 1 John:[16] temptations "of the flesh" (10.30.41–33.53); temptations "of the eyes" (10.35.54–57); and temptations brought about because of "the pride of life" (10.36.58–39.64).

Augustine begins his analysis by considering the memory of lustful acts: "But in my memory, of which I have spoken at length, there still live images of acts which were fixed there by my sexual habit" (10.30.41), referring to these persistent memories as "the glue of lust" (10.30.42), a continuation of the earlier trap that continues long after the original act is over. Five sections are then devoted to the temptation of excessive eating and drinking (10.31.43–47). The necessity of food is compared to the necessity of medicine, but "while I pass from the discomfort of need to the tranquillity of satisfaction, the very transition contains for me an insidious trap of uncontrolled desire" (10.31.44): desires are captivating in both their presence and in their satisfaction. Augustine acknowledges the allurement of perfumes (10.32.48), but describes how the pleasures of the ear had a more tenacious hold over him (10.33.49–50). But he also cannot advocate a complete austerity, noting that "sometimes, however, by taking excessive safeguards against being led astray, I err on the side of too much severity," and so (hesitantly) puts forward "the opinion (not as an irrevocable view) that the custom of singing in Church is to be approved" (10.33.50). Augustine acknowledges the pleasures of sight, "a delight to my eyes are beautiful and varied forms" (10.34.51), but he is also aware that the physical light can work "by a seductive and dangerous sweetness to season the life of those who blindly love the world. But those who know how to praise you for it . . . include it in their hymn of praise to you" (10.34.52). Any and every part of God's good creation can be twisted by concupiscence into a replacement for the love of God, but Augustine also acknowledges that every part should be included in the praise of God, gratefully accepted as a gift from and pointer to the Creator.

The second concupiscence is the "vain inquisitiveness dignified with the title of knowledge and science . . . the divine word calls it 'the lust of the eyes'" (1 John 2:16; *Conf.* 10.35.54). Unlike the concupiscence "of the flesh," this "lust of the eyes" is more cerebral, desiring *every* kind of experience, not merely the pleasurable: "Pleasure pursues beautiful objects—what is agreeable to look at, to hear, to smell, to taste, to touch. But curiosity pursues the contraries of these delights with the motive of seeing what these experiences are like, not with the wish to undergo discomfort, but out of the lust for experimenting and knowing" (10.35.55). Augustine includes under this second concupiscence the curiosity that drags people to see a corpse (even when they know and say that they are frightened of such a sight), or that causes them to engage in the magical arts, or even such seemingly harmless activities as listening to idle gossip, the empty distraction of gaming, or watching a spider catching flies. Such meaningless but not harmless temptations are so numerous as to make this concupiscence seem more pervasive and insidious than the first: "My life is full of such lapses, and my one hope is in your great mercy" (10.35.57).

The third concupiscence is "the pride of life," which "has not ceased to trouble me, nor during the whole of life can it cease" (10.36.59). At first Augustine seems to be minimizing the presence of this kind of sin in his life. He claims that even at his most wretched, he always valued the truth over praise: "What then, Lord, have I to confess to you in this kind of temptation? I cannot pretend I am not pleased by praise; but I am more delighted to have declared the truth than to be praised for it" (10.37.61). Augustine was never attracted or pleased by *false* praise, but he admits a love of praise nonetheless: "I have to admit not only that admiration increases my pleasure, but that adverse criticism diminishes it" (10.37.61). And the dangers of this love are again insidious and internal. This love threatens the bonds of friendship, because one cannot be sure if one loves being praised by one's friends because one is glad that they too value the truth, or because one enjoys being superior to them (10.37.61–62). And in a final ironic twist, Augustine considers the experience of false humility, of hoarding all the praise one has received, then privately gloating over how humble and disdainful one has been of such praise (10.38.63). This concupiscence can twist even the highest virtues of friendship and humility into an inner ugliness and emptiness, indulging in acquisitiveness and narcissism at their worst.

The analysis of the depth of human woundedness in the frame of 1 John 2:16 covers a long section of the second half of Book Ten (10.30.41–41.66). At the end of this discussion, Augustine looks forward to the cure to his sickness, the healing of his wounds: "So under the three forms of lust I have considered the sicknesses of my sins, and I have invoked your right hand to save me (Ps 102:3). For I have caught a glimpse of your splendour with a wounded heart" (10.41.66). This is immediately followed by a turn to the Mediator (10.42.67–43.69), who is vividly described as a Physician:

> Who could be found to reconcile me to you? (10.42.67) . . . The true Mediator you showed to humanity in your secret mercy. You sent him so that from his example they should learn humility. (10.43.68) . . . With good reason my firm hope is in him. For you will cure all my diseases (Ps 102:3) through him who sits at your right hand and intercedes with you for us (Rm 8:34). Otherwise I would be in despair. Many and great are those diseases, many and great indeed. But your medicine is still more potent. (10.43.69)

We see the same description of the healing of the concupiscences by the true Physician, the "one Mediator of God and men, Christ Jesus" (10.43.68),[17] in Book Thirteen in the context of Augustine's spiritual (or allegorical) exegesis on the sixth day of creation:

> The haughtiness of pride, the pleasure of lust, and the poison of curiosity (1 Jn 2:16) are the passions of a dead soul. The soul's death does not end all movement. Its "death" comes about as it departs from the fount of life, so that it is absorbed by the transitory world and conformed to it. But the Word, O God, is fount of eternal life (Jn 4:14) and does not pass away. A departure from God is checked by your Word, when it is said to us, "Be not

conformed to this world" (Rm 12:2) so that the "earth may produce a living soul" through the fount of life. (13.21.30–31)

The second half of Book Ten provides the crucial summary and pivotal point in the *Confessions* by analyzing the concupiscences that had kept Augustine running away from and toward God in Books One to Nine, at the same time as it anticipates and longs for the healing of his "wounded heart" at the end of the work.

CONCLUSION: THE SIGNIFICANCE OF BOOK TEN

Janus-like, Book Ten looks back on the narrative of Books One to Nine and looks forward to the scriptural reflection of Books Eleven to Thirteen. It looks back by drawing together themes and elements of the first nine books. Augustine begins Book Ten by drawing attention to the very title of the work, *Confessiones,* and then proceeds to write Book Ten in the form of the new spiritual genre that he has announced. The first part invites his readers to join him in his journey toward the truth of the "inner self":

> My Lord, every day my conscience makes confession, relying on the hope of your mercy as more to be trusted than its own innocence. So what profit is there, I ask, when, to human readers, by this book I confess to you who I am now, not what I once was? The profit derived from confessing my past I have seen and spoken about. But what I now am at this time when I am writing my confessions many wish to know, both those who know me and those who do not but have heard something from me or about me; their ear is not attuned to my heart at the point where I am whatever I am. So as I make my confession, they wish to learn about my inner self, where they cannot penetrate with eye or ear or mind. (10.3.4)

This journey through his "inner self" culminates in praising and giving thanks to the God for whom he had been seeking, has found, and has loved "so late" (10.27.38). From that point the confession takes an uncompromising turn toward the disquiet, a kind of vertigo, that continues to plague his "inner self": "for the present, because I am not full of you, I am a burden to myself" (10.28.39). This restless instability of will is unflinchingly explored in the frame of 1 John 2:16, the three concupiscences that wound the heart with sinful, restless loves. Augustine longs to "adhere" to God, the only place where there is true rest, and knows he is dissipated and agonized until then, as he vividly describes also in Book Eleven:

> "Because your mercy is more than lives" (Ps 62:4), see how my life is a distension in several directions. "Your right hand upheld me" (Ps 17:36; 62:9) in my Lord, the Son of man who is mediator between you the One and us the Many, who live in a multiplicity of distractions by many things . . . But now "my years pass in groans" (Ps 30:11) and you, my Lord, are my consolation. You are my eternal Father, but I am scattered in times whose order I

do not understand. The storms of incoherent events tear to pieces my thoughts, the inmost entrails of my soul, until that day when, purified and molten by the fire of your love, I flow together to merge into you. (11.29.39)

Augustine may well have been calling upon his Neoplatonic background[18] in evoking this paralyzing inner tension, this "distension" of the self, implicitly in Book Ten, and then explicitly in Book Eleven, but it is the voice of the psalmist that is nearest to him.

It is well to argue that Book Ten sums up the major themes and lines of argument running through the earlier books, and it is certainly true that in its subjective focus it belongs to that group of ten books "about me," as Augustine states. At the same time, Book Ten also points to, and logically prepares the way for, the last three books, which in themselves form one of the most remarkable reflections on a topic dear to the preaching and prayer of the early church, the six days of creation as a paradigm of the spiritual life, from the light of the first day to the entry into the rest of the seventh day: "This utterance in your book foretells for us that after our works which, because they are your gift to us, are very good, we also may find rest in you for the Sabbath of eternal life" (13.36.51). The quiet beyond disquiet, the rest beyond restlessness is the true conclusion of the many-stranded narrative and the multidimensional work.

How can one sum up the riches and the challenges of Book Ten of the *Confessions*? It may be argued that it is difficult to keep the whole in view, not because the literary unity of the book is so elusive, but because the jewel-like beauty of the individual pieces that make up the whole are so captivating.[19] However, there is a phrase toward the end of the book that is evocative of the whole: "For I have caught a glimpse of your splendour with a wounded heart" (10.41.66). There is the confession of the splendor and there is the confession of woundedness, and it is no more than a glimpse of the profundity of both. This double confession remains at the core of Book Ten and of the *Confessions* as a whole.

Chapter 11

Book Eleven: The *Confessions* as Eschatological Narrative

Robert P. Kennedy

INTRODUCTION

"You arouse us so that praising you may bring us joy, because you have made us and drawn us to yourself, and our heart is unquiet until it rests in you."[1] With this opening, Augustine indicates that the story of his life will not be complete until he himself has found complete rest in communion with God at the resurrection. He also indicates that his story does not begin with his own existence in time but with God's creation of him in eternity. The context of his life thus stretches from the eternity of God's creative act to the eternity of God's final redemption. From the standpoint of narration, Augustine is trying to tell a story whose beginning and end are shrouded in mystery, while the narrator himself is severely limited by the lack of completion and goodness in his own life.

At the beginning of Book Eleven, Augustine alludes to the words and themes in the first paragraph of Book One. The purpose of his confessions is "to arouse my loving devotion toward you, and that of my readers," so that they can praise God together in the scriptural words with which he began the work, "Great is the Lord, and exceedingly worthy of praise" (Ps 47:2 [48:1]). Because God has willed Augustine to confess, it is now Augustine who "arouses" himself and others to praise God. The voice of God, which alone can draw joyful praise from Augustine and his audience, speaks through Augustine's words and brings him and his listeners closer to finding their fulfillment in God. By confessing, the church lives out its hope, gradually ceasing to be "miserable in ourselves," so that it may "find our beatitude in you" (11.1.1).

In Book Eleven, as in Book One, his awe at God's greatness and mercy is counterbalanced by awareness of his difference from God (contrasting his own finitude with God's infinite and complete being), and by sadness at the distance he has put between himself and God by sinning. These themes—God's infinite

167

being versus our finitude, God's mercy versus our sinfulness—coalesce in the problem of confession: "I do not believe I could speak truthfully under inspiration from anyone other than you, since you are the Truth, whereas all human beings are liars. Thus anyone who tells lies is speaking from what is his own; and in order to speak the truth, I must speak from what is yours" (13.25.38; cf. 12.25.34). In order to confess truthfully, Augustine must somehow contain God in himself and he must then communicate this truth to others without distorting it by interjecting his own sinful habits of thought into his language.[2]

In the last three books of the *Confessions*, Augustine sets out a guide to transforming temporal and sin-laden habits of thought and language into confession. Book Eleven is the interpretive key to the *Confessions* because it sets out the groundwork for discovering the eternal within the temporal and for transforming the desire for God into the activity of attaining communion with him. Augustine first discovers the absolute incomparability between creation and God. His meditation on time brings home the complete impossibility of attaining God unless God himself has created a path that will guide his steps to God. That path is scripture. By uniting his mind with the words of scripture, he can shape his life for an identity that can sustain the vision of God. There, Augustine learns to hear God's voice speaking in human words and he learns to appropriate that voice so that it speaks in and through his own words. In describing how God's voice speaks in scripture through the words of Moses and Paul, Augustine is also describing what happens when he confesses. His life, reflected in his speech about it, becomes an allegory of the scriptures and a place where both he and others can make progress toward true peace.[3]

BETWEEN MATTER AND SPIRIT: BOOK ELEVEN
WITHIN BOOKS ELEVEN TO THIRTEEN

Near the end of the opening of Book Eleven, Augustine states the program of the last three books:

> See, Father, have regard to me and see and bless my longing, and let it be pleasing in your merciful eyes that I find grace before you, so that the inner meaning of your words may be opened to me as I knock at their door. I beg this grace through our Lord Jesus Christ, your Son, the man at your right hand, the Son of Man whom you have made strong to stand between yourself and us as mediator. Through him you sought us when we were not seeking you, but you sought us that we might begin to seek you. He is the Word through whom *you made all things, and me among them,* your only Son through whom *you called your believing people to be your children by adoption, and me among them.* . . . (11.2.4; italics added)

Through reading the words of Scripture with the help of God's grace, Augustine seeks their inner meaning, namely the truth that Augustine identifies as the second person of the Trinity. He is going to do this in Books Eleven and Twelve by a literal exegesis of the first two verses of Genesis, focusing on the doctrine of creation, and in Book Thirteen by a figurative exegesis of Genesis 1:3–2:2 as an allegory of the church. Augustine thus explicitly announces what he is doing in these books. Their topics are creation ("you made all things") and the church ("you called your believing people to be your children by adoption").[4] At the beginning of Book Thirteen, Augustine alludes to this structure again when he states, "you [God] command me to serve you and worship you that it may be well with me of your bounty, who have granted me first to exist [creation: Books Eleven and Twelve], that I may enjoy well being [church as community of the saved: Book Thirteen]."[5]

In the last three books of the *Confessions* Augustine is discovering himself by seeking God's will in the words of Scripture. The topics are not simply creation and church, but all created things "and me among them," and the people of God "and me among them." He has not stopped talking about himself, therefore. He is now exemplifying the search for himself in his search for the meaning of Scripture. As he penetrates the meaning of Scripture more deeply he is also developing a stronger understanding of the divine nature. As his knowledge of God strengthens, so does his knowledge of his own nature as a creature.[6] While Augustine's overriding personal desire is to attain full knowledge of God, this quest is inseparable from genuine self-knowledge. Moreover, Augustine has not forgotten his intention to exemplify the process of self-discovery for his readers.

Augustine's discussion of time is part of a broader project, to strengthen his understanding of God and himself, and the framework of this project specifies his definition of time. In Book Eleven, Augustine seeks to understand his creatureliness within the ultimate frame of reference, which is God's eternal knowledge of him. Scripture itself tells him that this is where he should begin: "In the beginning, God made heaven and earth" (11.3.5, *in principio fecit Deus caelum et terram*). Augustine interprets beginning (*principium*) to refer primarily to the eternal Word of God, who is the "principle," the source of meaning and existence, for all things, including Augustine himself. First and foremost, Augustine is a creature whose reality consists in the eternal knowledge God has of him in the Word. Yet Augustine is not eternal, he is a temporal creature. The problem he faces is how to reconcile his eternal existence in God with his created existence in time.

One way to resolve this is by identifying the self completely with his eternal existence in God and to deny the relevance of temporality for self-knowledge.[7] However, Augustine effectively rules out this option in Book Twelve. He cannot find out what he is by juxtaposing his created being and God's eternal being, because there can be no comparison between creation and God (see 11.4.6, 11.6.8, 11.11.13). God's being is incomparable to any other being; in addition, God is infinitely beyond our understanding. So Augustine, again following the lead of Scripture, locates himself in relation to the extremes within creation itself. At each extreme he finds a being that is timeless, but not eternal. The highest creation is the heaven of heavens, the harmonious unity of spiritual creatures who cling to God with all their love. The lowest is the formless void, which is pure potential for becoming any corporeal creature.

According to Augustine's interpretation of Genesis 1:1, "heaven" refers to the "heaven of heavens" of which the psalmist speaks in Psalm 113:16: "Heaven's heaven is for the Lord; but he has assigned the earth to humankind" (12.2.2). This heavenly communion is timeless because it is completely spiritual. The "earth" of Genesis 1:1 is also outside time because it lacks all form and order. Although it has real existence, formless matter can never appear except in some form. As temporal, Augustine is a creature inferior to the heavenly communion. But it is also precisely as a temporal creature that Augustine is superior to formless matter. Augustine aspires to be as much like the heavenly communion as he can be, for he is also a spiritual creation whose destiny is to cling eternally to God. Augustine also wants to be as distant from formless matter as he can get so as to be less changeable and more stable in giving his life to God. In this twofold desire, toward the status of the heavenly communion and away from that of formless matter, Augustine finds himself caught in a tension between a longing for one kind of timelessness and a rejection of another kind of timelessness. Because the stability that is a necessary condition for achieving the timelessness of the heavenly communion entails becoming more definitively part of the temporal order, Augustine has discovered that his spiritual quest must embrace temporality, not abandon it.

Augustine's discussion of the heavenly communion and formless matter brings two further considerations into view. First, although both of these creatures are outside time, they are nonetheless creatures and therefore subject to change. Only God is truly immutable. The mutability of formless matter is self-evident; such existence as it has is pure potentiality for becoming. As for the heavenly communion, Augustine insists that its exalted nature does not mean that it has the capacity for immutability from its own resources. In fact, it changed when God converted the unformed spirit to himself by his grace (13.4.5). Moreover, the heavenly communion continues in its adherence to God and the exalted status this confers only by God's continuous action on it. The heavenly communion, in other words, is immutable by participation and not by nature. What these two types of change (from formless matter to material things, and from unformed spirit to heavenly communion) have in common is that they occur outside time. So, all creatures are by definition mutable, but not all are temporal. Second, in his discussion of the creation of material things from formless matter, Augustine distinguishes between temporal change and time itself. All material forms are subject to time because they are constantly coming to be and passing away; temporal creation exists because it has forms that must pass away. The brute fact of change does not constitute time because the concept of time includes reference to the past and to the future, whereas change occurs only in the present.

At the beginning of Book Thirteen, Augustine draws out the lessons the church should take from examining the heavenly communion and formless matter. The most important of these is that the source of all goodness is God. A second lesson is that all creation is good, even formless matter. Formless matter is the lowest good, but it is good. A fortiori, temporal creation is good, as is time itself,[8] because time is also God's creation:

> Even in its unformed state the spiritual was of higher dignity than any formed corporeal thing, and a corporeal being, even unformed, had more dignity than if it had had no existence at all. Thus these formless things would have depended on your Word even had they not by that same Word been summoned back to your unity and received form, and become, every one of them, exceedingly good because they are from you, the one Supreme Good. (13.2.2)

In this paragraph Augustine establishes a hierarchy of being, equal in being utterly dependent on God, yet created in a hierarchical order. At the bottom is formless matter, which has bare existence and is outside time. Next are the material things made from formless matter, which have a higher goodness for the same reason that they are temporal, namely, because they have form (12.12.15, 12.13.16; 13.2.3). Finally, at the height, there is the spiritual creation, which by nature transcends time, but even this creature would be "dark and abysmal" (13.2.3; cf. 13.5.6) without God's grace constantly supporting it. The church takes its bearings from the order of creation revealed in Scripture. Its goal is to share the bliss of the heavenly communion, yet it will accomplish this ascent only by remembering that the form of ascent is pilgrimage to a future that can come only from God.

THE PURPOSE OF BOOK ELEVEN

Augustine has set himself two main tasks in Book Eleven. First, he is beginning his exegesis of Genesis. The subject of the book is the opening of the Bible: "In the beginning God made the heaven and the earth." What Augustine has before him in Genesis 1:1 is the juxtaposition of two phrases signifying two realities, "In the beginning" (*in principio*) and "heaven and earth" (*caelum et terram*). As noted above, he takes the first as referring to the Word of God who became incarnate in Jesus Christ, and he understands the second as the whole of creation, both nontemporal and temporal. In Book Eleven he will concern himself with temporal creation, with himself as its representative; and in Book Twelve he will discuss the nontemporal creation, namely "the heaven of heavens" (*caelum caeli*, equated with the heavenly communion of minds who turned to God and clung to him at their creation) and "the formless void" (*materia informis*, the matter from which all things were given form). In Book Thirteen he switches from literal interpretation to figurative and treats the days of creation as an allegory of the church.

Second, Augustine is introducing Scripture as the meaning of his own confession. In its proper context, the discussion of time serves as an exploration of the mystery of the incarnation. Augustine knows that he cannot understand how the eternal Word could become flesh, yet he also knows that he must strive to understand it. In doing this, he is providing the reader with an insight into the paradox of truthful speech by looking at the (logically) prior act of understanding. Here, in Book Eleven, he investigates why it seems impossible to use temporal speech to communicate truth about God. This problem of communication is the link between Augustine's words and the words of Scripture, and it is the question of how Scripture can communicate the eternal Word in temporal words that is the main theme of the discussion of time.

Augustine begins his interpretation of Genesis by asking how God "made heaven and earth in the beginning" (11.3.5). This is really two questions, because "beginning" (*principium*) refers both to the act that brought all creation into existence (11.5.7) and to the Word in whom God spoke in creating. Therefore, the question becomes how God spoke in making heaven and earth (11.6.8). The creation in which Augustine finds himself is the temporal expression of God's eternal will. This is why creation can serve to direct Augustine beyond itself to God. Augustine also knows that God created through the Word, the second person of the Trinity. Having identified the appropriate question, Augustine reaches an impasse: if God spoke outwardly to make the universe, then there would have to have been a temporal creature in which the sound of the words would take place. But this is impossible, because there was no creature before God started to create, and if we posit such a creature then we are left with the question of how God spoke in making that creature. More tellingly, if God's speech were mediated by a creature, then it would not be God's speech, because all God's activity is eternal, including God's speech:

> Then these words of yours, in their temporal expression, would be reported by the outward ear to the mind of any discerning listener whose inner ear was attuned to your eternal Word. The mind would then compare the words sounding in time with your silent Word in eternity, and say, "These are something different, totally different. They are far below me and have no being, since they are fleeting and ephemeral; but the Word of my God is above me and abides for ever." (11.6.8)

Augustine establishes that God's speech is identical with God's being, which is unchangeable and beyond human understanding. Rather than finding an answer, Augustine is showing that there can be no explanation of this. The manner of God's speech is as mysterious as God's eternity.

> However, God has bridged this infinite gap through the incarnation of the Word: [E]verything which begins to exist and then ceases to exist does so at the due time for its beginning and cessation decreed in that eternal Reason, where nothing begins or comes to an end. This eternal Reason is your Word, who is "the Beginning" in that he also speaks to us. The gospel records that he claimed this by word of mouth, making his claim audible to people's outward ears that they might believe him and seek him within themselves and find him in the eternal Truth where he, our sole teacher, instructs apt disciples. There it is that I hear your voice, O Lord, the voice of one who speaks to me, because anyone who truly teaches us speaks to us directly, whereas one who is no true teacher does not speak to us, though speak he may. (11.8.10)

All true meaning comes from the Word, who bestows genuine intelligibility on all creatures and who enables human beings to find the truth in the appearances. The incarnate Word is the center for understanding Scripture and, through its words, becomes the means for uniting our scattered lives.

Augustine has also found the answer to how God spoke in creating. It is the mystery of God's activity, and so the answer is not a proposition but a dynamic, the listening to God's voice in Scripture. The realization that God supplies the measure, not our mind, directs Augustine to the process of appropriating the words of Scripture and discovering the Word in those words. God's voice is both particular to these words and universal. The reader's task is to discern God's voice by refusing to reduce the meaning to the particular intention of the authors or to gloss over the specific form in which God has chosen to accommodate his Word to human temporality.

In summary, Book Eleven both begins the exegesis of Genesis and introduces it. The discussion of the problem of time arises from and is part of the exegesis of the first verse of Genesis. In beginning his reading, Augustine must face the question of how the eternal and unchangeable God creates a temporal and corruptible universe. Augustine's purpose in this discussion is to refute all attempts to bypass the literal meaning of the text and all attempts to reduce or remove the paradox of the eternal relating to the temporal. With this problem there also arises the parallel question of how the eternal Word could communicate in temporal words. Because the paradoxes of creation and revelation are the same, in resolving the mystery of God's autobiography Augustine will find the way to make his own autobiography truthfully.

PARADOXES OF TIME

Discussions of Book Eleven tend either to separate his proof that time is a distension of the mind from its context, or to focus on the larger themes he raises while denigrating or dismissing as irrelevant the arguments he gives about the nature of time. The key to understanding the book as a unity is, I believe, to train our attention on the transitions in the book and thereby to discover how the intention he states in the opening chapters emerges from the problems he encounters as he investigates what time is. Both groups are correct: Augustine does mean to give a definition of time,[9] so far as this is possible, *and* he wants to illustrate by this inquiry the emptiness and futility of human attempts to construct our lives on any other basis than the unfathomable mystery of God's incarnation. As Augustine brings the tools of dialectic to the "most intricate enigma" (*Conf.* 11.22.28) of time, he also frames this inquiry as a pursuit of an impossible goal. His conclusions about time are therefore severely limited in their claims to give a completely satisfactory resolution. They help to bring the problematic features of our existence in time into clearer focus, while at the same time exposing our inability to grasp their significance.

Augustine invites us to read his treatment of time as a series of problems or paradoxes. His purpose is to show how the realities that seem most familiar to us are not as easily understood as we take them to be: "What, then, is time? If no one asks me, I know, but if I want to explain it to someone who asks me, I don't know" (11.14.17). In this, he is continuing the reflections in Book Ten, which revolved around the theme that he does not know himself. Book Eleven broadens this theme to include the whole temporal creation. Roland Teske identifies three "paradoxes of time" in Book Eleven.[10] The first is Augustine's answer to those who ask what God was doing before he created heaven and earth. The second paradox concerns how there can be measurement of time if past and future do not exist and the present has no extension. Finally, there is the paradox that arises from the apparent conflict between his assumption (most clearly evident in his refutation of those who assume that there was time before God created [11.11.13–14.17]) that time is an objective reality, something that exists outside the mind, and his conclusion that time exists only as a distension of the mind (11.27.36).

A more comprehensive reading turns up more paradoxes. The greatest is how God's eternal Word produces non-eternal beings: "Thus in that Word who is coeternal with yourself you speak all that you speak simultaneously and eternally, and whatever you say shall be comes into being. Yet things that you create by speaking do not all come to be simultaneously, nor are they eternal" (11.7.9). Augustine began his exegesis of Genesis with the goal of understanding "how you made heaven and earth in the beginning" (11.3.5). If God is truly the creator of absolutely everything, then the word he spoke must be coeternal with him. Otherwise, there would have been a creature before God created, and the question of the source of that creature would arise. By identifying God's speech with the eternal Word, Augustine solved the problem of an infinite regression by removing any question of successiveness from God's creative activity, but this strategy does not, as it were, get Augustine from God's eternal and incorruptible being to our temporal and corruptible being. The closest he can get to an answer is to appeal to the order or plan of creation. Because we are aware of an order in things, we can also realize that there must be a source from which we learn eternal truths from ever-changing creatures: "When some changeable creature advises us, we are but led to that stable truth, where we truly learn as we stand still and listen to him" (11.8.10). Although the question of how the eternal Word creates mutable realities has uncovered an important truth about our relationship to the Word, reinforcing the lesson that there can be no truth apart from this Word, Augustine is under no illusion that he has explained the possibility of creation. Instead, Augustine continues in a different vein:

> In this Beginning you made heaven and earth, O God. You made them in
> your Word, your Son, your Power, your Wisdom, your Truth, wonderfully
> speaking and in a wondrous way creating. Who can understand this? Who
> can explain it? What is this light that shines through the chinks of my mind
> and pierces my heart, doing it no injury? I begin to shudder yet catch fire

> with longing: I shudder inasmuch as I am unlike him, yet I am afire with
> longing for him because some likeness there is. (11.9.11)

Rational interrogation and examination yield to awestruck wonder and praise.

Augustine's search for understanding has given way to the acknowledgment
of mystery, and with it the recognition of his own unfitness to perceive the truth
clearly. While Augustine accepts his limitations, learning patience from the hope
of God granting full understanding (11.9.11), others have sought to cut down
the problem to their own capacities. Augustine turns rather abruptly from the
question of the eternal creation of mutable creatures to the false question "What
was God doing before he made heaven and earth?" (11.10.12). The connection
with Augustine's question becomes apparent at the end of the same section. If
God's will is the same as God's substance, as Augustine contends, and something
new appears, then we are left with a dilemma, for "if some element appears in
God's substance that was not previously there, that substance cannot accurately
be called eternal. On the other hand, if God's will that creation should occur is
eternal, why is creation not eternal as well?" According to this objection, Augustine must either give up the idea that God created everything from nothing,
and thus allow the possibility in principle of a reality coeternal with God, or he
must admit that God is subject to change. In sum, either there was something
for God to work with or God decided to create at some point, and thus under-
went some change.

Historically, the source of this objection was the Manichees, who held that
there were two coeternal and opposed principles and that the conflict between
them led to the formation of the world as we know it.[11] In the context of Book
Eleven it has the dialectical function of clarifying what it means for God to be
eternal. God's act of creation evokes awe and wonder only if there is genuine
appreciation of its mysteriousness, and so Augustine refutes a false understanding of eternity. The Manichees' mistake involves an equivocation on the meaning of "before." If God is eternal, Augustine points out, then he is outside time
and there can be no temporal successiveness for God.[12] In eternity, all times are
equally present, so that God's "years are a single day [see Ps. 90(89):4; 2 Pet. 3:8],
and this day of yours is not a daily recurrence, but a simple 'Today,' because your
Today does not give way to tomorrow, nor follow yesterday" (11.13.16).[13] This
amounts to a reaffirmation of the Christian doctrine of creation, which, for
Augustine, does not tolerate any reality alongside God in the act of creating. It
follows that God made time itself, not creating *in* time but creating the material
universe and time *with* it.[14]

With the opening sentences of chapter 14, Augustine has resolved the inquiry
into how God's eternal act of creation in his eternal Word produces temporal
things: "There was therefore never any time when you had not made anything,
because you made time itself. And no phases of time are coeternal with you, for
you abide, and if they likewise were to abide, they would not be time" (11.14.17).
At this point, Augustine begins his long investigation into the nature of time.

AUGUSTINE ON TIME: MEDITATION AND DIALECTIC

It is not immediately clear why Augustine launches into this extended and problematic discussion. From what we have seen, he has answered as fully as possible the question of how God spoke in creating (11.6.8) and why God's eternal speech does not produce eternal realities. Once he has shown that the issue of God's activity prior to creating is fallacious, because based on a misunderstanding of eternity, he has reached an appropriate conclusion to the interpretation of the Bible's opening words. Why, then, does he pursue the question of the nature of time?

One way to approach the discussion of time is as a continuation of the dialectic he has been employing in his refutation of objections to the Christian doctrine of creation. He is broadening its scope to address a number of possible illusions a temporal creature might fall prey to in attempting to understand the relationship between God and creation.[15] As I shall argue below, Augustine exemplifies the temptation to claim more room than is warranted for human control by repeatedly advancing the idea that the ability to measure time arises from noting things as they pass. If we do measure time as it passes, then there would be a standard for temporal creation within itself, and this in turn would legitimize finding a value in things that does not depend on referring their goodness back to God's. That there is a moral purpose in Augustine's analysis of time would seem likely, given the conclusion to his earlier refutation of the Manichean idea that something outside of God must have caused God to decide to create. Understanding the reason for creation, he tells them, comes only "by the highest purity of morals and by that goal of the command, of which the Apostle speaks, 'The goal of the command is charity from a pure heart and a good conscience and faith unfeigned' [1 Tim. 1:5]." In Book Eleven, the moral purpose of Augustine's discussion of time emerges out of the dialectic,[16] the back-and-forth argumentation he uses to arrive at his definition of time as the mind's power both to stretch itself out and to contain the past and the future in the present. In order to grasp his purpose accurately, therefore, we must look closely at his arguments and discern in them how they serve Augustine's intention.

The investigation into the nature of time has three parts. The first (11.14.17–20.26) is a clarification of what we mean by "time." Augustine assumes that our references to past, present, and future are meaningful, and that the tenses must therefore have some basis in reality. His first move is to refine our language in order to determine more precisely what that reality is. At the end of this part, Augustine has elucidated how it is possible to measure time. In the second part (11.21.27–26.33), Augustine takes up his own suggestion that "we measure periods of time as they pass" (11.21.27) and asks what it is that we measure. After taking two chapters (11.23.29–24.31) to refute the suggestion made by some anonymous "learned man" that "the movements of the sun, moon and stars themselves constitute time" (11.23.29), Augustine tentatively concludes that time is a distension of the mind (11.26.33). Finally, in the third part of his analysis of time (11.27.34–28.38), Augustine again takes up the idea that we measure time as it passes by and discovers that this is not, in fact, the case. It is interesting to note that in the first two parts, Augustine has been refuting others' misunderstandings of time, but here he turns on his own assumption, tentatively asserted in 11.16.21 and 11.21.27 and mentioned at the end of 11.26.33, and shows its fallaciousness. Augustine concludes his discussion with an explanation and defense of his thesis that time, properly speaking, exists only in the human soul.

First Movement: Time as the Present Extended in the Mind

Like the Manichees, all of us are prone to make the mistake of thinking that God, like a human artisan (11.5.7), had to undergo some change in order to create. This cannot be true, for it is definitive of God that he does not change, indeed, that he is incapable of change. As God is necessarily immutable, time has to be a creation. If it were not created, then either there would be something that God had not created, which contradicts the notion of God as creator of all, or time would be immutable, which contradicts the nature of time (cf. 11.14.17). The reason we are tempted to draw this conclusion is that we cannot engage in any activity which pertains to time without subjecting ourselves to the effects of time.

After disposing of this misapprehension about God's activity, Augustine inquires into what time is. He begins by noting that neither future nor past times have any existence, because the future does not yet exist and the past has gone out of existence. This would seem to leave him with only one option, that time exists only as present time. But the present does not provide any footing or vantage that would allow us to examine what time is:

> As for present time, if that were always present and never slipped away into the past, it would not be time at all; it would be eternity. If, therefore, the present's only claim to be called "time" is that it is slipping away into the past, how can we assert that this thing *is*, when its only title to being is that it will soon cease to be? In other words, we cannot really say that time exists, except because it tends to non-being. (11.14.17)

Because present time does not give anything for the mind to grasp, Augustine turns to the question of what we measure when we measure time. Present time is ruled out because it has no extension, and what has no extension cannot be measured (11.15.20). However, periods of time in the past do not exist because they have passed from existence, and periods of time in the future do not exist because they have not yet come into existence (11.16.21). Therefore, we cannot measure time itself because time is either extensionless (present time) or non-existent (past and future times).

Yet, Augustine cannot deny that we do measure times, comparing longer and shorter times, and he takes this as evidence that time does exist in some sense. In order to determine how time exists and what time is, Augustine focuses on the question of what we measure when we measure time. Again, he appeals to the nonexistence of both time past and time future to establish that neither past nor future is what we measure, for the reason that one cannot measure anything that does not exist. This leaves time present as the only time capable of being measured. But because present time has no extension, existing only as passing, Augustine must conclude that the present cannot be what we measure when we measure time. If time cannot be measured as past or as future because these don't exist, and if time cannot be measured as present because the present has no extension, then it seems either that it is impossible to measure time or that it is impossible to explain how we do measure time.

However, this impasse is only apparent. The problem is with our language, not with the consciousness that time exists and that we do measure it. So if time exists, and if the present is the only time that exists, then in measuring time we must be measuring the present. However, because the present has no extension, it is not measurable in itself. Time becomes measurable if we understand time present as containing time past and time future, which can be divided and therefore measured:

> What is now clear and unmistakable is that neither things past nor things future have any existence, and that it is inaccurate to say, "There are three tenses or times: past, present, and future," though it might properly be said, "There are three tenses or times: the present of past things, the present of present things, and the present of future things." These are three realities in the mind, but nowhere else as far as I can see, for the present of past things is memory, the present of present things is attention, and the present of future things is expectation. (11.20.26)

Augustine has found the existence of time in the present and he has found its extension in the past and the future as contained in the present. Because the human soul can stretch out the present and draw nonexistent things, whether past or future, into the present, it is possible to measure periods of time.

Augustine is already hinting at his answer to the question, What is time? He has found that the meanings we discover in the past and the future depend on the mental operations of memory, attention, and expectation. In order to understand what time is, therefore, we must examine these operations. In the next section he addresses the assumption that our ability to measure time is not based on the nature of the human soul but on the motions of bodies. His refutation of this view vindicates his insistence that past and future do not exist in external things. He does not deny that everything that we can perceive by our senses is temporal. The point is that external, physical time cannot provide a meaningful account of time; it has no significance because it is simply the tendency of things to undergo change. If time were merely the succession of changing forms as they pass into and out of existence, then the meaning we find in temporal things would be either unexplainable or completely arbitrary.

Some readers have accused Augustine himself of reducing time to a subjective and, by implication, arbitrary reality.[17] In fact, the opposite is true. It is crucial that time have significance because it is through the incarnation of the Word in time that Augustine, and all temporal creation with him, can gain salvation. If time were subjective in the sense of being merely a figment of our minds, then there would be no value in the historical narratives in Scripture, nor would its prophecies or promises have any validity (see 11.17.22). The prospect of emptying the words of Scripture of their truth leads Augustine to address God as his hope, a hope that relies on the truthfulness of the scriptural witness to the past and its expressions of hope in the future (18.23).[18]

Second Movement: The Mind as the Measure of Time

In the second section, Augustine focuses on how we measure time. He hypothesizes that if he can grasp how we measure time he will also gain insight into what time is (11.23.30). His discussion of the idea that time is identical to the movements of certain bodies raises the issue of the relationship between physical time and time as a mental reality. He points out that the twenty-four-hour period of time we call a day does not depend on the motion of the sun because if the sun's motion were to slow down or speed up, we would still be able to compare these different periods of time and determine that the one was longer and the other shorter than our "day" (11.23.30). We determine "some agreed standard" of duration (11.24.31) and use this to measure the motions of various bodies. It is not that human beings discover a standard in nature but that they agree to use certain motions as signs (11.23.29, *in signis*, citing Gen. 1:14) to indicate durations that they have set for themselves.

Yet there seems to be a discrepancy between Augustine's statements that time existed before the creation of human beings and his contention that time does not exist outside the human soul. If time is a distension that takes place within the soul of a temporal creature, then there cannot have been any time before that creature came into existence. But Augustine clearly and repeatedly states that time was created with the first material creatures, before the appearance of humankind. Rather than searching out some arcane resolution to this issue, it seems altogether justifiable simply to distinguish between a strict and a broad definition of time. For Augustine the word "time" refers to a reality that includes three dimensions, namely the past, the present, and the future. Since there is nothing of which Augustine is more certain than the nonexistence of things that have passed away and things that have not yet come to be, time cannot, strictly speaking, exist outside the mind.[19]

The second part ends on a note of failure. Augustine declares that "even today I am ignorant of what time is" (11.25.32; see 11.26.33: "though I can measure [time], I do not know what I am measuring"). He has searched outside himself for a reality that would anchor his sense that time does in fact exist. Despite the apparent uselessness of this inquiry, Augustine still praises God for making him capable of measuring time (11.26.33). Moreover, his inability to find an objective standard leads him back to a consideration of his own soul, a turn that sets him on the right track.

Third Movement: Time as a Reflection of God's Image

Augustine begins the third part of his discussion of time by dispelling the illusion that we measure time as it passes. Using the example of a sounding voice, he shows that this cannot be true. We have to have marked the beginning of the sound and the voice has to end before we have a definite length of time, a duration, to measure: "Hence the sound of a voice which has not yet finished cannot be measured in such a way that anyone can say how long or short it is, nor can it be declared to be of the same length as something else, or half the length, or anything of the kind" (11.27.34). The duration of a completed sound is stored in memory as an impression (11.27.35). We commit this duration to memory by paying attention to when the sound begins, waiting attentively while it continues, and noting its conclusion. It is through constant attention to some transient thing that we form the impressions that we can then use to assign values to different movements (11.27.36) and thus determine that one duration is longer or shorter than another. Time is a product of our attention, the "vital energy" of the mind that transforms the expectation of the future into memory of the past, and, in so doing, enables us to measure and give meaning to ephemeral things (11.28.38). This is the process by which we give meaning to our lives and create history.

Since time is an activity of the human soul, it is more accurate to say that we contain time than that we are bound by time.[20] Augustine has already implied that reflection on the meaning of time leads to an acknowledgment of human dignity.[21] Although we, along with all temporal creatures, are ephemeral, we also transcend the process of birth and death through the ability to tell our own story. Each time someone makes a sentence, she or he gives shape to sounds that are in themselves meaningless. In a real way, every time we use language, therefore, we transcend our temporal condition.[22] Thus, incredible as it may seem,[23] the very fact of our ephemerality points toward our superiority over time's effects. The distension of the mind, by which we create narratives and discover meaning in our individual and collective lives, is evidence of the divine image in us.

Augustine uses the analogy of reciting a poem to show how the human mind is capable of stretching itself out to contain passing things and so to bring order to them. He concludes his discussion of time by extending the analogy to the creation of history:

> What is true of the poem as a whole is true equally of its individual stanzas and syllables. The same is true of the whole long performance, in which this poem may be a single item. The same thing happens in the entirety of a person's life, of which all his actions are parts; and the same in the entire sweep of human history, the parts of which are individual lives. (11.28.38)

Even as he moves toward this affirmation of human creativity, Augustine continually warns against the temptation of thinking that our minds are the standard of truth. Throughout his discussion of the measurement of time, Augustine himself has fallen prey to the illusion that we measure time as it passes by (11.16.21, 11.21.27, 11.26.33). This is the equivalent of measuring our lives by an external, material standard. We are constantly in danger of setting an absolute value on passing things, thereby forgetting the fact that there can be no comparison between the eternal value of our soul and any temporal good. But there is also the further danger of worshiping our own creativity, so that we substitute our own narratives, our own constructions of order, for the order set by God and revealed in the Scriptures.[24]

In reality, human control is severely limited by the fact that we do not know how our lives are going to end. Still less do we know the end to which human history is tending. Without knowledge of the completion of a sentence, we do not know what it means. The same is true of our lives. At the midpoint of his little treatise on time, Augustine inserts a prayer, in which he confesses his ignorance and prays through Christ for light to understand the "most intricate enigma" of how we measure time (11.22.28). This paragraph reminds the reader that he is seeking the meaning of the Scriptures, but it also serves as a reminder that God has revealed the meaning of time in the Scriptures. In other words, it is God who sets the true meaning of our lives, not ourselves. It is only through love, inspired by faith, that Augustine will grasp the truth of his life, and discriminate that truth from the false narratives he is prone to construct: "Give me what I love; for I love indeed, and this love you have given me" (11.22.28). At this point, his prayer for understanding the Scriptures, quoted verbatim from chapter two (11.2.3), becomes a prayer for self-knowledge, recalling the famous prayer of Book Ten: "Give what you command, and command whatever you will" (10.29.40).

In his meditation on time, Augustine has been speaking of himself as created in the divine image. As a temporal creature, he longs to be at rest with God: "I begin to shudder yet catch fire with longing: I shudder inasmuch as I am unlike him, yet I am afire with longing for him because some likeness there is" (11.9.11). But he has not left his history and the habits of sinfulness behind. His yearning for God coexists with revulsion at the ways in which he has deformed that image. As he gives the account of his search for the meaning of time, he exemplifies the temptation of concluding that we can make our own lives. Augustine wants to affirm both our created dignity and our fallen condition. The unquiet in our hearts is not a regrettable limitation, but the source of our creativity. This longing drives us to make meaning and reveals our transcendence. It is only when we decide to make our own creations the measure of reality, setting a standard other than God's as the source of truth, that we experience time as negative. This prideful and destructive self-assertion appears in its ugliness only when we compare it with the goodness that it might have been. Creating meaning apart from God is false dignity, and thus not real dignity at all.

THE MEANINGS OF DISTENSION

Many commentators have noted a significant change of tone as Augustine concludes Book Eleven. James Wetzel proposes that Augustine puns on the meanings of *distentus* as "stretched out" (from the verb *distendo*) and "kept apart" or "distracted" (from the verb *distineo*).[25] Whether Augustine had these different words in mind or not, he begins his conclusion on a wistful note: "But since your mercy is above many lives, behold, distension is my life; all the while, your right hand has sustained me in my Lord, the Son of Man, the mediator between you, the one, and us, the many, who are pulled in many ways by many things" (11.29.39, my translation). The mention of mercy recalls Augustine's need for forgiveness and healing, so that he "may be gathered in from dispersion" as his "years waste away amid groaning" (11.29.39; cf. Ps. 30:11). As he leaves behind the discussion of his status as a temporal creation, Augustine unites the persona of the perplexed inquirer into time with his status as one who has been redeemed but who awaits final redemption. In the incarnate Word, God's right hand "holds me fast, so that I may grasp that for which I have been grasped myself, and may be gathered in from dispersion in my stale days to pursue the One, forgetting the past and stretching undistracted not to future things doomed to pass away, but to my eternal goal" (11.29.39).

There are several meanings of distension at work here. The references to Christ as God's right hand and as the Son of Man refer us back to chapter two (11.2.4), where the theme was the utter difference between God's eternity and human temporality. This emphasis on the distance between divine and human existence moderates the potentially misleading accent on distension as indicating the divine image present in human creativity that was the theme throughout the preceding chapters. Augustine will reinforce this meaning in the final chapter, where he contrasts a person able to hold all history in his memory with God's stable and *un*distended knowledge. Second, Augustine acknowledges the effects of sin in his experience of time. He has allowed himself to get caught up in passing things to the point of forgetting God. His comment that he has "leapt down into the flux of time,"[26] where his thoughts are "torn to fragments by tempestuous changes" (11.29.39), refers to the tendency to lose oneself in passing things, a tendency he exemplified in his investigation into the nature of time. Third, Augustine acknowledges that he still reaches for "future things doomed to pass away." He needs constant help to avoid putting his own judgment before God's and replacing the order of things set by God with his own constructions of reality. Finally, and most importantly, Augustine presents a distension transformed by the fire of God's love into a river that flows into God. He concludes on a note of eschatological hope. Through the mediation of the incarnate Word, Augustine can learn to make all his activities acts of praise: "With no distracted mind but with focused attention I press on to the prize of our heavenly calling, to that place where I yearn to hear songs of praise and contemplate your delight, which neither comes, nor slips away" (11.29.39).

CONCLUSION: BETWEEN CREATION
AND CONSUMMATION

Augustine's *Confessions* begin with him setting out on a quest for repose and stability. It ends by looking forward to the peace and rest God has promised in Scripture, represented by the Sabbath rest of God after the six days of creation (13.35.50). Book Eleven explores the significance of human existence, in tension between God's gift of the way to the heavenly Jerusalem in the incarnation of the Word, and the full realization of that gift at the end of time.[27] From the eschatological tension of Christian life there flows the basic moral tension between affirming the goodness of creation, especially ourselves, and not forgetting that the source and goal of all goodness is God. In his yearning to attain that final rest, Augustine reminds himself and his readers both of their difference from God and of their intrinsic dignity. Because of its orientation to completion in God, there is a distinctively Christian temptation to denigrate temporal existence. Augustine's meditation on time counters this tendency by affirming that God created us with the ability to find stability and meaning in our lives by organizing sounds into words, words into sentences, and sentences into narratives. These narratives, in turn, give shape to our lives. On the other hand, Augustine is acutely aware of the human tendency to claim ultimacy for our own inventions.

It is in the text of Scripture that Augustine finds the means to use these tensions so that his life will flow into God. The very fact that the words of Scripture are both temporal and yet the perfect expression of God's eternal will shows that the incomparability between time and eternity does not imply any opposition between them. Progress in understanding the human words of Scripture is, at the same time, progress in understanding eternal truth and in attaining union with God. Further, Scripture points beyond itself to eternal rest in God. When Augustine ends his work with the word *aperietur*, "shall be opened" (13.38.53),[28] he is reflecting the prophetic nature of the scriptural narrative itself. In uniting his voice with the temporal expression of God's voice in Scripture, Augustine is given the grace to make his distended life a confession of praise that will arouse in himself and his readers a stronger love of God.

Chapter 12

Book Twelve:
Exegesis and *Confessio*[1]

Thomas F. Martin, O.S.A.

> *My heart is occupied about many things, Lord, when in the neediness of this my life the words of your Holy Scripture strike upon it.*
>
> (12.1.1)

INTRODUCTION

Perhaps only a very inattentive reader of the *Confessions* would not by now have been both struck and intrigued by what Augustine is doing with that book sacred to Christians called the Bible. The very first lines of the *Confessions* are not Augustine's, but Scripture's words: isn't this Augustine's story? And as the narrative unfolds, this intersection of Augustine's voice and the biblical voice progresses in such a way that it is not always evident where one ends and the other begins. The attentive reader would also have noted that at certain key moments of the narrative the Bible becomes a key player in the narrative. When Cicero's *Hortensius* enflames Augustine to long for wisdom, the first thing he does is to take up the Bible. Of course it is not a felicitous encounter since Augustine, the aspiring "word artist" or "rhetorician," finds the inelegant and unpolished Latin Bible he picks up no match for Cicero's Latin (3.5.9). The status of the Bible for Augustine only worsens as he turns to the Manichees, who try to teach him that the Christian Bible is hopelessly corrupted (5.11.21). Augustine remains "biblically conflicted" until Ambrose opens him to new possibilities through a more spiritual reading of the Bible (5.14.24).

At this point in the narrative of the *Confessions* the Bible begins anew to attract and entice Augustine, now no longer viewed as crude literature, but rather as alluring mystery. Unexpectedly, intimations of even a budding passionate relationship with the Bible bring Book Seven to a close: "So now I seized upon

(*arripui*) the sacred writings of your Spirit and especially the apostle Paul"
(7.21.27).[2] Augustine deliberately chooses a charged word (*arripui*) to describe
his experience. This is no ordinary or casual picking up of a book as he describes
his intense "new" encounter with the Scriptures. And the attentive reader may
have already noticed that throughout Book Seven, even before he finally "seizes"
Paul, Augustine has been carefully using Paul's own words from Romans to
describe his own interior struggles (see esp. 7.21.27). Thus, it ought to come as
no surprise to the reader when it is not only the Bible, but the words of Paul himself that provide the centerpiece for his conversion narrative. "Pick it up! Read!—
Tolle! Lege!" (8.12.30) leads him to Paul and Romans once again, and this time
only a few sentences from Scripture do for Augustine what he has not been
able to do for himself over the course of almost two decades: "For in that instant,
with the very ending of the sentence [of Paul], it was as though a light of utter
confidence shone in all my heart, and all the darkness of uncertainty vanished
away" (8.12.29).

For that conversion to come about Augustine had once more to "seize upon"
the Bible: he deliberately employs *arripui* again to describe his "grabbing Paul"
to read, a grabbing so intense as to change his life once and for all. Yet, this is not
an end to that intensity. In Book Nine we find him "inflamed" by the psalms, his
reading of them filling his heart with both delight and remorse (9.4.8ff.). All of
this has a startling outcome. Augustine's own instincts to "flee to the desert" at
the outset of this profoundly religious and biblical experience are challenged by
those same words of Scripture to undertake an unanticipated course: "You forbade me and comforted me, saying to me: 'Christ, therefore, died for all, so that
they also who live may no longer live for themselves but for him who died for
them' (2 Cor 5:15)" (10.43.70). The unexpected outcome is that Augustine is
now a preacher of the Word and a dispenser of God's sacrament (11.2.2), and it
is from this position that he has been writing his *Confessions*, doing so with the
very words and themes of the Bible, previously rejected but now become his very
own words and themes.

After eleven books of an indeed remarkable and highly original approach to
the Scriptures (more about this to come), an approach that has been operative
but not really explained, Augustine finally turns his explicit attention to the fact
that what he has been about from the very first words of the *Confessions* has been
a biblical project that he now must explain, justify, and, if necessary, defend. In
Book Twelve Augustine at last offers to us, his readers, the invitation to consider
his *Confessions* as a work of *exegesis*, a way of reading and interpreting the Bible.
And this biblical intention is by no means haphazard. I would like to explore both
what Augustine tells us about the nature of this biblical project that is the *Confessions*, its context and controversial scope, as well as its provocative implications
for anyone who, like Augustine, seeks to discover the Bible's *truth*. Book Twelve
offers us a reading key to the *Confessions* that turns out to be a reading key for
the Bible.[3]

CONTEXT AND CONTROVERSY

The early narrative of the *Confessions* does not hide the fact that Augustine had a history of personal difficulties with and concerns about the Bible. As a young man he found its prose no match for the eloquence and artistry of Cicero's elegant Latin. A first glance at the Bible did little to capture the interest or imagination of someone with a sense of culture or a liberal education; in fact, it seemed to repel such intellectuals. The *Confessions* can be viewed as Augustine's creative response to those difficulties and challenges. That same young man was taught by the Manichees that the text of the Bible had been hopelessly corrupted: it was not a reliable book. Throughout the *Confessions* Augustine challenges the biblical project of the Manichees. Finally, Augustine the Catholic bishop found himself in the midst of a divided Christianity in Roman North Africa, his own community vying with Donatist Christians for the claim to be the "true Church of Christ." Given these diverse scriptural challenges facing Augustine—from his culture, from the Manichees, from the Donatists, and, as will be seen, even from the ignorance of his own clergy and laity—I would like to propose that the *Confessions* (supported by a host of surrounding works) can be viewed as the cornerstone of a grand and challenging biblical project undertaken by Augustine. He is seeking to encourage, teach, and support a true reading of the Bible, one that will appropriately nourish and support the demands and challenges of Christian living, as well as answer the arguments and objections of opposing and alternative ways of reading the Bible. It is to the details of these challenges I now turn.

Classical Culture versus the Bible

Augustine was what we might call a professional word master, a rhetorician. In an ancient world that was still fundamentally *oral* in its approach to *words* (literature abounded and was highly regarded, but was expensive since all texts had to be handwritten, and most often *written* to be read aloud, to be *heard*), one's ability to be eloquent and persuasive opened the door to power, prestige, and wealth, everything necessary for a secure and leisurely retirement. The rhetorician flourished in both government and law courts and Augustine followed the governmental path, attaining to the post of Imperial Rhetor, where his words, eloquence, and persuasion served the interests of the imperial throne itself. As a young student rhetorician, inflamed by Cicero's eloquent persuasion to pursue immortal wisdom upon reading his *Hortensius* (4.4.7), Augustine turned to the Bible. He was terribly disappointed. It seemed "unworthy" when he compared it to the "worthiness" of Cicero (3.5.9).[4] Augustine could indeed have extended his critique even further, to say that the Bible he took up could not compare with Virgil, Seneca, and a host of other revered authors who provided Augustine's culture with its "classical canon," setting the standard for proper language and literary expression. From what Augustine tells us on a variety of occasions and from what scholars know about the ancient Latin Bible in Augustine's day, it was a rough and inelegant translation of the original Greek that would surely have been a stumbling block for the more cultured and literate.[5] In his culture there was a strong *aesthetic* assumption that truth and beauty (style) had an important reciprocal relationship. The poor style of the Latin Bible made it seem unconvincing and, as Augustine himself describes it, unworthy. One could surmise that the "unworthiness" ran in two directions. If it seemed "beneath the dignity" of the intelligentsia of Augustine's day, it would also seem to be "beneath the dignity" of God. How could such a clumsy and crude text claim to be "divine," "inspired," "words of salvation"?

It is precisely this background that makes all of the *Confessions* "biblically" remarkable and gives Book Twelve its own uniqueness. The Latin of Augustine's *Confessions*, a language far different from English and in those differences often virtually untranslatable, is polished, poetic prose (I have chosen deliberately to alliterate here as a sample of what Augustine does all through the work).[6] However, Augustine drenches his eloquent prose of the *Confessions* with biblical words and themes, weaving both together into a single, seamless narrative tapestry. (12.10.10 in the Latin is a stunning example of this artistry, where Augustine takes the tools and devices of eloquence such as dramatic statement, repetition, parallelism, assonance and alliteration, etc., with texts, words, and themes from the Scriptures and creates a rapturous declaration of faith and love.)

The "wonderful profundity of your eloquence" Augustine will ecstatically exclaim three times in one paragraph (12.13.16) in response to Genesis 1:1, "In the beginning God made heaven and earth." What has become of that initial clumsy and crude Bible tossed aside since it seemed to offer no promise of wisdom by its very inelegance? Augustine remarked in his initial comments about his "Ciceronian" rejection of the Bible that he was not yet humble enough to accept its inelegant prose (he describes himself as "swollen with pride" so that he could not, we might say, "squeeze" into the Bible's simple, "small" language). Throughout the *Confessions* and in Book Twelve in particular, that narrow door of simplicity has opened out into a vast field of biblical eloquence and artistry. This is not in any way to lose sight of Augustine's constant emphasis on humility and simplicity as the necessary lens for viewing those very words of Scripture that he is exploring and explaining. Yet for the reader of Augustine's day, there could be no mistaking what an elegant and eloquent text this biblical tapestry of Augustine's *Confessions* is. This very effort will not be without exegetical implications, something to be returned to later. At this point it is simply to be noted that to a cultured reader of Augustine's day, the *Confessions* offer a vehicle for encountering the Christian Scriptures, showcasing the "wonderful profundity of God's eloquence" called the Bible.

The Manichees

If "Bible and culture" is one issue implicitly yet unmistakably present in the narrative of the *Confessions*, an even more obvious issue concerns Augustine and the

Manichees, a religious movement that held Augustine for a decade or so and whose origins were Persian and doctrine dualistic.[7] Once again the question of the Bible is at the heart of Augustine's ongoing polemic against the Manichees that permeates the *Confessions'* narrative from beginning to end, but finds exegetical focus in Book Twelve. The question "What did Moses mean?" echoes all throughout Book Twelve. It was a central question for the Manichees, as Augustine recounts how he turned to them following upon his disappointing reading of an inelegant Bible. Augustine notes how it was precisely their interpretation of the books of Moses (Augustine, along with all his contemporaries, but unlike contemporary biblical scholars, believed Moses to be the real author of the Pentateuch, the first five books of the Hebrew Bible) that led him to reject the Old Testament as a whole. Their interpretation was intended to "scandalize," as they accused the ancient Hebrew patriarchs of immorality and unholiness (see 3.7.12). It is important to keep in mind that the Manichees were part of a larger movement on the fringes of ancient Christianity that preached a wholesale rejection of the Jewish Scriptures as the product and story of a God other than "the God of Jesus Christ." Their preaching especially highlighted what they considered to be the dissonance between Old and New Testament morality, that the former permitted behaviors that the latter condemns. If it was the same God of both Testaments, that God would have to be "unstable and changeable" (ibid.) and thus "not God." Augustine laments his credulousness and his inability to see through their biblical critique that resulted in his dismissal of the Old Testament.

He also addresses them directly in Book Nine as he lashes out against their disdain for the Psalms, a particular consequence of their general rejection of all the Old Testament books. It is not at all incidental or casual that more than any other scriptural text, the book of Psalms is the most quoted biblical text in the *Confessions*. That very practice is a constant reminder to Augustine and to his audience that these "songs of faithfulness and devotion" (9.4.8) were, for the Manichees, songs of faithlessness and impiety, what he calls the Manichean "insanity." "My heart is occupied about many things, Lord, when in the neediness of this my life the words of your Holy Scripture strike upon it" (12.1.1). As gentle and seemingly "casual" as these opening words of Book Twelve are, they fly in the face of the Manichees and are a stinging denial of their biblical posture. But it was not only the Psalms that were the target of their rejection, they especially dismissed the Genesis creation narrative, or perhaps better, reinterpreted it to identify materiality with evil, thereby distorting any true appreciation of "the image of God" (Gen. 1:27) within us (3.7.12). It is no surprise then that the creation story takes on such importance in the final books of the *Confessions*, as Augustine demonstrates various possibilities for a true understanding of the Genesis accounts of creation: "You created heaven and earth" echoes throughout Book Twelve, the exact opposite of Manichean insistence that "heaven and earth" are unfortunate by-products of a great cosmic struggle between good and evil, resulting in "God's spiritual particles" being entrapped in the evilness of material reality (3.10.18). Genesis is thus no mere casual choice by Augustine:

his very act of interpretation is part of a "dislodging process" that he has been engaged in since the time of his conversion, wresting this text away from the vise grip of Manichean exegesis. The Manichees are right, perhaps Augustine would say, in seeing that this is a difficult text. But what they fail to grasp is that this is not a sign of "untruth" but a call to pursue its deeper "truth." This is why an important New Testament text for Augustine appears in the opening lines of Book Twelve:

> "If God is for us, who can be against us" (Rom 8:31). "Ask and you will receive; seek and you will find; knock and it will be opened for you. For everyone who asks, receives; and in seeking, finds; and by knocking, has it opened" (Matt 7:7). These are your promises, and who fears to be deceived when Truth so promises? (12.1.1)

The text of Matthew 7:7–8 both opens and closes the *Confessions* (1.1.1 and 13.38.53),[8] and here becomes the charter for what Augustine has been doing scripturally throughout the *Confessions*, and what he will do even more explicitly in Book Twelve.[9] The Manichees are guilty of the same "arrogance" that infected a young and foolish Augustine when he first took up the Scriptures in response to Cicero's *Hortensius* and its call to pursue wisdom. Just as Augustine tried to "bend" the Scriptures to his pride rather than allow the Scriptures to bend him to their humility (it is this "bending language" that Augustine employs in 3.5.9), so too the Manichees bend and twist the Scriptures, in particular Genesis and the story of the "creation of heaven and earth." The tasks of *asking*, *seeking*, and *knocking* of Matthew 7:7–8 are precisely a humble bending to the truth and power of the Scriptures, knowing that the multiplicity of human words can never match the "wonderful profundity of the divine word." "For seeking is more long-winded than finding, and longer still is asking than obtaining, and more laborious for the hands is knocking than receiving" (12.1.1). Augustine is insisting here that it is only a humble seeking, asking, and knocking that at last open Scripture's *truth* to anyone seriously desiring to embrace it.

However, Augustine insists, the Manichees were not content to dismiss the Old Testament. They likewise considered the New Testament to be infected with Judaizing corruptions (5.11.21). Once again, Augustine's early *Confessions* narrative shows how he succumbed to such arguments, acknowledging that he had to take their word for it since they produced "no uncorrupted scriptures" (ibid.). The very tapestry of scriptural texts that permeate the entire narrative where Old Testament verses and allusions are inextricably intertwined with New Testament verses and allusions becomes an operative demonstration of the unity between the Old and the New Testaments and the vitality of their interrelationship. Book Twelve's exploration of the opening words of Genesis is done by way of a deluge of New Testament citations, and once again the careful reader knows that this is not simply rhetorical amplification or incidental ornamentation. What is being demonstrated is the unity of the Bible, the very antithesis of a Manichean reading of the Bible.

To the uninformed or perhaps inattentive reader of Augustine's *Confessions* it may almost seem that the abundance of Scripture gets in the way of the "real" narrative. So often has the work been depicted as "autobiographical" that a "careless" reader might consider the constant recourse to Scripture to interfere with the autobiography. Hopefully by this point it is clear that there is more here than meets the eye. While the *Confessions* are "autobiographical," they are certainly not "autobiography," and that distinction becomes critical regarding what exactly Augustine is about in this unique work. My contention is that Book Twelve provides a reading key to the *Confessions* precisely because it is where Augustine formally addresses "exegesis," that all along he has been "interpreting the Bible" and that this is, in the long term, even more important than the "autobiographical" elements of the work. I've further proposed that this biblical concern is multifaceted. Augustine is showing, but most often in a very subtle and indirect way, that the Christian literature that is the Bible is as eloquent and certainly more profound than anything Cicero has to offer. Augustine is demonstrating to the intellectuals and cultured of his own day and age that to turn to Christianity does not demean the intellectual or the artful, though the way of humility alone provides access to this biblical aesthetic. Further (and Augustine is rarely one to have a "single story line"), he is likewise deconstructing Manichean biblical arguments, most often quite explicitly as we have seen, but likewise by way of implication: the very Old Testament they discredit and reject provides the support structure for the textual narrative of the *Confessions*. Yet, as I have already briefly indicated, Augustine's biblical concerns are not confined to "the Pagans" or "the Manichees." There is yet another group that Augustine is confronting right within this deeply scriptural narrative of the *Confessions*, perhaps in a more discreet way, but nonetheless, with a much deeper personal stake involved.

The Donatists

At the time of his writing of the *Confessions* the main Christian opponents to Augustine's "Catholic"[10] church were the Donatists, fellow African Christians who claimed to be the only true Christians, the only true church.[11] The division into "Catholic" and "Donatist" churches was a direct result of the persecutions under the emperor Diocletian that lasted from 305 to 311. Under the threat of imprisonment and torture, the imperial government demanded that Christians hand over their books (thus "outsiders" knew how important the Bible was for the Christians). Those who succumbed to this edict and its threats became a serious problem for the Christian community after the persecution ceased. What should they do with these "traitors"? Could they be forgiven? Were they disqualified from office if they were clerics? Did such clerics render the sacraments they administered invalid? The answer to these and other questions, both sides agreed, was to be found in the Scriptures, which, however, could be read in a variety of different ways: the church is a pure community (see Eph. 5:27), insisted the Donatists; the church is a "mixed" community of wheat and weeds (Matt.

13:24–30), insisted the Catholic Augustine. While it is not possible here to explore many of the complex details of this Catholic/Donatist conflict, what is important to note regarding the *Confessions* is that these disputes were profoundly biblical in their content. This ongoing scriptural debate with the Donatists provides another key for understanding the profoundly biblical texture of the narrative of the *Confessions*, and it does so in a variety of ways. One reason for the ascendancy of Donatism in North Africa was an ill-equipped clergy: the Catholic clergy did not know their Bible. A direct result was an ill-informed laity: the Catholic laity did not know their Bible. Augustine is laying out a biblical spirituality that has profound implications for both the clergy and the laity of his Catholic church.

When Augustine returned to his homeland after conversion and baptism, the Catholic Christians were in a minority (and all that will dramatically change during the almost four decades of Augustine's episcopacy). The tensions between the two groups verged on what might be called a religious civil war, leading even to acts of violence and murder. The issues dividing these two communities were complex, and continue to be hotly debated.[12] For our purposes, it is most important to repeat that "interpretation of the Bible" was a central component of their theological debates with one another.[13] As noted above, the roots of the conflict go back to accusations concerning *traditores* (traitors),[14] Christians who handed over the Scriptures to the Roman officials during persecution. The very act of such an unholy treason demonstrated that the traitor never was "holy," was always "without the Holy Spirit," and so could not even be considered "baptized," let alone a leader of the community. There were exegetical implications here.

Donatist charges that the Catholic Christian community was "without the Holy Spirit" had the inescapable consequence of proving that they were incapable of truly interpreting the Scriptures.[15] In Augustine's case the charges went even further. They spread rumors that he was not even a Christian but remained a crypto-Manichee, and we have already seen what the scriptural implications of that accusation would mean. Thus Donatist accusations had both a public and personal dimension for Augustine, challenging both the general authenticity of Catholic practice, as well as the specific integrity of Augustine's own practice. Through the narrative of the *Confessions* Augustine has already made clear his past sins (he has nothing to hide and has publicly renounced his past errors). He has further informed his readers that his public instruction (in the Scriptures) as well as his Easter 387 baptism were done at the hands of none other than Ambrose of Milan. In fact it was Ambrose who first opened the Scriptures to him. This is the warrant behind the present Augustine, Catholic bishop, whose primary task is to interpret the Scriptures and administer the sacraments (11.2.2), and it is that first responsibility that he is legitimating in this precise act of composing the *Confessions*. His very "success" in reaching the hearts of his readers serves as a veritable "proof" that the Holy Spirit is indeed present with Augustine, and in that very act he is dismantling Donatist accusations against him and his church.

Thus, O God my helper, You had broken my chains . . . and despite all the ebb and flow of my thinking did not let me be carried away from the faith by which I believed You existed, and that Your substance is unchangeable and that You care for and judge us, and that in Christ Your Son, our Lord, and in the Holy Scriptures which the authority of Your Catholic Church commends, You had established the way to that life. (7.7.1)

That is why the Holy Spirit, the teacher of Your servant . . . (12.9.9)

I consider all these things as far as You give me the power, O my God, as far as You incite me to knock and open to my knocking. (12.12.15)

I wish to speak with these [critics of me] before You, my God, since within, in my mind, Your Truth does not remain silent. (12.15.23)

It is important to note the power of these affirmations regarding Augustine's actual practice of interpreting the Scriptures. These may be called "licensing statements," "showing one's credentials." They affirm Augustine's qualifications to interpret the Scriptures.

First of all, he is doing this as a "Catholic bishop," drawing upon and dwelling in "the authority of God's Catholic Church." It is exactly this authority that is intimately linked with "the authority of the Holy Scriptures." He will say elsewhere in speaking against the Manichees that "Indeed I would not have believed the gospel unless I had been persuaded by the authority of the Catholic Church."[16] Augustine's "Catholic" affirmations, however, ought not be seen as only anti-Manichean. They likewise serve as ongoing reproach directed against the Donatists and, as a result, go to the heart of the very "exegetical activity" under way in the *Confessions*. It is precisely this Catholic authority that empowers and even demands of its Catholic bishops that they undertake the task of explaining the Scriptures. While acknowledging that it is indeed "rather discreet but nonetheless persistent,"[17] if one is aware of the acute nature of the Donatist conflict confronting Augustine as a *Catholic* bishop, along with more stinging personal attacks against Augustine precisely at the time of the writing of the *Confessions*, then one should see Augustine's striking personal claims for "inspiration" ("the Holy Spirit, the teacher of Your servant," 12.9.9) as refutation of Donatist accusations and slander. But there are further biblical implications to the Donatist critique.

Reforming Catholics

It is precisely because of the Donatist controversy that the most important audience Augustine is addressing is his own Catholic Christian community. Based upon their interpretation of certain biblical texts, Donatists charged Catholic Christians with spiritual mediocrity and toleration of sinners. This accusation was intended to disqualify the Catholic Church from any claim to spiritual authority. I have already referred to a Donatist campaign directed against Augustine himself (that he was, for example, a crypto-Manichee). These allegations were not only meant for Augustine, but were also intended to fall back upon his own Catholic community: a "compromised" Catholic bishop also meant a "compromised" Catholic community. It is thus not a casual comment when Augustine insists that neither he nor his community has arrived at perfection of holiness: "my dispersion and deformity" is how he describes even his present "episcopal" condition (12.16.23). That is not meant to encourage imperfection, but simply to remind his audience, Catholic and Donatist (and himself), that such perfection awaits eternity. He takes it even a step further, insisting that God alone should be the judge in matters of the heart: "You, our God, be the Judge" (ibid.).

Yet these reminders of the "unfinished" holiness that marks all Christians are complemented by a scriptural technique and artistry intended to awaken his own Catholic people from spiritual mediocrity to renewed faith and fervor. He reminds us in his late-in-life *Retractationes* that the *Confessions* were written to arouse (*excitare* is the term he uses in Latin) intellect and affect.[18] But to what end? Toward God, that is, conversion, renewed faith, holiness of life. Augustine is writing his *Confessions* to "excite" his audience to turn anew and ever more passionately to God, and Scripture is at the heart of this effort at "spiritual arousal." Thus Augustine insists upon the "unfinished" nature of Christian holiness, on the need to not judge another's heart, on the fact that the source of his Catholic community's integrity is not in Bishop Augustine, but in God, and this is paralleled by an equal insistence on the need for dedication, faithfulness, commitment, passionate striving for union with God. Augustine combines biblical text and rhetorical artistry to weave together both affirmations: tolerance *and* fervor, religious patience *and* religious passion. He wants his Catholic community to know that the Donatists are wrong in their expectations of an "already perfect" church, but he equally wants his Catholic community to be ardent in their own living of the Christian life. His own passionate prayer in 12.10.10 that weaves Scripture and rhetorical intensity delicately holds together these arguments:

> O Truth (John 14:6), Light of my heart (John 8:12), speak to me, not my own darkness (Gen 1:2)! I tumbled down into that darkness and fell into oblivion, Yet from there, even from there, I loved you. I lost my way (Ps 118:179),[19] but remembered you (John 2:8). I heard your voice calling after me to return (Ezek 3:12), but I scarcely heard you because of the tumult of restless things. But now, behold, I am returning, burning and longing, to your fountain (Ps 41:1). Let no one get in my way: at this fountain may I drink, at this fountain may I live. Let me not be my own life: I lived evilly from myself, I was death for myself: in you I am revived (Lk 15:24). Speak to me, converse with me. I have believed in your books, and their words are profoundly mysterious (2 Cor 12:4).

This prayer is loaded with scriptural words and themes and is rhetorically crafted with emotion and intensity. Augustine confesses both his past sin and his present love. It ends on an explicitly biblical note: the need to believe in "God's books," the Bible, yet with an insistence upon the hiddenness of these same biblical words. What Augustine is offering here is "the prayer of an exegete," the prayer of one who seeks Scripture's hidden meaning, not for the sake of his life alone, but for the sake of those who find themselves invited into the discourse of this prayer, so that they might make it their own. In this thoroughly scriptural prayer, Augustine makes clear to his readers that he will not be life nor truth for them. God alone can fulfill that need. But one must keep in mind what all this means for Augustine's Catholic Christian community. They are being called to respond to Donatist criticism by their own witness to holiness and conversion; they are being reassured and even emboldened by their bishop's "scriptural performance"; they themselves are learning the Scriptures and discovering how they apply to their journey and not just Augustine's: "Pay heed, O excellent Judge, O God, Truth itself, pay heed . . . for I speak in your presence and in the presence of my brothers and sisters" (12.25.35). Finally, and especially (but in a clearly "anti-Donatist" way), they are being reminded that their holiness does not depend upon Augustine, but upon their God, their Truth, the only one who can really judge.

In that sense, the choice and importance of the book of Genesis in this narrative is not incidental.

> Let me not waver from my course before you have gathered all that I am, my whole disintegrated and deformed self, into that dearly loved mother's peace, where are lodged the first-fruits of my spirit and whence I draw my present certainty, that so you may reshape me to new form, new firmness, for eternity, O my God, my mercy. (12.16.23, Boulding)

Augustine's taking up of the book of Genesis now and his exploration of the meaning(s) of the creation story therein provide a deliberate complement to the narrative of Augustine's own "Genesis" that has been under way since the very first lines of the *Confessions*: God has been making Augustine anew. And one might suggest that Augustine deeply desires a similar "Genesis" for his own Catholic community. They are being confirmed in their own faith in the very unfolding of a "Catholic meaning" of the Scriptures. Further, they are being aroused and awakened to deeper conversion, to greater faith, to steadfastness and fidelity. Those very texts of Scripture that taught Augustine, that brought him to conversion, that consoled him while awaiting baptism, that continue to enlighten his present journey, those same texts are intended to be received by Augustine's readers in the same way. And yet Augustine will never allow his "Catholic audience" to forget that it is not Augustine who matters here, it is not even Augustine who instructs here. Rather, the One who teaches Augustine will also teach those to whom he speaks: "O Truth, Light of my heart, speak to me, not my own darkness" (12.10.10). Augustine reminds both himself and his audience that it is the light of God's Word and not the bishop of Hippo who will illumine this and every other Christian community.

A Biblical Campaign

The *Confessions* can thus be rightly understood as the cornerstone of what I would like to call a biblical campaign on the part of Augustine, in league with his fellow Catholic bishops,[20] to reinvigorate the Catholic community in Roman Africa, to counter Donatist accusations that seek to undermine the very integrity of "Catholic" claims, to woo reluctant pagans still leery of a populist and accordingly "uncultured" Christianity, and finally to confront the continuing challenge of Manicheism that still seems to offer itself as an attractive alternative to both Donatist and Catholic alike.[21]

In this light it is important to realize that the *Confessions* do not stand alone. They are surrounded by works written immediately before, concurrently, and after that show an Augustine intensely interested in biblical questions from a variety of diverse perspectives. The *Confessions* are preceded by the beginning of an almost lifelong project of a commentary on all 150 of the Psalms; by an intense study of St. Paul, the product of which will be what many commentators call a veritable conversion to a new understanding of the power and mystery of grace;[22] and a continuing series of anti-Manichean treatises, all of which are fundamentally exegetical in character. Perhaps most significantly, he begins the writing of *Christian Instruction*, a groundbreaking work on the interpretation of Scripture, a work to which we will return shortly.[23] Concurrent with the extended writing of the *Confessions*,[24] Augustine pens two works on the Gospels, a treatise on monastic labors that is a veritable Pauline commentary, a continuing barrage of anti-Manichean works with the ongoing concern to dismantle their ridiculing rejection of the Old Testament, and a work on religious formation that places the Scriptures at the heart of Christian instruction.[25] Immediately after he finishes the *Confessions*, he continues the same activity, and most importantly attempts for a third time to undertake a commentary on Genesis, a project that will extend for the next fifteen years or so.[26] All the while, Augustine the bishop has been preaching on a regular basis, both in his home see of Hippo Regius, on the road throughout his Roman province, and in the capital, Carthage, where he must travel frequently for bishops' meetings and other church matters that require his attention and services.[27] Thus the *Confessions* do not stand alone, but certainly stand out as the most original and most personal work in this array of biblical and exegetical writings. More than any of these other texts, the *Confessions* reveal the inner workings of Augustine the biblical scholar, teacher of Scripture, and preacher of the Word. We find out how the Scriptures led him to conversion; how they continue to call and nourish, challenge and encourage him daily; how they remain simultaneously inviting and mysterious, provoking Augustine's own asking, seeking, and knocking.

This personal testimony is strikingly complemented by his more theoretical biblical work *Christian Instruction*, which virtually coincides with the writing of the *Confessions*. There Augustine proposes to lay out "rules for dealing with the scriptures,"[28] and proceeds by offering guidelines and principles for those who wish to understand and teach the Scriptures. Yet the two works shed light on one another. Someone like Augustine who has the responsibility of interpreting and preaching the Scriptures must not approach this task in an arbitrary way: *Christian Instruction* responds precisely to this demand. Yet someone who has the responsibility of interpreting and preaching the Scriptures must be guided by the Holy Spirit, must be in communion with the church catholic, and must be aware that he or she is a sinner in need always of God's mercy: the *Confessions* respond precisely and provocatively to this demand. There is not only a need for "rules" to interpret the Scriptures, there is always the question of the one who does the interpreting. And it is time to turn to this dimension.

CONFESSIO AND EXEGESIS IN THE *CONFESSIONS*

From the first lines of the *Confessions*, Augustine has been interpreting the Scriptures in an original and provocative way. Up until this point in ancient Christianity, no previous author has allowed the text of Scripture to intersect so publicly and yet so personally with his or her own life in such a dramatic and direct way. Thus at every point of this intersection we have been learning about Augustine, but even more importantly we have been learning the Scriptures, especially since the Scriptures themselves provide the very lens through which Augustine comes to know himself, and through which we are coming to know Augustine. He is showing "in practice" what it takes to interpret the Scriptures. And in a provocative way he is demonstrating what it means to be an interpreter of the Scriptures. The importance of Augustine the exegete must not be underestimated. There is no doubt that Augustine is "showcasing" himself in the *Confessions*, but from what we know of his adversaries, they had already taken the first steps to showcase Augustine in the worst possible light (this former Manichee, fornicator, and who knows what!). Augustine is fighting for his own reputation (and that of the community whose bishop he is).

But despite the persistent temptation to place Augustine at the center of this narrative, he is always being "pushed aside," overshadowed, even drowned out by his dialogue partner. For after all, from the outset this work has been a conversation, a discussion, sometimes even a debate or argument, but always a unique kind of dialogue between Augustine and God. And how does God speak to human beings, how does Divine Word come to human ears, how can Divine Word fit into the fragile vehicle of human words? For Augustine, there is no doubt about the answer. The Word of God has already taken the initiative and addressed humanity in the Word of God, Son of God, coeternal with the Father (12.20.29), and the Word of God, the Holy Scriptures (12.1.1).[29] Certainly God's Word has been at the center of this narrative, and this divine address to humanity is fraught with mystery, wonder, and even dismay: "the wonderful profundity of your word" (*o mira profunditas*, 12.14.17). Book Twelve brings to the forefront this mystery, wonder, and dismay, laying out the demands and challenges involved in his and any human engagement with this Divine Word. Unlike some of his works mentioned above, in particular *Christian Instruction*, the *Confessions* do not give us precepts for interpreting the Scriptures, but show us exegesis in action, an exegete in action, impelled by underlying principles and values that one must bring to the task of interpretation. Throughout the narrative, Augustine himself struggles to embody these principles. I would like to highlight four in particular, since they suggest Augustine's primary framework for any and all exegetical activity (his own included). These four principles guide Augustine's reading of Scripture, and I would like to suggest that he proposes them as a perennial guide for anyone who seeks to take up the Scriptures responsibly and correctly.

Incommensurability

> Behold, O Lord, my God, how much we have written, how much, I pray you, about so few words. Where will we find the strength, where the time to consider all your books in such a way as this? (12.32.43)

In so many ways, the whole of Book Twelve has been a profoundly rich and complex exploration of only two words: heaven and earth (12.17.25). As Augustine concludes the book, he makes explicit for one final time an awareness that has echoed throughout, namely the disproportionality, the gap, the profound abyss that separates the simplicity and power of the Divine Word from the multiplicity and fragility of human words. If there is one thing Augustine insists upon again and again in this book, it is this "incommensurability" that both prompts the search for the meaning and truths of "the words of Your Book" (12.23.31) and precludes every mistaken claim to have ever "captured" that meaning and truth once and for all.

> How amazing is the profundity of your words. We are confronted with a superficial meaning that offers easy access to the unlettered; yet how amazing their profundity, O my God, how amazingly deep they are. To look into that depth makes me shudder, but it is the shudder of awe, the trembling of love. I regard with intense hatred all those who attack the scriptures; if only you would slay them with your double edged sword, that they might be enemies no longer. How dearly would I love them to be slain in that respect, that they might live to you. (12.14.17)

These words ought to disturb us, and I would argue they were deliberately intended to provoke. Augustine wants his readers at this point to shout "stop," forcing them to return more carefully to his words in order to see whether he or she has heard correctly. What the reader discovers is that this is yet another densely constructed "scriptural" assertion, held together by diverse biblical texts: the "hatred" declaration is, in fact, the psalmist speaking (Ps. 138:21–22); the two-edged sword that slays is not in Augustine's hand, but in God's (Ps. 149:6); and the death penalty inflicted is, in reality, life bestowed. Thus hatred here is really love, the slaying is really life-giving, and the seeming violence is, in fact, restoration. Augustine is powerfully reminding his readers that in this intersection of Divine Word and human words, our own world of meaning and words is turned upside down. The interpreter of Scripture can never claim to have cornered or domesticated God's word, it even seems to do us violence, but this is divine violence that restores us to life! This, I would propose, is Augustine's own way of insisting upon incommensurability, the painful abyss between Divine Word and human words. The interpreter of the Scriptures must never lose sight of the incommensurability: there will never be a perfect fit. It is precisely this "gap" that keeps the interpreter of Scripture humble yet driven, never claiming to have arrived at Scripture's final truth, yet never ceasing passionately to search for even a fleeting glimpse of it.

The Dialogue

One of the most intriguing and provocative elements in the narrative of the *Confessions* is its dialogical character. Augustine is directly speaking to and conversing with God. God is directly speaking to and conversing with Augustine. The divine part of this dialogue takes the form of Scripture.

> Loud and clear have you spoken to me already, in my inward ear, O Lord, telling me that you are eternal, and "to you alone immortality belongs" [see 1 Tim. 6:16]. . . . Loud and clear have you spoken to me once more in my inward ear, to tell me that no creature is coeternal with you, not even a created being whose entire pleasure is in you alone. (12.11.11–11.12)

Augustine boldly and passionately addresses God with praise, with questions, with affirmations, with protestations of love, with petitions for mercy and grace. And just as boldly and passionately God addresses Augustine: "loud and clear have you spoken to me." Augustine has taken up one of the mainstays of ancient pedagogy and of ancient friendship and incorporated it into his *Confessions'* narrative as its framework: the discipline of the dialogue.[30]

Anyone familiar with ancient literary and philosophical culture is well aware of the importance of the dialogue as an essential vehicle for the pursuit and communication of truth. It reminds us that the ancient world was, despite its great literature, fundamentally an oral world, where the spoken word had prominence of place. In a modern world where words are cheap and "chatting" predominates, it is perhaps difficult to appreciate the importance and seriousness of "the dialogue" for the ancients. The dialogue placed great demands upon its participants: to listen attentively, to remember carefully, to respond thoughtfully. This is certainly why it was so important as an ancient pedagogical method and practice. The challenge of the student engaged in a dialogue with his or her teacher was to hold the course of the conversation. To take the mind's eye off that course was to lose the road, ending up, one might say, in the ditch of falsehood.

All of Augustine's earliest works take the shape of formal dialogues,[31] and while the dialogical nature of the *Confessions* would have been immediately recognized by the ancients, the non-Christian would perhaps have been amazed if not dismayed that the "dialogue" partner here is none other than God. God addresses Augustine through scriptural words; Augustine hears and responds through his own words. The bishop of Hippo here takes up a revered ancient pedagogical practice and reshapes it into a framework and tool at the service of exegesis. One begins to understand the biblical word to the extent that one truly listens "from the heart" as God speaks: "My heart is occupied about many things, Lord, when in the neediness of this my life the words of your Holy Scripture strike upon it" (12.1.1). The words that begin this book and with which I began this essay are vivid reminders that Augustine is deeply aware of the wonder and demands of this dialogue: "This is what I'm thinking now, as I hear your scripture speaking" (12.13.16); "And now will you say these things are false which Truth speaks loudly into my interior ear" (12.15.18); "Speak truly within my heart, for only you speak in such a way" (12.16.23). The references could be multiplied in abundance as Augustine leaves no doubt regarding the power and impact of this dialogue taking place within his own heart. And yet he is speaking aloud and we, his listeners, cannot help but overhear. Augustine has enticed us into his dialogue, wanting us, as it were, to eavesdrop, only to find ourselves actual partners in this serious conversation. And once invited in, we begin to discover the truth that is at stake in this volley and exchange of words. Further, there are those others who are being, perhaps rather reluctantly, dragged into this dialogue. Augustine calls them his *contradictores* (12.15.22); the Latin hardly needs translation.[32] Those who contradict him, those who accuse him of being mistaken, are chidingly invited to become part of this disciplined and demanding exchange: "In your presence, O my God, I want to discuss some matters with those who acknowledge as true what your Truth never ceases to tell me within my own mind" (12.16.23). Augustine asks God's permission to turn away for a moment and to engage in a dialogue with his "opponents," but with both parties, Augustine and his *contradictores*, well aware that as they speak God listens. There is no room for petty or small talk here, nor is there room for contention. "Having heard and weighed all these things I have no wish to contend in words. All that will do is ruin those who are listening [see 2 Tim 2:14]" (12.18.27). Augustine does not want this to be an acrimonious debate with the potential to scandalize the guests he has invited into this dialogue, ourselves included. What is or ought to be clear is how *dialogue* both provides the context for understanding God's word and offers in its discipline the very means to be able to do so. To understand the Scriptures, Augustine has been saying, one must enter into a serious conversation with God; to understand the Scriptures one must even be willing to dialogue with one's *contradictores*.

Truth

Augustine addresses God throughout the *Confessions* using a rich array of biblical titles and names. In Book Twelve God is above all Truth, from opening to final lines: "these are your promises; and who need fear to be deceived by the promises of Truth himself?" (12.1.1); "may I at least say what your Truth wills to reveal to me through the words of Moses, since it was your Truth who communicated to him also whatever he willed" (12.32.43). Throughout this book the words *truth*, *truthful*, and *true* echo incessantly, one reason why it has captured the attention of many a modern philosopher fascinated and intrigued by Augustine's study of truth and meaning here. But it is not an abstract or poetical Truth that Augustine evokes when his God is addressed as Truth. It is the "God of meaning," and yes, "the meaning of God" that Augustine is about when he takes up and seeks to understand the Scriptures. From the outset of the *Confessions* "Truth" has been Augustine's quest, supported and nuanced by a further series of "truth"-related images and themes—"light and knowledge," "darkness and lies," just to name two. Augustine desperately wants to know his Creator and his Beloved, he abhors the notion of being deceived, and he is profoundly aware that his encounter with the God who is Truth will also show Augustine to himself. Perhaps this has no more powerful statement than Augustine's comments after his garden crisis and his dramatic encounter with Paul speaking to him in Romans 13:13–14. "I had no wish to read further, nor was there need. No sooner had I reached the end of the verse than the light of certainty flooded my heart and all dark shades of doubt fled away" (8.12.29). The Scriptures are for Augustine the place of encounter with Truth, both divine and personal, which is why his conversion prompts Augustine to abandon what he calls the "Chair of Lying"[33] and retire from public life. In his own quest for Truth, Augustine accuses himself of having become a *professional liar*, another indication of the intensity of heart Augustine brings to his searching for truth. But if Augustine is unwilling to be satisfied with anything less than the Truth, Book Twelve is also a striking reminder that Truth bears no domestication.

Reminiscent of modern quests today for the historical Jesus that dominate certain fields of biblical studies, Augustine engages in a quest for "the historical Moses" as a strikingly original vehicle for pondering the mystery of Truth. "Let no one henceforth try to pick a quarrel with me by telling me, 'Moses did not mean what you say; he meant what I say'" (12.25.34). From the outset of Book Twelve, Augustine has been exploring the meaning of the opening words of the book of Genesis, "Moses' book": "God made heaven and earth." Augustine has no doubts but that God, Truth, wants him to seek, ask, and knock in order to come to the correct knowledge and understanding and meaning of these words. His exploration of Genesis offers a test case for how he or we will come to any and all scriptural truth, so that what he concludes regarding Genesis ought to be understood as applying to all scriptural words.

Augustine has some unique rhetorical methods for emphasizing this truth. Every sentence in chapter nineteen of Book Twelve begins with the same word: true (*verum*). He uses it ten times in the course of nine sentences, a literary assertion of what is more than simply a literary truth, as he affirms ten truths about what it means to say that "God made heaven and earth." God who is Truth gives humanity a true word, and so the task of the reader of that word is to discover its truth, a daunting task since this truth reflects the greatness and eternity of God. So in chapter twenty that follows, this truth explodes into a pluriformity and multiplicity of meanings and understandings. Each interpreter may choose one meaning or one understanding, but these are always connected and interconnected, linked and bonded together by and with the One Truth: "from all of these true things, concerning which they have no doubt, those to whom you give to see those things by their interior eye, and who unswervingly believe that Moses, your servant, spoke them in the spirit of truth" (12.20.29). Surprisingly, this passion for truth does not limit or close, but opens and frees. The Truth that is God breaks out into a lush and lavish abundance of truths, a surplus of meaning,[34] that creates a Communion of Truth, a Community of Truth, where what is true cannot be claimed as private property or personal possession: If they love their understanding because it is true, it already has become theirs and mine, since truth is in common for all lovers of truth . . . (12.25.34).

From Augustine's own pursuit of the truth of God's Scriptures, to Augustine's fellow and even rival pursuers of the truth of God's Scriptures, neither one is engaged in a private or possessive truth quest. Intensity and commitment to truth do not divide but unite. At this point Augustine makes one of his most remarkable truth affirmations, dazzling, provocative, and demanding:

> This is why we must tremble before your judgments, O Lord, for your Truth is not mine, nor his, nor hers, but belongs to all of us whom you call to share it in communion with him, at the same time giving us the terrible warning not to arrogate truth to ourselves as private property, lest we find ourselves deprived of it. For anyone who appropriates what you provide for all to enjoy, and claims as his own what belongs to all, is cast out from this commonwealth, cast out to what is truly his own which is to say from truth to a lie; for anyone who lies is speaking from what is his own. (12.25.34, Boulding)

As remarkable, provocative, and demanding as this statement is, Augustine is simply laying out what has been his fundamental assertion all throughout the *Confessions*: God is Truth. To participate in anything true is to participate in God's Truth. This Truth is meant for all, just as God can never be claimed as someone's private possession. A few paragraphs later he will use the image of a wellspring, which often seems to bubble up from a tiny source and yet provides unlimited waters to all who are drawn to it. The same holds for God's Truth. It is precisely in this "surplus of truth" that Augustine resolves the contentious problem of a "surplus of meanings" when trying to understand Moses' meaning. One ought to expect plurality of meanings, polysemy, precisely because it is God's Truth that is the intention of Moses: "I am convinced that when Moses wrote those words what he meant and what he thought was all the truth we have been able to discover there, and whatever truth we have not been able to find, or have not found yet, but which is nonetheless there to be found" (12.31.42, Boulding). Augustine is not relativizing truth here, but grounding it deeply in its own deepest source. It is a perhaps dangerous and even potentially reckless affirmation, until we realize how love serves as its boundary and goal. Above all, the interpreter of the Scriptures must be someone who loves.

Charity

All throughout the *Confessions*, but most especially in Book Twelve, Augustine has been insisting on a reciprocity between truth and love. It pertains to the way others "read" Augustine.

> Yet "love believes without hesitation," at least among those who are bonded together by love, and so I also confess to you, Lord, in such a way that people to whom I can offer no proof may discern whether I confess truthfully. I cannot prove it, but all whose ears are open to me by love will believe me. (10.3.3)

Augustine takes the principle that introduces this statement directly from St. Paul: "love believes without hesitation" (see 1 Cor. 13:7). Love provides the "interpretative lens," the hermeneutical perspective, through which we are invited to read Augustine, as well as Augustine's reading of Moses. But if it applies to Augustine, it applies even more to the Scriptures. If one does not approach the Scriptures with love, if one does not approach those who interpret the Scriptures with love, Truth will never be attained: "You, O God, show yourself to anyone who loves you according to your bidding, and are wholly sufficient to him or her, so that such a one neither turns aside from you nor turns to themselves" (12.15.19). Notice here how love not only opens one to the Truth of God, but also prevents that very pursuit from deteriorating into selfishness. Love and Truth are, for Augustine, inseparable. In searching for God's Truth, love always ends up as the surprising and unexpected reward:

> O lightsome house, so fair of form, I have fallen in love with your beauty, loved you as the place where dwells the glory of my Lord, who fashioned you and claims you as his own. My pilgrim-soul sighs for you, and I pray him who made you to claim me also as his own within you, for he made me too. Like a lost sheep I have gone astray, but on the shoulders of my shepherd, your builder, I hope to be carried back to you. (12.15.22)

Right in the very midst of seeking the true meaning of "God made heaven and earth," Augustine the lover of Truth breaks out into a lightsome declaration of true love. He draws here upon the pilgrimage love canticles (see Pss. 25:8; 26:4), where searching and loving are one, beauty and truth are one.

As above in our comments about Truth shared, Augustine is preparing the way for his remarkable assertions about the communal nature of truth, which is simply another way of insisting that Truth and Love are inseparable. All too easily my meaning is set over and against your meaning, and selfishness is the only victor in such a contest.

> Let us not "go beyond what is written, inflated with pride and playing one off against another" (1 Cor 4:6). Rather let us love the Lord our God with our whole heart, our whole soul and our whole mind, and our neighbor as ourselves. Unless we believe that Moses meant whatever he did mean in his books with an eye to those twin commandments of love, we should make the Lord out to be a liar, by attributing to our fellow-servant a purpose which is at odds with the Lord's teaching. Since, then, so rich a variety of highly plausible interpretations can be drawn from those words, consider how foolish it is to rashly assert that Moses intended one particular meaning rather than any of the others. If we engage in hurtful strife as we attempt to expound his words, we offend against the very love for the sake of which he said all those things. (12.25.35, Boulding)

In the already mentioned *Christian Instruction* Augustine has "reduced" or perhaps better "raised" all meaning of Scripture to the twofold love commandment of Jesus: "Whoever thus thinks that they understand the divine Scriptures or any part of them so that it does not build up the double love of God and of our neighbor does not understand the Scriptures at all."[35] Is the exegete in pursuit of Truth or Love? For Augustine the answer is *both*, for the God who is Truth is the God who is Love. Reading the Scriptures both demands the "love of truth" and reveals the "truth of love."[36] It is a challenge that will ever tax Augustine, as his future scriptural and theological activity will engage him in passionate but sometime bitter argument and polemics on behalf of that truth. Augustine is certainly setting the highest standard possible both for himself and for his fellow searchers. In the paragraph that follows he thus prays God that he might seek Moses' truth in such a way that it would not overlook or demean others, but would, in fact, be a home for their sharing of the Truth: "I would hope to have written in such a way that if anyone else had in the light of truth seen some other valid meanings, that too should not be excluded, but present itself as a possible way of understanding in what I had said" (12.26.36). Augustine's truth resides in the truth of the other interpreters, and vice versa. Thus the seeming diversity and disparity of many truths can and must be held together and harmonized on a deeper level by the law of love: "In this diversity of true meanings let Truth Itself give birth to concord; may our God be merciful to us in order to rightfully use that law, the end of the precept, a love that is pure" (12.30.41). Diversity and concord—they are not at odds, but are framed by the very law of love. Augustine makes clear that this "law" must be used rightfully. It does not tolerate falsehood. It is not an escape from the demands of truth. It does, however, preclude contentiousness (12.18.27). And it generates a multiplicity of meanings (ibid.). It is this very love that puts Augustine in communion with Moses: there is a community of interpretation that extends from Moses to Augustine, bound together by the law of love.

Augustine's Genesis

Incommensurability, dialogue, truth, love: these guide, shape, direct, and control Augustine's exegetical searching. He applies them throughout the *Confessions* to the exegesis of his own "Genesis," his "creation" story. He applies them now, in the final books of the *Confessions*, to Moses' Genesis, the creation story.[37] Augustine fashions a provocative connectedness between both "Genesis" narratives: it is the same Creator at work, the same Word creating and speaking, the same mystery of God's love transforming chaos to order, death to life. Both Augustine and Moses seek to speak "in the spirit of truth" (12.20.29); both Augustine and Moses have the same Holy Spirit, teacher of God's servants (12.9.9); both Augustine and Moses know their words can be misconstrued (12.17.24); both Moses and Augustine are unwilling to separate truth and love (12.23.32); both Moses and Augustine carry out "a service of heart and tongue so that God's word may be shared" (12.26.36); both Moses and Augustine love those for whom they carry out this service (12.30.41); both Moses and Augustine yield to God's purposes that always transcend their own (ibid.). In the end, there is a remarkable bond between Moses and Augustine, more a statement of the power of God's Truth and Love than of the power or genius of either Augustine or Moses: "may I at least say what your Truth willed to say to me through his [Moses'] words, just as [Truth] said what He willed to Moses" (12.32.43). Truth has only one voice and it speaks both to and through Moses, to and through Augustine.

CONCLUSION

There remains something profoundly "unprogrammatic" about the *Confessions*, not in the sense of it being haphazard or poorly composed, but rather in that it addresses a God who speaks to humanity in ways that can never be contained or confined by human interpretative schemes. In proposing exegesis, the center of Book Twelve, as the central concern of the *Confessions*, I would like to suggest that Augustine intends this to be taken inclusively and not exclusively, not sweeping away other purposes or intentions, but uniting them into a grand and mysterious dialogue between God and humanity, where God speaks first, where God's Word takes flesh, where humanity humbly responds. Understanding Scriptures is not a narrow or restrictive concern for Augustine, since the Bible is not "narrowly" or "restrictively" true. Genesis, as a case in point, does not only speak to Moses' generation, but speaks to Augustine and his generation, and to all future generations. God's Word, for Augustine, is boundless in its truth and boundless in its application. Exegesis thus is not only concerned with *text*, it is equally concerned with a *community of truth*, those who read or hear the text, and take it into their heart. Its truth thus extends to the "truth" of the exegete, those seeking to understand the text—their need for a loving heart, humility, a genuine seeking of God's Truth. Augustine has throughout Book Twelve been reminding his own readers of the transcendence of this text, precisely because it is God's Word. This awareness engenders awe, fear, and a call to conversion, but it also awakens inquisitiveness. It is an inviting word that beckons, a demanding word that chastens, a vital word that is life-giving. We have seen multiple audiences envisioned by Augustine, multiple interpretative practices laid down by Augustine, leading to multiple truths and meanings engendered by the very Truth that is being sought. Augustine himself embodies all of these audiences: the lover of Cicero, the former Manichee, the African (Donatism did indeed claim to be "African"), the Catholic. Here in the *Confessions* and throughout his life, Augustine's own practice struggles with the values and principles he has laid out: incommensurability, dialogue, truth, and love. The "wonderful profundity of God's eloquence" (12.14.17) is itself the source of the wonderful eloquence of Augustine's profundity. It is precisely why Augustine exclaimed at the beginning of Book Twelve: "My heart is occupied about many things, Lord, when in the neediness of this my life the words of your Holy Scripture strike upon it" (12.1.1). It is Augustine's invitation that we will find our own Genesis here, and thus not just read Augustine, but imitate him in our own practice of both *exegesis* and *confessio*:

> May I be with my readers and hearers in You, Lord, and rejoice with them in You who themselves are nourished by your Truth in the wideness of your Love; and may we seek together in Moses' words your will through what your servant Moses wanted to say, by whose pen You have dispensed those words to us. (See 12.23.32.)

Book Twelve reminds Augustine's readers and Augustine himself that to embrace the Truth of the Scriptures demands a concurrent embracing of those seeking after Truth. Exegesis can only take place in a community of truth; in fact, its final aim is nothing less than to create this community of truth.

Chapter 13

Book Thirteen: The Creation of the Church as the Paradigm for the *Confessions*

Robert McMahon

INTRODUCTION

The *Confessions* concludes with Augustine's allegorical interpretation of the first chapter of Genesis as the creation of the church. These twenty-seven chapters not only close the work but mark a new departure within it. For one thing, Augustine has been reflecting on Genesis 1 for seventy-two chapters, since 11.3.5, and his progress has been quite slow, as he observes at the end of Book Twelve (12.32.43): in those seventy-two chapters he has gotten no farther than Genesis 1:2a. But when he begins his allegorical interpretation in Book Thirteen, chapter twelve, he begins again, with the beginning of Genesis, and he moves much more quickly, as though he were inspired. Speed is not the only index of inspiration, for his style, too, is altered. His writing is suddenly crowded with quotations from Scripture, mingling texts from the Old and New Testaments. So dense are these quotations that the writing often becomes difficult to follow, and we must read carefully just to grasp its surface meaning. Moreover, the hesitations that marked his groping exposition in the previous ninety-nine chapters have vanished, for he expounds a difficult allegory with sublime assurance. Augustine has a new subject for the creation story, the church, and he treats it with a new style and sudden confidence in his exposition. Within twenty-seven chapters, he completes an allegorical exposition of the creation of the church that finds all of Scripture, from creation to apocalypse, in its first chapter.

I intend to show how Augustine's allegory at the end of the *Confessions* provides the paradigm for the whole work, in one way for Books One through Nine, in a different way for Books Ten through Thirteen and the work as a whole. Augustine distinguishes what I shall call nine "acts" in the creation story. God creates twice on both the third and sixth days, making eight creative acts in the six days of Genesis 1, followed by the creation of the Sabbath. Augustine counts

207

God pronouncing his work "good" seven times, followed by an eighth "very good" (12.38.43), and the seventh day of rest makes nine acts, all told.[1] In the first part of this essay, I will show that the sequence of these nine acts in Augustine's allegory underlies the sequence of the nine books in his autobiography. That is, parallel images and themes link Book One of the *Confessions* and Augustine's allegory on God's first act, Book Two and the allegory on God's second act, and so on. The next part of this essay shows that the allegory in Book Thirteen describes the pattern of "return to the Origin," and this Christian-Platonist structure underlies Books Ten through Thirteen and the work as a whole. My final part relates this large-scale structure to the work's small-scale, meditative texture as a dialogue with God, and thereby indicates the unity of the *Confessions*.

BOOK THIRTEEN AND BOOKS ONE THROUGH NINE

It would take a long account to show how Augustine's allegory for each successive act in his allegory of the creation story corresponds to each successive book in his autobiography.[2] Because space does not allow this, I will treat the books from the beginning, middle, and end—Books One, Five, and Nine. In each instance, I will summarize Augustine's allegory before showing how it relates to the corresponding book. In each case, the imagery and themes of the allegory prove fundamental to the corresponding book. Nevertheless, because each book is much longer than its corresponding allegory, each book necessarily explores themes and uses images beyond those in Book Thirteen. The parallels between Augustine's autobiography, in Books One through Nine, and his allegory of God's nine creative acts, in Book Thirteen, prove significant and illuminating, but not comprehensive. The allegory is a paradigm for the autobiography, not a mold.

God's first act in Genesis 1 is the creation of light: as the Spirit broods over the dark waters of chaos, God creates light by the power of his word. Allegorically, the darkness is our ignorance and the chaotic waters represent the world, unredeemed human life. Augustine also calls this unredeemed and chaotic life "our earth, disordered and formless," before it receives "the form of doctrine" through God's word in Christ, the light of the world, calling us to repentance. In this creation of the church, God's "mercy," linked with the Spirit and with Christ, "did not abandon our misery," associated with the formless and dark waters (13.12.13). The Spirit, which is within us, "is borne above our dark and fluid inner being," calling us to be "children of light," rather than "children of darkness" (13.14.15).

Book One features the chaotic waters of "this world" and its values in several passages. Though Augustine treats his language learning as the effort to express his desires and so to exert some control of the world, the chapter concludes by saying that he thereby "entered more deeply into *the stormy society* of human life" (1.8.13, emphasis added). Evidently, the child's capacity for language not only enables him to express his desires, but also enables the words of others to enter into him and so to form his desires. The child Augustine's ability to speak made him more susceptible to the words and values of others: their worldly values entered "more deeply" into him and swept him into the "storm" of society.

From this arises the bishop's polemic against the classical education that he received, and its worldly, non-Christian values, portrayed as violent, and therefore chaotic, waters. He inveighs against "the torrent of men's ways," for worldly custom is a "mighty and hideous ocean" (1.16.25), and men are eager to hurl their sons into "the hellish flood" of a pagan education (1.16.26), because it leads to worldly success. Book One features three examples from this education that all use or imply water imagery. First, the boy Augustine weeps passionately over the death of Dido: the Latin rings with variations on the root *miser*, for the boy pities (*miserare*) the wretched (*miser*) Dido (1.13.21). In the imagery of Book Thirteen, his copious tears reveal that he is immersed in the dark waters of "our misery" (13.12.13) indulging his emotions and ignoring God's light calling him to conversion. Second, in a play by Terence, a youth "arouses himself to lust, and by heavenly instruction" when he sees a painting of Danae and Jove's "shower of gold" (1.16.26). In both of these, the water imagery has sexual overtones: "the fornication away from God" that is "the friendship of this world" (1.13.21; Jas. 4:4). Finally, the boy Augustine wins a prize for composing and presenting orally a prose version of Juno's irate speech in *Aeneid* One. In the *Aeneid*, the "storm" of Juno's passions leads her to cause a sea storm against Aeneas's fleet: the boy Augustine is rewarded for his compelling re-creation of these violent feelings (1.17.27). Because the boy Augustine was responsive to the worldly voices of his teachers and other adults, he was far from God "in the darkness of [his] passions" (1.18.28), and in "a whirlpool of filth" (1.19.30), floundering in the dark chaos of the "waters below."

In a happier vein, the imagery of Book Thirteen may be found in Augustine's portrayal of his infancy (1.6.7–10). In early infancy, the child is governed wholly by sensations and desires, for he knows "only how to seek the breast, to be satisfied with pleasant things, to cry at bodily hurts, nothing more." Above this moral formlessness, like the Spirit above the waters, are the love and care of his parents and nurses. Augustine emphasizes that it is God who gives nourishment to the infant by means of his mother and nurses, and this is one of God's mercies (1.6.7). Just as, in the allegory, the people of God take rest and joy in the flood of God's gifts coming through the Spirit (13.13.14), so does the child find comfort in the flow of milk and love that comes "from above," from God through caring adults, in "an orderly affection" (1.6.7). In this way, the Spirit "is borne above the dark and fluid inner being" (13.14.15) of the infant, giving it the ordering form of love.

More generally, as Robert M. Durling has shown, the structure of the first day of Genesis governs the structure of Book One, which falls into two parts, infancy and boyhood.[3] Augustine has no personal memories of infancy, which "belongs to the dark regions of forgetfulness" (1.7.12), while he does recall and record how he learned to talk. Clearly, the "darkness" of infancy proves analogous to the darkness before God speaks, and just as God's word creates light, so does the child's language learning bring forth the light of memory amid the "dark regions of forgetfulness." Durling also points to correspondences with God's seeing the light as good. Augustine argues that the elementary skills of reading and writing are good, far better than their purportedly "higher" use in studying pagan literature (1.13.22), or in using rhetoric to fulfill vain ambitions (1.17.27–19.30). Moreover, Book One closes by emphasizing the goodness of the boy Augustine, a growing unity derived from God's unity (1.20.31).

By these parallel images, Augustine links the first day in Genesis, its allegorical interpretation as the creation of the church, and his own beginnings in this life. Analogously, Book Five, at the center of his autobiography, parallels his allegory on the central act of the creation, that of the "lights in the firmament of heaven" on the fourth day. Augustine's allegory on God's second act, the creation of the "firmament of heaven," associates it with Scripture (13.15.16–18), "a firmament of authority over us," and he maintains this link in his allegory on God's fifth act (13.18.22–19.25). Just as the stars adhere to the firmament of heaven, so should Christians "appear like lights in the world, holding fast to the firmament of Scripture" (13.18.22). Augustine goes on to link the heavenly fires above to the heavenly flames of Pentecost, when the apostles "were made lights in the firmament of heaven, holding the word of life," and then went forth to preach the gospel to all nations (13.19.25). The creation of the stars is thereby linked with the spiritual or allegorical interpretation of Scripture and with preaching its truth. According to traditional doctrine, the apostles became the first bishops at Pentecost, when they were "anointed" by the Holy Spirit (Acts 2:1–4); Peter then gives the first Christian sermon, interpreting scriptural texts allegorically, in light of Jesus' crucifixion and resurrection (Acts 2:14–36). Augustine's allegory implies the ecclesiastical practice of his day: the spiritual interpretation and preaching of Scripture belongs especially to bishops, the successors of the apostles. His allegory also associates the "lights in the firmament" with the gifts of the Holy Spirit (1 Cor. 12:7–11), especially the moon with "knowledge" and the sun with "wisdom."[4]

The true spiritual understanding of Scripture proves crucial to Book Five, which describes the young Augustine's movement away from Faustus and the Manichees (5.3.3–7.13) toward Ambrose and Christianity (5.13.23–14.25). Ambrose expounds Old Testament passages allegorically, and his interpretations "in the spirit" revolutionize the young Augustine's understanding of Christianity. He discovers that "the Catholic faith can be maintained without being ashamed of it," for passages that were unacceptable when taken literally proved illuminating and true through Ambrose's spiritual exposition (15.14.24). Ambrose's preaching enables the young Augustine to understand how "the letter kills, but the Spirit gives life" (2 Cor. 3:6 NRSV; cf. *Conf.* 5.14.24–25; 6.3.3–4.6). Clearly, Ambrose is a true spiritual descendant of the apostles, for like them he interprets the Old Testament allegorically and preaches the true faith.

In terms of the allegory in Book Thirteen, Ambrose proves a genuine spiritual luminary, because he holds fast to the firmament of Scripture. Hence, the light of his preaching proves brilliant with "the gifts of the Holy Spirit," especially "the word of wisdom" and "the word of knowledge," the allegorical sun and moon (13.18.23). Faustus the Manichee, in contrast, proves a false luminary, because the Manichees do not interpret the Old Testament spiritually and so they do not hold fast to the firmament of Scripture. In this way, Faustus's spiritual light is phantasmal, a vain imagination, just like the "corporeal phantasms" of the sun and moon in Manichean teaching, which shed no light at all (3.6.10). Among the Manichees, Faustus was considered a sage, and the young Augustine long looked forward to learning from him how to resolve certain questions (5.6.10). But when they finally meet, Augustine finds him to be of limited attainments, and Faustus soon undertakes studies under his direction (5.7.13)! Book Five turns on the contrasts between Faustus, the Manichean false luminary with a pleasing style of speech but no substance, and Ambrose, whose eloquence is filled with the true light of the Catholic faith.[5]

The allegory in Book Thirteen also informs Augustine's critique of the astronomers: they make true predictions of eclipses, but become puffed up with foolish pride in their knowledge (5.3.4). The critique turns on the etymological link between *defectus*, "eclipse," and the verb *deficere*, "to fail, fall away": "Out of an impious pride they *fall back* from you and suffer an *eclipse* of your light, so early can they foresee a coming *eclipse*, but their own present *eclipse* they do not see" (5.3.4, my emphasis). Their pride in predicting a physical eclipse of the sun leads to their spiritual eclipse. Though Augustine's general criticism proves clear enough, its details depend on the allegory in Book Thirteen, for these are not made explicit in Book Five. A solar eclipse occurs when the moon passes between earth and the sun, blotting out its light. When astronomers become puffed up with pride at predicting an eclipse, they are putting the moon of their own knowledge (*scientia*) before the sun of divine wisdom (13.18.22–23). "Knowledge" concerns "sensible things," which vary in their seasons like the changeable moon and are analogous to the night (13.18.22). "Wisdom" concerns the eternal light of God's truth, found in Scripture and the church. Hence, the astronomers' pride in their own knowledge not only blots out the sun of divine wisdom but also darkens the "moon" of their knowledge, for they "do not see their own present eclipse" (5.3.4). The eclipse imagery in Book Five is both precise and morally instructive, but the precision of its terms can only be discovered by reading it in light of Augustine's corresponding allegory in Book Thirteen.

The correspondences between Book Nine and the allegory on God's ninth act may be treated more briefly, because they prove more readily grasped. God's ninth act is the blessing of the Sabbath, which Augustine interprets as "the Sabbath of eternal life" with God (13.36.51). The "peace of rest" (13.35.50) is a recurrent theme in Book Nine. The book begins with the young Augustine taking a vacation (9.4.12) at Cassiciacum after retiring from his post as a teacher (9.2.2–4)— a time of "respite" (9.4.7) and "leisure" (9.4.8). It ends with the death of Monica (9.11.27–12.33) and Augustine's prayer for the eternal rest of her soul with God (9.13.34–37). Only two earlier passages in the *Confessions* record deaths: that of Augustine's father (3.4.7), mentioned in passing, and that of his friend, explored in Book Four (4.4.7–12.19). In Book Nine, Augustine records five deaths: those of his mother, of his father (now named: 9.13.37), of his son Adeodatus (9.6.14), and of his friends Verecundus (9.3.5) and Nebridius (9.3.6). The last two passages mention the delights of paradise now enjoyed by these faithful souls in God's eternal Sabbath. Book Nine also records five baptisms, the sacramental death and rebirth into the mystical body of Christ that looks forward to life with God in his eternal Sabbath. Augustine speaks of his own baptism as a "release from anxiety" entailing "wondrous sweetness" (9.6.14), a foretaste (as it were) of eternal peace. But the keenest foretaste of the eternal Sabbath comes in the vision at Ostia (9.10.23–26), when Augustine and Monica ascend beyond all things to hear God's Word in beatifying silence. That chapter ends with Augustine looking forward to the general resurrection on the last day. The whole vision, in fact, arises from, concludes in, and is richly informed by the theme of rest in God, "the Sabbath of eternal life" (13.36.51).

STRUCTURE: RETURN TO THE ORIGIN

The *Confessions* undergoes an obvious change in Book Ten, from the narrative in Books One through Nine to philosophy and theology in Books Ten through Thirteen. Though the autobiography is filled with philosophical and theological reflections, and Books Ten through Thirteen naturally have a certain "narrative" progress, the differences between the two blocks are obvious. To see how the allegory in Book Thirteen provides a paradigm for the final books, then, we must understand it in a new way, no longer as a narrative of acts, but as a theological whole.

The pattern of this theological whole has long been understood, for it was described by Solignac over forty years ago. Solignac argues that in this allegory Augustine "has considered the *totality* of creation in its material reality and in its spiritual signification, as a figure of the Church" (emphasis in original). He summarizes the whole as a movement from eternity, through time, to eternity: "time is opened for us out of eternity by the *fiat* of the Creator and it is closed in the eternity of the heavenly rest, without ceasing to be governed by the transcendence of this divine eternity."[6] Solignac emphasizes the scope of Augustine's allegory, encompassing the totality of creation in the sweep and direction of all time, proceeding from God's eternity and returning to it. The pattern of the allegory, then, may be described as the "return to the Origin."

"Return to the Origin" describes a pattern fundamental to all of Augustine's thought: it names a Christian-Platonist principle, with ontological, epistemological, moral, and historical meaning. Ontologically, all things proceed from and return to God, and all things are ontologically dependent on God. Epistemologically, the order of the cosmos can be rightly understood only by a person who seeks this return to the Origin through spiritual discipline. The "carnal" human being, oriented by the lower appetites, cannot properly apprehend the cosmic order. Morally, therefore, one's life should be directed toward that journey of return. Finally, Christians understand that all human history is engaged in an exodus toward the heavenly Jerusalem, when the dead shall rise and God shall be "all in all" (1 Cor. 15:28 NRSV). The outline of this salvation history can be found in the Christian Bible, with its movement from creation, in Genesis 1, to the "new heaven and earth" of Revelation 21–22. The sacrament or sign of this universal and historical return to the Origin is the church. For a Christian-Platonist, the church teaches the "return to the Origin" as an ontological, epistemological, and moral principle because the church embodies that return in history.

"Return to the Origin" also points to a literary-philosophical genre, the Platonist ascent to principles ("first things"). This genre is based on the Christian-Platonist *exitus-reditus* scheme: as all things come forth (*exitus*) from God, so do all things return (*reditus*) to him. A work in this genre enacts the "return to the Origin" by ascending reflectively to principles always logically prior and, therefore, ontologically higher. These Platonist principles are not merely ideational abstractions, but universals, and they thereby name realms of being. Hence, the ascent moves not merely to categories progressively more general, as in our nominalist way of thinking, but to realms of being more universal and real, because they comprehend more of reality. In this Platonist ascent to the Origin, then, the way forward is the way back, and what comes last in the narrative sequence is actually first in the ontological order. At the same time, the Platonist arrives at these realms "above himself" after taking the inward turn, away from things "outside him" to the principles of the soul within. In *True Religion*, Augustine urged this inward turn: "Do not go outside, return within yourself, for truth dwells in the interior man."[7] The Platonist ascent, then, moves not only "upward" but also "inward," to universal principles ontologically higher because more interior. In this way, the meditator moves toward the divine presence dwelling "more inward than my innermost and higher than my uppermost" (*Conf.* 3.6.11).

Let us see how this pattern works itself out in the *Confessions*, first as a progress to what is prior, logically and ontologically, and then as an interior movement.[8] After examining certain memories in his autobiography (Books One through Nine), Augustine explores the faculty of memory, in Book Ten, and time, in Book Eleven. Memories cannot exist without memory, and memory cannot exist without time. Though today some might say that the faculty of memory is formed by the accumulation of individual memories, for Augustine there can be no memories without the innate capacity of memory. The faculty of memory, in his understanding, is the logical and ontological precondition for having any memories at all: memory is the ground of memories. Similarly, time is the logical and ontological precondition of memory, for without time there could be no memory. Because memory proves but one aspect of time, time is the ground of memory. In short, as the *Confessions* progress from memories (Books One through Nine), to memory (Book Ten), to time (Book Eleven), Augustine moves to universals ever "higher," because more general and encompassing, and prior, because preconditioning what came before. His relentless questioning carries him on a Platonist ascent to principles, a return to the Origin.

Book Twelve is largely taken up with Augustine's interpreting "heaven and earth" in Genesis 1:1. He holds that "heaven" refers to the "heaven of heavens," the "incorporeal creation" (12.8.8–9.9), and "earth" refers to the "formless matter" from which the world would be made (12.3.3–7.7). Both of these, he argues, exist prior to time, though neither is eternal, properly speaking (12.12.15–13.16). Before the world exists, there is no time. "Heaven and earth" in Genesis 1:1, according to Augustine, are pure form and pure matter, the pretemporal constituents of the world. Hence, "heaven and earth" in Book Twelve are logically and ontologically prior to time, which was discussed in Book Eleven: they are "higher" aspects of being, because they are more fundamental and encompassing. As Augustine moves forward in his *Confessions* he progresses to ever more original realms of being because he is returning to the Origin.

Book Thirteen concludes the work, and it concludes by interpreting the seven days of creation as an allegory for the creation and growth of the church (13.12.13–38.53). According to Augustine, the church represents God's purpose for creating the universe. Summarizing his treatment of the six days in chapter thirty-four, Augustine begins, "We have seen into (*inspeximus*) these things according to the mystical purpose (*figurationem*) with which Thou willedst (*voluisti*) them to come into being in such an order, or to be written in such an order" (13.34.49, my translation). Augustine is claiming that his allegory for the church reveals God's purpose in creating the world, or God's purpose in inspiring the creation story. Odd though Augustine's allegory and claim may be to us, the fundamental point has considerable support in early Christianity. *The Shepherd of Hermas* affirmed that "the world was created for the sake of the Church." Clement of Alexandria explained it this way: "Just as God's will is creation and is called 'the world,' so his intention is the salvation of men, and it is called 'the Church.'"[9] In this traditional understanding, the church is the divine origin and the goal of all things: God created the world for human beings, and human beings for himself, to share his life with them.

For Augustine, then, the allegory of the church in Book Thirteen reveals God's purpose in creation, or in inspiring its account in Genesis. Since purpose is ontologically and logically prior to act, the church, as God's purpose, is logically and ontologically prior to creation. Moreover, as the mystical body of Christ, the church is understood to be eternal: it preceded the world in God's mind and will endure beyond the end of the world in the "eternal Sabbath" (13.35.50–38.53) of his presence. God's purpose in creating is logically prior to and ontologically higher than all created things. Augustine's meditative ascent can go no further than his vision into the providential order of creation and church. His return to the Origin is complete, and his *Confessions* come to a close.

Now let us consider the work as a progressively interior movement.[10] This inward movement proves obvious in the progress from memories, in Books One through Nine, to memory, in Book Ten, for the faculty of memory proves deeper than its contents. In Books Eleven, Twelve, and Thirteen, the interior progress of Augustine's ascent emerges in the final chapters of each. Near the end of Book

Eleven, Augustine concludes that time contains memory as one of its aspects. Discovering that only the present exists, because the past has vanished and the future does not yet exist (11.14.17–15.20), he comes to analyze our experience of time psychologically, as present "attention" (11.28.37–38) to various things: memory is attention to things past, the present is attention to things present, and expectation is attention to things future. Attention, then, is necessary to memory, prior to it and deeper in the soul. That is why its scope extends not only to things past but also to things present and things future. Hence, when Augustine moves from memory, in Book Ten, to "attention," in 11.28.37–29.39, he progresses more deeply into the ground of his soul. Attention proves the psychological ground of memory, its origin within Augustine's interior powers.

From "attention," near the end of Book Eleven, the ascent moves to "the will" (*voluntas*) in the final chapters of Book Twelve. After treating his own and various other interpretations of "heaven and earth" in 12.2.2–22.31, Augustine begins to reflect on hermeneutic principles. These all turn on the moral disposition (*voluntas*) of interpreters attempting to understand the intention (*voluntas*) of Moses and of God in Genesis 1 (12.23.32–24.33). Because Augustine refuses to consider the views of heretics or unbelievers (12.14.17; 12.16.23; 12.23.32), the "rule of faith" governs his whole discussion: all the differing interpretations are true, because the rule of faith excludes false ones. He goes on to develop the "rule of charity": no exegete should prefer his interpretation to other true ones simply because it is his (12.25.34–35; 30.41–31.42). Because charity is the end of Scripture, charity should bring concord to exegetes with differing views.

Now faith and charity are dispositions of the rightly oriented will. Clearly, the directing of attention (11.28.37–29.39) depends on the will, and right attention depends on a rightly oriented will. Hence, the will is an interior principle logically prior to attention, and ontologically deeper than it. Attention is grounded in the will. Hence, the will is more important and more powerful than attention, because deeper in the soul. When Augustine moves from attention, near the end of Book Eleven, to the will, near the end of Book Twelve, he progresses to a deeper, more interior, principle in the soul.

Book Thirteen, as we have seen, closes with the purpose God wills in creation. Obviously, God's will (*voluisti*, "Thou willedst," 13.34.49) is prior to and higher than the will (*voluntas*) of human beings. At the same time, the purpose that God wills in creation is the church, to share his life with human beings made in his image, and this divine desire is stamped by its presence within the restless human heart. This divine presence is the ground of the soul, "more inward than my innermost" (3.6.11), and so Augustine affirms, "Thou hast made us toward thyself and *our* heart *is* restless until it rests in Thee" (1.1.1, my translation and emphasis). This formulation points toward the church: not only is every human heart restless toward God, but also a single corporate heart seeks rest in the divine presence. In the church, the divine creation continues in the divine providence guiding our restless heart, individually and corporately, toward its eternal rest in God's eternal Sabbath (13.35.50–38.53). In other words, when Augustine recognizes the church as God's purpose in creation, at the end of Book Thirteen, he recognizes the deepest aspect of himself. Here is the divine ground of the longing that animates his will (Book Twelve), his attention (Book Eleven), and his memory (Book Ten). Augustine's return to the Origin comes to a close with his allegorical vision of God's will in the church as his own Origin and End. Further inward he cannot go. His innermost is also his uppermost, for God is "more inward than my innermost and higher than my uppermost" (3.6.11).

In short, as a Christian-Platonist ascent, the *Confessions'* end is its beginning. At the literary level, church governs the work from its first sentence to its last: as a prayerful dialogue with God, the *Confessions* enacts church throughout. But church also functions at the level of universal history: as God's purpose for creating, the church is his original intention and ultimate end for the world and human beings. Most obviously, Augustine discovers the meaning of his life in church: God's presence is the origin and goal of his "restless heart." Just as God led the young Augustine, despite all his errors, to Christian faith, so does he direct human history, despite all its vagaries, to salvation in himself. The providence guiding Augustine's life and his dialogue with God in the *Confessions* leads him finally to envision the providence guiding all human history. Augustine's life and *Confessions* prove, in the end, instances of church, the divinely guided universal movement that begins before time and ends after it.

The allegory of Book Thirteen thereby completes Augustine's understanding of the "restless heart" in the work's very first chapter. The meditative structure of the *Confessions* moves to progressively deeper, and therefore more universal, self-understandings. Augustine would have us recognize deeper and deeper aspects of ourselves in this movement, and so come to see ourselves as he does, stamped in his origin, longing, and end as God's. In the *Confessions*, the church proves at once the deepest, highest, and most universal form of self-knowledge. As the providential origin and goal of the world, the church is the ground of creation, of Augustine's restless heart, of his dialogue with God, and of his Christian-Platonist ascent.

Within this movement of the *Confessions* as a whole, the autobiography in Books One through Nine enacts, in its own ways, a return to the Origin. For one thing, it tells the story of the young Augustine's conversion, and as a turning toward God, a conversion is necessarily a return to the Origin. Also, the autobiography moves climactically to gradually deeper, or higher, returns to the Origin: the young Augustine's experience of God as a spiritual substance (7.9.13–11.17), his conversion to faith in the incarnation and to chastity (8.12.28–30), and his entry into the church in his baptism (9.6.14). Each of these proves a return to the Origin by the young Augustine: in his intellect (7.9.13–11.17), in his intellect and will (8.12.28–30), and in his whole person through the sacraments of the church (9.6.14). Book Nine also features his return to the Origin in the meditative ascent of his vision at Ostia (9.10.23–26), and it concludes with the saintly death of his mother: his earthly origins returning to their divine Origin.

Books One through Nine also enact this return in their formal structure as a chiasm. A simple chiastic structure may be represented schematically in this way:

A B C B A. This schema clearly shows a movement that enacts a return. William A. Stephany has shown how this structure functions in Augustine's autobiography with thematic parallels between Books One and Nine, Two and Eight, Three and Seven, and Four and Six.[11] Books One and Nine, according to Stephany, emphasize physical birth and spiritual birth, respectively. Augustine's narrative of his own life begins with his physical birth (1.6.7), and ends with his spiritual rebirth in baptism (9.6.14). Book Nine also records the baptisms—the sacramental births—of Verecundus, Nebridius, Adeodatus, and Alypius. All except the last are dead when the *Confessions* is written, and Augustine envisions each as born into eternal life. Also, it may be noted, Book One recurrently criticizes the boy's classical education, while Book Nine begins with the young convert's decision to give up his profession as a teacher of the classics (9.2.2–4), and his immersion in the prayerful reading of Scripture (9.4.7–12).

Let one other set of parallel books illustrate the chiastic pattern of the autobiography. Stephany observes that Books Two and Eight feature events around a fruit tree in a garden. Both treat the perversity of human will after the fall, whether inclined toward evil (Book Two), or unable wholly to will the good (Book Eight). The two books also feature contrasting roles for friendship: in Book Two, the young Augustine's companions lead him to sin, while in Book Eight the Christian friendship of Simplicianus and Ponticianus leads to his conversion.

In this chiastic structure of thematic parallels, then, the later books rework themes of the earlier ones in a higher way, a way that points to and includes conversion. Book Eight returns to, or echoes, the themes of Book Two, but orients them toward conversion of the will, rather than its perversion through sin. Similarly, Book Nine returns to certain themes in Book One, but they now appear as spiritual rebirth and Christian studies, rather than physical birth and classical studies. In this way, the formal, chiastic structure of parallel or returning themes participates in the progress of the narrative as a return to the Origin. Books One through Nine thereby enact a return to the Origin, not only as the story of Augustine's conversion, but also in their formal structure as an unfolding chiasm of returning themes, which may be graphed as A B C D E D C B A for the nine books. And since a chiasm is traditionally understood to be a cross structure, from the Greek letter *chi* (X), Augustine's autobiographical return to the Origin is thereby marked with the sign of the cross and the emblem of the name of Christ.

CONCLUSION: MEDITATIVE TEXTURE AND THE UNITY OF *CONFESSIONS*

In this large-scale way, the *Confessions* unfolds as a return to the Origin. It progresses, however haltingly, to higher, more comprehensive perspectives. These culminate in the church as God's purpose for creating, the divine origin and goal of the visible universe and of human history. The church, as the mystical body of Christ, thereby embraces time and participates in eternity, because it manifests the purpose of God. Augustine's allegory in Book Thirteen considers the most comprehensive category of being within the *Confessions* and, for that reason, provides the paradigm for the unity of the whole, both in theme and in its unfolding structure.

Augustine scholars have been reluctant to acknowledge this large-scale movement of the *Confessions*. They have shown keen interest in meditative ascents within the work (e.g., 7.10.16; 7.17.23; 9.10.23–26; 10.7.11–8.15), but not the ascent of the work as a whole.[12] This ascent is not clearly and explicitly marked, like those within the work, or like that in Bonaventure's *The Journey of the Mind to God*. Hence, there is no scholarly agreement on what constitutes "the unity of the *Confessions*," and many have argued that the work has little or no unity.[13] There can be no doubt that the work is filled with digressions, as Augustine puzzles out various problems, and so its progress is often halting, on a small scale. In order to grasp the unity of the *Confessions* more fully, we must understand how its large-scale structure as an ascent relates to its small-scale textures.

It is well understood that the *Confessions* presents itself as a prayer, a dialogue with God. Peter Brown notes Augustine's originality in making prayer the literary form of so long a work and terms it "a lively conversation."[14] Solignac also calls the work "a dialogue with God" and, arguing that God is present throughout as "an invisible interlocutor," insists that "throughout these thirteen books, Augustine *allows himself to be taught by God*" (emphasis in original).[15] G. Boissou describes the *Confessions* as "a dialogue in one voice," because "only Augustine speaks—or rather, we only hear his voice—but from his language, his feelings, the tone of his discourse, and in a certain sense the reactions of his countenance, we sense the divine replies."[16] Augustine scholars have often recorded their understanding and appreciation of this aspect of the work.

But they have not fully understood its implications: we must distinguish Augustine the narrator, the voice of the unfolding prayer, from Augustine the author, who designed, wrote, and revised the *Confessions* as a whole.[17] The work presents itself as an oral prayer that unfolds in an ongoing present, in which the narrator is guided by the spontaneities of his dialogue with God. The etymology of its title implies as much: *confessio* derives from *con-fari*, "to speak with." As an oral and spontaneous prayer, it necessarily presents itself as unrevised: a dialogue, by definition, cannot be revised by the speakers in it. An oral speaker cannot erase an utterance to correct it: he can only rephrase or qualify it by speaking further. So, too, the narrator of the *Confessions* may correct an earlier statement on, say, the nature of time, not by erasure and revision, but only by adding to what he has said. The narrator can and does come to new understandings in his quest for truth, and we see this happening over and over in the *Confessions*. Though the narrator makes discoveries, Augustine *the author* did not: by definition, he comprehended the finished work as a whole, for he has shaped and revised it. I write of Augustine the author in the past tense, because I identify him with the historical Augustine. Augustine the narrator, however, is a figure who functions in the literary present, for he continues to pray his *Confessions* "now" every time we read it. This narrator was created by Augustine the author as a literary, and therefore partial, representation of himself.

Augustine the narrator should be distinguished, but not separated, from Augustine the author. Augustine the author created this narrator partly to state his views on certain things, partly as an example of prayerful self-examination and the quest for truth. We always know what Augustine the narrator is thinking, because he is a function of what the work is saying at any moment: the narrator's thoughts are wholly explicit, by definition. Augustine the author, by definition, comprehended the total movement of his narrator's thinking: he thereby implied understandings beyond what the narrator explicitly says. One such understanding I have already set forth: the *Confessions* as a whole unfolds as a Christian-Platonist ascent, a return to the Origin. Scholars have tended to miss this because they recognize only one Augustine in the work, and so they identify the narrator's voice *in* the work with Augustine the author's understanding *of* the work. They thereby miss larger structures, and the understandings they imply, created by Augustine the author.

The *Confessions* presents itself as the record of a narrator's oral dialogue with God, not as an author's written treatise. In this regard, we may contrast it with the self-presentation of individual books in the *City of God*, for these present themselves as written by an author. For the most part, each of these twenty-two books has a prospectus near its beginning and a summary near its end. Hence, each book presents itself as *framed* by an *author*: each has been written and revised by an author who knows where the argument is going. Thus framed in the manner of a written treatise, the argument of each book is presented as containing no spontaneous discoveries.

In the *Confessions*, in contrast, no book contains a treatise-style prospectus introducing its argument. Many of the books begin with a prayer, not a prospectus or summary, for they are meant to invoke and praise, not argue or prove. At the most, one finds a suggestive promise, as at the beginning of Book Eight: "'You have broken my chains. . . .' I will tell how you broke them" (8.1.1). For the most part, the opening of each book tells us little or nothing about what will come. In Book Eleven, for example, Augustine the narrator says that he will meditate on Scripture (11.2.3), and he begins with the first verse of Genesis (11.3.5). But he does not say that he will reflect on "time," as he winds up doing for half the book, because he does not know that he will do so: the question "What is time?" (11.14.17) emerges through the dynamism of his dialogue with God. Hence, when Augustine the narrator begins to think about time, he does not yet know the answer he will eventually arrive at: he prays his way through preliminary answers before his dialogue with God brings him to a satisfactory conclusion (11.28.37–38). Augustine the author, however, comprehended this whole movement, by definition: he knew the narrator's final position, and he dramatized the narrator's prayerful progress to it.

If there were only "one Augustine" in the *Confessions*, the following problem would be insuperable: did he know his conclusions about "time" before he began writing Book Eleven? If he did, then his perplexities and his prayerful search for truth are a sham: he knew his final answer already. As far as I know, no scholar has ever accused the prayer of the *Confessions* of being a sham. On the other hand, if Augustine did not already know his conclusion, then his perplexities and prayer were genuine, and he worked his way to his conclusions in the course of praying chapters fourteen through twenty-eight, with precisely those stages and that line of reasoning. As far as I know, no scholar has suggested this, either.

I would argue that the historical Augustine did know his conclusion when he started to write Book Eleven, and he dramatized there the perplexities and prayer of his narrator. Augustine the narrator's prayerful perplexities are genuine, and they reflect and telescope a process of thinking that took the historical Augustine much longer than chapters fourteen through twenty-eight. After all, Augustine the narrator resolves his difficulties about "time" in something less than two hours, the time it takes to read these chapters aloud as a prayerful quest for truth. Like nearly all literary works, the *Confessions* rouses interest by eliminating everything irrelevant and by concentrating on essentials. Augustine the narrator, the voice in the work, never calls a break in his prayer to eat, or sleep, or attend to his ecclesiastical duties. His quest for the truth about "time" begins in 11.14.17 and continues without a stop until 11.28.37–38. In my view, the historical Augustine condensed here an intellectual development through prayer that probably took place over years.

If there is only "one Augustine" in the work, then he made all the discoveries of the *Confessions* while he composed it. But this seems implausible. For example, near the beginning of Book Two, the narrator complains that, when the adolescent Augustine was "spilt, scattered and boiled dry in [his] fornications," God was silent (2.2.2). In the following chapter, he realizes that this accusation was incorrect: in truth, God was speaking to him through his mother (2.3.7). Here is an instance of the narrator's making a discovery in the course of his unfolding dialogue with God: his earlier accusation against God's silence was wrong, and he accuses himself instead, "Wretch that I am" (2.3.7). I cannot believe that the historical Augustine, who had been a self-examining Christian for over a decade before he began his autobiography, made this discovery about his adolescence only when he composed Book Two. In my view, Augustine used his narrator to dramatize a discovery he himself made some years earlier through prayerful confession.

We may rightfully assume that the historical Augustine did make discoveries as he composed the *Confessions*, as writers normally do when they work. But since we do not have his working papers, we cannot know what these discoveries were. We do know what Augustine the narrator discovers, and how he does so, but we cannot know whether the historical Augustine learned these things while he composed the *Confessions* or before. We can be sure that he created a narrator for the *Confessions* as a literary version of himself, and this narrator's process of discovery through prayer imitates what Augustine himself practiced over many years. Distinguishing the historical Augustine, the author *of* the *Confessions* as a completed whole, from Augustine the narrator, the praying voice *in* the work, enables us to appreciate more fully its meditative texture, the dynamism of its dialogue with God.

This meditative texture is filled with surprises for the reader because it is full of surprises for the narrator, praying in an ongoing present. The entire work, from its first sentence to its last, uses the present tense for Augustine the narrator's activity as he prays. Open it to any page: the narrator is praying "now," in a literary present, remembering his past life "now," unfolding his quest for truth "now," as you read. Moreover, he insists recurrently that he is not in complete control of his utterances, for God "recalls these things to my memory" (2.7.15). He expresses surprise at what is happening as he prays: "Why do I speak of these matters? Now is the time not to be putting questions but to be making confession to you" (4.6.11). He affirms that God leads his prayer in surprising directions: "From what starting point and to what end have you led my memory to include even these events in my confession to you, when I have passed over so much that I have forgotten?" (9.7.16). Augustine the narrator is not in full control of his *Confessions*, because the work unfolds as a dialogue with God. Augustine the author, however, was in full control of the work, by definition: because he stood beyond the completed whole, as its composer and reviser, it contained no surprises for him.

The interpretive consequences of this distinction illuminate a long-standing debate about the pear theft in Book Two. Immediately after recounting the theft, Augustine the narrator insists that he had no rational motive for the act: "I had no motive for my wickedness except wickedness itself" (2.4.9). In other words, he loved rebellion for its own sake, for its purely negative self-assertion. But five chapters later, he arrives at a new understanding of his motives: because he would never have done it alone, he did it out of friendship, to be one of the gang. In other words, the adolescent Augustine did have a positive, rational motive for the theft: it was not purely negative self-assertion, but arose from his love for the love of others. Moreover, the narrator insists that this realization was brought about by God's grace, exclaiming "See, before you, my God, is the living memory of my soul: alone I would not have committed that crime" (2.9.17).

Scholars have argued about which was "Augustine's view" on his motives for the theft.[18] Because they fail to distinguish Augustine the narrator from Augustine the author, they tend to argue for one or the other. But when we make this distinction, we can point to a resolution of the issue. Clearly, the narrator progresses prayerfully from a negative understanding of motives—pure rebellious self-assertion—to a positive one—the friendship of others. Hence, the latter deserves primacy. But Augustine the author crafted this movement so that the latter understanding *qualifies*, but does not *cancel*, the earlier one. The narrator does not revisit his earlier understanding and attempt to reconcile it with his final realization, for the dynamism of his dialogue with God carries him forward. But these two understandings are dialectically related, and Augustine the author has left us the task of working out their relations. If we recognize only one Augustine in the *Confessions*, we do not grasp how unresolved differences in the narrator's positions prove a philosophical task set for us by Augustine the author. In other words, when we identify "Augustine" only with the narrator's voice, and so with the explicit utterances in the work, we tend to miss what Augustine the author implied by relations between parts of the work, and we fail to interpret adequately his achievement in the *Confessions*.

Though the oral character of Augustine the narrator's unfolding prayer may seem strange to us, we do well to remember the habits of composition and oral reading in late antiquity. Augustine probably dictated the *Confessions*, as he did other works, and his contemporaries certainly read it aloud. His first readers would thereby have been responsive to the spontaneities of its dialogue with God as unfolding in an ongoing present: the "now" of reading imitates the "now" of the narrator's prayer, and every reader would have given present voice to the work's utterances. Also, we do well to remember that ancient readers would not have had the "helps" featured in almost all of our translations and editions: no table of contents, no book titles, chapter titles, or page headings. These helps inform first-time readers today that Book Ten concerns "Memory," and Book Eleven, "Time," even though these subjects take up only about half of each book. Without these helps, no first-time reader of Book Eleven could possibly know, from reading chapters one through thirteen, that "time" would take up the inquiry in chapters fourteen through twenty-eight. Augustine's original audience, then, would have experienced directly the oral character of his narrator's dialogue with God, its spontaneities and surprises and, hence, its self-presentation as unfolding without revision in the order of our reading, from 1.1.1 to 13.38.53.

In sum, if we wish to appreciate both the unfolding dynamism of the *Confessions'* dialogue with God and the structure of the whole as a planned ascent, we need to distinguish Augustine the narrator from Augustine the author. Only from this perspective can we see the crucial parallel between the young Augustine's life and the narrator's prayer: just as God led the young Augustine to Christian faith, even through all his moral wanderings, so does God guide the narrator's "Confessions," even through all its digressions. Just as the young Augustine's life revealed God's providential guidance, so does the unfolding of the *Confessions*: its large-scale structure as a return to the Origin emerges, not from Augustine the narrator's plan, but through God's guidance.

In other words, the *Confessions* does not merely tell a story about God's providential grace in Augustine's life. Rather, its very literary form enacts, moment by moment, the dialectic between divine grace and human freedom in its unfolding prayer. Augustine the narrator does not always know where his prayer is going, but its course emerges from the dynamism of his dialogue with God and so that course proves providential. In this way, the *Confessions* unites speech about God with the action of God: as a dialogue with God, the work does what it says, is what it talks about. Its literary form embodies providence and grace. A treatise, featuring its author's control of his argument, can analyze the dialectic between grace and freedom but cannot embody it. Only the meditative texture of a "dialogue with God" can embody and enact the dialectic between divine grace and human free will. The *Confessions* thereby unites indissolubly content and form.

As we have seen, the providential course of the *Confessions* as a whole follows a Christian-Platonist ascent and culminates in an allegorical discourse about the church as God's purpose in creation. Like every return to the Origin, its end reveals its beginning: Augustine the narrator turns to his Origin at every point in the work, because it unfolds as a prayer. Because the narrator turns to his Origin at every point in the work, God guides his *Confessions* as a return to the Origin over the whole. The dynamism of its meditative texture as a dialogue with God generates its structure as a Christian-Platonist ascent. Here, again, form and content are indissolubly united.

We know how important "unity" was for Augustine, and yet scholars have often thought that the *Confessions* lacks unity. In my view, this error arises because scholars see only "one Augustine" in the work and identify him wholly with the narrator's voice. To be sure, Augustine the narrator has no plan for his prayer, for it unfolds in the dynamism of his dialogue with God, with all its digressions and discoveries. But Augustine the author had a plan for the whole, for he structured it as a return to the Origin. The *Confessions* thereby reflects human experience as Christians understand it: the seeming planlessness in its small-scale movements is taken up into God's providential structure over the whole. If we think there is only "one Augustine" in the work, we cannot see this structure, because Augustine the narrator never remarks on it. In order to grasp the unity of *Confessions* and Augustine's achievement in designing it, we must distinguish what its narrator says from the large-scale structure designed by its author. Once we have distinguished them, we can see the *Confessions'* unity of texture and structure, planlessness and plan, in the narrator's turning to God at every moment and his return to the Origin enacted over the whole.

Notes

Chapter 1: Book One

1. I do not want to identify what I am calling "autobiography" here with the genre of autobiographical writing. One can write a memoir that struggles more or less successfully (and more or less directly) with the autobiographical temptation; think of Philip Roth's book *The Facts: A Novelist's Autobiography* (New York: Farrar, Straus & Giroux, 1988) or, in a fictional form, David Markson's *Wittgenstein's Mistress* (Elmwood Park, Ill.: Dalkey Archive Press, 1988). I thank Lauren Winner for conversations on this issue.

2. By "presume" here I obviously mean something other than a fully self-conscious postulation of the above sentence as a proposition to be affirmed after due reflection; the tenuous grip of the proposition, so baldly stated as above, conflicts with the tenacity with which we hold it, and so we act out of it while never letting ourselves recognize that that is the belief we practically affirm.

3. James J. O'Donnell puts it well: "the relationship of this text to Augustine's life is not that of signifier to signified." James J. O'Donnell, *Augustine: Confessions,* 3 vols. (Oxford: Oxford University Press, 1992), 2:3.

4. This raises interesting questions about the reception of grace and the eschatological nature of hermeneutics, which I cannot address here.

5. Throughout this essay I use the Maria Boulding, O.S.B., translation of the *Confessions* in pt. I/1 of *The Works of Saint Augustine: A Translation for the 21st Century* (ed. John E. Rotelle; Hyde Park, N.Y.: New City Press, 1997), and all departures from Boulding's translation are explained in the notes.

6. For historical evidence, see Nicholas D. Paige, *Being Interior: Autobiography and the Contradictions of Modernity in Seventeenth-Century France* (Philadelphia: University of Pennsylvania Press, 2001); for recent philosophical examples, see Charles Taylor, *Sources of the Self* (Cambridge, Mass.: Harvard University Press, 1989); Stephen Menn, *Descartes and Augustine* (New York: Cambridge University Press, 1998); and Phillip Cary, *Augustine's Invention of the Inner Self: The Legacy of a Christian Platonist* (Oxford: Oxford University Press, 2000).

7. See Augustine's discussion of this in *De Trinitate,* and my essay "Augustinian Anthropology: *Interior intimo meo,*" *Journal of Religious Ethics* 27:2 (June 1999): 195–221.

8. I have slightly modified Boulding's translation here, to cleave more closely to the Latin: *A quo est omnis modus, formosissime, qui formas omnia et lege tua ordinas omnia.*

9. "Friday's Child," in W. H. Auden, *Collected Poems* (London: Faber, 1991).

10. O'Donnell, *Augustine: Confessions,* 2:23.

11. Ibid., 2:17.

12. Heidegger's misunderstanding of Augustine on this point was part of what led him to speak of ontotheology as suffusing the western metaphysical tradition.

13. Again, modifying Boulding: *Sed quis te invocat sed nesciens te?*

14. Ludwig Wittgenstein, *Philosophical Investigations* (3rd ed.; trans. G. E. M. Anscombe; New York: Macmillan, 1958), pt. I § 32, 15–16.

15. See Myles Burnyeat, "Wittgenstein and Augustine *De magistro*," in *The Augustinian Tradition* (Berkeley, Calif.: University of California Press, 1999), 236–303.

16. André Malraux, *Antimemoires* (trans. Terence Kilmartin; New York: Holt, Reinhart & Winston, 1968), 1.

17. See Augustine's discussion of judgment in *Civ.* 19.6.

18. Where I have "fornication," Boulding several times uses "troth-breaking," which seems to me unhappily archaic. It is worth noting here the way that this deformation was properly *triune*: he learned to love games, he aimed to win victory (*superbas victorias*), and he was ridden by curiosity (1.10.16). This reflects, again, the triune nature of creation, as well as suggesting that, for Augustine to be healed of his sickness, only a triune medicine, administered by a triune agent, will do.

19. On rule-following, I have found the work of Stanley Cavell and John McDowell especially helpful: see Cavell's *Must We Mean What We Say?* (Cambridge: Cambridge University Press, 1976), and *The Claim of Reason: Wittgenstein, Skepticism, Morality, and Tragedy* (New York: Oxford University Press, 1979); and McDowell's "Non-cognitivism and Rule-Following," in *Mind, Value, and Reality* (Cambridge, Mass.: Harvard University Press, 1998), 198–218. This issue speaks to the deep question of who is doing the teaching—with Augustine claiming that we do not teach one another, but rely on God behind both teachers and learners. This is an old theme in Platonic thinking, going back to Plato's Socrates's description of himself as a "midwife," and Augustine himself exploits the thought in his early dialogue *De magistro*, where ultimately the *only* teacher is Christ.

20. My thanks go to Kim Paffenroth for suggesting this example to me.

21. On this see Leo C. Ferrari, "The Theme of the Prodigal Son in Augustine's *Confessions*," *Recherches Augustiniennes* 12 (1977): 105–18.

22. I thank Jennifer L. Geddes for conversations relating to this essay, and for reading an early draft of it.

Chapter 2: Book Two

1. In a letter to a friend, Friedrich Nietzsche, *Nietzsche Briefwechsel: Kritische Gesamtausgabe* (Berlin and New York: Walter de Gruyter, 1982), 3.3.34, singled out Augustine's comments on his theft of the pears and his expression of grief for his childhood friend (*Conf.* 4.7.11). He is a kind of forerunner of the twentieth-century critiques we will mention. At one point he exclaims in exasperation, "Oh these ancient rhetoricians! How false! How outlandish!" and Nietzsche goes on to criticize Augustine's high-flown rhetoric and "psychological falsity." These passages are cited in James J. O'Donnell, *Augustine: Confessions* (Oxford: Oxford University Press, 1992), 2:227.

2. For example, see Peter Brown, *Augustine of Hippo: A Biography* (Berkeley, Calif.: University of California Press, 1967), 39. See also the comment of O'Donnell, *Augustine: Confessions*, 2:104: "There is little here that is so unusual: adolescent sexual profligacy of a sort that seemed inconceivable to some of our pious ancestors, but that is less so today and was certainly far less so in antiquity."

3. When it came time to brag about them, he seemed to find his libidinous behavior not quite up to standards: "and when I had no indecent acts to admit that could put me on a level with these abandoned youths, I pretended to obscenities I had not committed, lest I might be thought less courageous for being more

innocent, and be accounted cheaper for being more chaste" (*Conf.* 2.3.7), translated by Maria Boulding, *The Confessions*, pt. I/1, *The Works of Saint Augustine: A Translation for the 21st Century* (ed. John E. Rotelle; Hyde Park, N.Y.: New City Press, 1997). Unless otherwise noted, all translations are Boulding's.

4. E.g., Charles Kligerman, "A Psychoanalytic Study of the *Confessions* of St. Augustine"; David Bakan, "Augustine's *Confessions*: The Unentailed Self"; and James E. Dittes, "Continuities Between the Life and Thought of Augustine"; as well as the interesting critique by David Burrell, "Reading the *Confessions* of Augustine: The Case of Oedipal Analyses"; all four to be found in *The Hunger of the Heart: Reflections on the* Confessions *of Augustine* (ed. Donald Capps and James E. Dittes; Society for the Scientific Study of Religion Monograph Series 8; West Lafayette, Ind.: Society for the Scientific Study of Religion, 1990), 95–108, 109–15, 117–31, 133–42.

5. For one example, see Margaret Miles, *Desire and Delight: A New Reading of Augustine's* Confessions (New York: Crossroad, 1992), 98.

6. Pierre Courcelle gave this the most prominence of anyone, without necessarily drawing the conclusions above about marriage. See his "Le jeune Augustin, second Catalina," *Revue des Études anciennes* 73 (1971): 141–50.

7. Frederick Crosson, "Structure and Meaning in St. Augustine's *Confessions*," *Proceedings of the American Catholic Philosophical Association* 63 (1989): 84–97; and O'Donnell, *Augustine: Confessions,* 1:xxxv–xxxvi, 2:127.

8. This seems to be the implication of O'Donnell's mention of the fall passage (*Augustine: Confessions,* 2:126–27: "The parallel to the fruit of the tree of good and evil in the Garden dominates. . . . The result for Adam and Eve was that their eyes were opened '*ad invicem concupiscendum*' [citing *Gen. litt.* (*On the Literal Interpretation of Genesis*) 11.31.40]"). But O'Donnell is right to point out that the belaboring of the incident is not out of an exaggerated sense of guilt on Augustine's part (2:127).

9. Nowhere insisted upon more strongly perhaps than in his *De doctrina christiana* (*Christian Instruction*), though in Book IV, which is much later than the *Confessions*. A more nearly contemporaneous statement of the principle would be in *De catechizandis rudibus* (*Catechizing the Uninstructed*), 1.15.23, 1.8.12–9.13, written some five years after *Confessions*.

10. *Factus sum mihi regio egestatis, Conf.* 2.10.18, my translation.

11. Compare the closing of Book One, with its image of the beautiful little boy who is totally God's gift, and on the other hand the emptiness left by the time we get to Book Two. Moving from one image to another, we can gauge the depth of the sadness on which the rhetoric of Book Two flows.

12. The evocations of the mercy of God in retrospect lend to the prose the invitation to mercy or pity on the hapless subject of the narrative, upon whom God is taking mercy even in God's seeming silence, and in Augustine's ignorance of it (see *Conf.* 2.3.7).

13. On the theme of the Prodigal Son (Luke 15:11–32) in the *Confessions*, see Leo C. Ferrari, "The Theme of the Prodigal Son in Augustine's *Confessions*," *Recherches Augustiniennes* 12 (1977): 105–18. See also O'Donnell, *Augustine: Confessions,* 2:95–98. As with all scriptural texts except for the Psalms, this passage is present by allusion only in Book Two: in the image of the young man exiled from his father's house (2.2.4), the reference to the pigs (2.4.9), and the closing image of the land of want. Augustine had introduced this parable explicitly at *Conf.* 1.18.28, so these echoes refer back not only to the parable itself but to Augustine's preparation for them in Book One.

14. We don't have to wait for Book Ten for this pole of memory to appear: here it is in Book Two, which first sets out the narrative poles of the rhetoric. "O my joy,

how long I took to find you!" (*o tardum gaudium meum!*), the narrator laments at 2.2.2 (literally, "O my late Joy"; cf. 10.27.38, *sero te amavi*, "late have I loved you!").

15. *Conf.* 2.3.5, echoing Ps. 129:1, my translation (*ut videlicet ego et quisquis haec legit cogitemus de quam profundo clamandum sit ad te*).

16. *Conf.* 2.1.1, my translation.

17. Cf. Miles, *Desire and Delight*, 50. The vagueness has even led to speculation that Augustine's youthful lust was homosexual in orientation: W. T. Smith, *Augustine: His Life and Thought* (Atlanta: John Knox Press, 1980), 34–36.

18. Note the language of sterility that pervades the book (see, e.g., also at 2.3.5 the image of Augustine's self as a desert or wasteland, and the final image of the empty land of want). Cf. O'Donnell, *Augustine: Confessions*, 2:111, on the phrase *sterilia semina* ("sterile seeds") in 2.2.2.

19. *Conf.* 2.6.14, *ita fornicatur anima, cum avertitur abs te et quaerit extra te ea quae pura et liquida non invenit, nisi cum redit ad te.*

20. *Conf.* 2.2.3, *amplexus.*

21. In the *Confessions* itself we should note at least that it has already occurred in Book One, in a context where there is no question of literal fornication, 1.13.21. See O'Donnell's comment (*Augustine: Confessions*, 2:78). See my article on pride in Allan D. Fitzgerald et al., eds., *Augustine through the Ages: An Encyclopedia* (Grand Rapids: Eerdmans, 1999), 679–84. Note the connection between *libido* and the wanderings of the prodigal at 1.18.28, exhibiting the same connection between lust in its sexual sense and wandering from God. As an example of what happens when the rhetoric denouncing fornication is taken too literally and then applied directly to sexual ethics, here is a comment by Lisa Sowle Cahill: "Margaret Miles even describes Augustine as a sex addict, although it is difficult to weigh his level of actual compulsiveness against his overwhelming revulsion in the face of sexual drives and reactions, especially in view of the fact that they represented to him a shameful lack of control" (Lisa Sowle Cahill, "Sex, Marriage, and Family in Christian Tradition," in Paulinus Ikechukwu Odozor, C.S.Sp., ed., *Sexuality, Marriage, and Family: Readings in the Catholic Tradition* [Notre Dame, Ind.: University of Notre Dame Press, 2001], 188 [citing Margaret Miles, "The Erotic Text: Augustine's Confessions," *Continuum* 2/1 (1992): 134]). Both the ascription of sexual addiction and the qualification of it in terms of revulsion take Augustine's rhetoric as referring to the literal sin alone. In the case of the charge of sexual addiction, this assumes the rhetoric matches the literal reality; in the case of "overwhelming revulsion," this assumes the rhetoric is meant to refer to literal events that either did not happen or are grossly exaggerated (by revulsion).

22. *Conf.* 2.6.14: *ecce est ille servus fugiens dominum suum et consecutus umbram.* Cf. Job 7:2, a text Augustine connected to Gen. 3:8 elsewhere: see O'Donnell, *Augustine: Confessions*, 2:139. The *Ecce est* tells us that somehow this servant, Adam, is present in this, the narrative of Augustine that the reader is reading or to which the listener is listening.

23. Clearly mentioned ("the punishment for my soul's pride," *poena superbiae animae meae*) in 2.2.2, where the phrase "abased by my pride," *superba deiectione,* also connects pride with the ejection from God's face, which is an allusion to Gen. 3:8, 10. The infrequency with which this sin, underlying all other sin, is named is related to the way in which Augustine wants to depict the essence, or really the anti-essence, of sin as precisely shadowy, precisely *not* a substance. If there is a trinity of sin taken from 1 John 2:14, each of these "personae" are connon-substantial in the underlying non-essence of sin, pride, if I may speak so archly. On words used for pride in the *Confessions* in the sense meant here, see O'Donnell, *Augustine: Confessions*, 2:170.

24. The story, with Augustine's reflections on the incident, takes up chapters four through nine (2.4.9–9.17). See Leo Ferrari, "The Pear-Theft in Augustine's *Confessions*," *Revue des études augustiniennes* 16 (1970): 233–42.

25. Cf. *Conf.* 3.5.9: Scripture is "something veiled in mystery" (*rem velatam mysteriis*) such that it is "not accessible to the scrutiny of the proud." For this reason, Augustine could not appreciate it: "My swollen pride recoiled from its style and my intelligence failed to penetrate its inner meaning" (*tumor enim meus refugiebat modum eius et acies mea non penetrabat interiora eius*).

26. *City of God*, Book Fourteen, chapter twelve, written ca. 418. (For the date, see Brown, *Augustine of Hippo*, 284.)

27. Any account that would give a reason for it has to deny the story, has to say he really *was* after something, and it's *this*. The link to the biblical account precludes these reductionisms in favor of exegesis of that account.

28. "How can I repay the Lord for my ability to recall these things without fear?" (*Quid retribuam domino quod recolit haec memoria mea et anima mea non metuit inde?*) *Conf.* 2.7.15, cf. Ps. 116:12.

29. *Quid enim non facere potui, qui etiam gratuitum facinus amavi?* (*Conf.* 2.7.15), here disagreeing with Boulding's translation of "wanton" for *gratuitum*, for it is precisely the gratuitous character of his sin that he has been emphasizing all along, not its unruliness (which is present but as a feature derivative from its primary character as irrational).

30. *Quis est hominum qui suam cogitans infirmitatem audet viribus suis tribuere castitatem atque innocentiam suam, ut minus amet te, quasi minus ei necessaria fuerit misericordia tua, qua donas peccata conversis ad te?* (*Conf.* 2.7.15), disagreeing again here with the translation of Maria Boulding which seems to miss the parallelism of purpose between the *ut* of the opening *ut amem,* and this *ut.* The parallelism highlights the perversity of wanting to do something *in order to* love God less.

31. "What fruit did I ever reap . . . from that theft in which I found nothing to love except the theft itself, wretch that I was? It was nothing, and by the very act of committing it I became more wretched still." (*quem fructum habui miser in illo furto in quo ipsum furtum amavi, nihil aliud, cum et ipsum esset nihil et eo ipso ego miserior?*) *Conf.* 2.8.16.

32. See *Civ.* 14.12.

33. *ea [voluptas mihi] erat in ipso facinore quam faciebat consortium simul peccantium* (*Conf.* 2.8.16).

34. *Conf.* 2.9.17, and who understands sins anyway, he adds rhetorically, *delicta quis intellegit?* echoing Ps. 18:13 and using it to state the rhetorical problem of the book.

35. *Conf.* 2.9.17: "The theft gave us a thrill, and we laughed to think we were outwitting people who had no idea what we were doing, and would angrily stop us if they knew. Why could I not have derived the same pleasure from doing it alone?" (*risus erat quasi titillato corde, quod fallebamus eos qui haec a nobis fieri non putabant et vehementer nolebant. Cur ergo eo me delectabat quo id non faciebam solus?*)

36. *Conf.* 2.9.17: *Cum dicitur, 'eamus, faciamus,' et pudet non esse impudentem.*

37. As such it is an image in miniature, not to mention parody, of the society described in Book One, bound together in a lust for praise (apart from the praise of God), where the social bonds, located in this shared desire for praise, are collectively "fornication" (1.13.21). This is the "friendship of this world" (*amicitia enim mundi huius fornicatio est abs te*) and the *consortium* of teenage thieves, their *nimis inimica amicitia,* is an image of it meant to deglamorize the quest for praise and prestige so pointedly described in Book One.

38. *Conf.* 1.13.22, 1.18.29.

39. *Conf.* 2.3.7: *inter coaetaneos meos puderet me minoris dedecoris, quoniam audiebam eos iactantes flagitia sua et tanto gloriantes magis, quanto magis turpes essent, et libebat facere non solum libidine facti verum etiam laudis.*

40. See, e.g., *Conf.* 1.18.28.

41. *Conf.* 2.2.3: *accepit in me sceptrum vesania libidinis, licentiosae per dedecus humanum, inlicitae autem per leges tuas.*

42. *Conf.* 2.2.3: *Non fuit cura meorum ruentem excipere me matrimonio, sed cura fuit tantum ut discerem sermonem facere quam optimum et persuadere dictione.*

43. Augustine's *concupiscentia carnis* could be tied to the praise of the Creator by letting it wash up on the shores of the marriage bed (*Conf.* 2.2.3), where it would be turned to the "use" of procreating children. This "use" is part of the work of Creator and Redeemer, because the lust as such is not formative but dissipative, yet the Creator "forms the offspring of our mortality" through it, and so through marriage lust tends toward form. But in this text this possibility recedes into the withering power of the rhetoric Augustine generates to describe the spilling out of the self that lust both is and stands for. Lust is the most intimate symbol or sacrament of the fall, the one that brings it closest to our persons, and so the one that gives rise to the saddest cases of illusion and self-deception, as Dante will show as he portrays himself fainting at Francesca's story, the only sinner's story that causes such a reaction in the *Inferno*.

44. *Conf.* 5.13.23: "this man of God welcomed me with a fatherly kindness" (*suscepit me paterne ille homo dei*).

45. I would like to thank Nancy Cavadini, Larry Cunningham, Cyril O'Regan, and Jean Porter for reading this paper and offering advice and assistance.

Chapter 3: Book Three

1. *Conf.* 3.1.1. The translation is Henry Chadwick's, *St. Augustine: Confessions* (Oxford: Oxford University Press, 1998). All translations are my own unless otherwise noted. I have used the revised Latin text by James J. O'Donnell, *Augustine: Confessions*, vol. 1 (Oxford: Oxford University Press, 1992), and refer frequently in the notes to his commentary (vol. 2) on Book III. The best general introductions to Augustine's life and thought are: Peter Brown, *Augustine of Hippo: A Biography* (Berkeley, Calif.: University of California Press, 1967; revised edition with a new epilogue, 2000); James J. O'Donnell, *Augustine,* Twayne's World Authors (Boston: Twayne, 1985); Garry Wills, *Saint Augustine*, Penguin Lives (New York: Viking, 1999); and Henry Chadwick, *Augustine*, Past Masters (Oxford: Oxford University Press, 1986).

2. The translation is Rex Warner's, *The Confessions of St. Augustine* (New York: New American Library, 1963).

3. *Conf.* 3.6.10. The quotation is from James 1:17, and is repeated at *Conf.* 4.15.25. The verse in full reads: "Every good endowment and every perfect gift is from above, coming down from the Father of lights with whom there is no variation or shadow due to change" (RSV).

4. First John 2:16: "For all that is in the world, the lust of the flesh and the lust of the eyes and the pride of life, is not of the Father but is of the world" (RSV).

5. In *De doctrina christiana* (3.8.16), Augustine charts the antithetical motions of *caritas* and *cupiditas*. Book Three can be read as a microcosm of the soul's oscillation between *caritas* and *cupiditas* described in the whole of the *Confessions*.

6. The paragraph divisions appeared in the Maurist edition of 1679.

7. Book Two, in its inquiry into the mystery of evil that lies at the root of even banal material theft, has already set the stage for understanding the spiritual foundations of illicit material loves; Book Three analyzes that spiritual dynamic with

greater detail and refinement, and looks forward to Book Four in suggesting that spiritual loves too can be misdirected.

8. *secretiore indigentia* (*Conf.* 3.1.1); this poverty becomes a hidden bondage (*occulte ad vinculum*).

9. *oderam me minus indigentem* (*Conf.* 3.1.1).

10. *Conf.* 3.1.1 (trans. Chadwick).

11. See also the bitter sea of heresy (13.17.20) contrasted with God's sweet and hidden spring (13.17.21). These and other images are traced masterfully in Robert McMahon, *Augustine's Prayerful Ascent: An Essay on the Literary Form of the Confessions* (Athens, Ga.: University of Georgia Press, 1989), 58ff. McMahon notes (p. 69) Augustine's etymological association of taste (*sapor*) with wisdom (*sapientia*). Augustine often contrasts God's sweetness with the restless heart which gives this life a bitter taste (see *Mor. eccl.* 1.53; *Retract.* 1.7.4; *Tract. Ev. Jo.* 25.14; *Serm.* 57.11, 88.7, 295.3); see also Josef Lössl, "dolor (dolere)," *Augustinus-Lexikon*, vol. 2, fasc. 3/4, col. 582.

12. Lovers of imaginative literature will understandably view Augustine's apparent dismissal of all imaginative literature with some frustration. There is, additionally, an element of misdirection in Augustine's criticism, for he himself is a master of the literary imagination and its use to effect change in his reader. In this, as with Tolstoy (in *What Is Art?* [trans. A. Maude; New York: Bobbs-Merrill Co., Liberal Arts Press, 1960]), one marvels at the artist's readiness to dismiss his art, particularly art that discloses the possibilities of redemption. Yet, what is the spiritual reality of habituating the soul to the enjoyment of suffering? Such art is dangerous indeed—art can participate in redemption, but it can also insulate the soul against the reality of human suffering.

13. *Conf.* 3.2.2. On the theater and love of sorrow, see Kim Paffenroth, "The Young Augustine: Lover of Sorrow," *Downside Review* 118 (July 2000): 221–30.

14. Chadwick (p. 36 n. 3) is right to note Augustine's objection to the Roman theater's fictional character and erotic content, and to see Augustine's discussion of theater as a (perhaps unknowing?) disagreement with Aristotle on tragedy. But Augustine here is concerned with what one sees only insofar as it forms and exhibits what one loves.

15. *in quos ipsa mutatur et vertitur per nutum proprium de caelesti serenitate detorta et deiecta* (3.2.3). See Lössl, who observes that *dolor* is "a rather ambiguous term," for it may be "a sign of hope" insofar as it stimulates spiritual reform (cols. 582–83). Yet, *dolor* "indicates not only a privation of being, but also <*resistentia*> against it and <*difficultas*> to maintain and retain <being> in its integrity" (col. 586).

16. See *Conf.* 4.6.11 with McMahon, *Augustine's Prayerful Ascent*, 67–71.

17. "Only if there were a malicious goodwill (which is impossible) is it possible for someone who truly and sincerely felt mercy to wish wretches to exist so that he might show mercy" (*Conf.* 3.2.3).

18. There is implicit here a criticism of the Christian's excessive devotion to Christ's agonies, and perhaps to Monica's own (somewhat) indulgent suffering over the fate of her son. Immoderate or misdirected asceticism, whether orthodox or Manichean, may also be implicated. On Monica's tears, see McMahon, *Augustine's Prayerful Ascent*, 63–65; and Kim Paffenroth, "Tears of Grief and Joy: Chronological Sequence and the Structure of *Confessions* Book 9," *Augustinian Studies* 28 (1997): 141–54.

19. *nonnullus itaque dolor approbandus, nullus amandus est* (*Conf.* 3.2.3); see also *Conf.* 10.28.39.

20. *in quantas iniquitates distabui et sacrilega curiositate secutus sum* (*Conf.* 3.3.5). Chadwick's rendering "a sacrilegious quest for knowledge" unduly narrows the

sense of *curiositas* and ignores the ablative of manner (see O'Donnell, 2:158). *Distabesco* can mean "melt away" as well as "consume" and so evokes both the earlier water imagery and the self-squandering of the prodigal son (Luke 15:11–32), which follows shortly.

21. *Conf.* 3.3.5 (with Warner).

22. *Conf.* 3.3.5; Chadwick's rendering—"The liberty I loved was merely that of a runaway"—provides an accurate and vivid image, but risks missing the sense that the liberty itself is fleeting and elusive as an object of love.

23. See Chadwick, p. 38 n. 7.

24. The image of the prodigal son echoes the muddied springs of lust of *Conf.* 3.1.1. The classic article on the theme of the prodigal son in *Confessions,* is Leo C. Ferrari, "The Theme of the Prodigal Son in Augustine's *Confessions,*" *Recherches Augustiniennes* 12 (1977): 105–18.

25. *malivolas laetitias suas* (*Conf.* 3.3.6, with Chadwick).

26. *per gaudia vanitatis humanae* (*Conf.* 3.4.7). Augustine writes at greater length of a similar vanity in dedicating a book to a Roman orator whom he admired but had never met (*Conf.* 4.14.21–23).

27. Cicero's *Hortensius*, a protreptic work, does not survive; much of our knowledge of it comes from Augustine's own account and quotations.

28. *ille vero liber mutavit affectum meum, et ad te ipsum, domine, mutavit preces meas, et vota ac desideria mea fecit alia* (*Conf.* 3.4.7). With due respect to the contemporary feel of Chadwick's translation, to say that the *Hortensius* "changed my feelings" and modified his "values and priorities" deprives the passage of its force; Brown's rendering, "it changed my way of feeling" is similarly inadequate (see Brown, *Augustine,* 169). *vota* is only weakly rendered by "longings," for it has the force of vow, usually religious vow, but sometimes also a matrimonial vow; *desiderium* is, for Augustine, a fundamental appetite. See Jean Doignon, "Desiderare, desiderium," *Augustinus-Lexikon*, vol. 2, Fasc. 1/2 1996 (cols. 306–9).

29. *viluit mihi repente omnis vana spes, et immortalitatem sapientiae concupiscebam aestu cordis incredibili, et surgere coeperam ut ad te redirem* (*Conf.* 3.4.7).

30. The beauty of words intimates more than the hollow echoes of his desire "to distinguish myself as a puffed-up orator" (*Conf.* 3.4.7). Words—like the body—may either cloak or disclose the contents of the heart. Cicero himself was admired, Augustine tells us, for his tongue but not his heart (*pectus,* on which see O'Donnell, 2:165, who suggests that Augustine is criticizing Cicero's excessive *ambitio saeculi*—"not an unverisimilar charge in Cicero's case"). Beneath the pride of human vanity lies a desire for the heart to measure up to the good. Can words signify things that neither change nor deceive?

31. *Conf.* 3.4.8; and yet, Augustine continues, "I did not know what you were doing with me (*et nesciebam quid ageres mecum!*)."

32. See Plotinus, *Enn.* 5.1.1.

33. Perhaps because of its punctuated brevity—and because it results in a "misconversion" (O'Donnell, 1:xxxiii n. 36)—the reading of the *Hortensius* is typically not viewed alongside the tentative ascents of Book Seven or the vision of Ostia in Book Nine.

34. "There are those who seduce others with philosophy" (*Conf.* 3.4.8), as the Manichees will indeed do, as Augustine soon relates.

35. *Conf.* 3.4.8 (with Chadwick).

36. See especially *Conf.* 10.24.35–26.37.

37. Having learned the lesson that eloquent words conveying substance are to be preferred to empty eloquence, Augustine has not yet learned to prefer spiritual substance, however inelegantly expressed. He is still too proud to divorce himself

from concerns of style. Conceit inhibits his gaze—eternal things are rendered invisible to the mental eye.

38. Though it does not figure explicitly in his account, it would seem that Augustine resisted the dissociation of philosophy from *cultus*. Despite his independence of mind, the young Augustine, it seems, recognized that the solitary pursuit of wisdom was untenable apart from communal practice.

39. Unduly attached to the fleshly sense of words, Augustine's intellect was blinded by pride, by confusion about corporeal things (especially the corporeal sense of words), and (related to pride) by the magical, secret character of Manichean doctrine and practice. All of these are misdirections of attention to external things, rather than the internal discernment of the "life of soul" and "the life of lives." On Augustine's expectation of secret doctrines among the Academics and in Christianity, see O'Donnell, 1:xxix and 2:175.

40. The intonations of magical practice (whether representative of Manichean ritual or an attempt to tarnish the Manichean image) are clear here. Both potions and the use of names in spells or theurgy operate on a mechanistic, which is to say material, rather than spiritual model. On the magical importance of names in late antiquity, see J. Dillon, "The Magical Power of Names in Origen and Later Platonism," in *Origeniana Tertia* (ed. R. Hanson and H. Crouzel; Roma: Edizioni dell'Ateneo, 1985), 203–16.

41. O'Donnell, 2:185, remarks: "When in after years, A. would be accused of retaining a Manichean outlook, the justice of the charge would lie in the way he remained in the power, not of the answers the Manichees offered, but of the questions (e.g. *unde malum*) on which they insisted with such effect." Yet this presupposes that Augustine had not already (before or after reading *Hortensius*) posed these questions to himself. This section, a weighty part of Book Three, is often read as the beginning of Augustine's anti-Manichean polemic in *Confessions*, but the obliqueness of Augustine's treatment indicates that he does not wish his audience to read it as such. In so doing, Augustine remains true to the Ciceronian injunction to seek truth where it may be found, and remains true to truth itself in refusing to dismiss a set of ideas prima facie because of the sect that holds them. To discredit the sect is not necessarily to discredit the philosophical force, or weakness, of the ideas themselves.

42. Augustine also wrestled with questions of Manichean authority, and this may be one reason for his refusal, over nine years, to join the Manichees formally through the rite of baptism. Augustine writes that he threw off the "darkness" of Manichean authority and "learned to trust more in those men who taught [i.e., in the Academics] than in those who ordained obedience" (*Beat.* 1.4). Indebted to Academic skepticism for his deliverance from Manichean superstition, Augustine's argument against skepticism's radical formulation is found in his *Contra Academicos*.

43. These questions are mooted here and then refined and given their definitive and precise expression, effectively *in medias res*, at *Conf.* 3.7.12. As O'Donnell notes, 2:185, the three central questions identified at *Conf.* 3.7.12 are taken up in reverse order in the narrative: where does evil come from? (*Conf.* 7.12.18); is God confined within a corporeal form? (*Conf.* 7.1.1–2.3); can the patriarchs be considered just? (*Conf.* 5.14.24 and 6.4.6). To this it must be added that this latter question is taken up immediately (in *Conf.* 3.7.13–8.15) in the exploration of the tension between human custom and divine truth.

44. Augustine offers his own account of creation in Books Eleven through Thirteen.

45. *Conf.* 3.6.10 (with Warner); the word *ferculum* (food tray, platter) also refers to the litter for carrying the spoils of war in a victory parade or cult images in a religious procession.

46. *Conf.* 10.6.9–10.

47. *Conf.* 3.6.11 (with Warner). The passage anticipates a similar combination of visual and edible imagery: "memory is, as it were, the stomach of the mind, whereas gladness and sadness are like sweet and bitter food" (*Conf.* 10.14.21). On memory and conversion, see my "Memory and Imagination in Augustine's *Confessions*," in *Literary Imagination, Ancient and Modern: Essays in Honor of David Grene* (ed. T. Breyfogle; Chicago: University of Chicago Press, 1999), 130–54.

48. See *Conf.* 4.16.28–30 for a similar misdirection after reading Aristotle's *Categories.*

49. *tu autem eras interior intimo meo et superior summo meo* (*Conf.* 3.6.11); cf. *Conf.* 10.19.28.

50. *non secundum intellectum mentis, quo me praestare voluisti beluis, sed secundum sensum carnis quaererem* (*Conf.* 3.6.11). This is, as O'Donnell notes, the first appearance in *Confessions* of that central word *intellectus* (1:xxxiii n. 36) and the only significant appearance in Book Three of the terms *intellectus* and *quaerere* (2:183). See my "*intellectus*" in *Augustine through the Ages: An Encyclopedia* (ed. Allan D. Fitzgerald, O.S.A., et al.; Grand Rapids: Eerdmans, 1999), 452–54.

51. *Conf.* 3.7.12 (trans. Warner).

52. This issue troubles him again at *Conf.* 4.16.31 and 7.1.1–2.3.

53. Chadwick (p. 43 n. 25) notes the affinities between Augustine's language here and at *Conf.* 7.1.1 and that of Plotinus's discussion of physical diffusion in *Enn.* 6.4 and 6.5.

54. For a recent treatment of the disordered soul informed by theology and contemporary social science, see Sandra Lee Dixon, *Augustine: The Scattered and Gathered Self* (St. Louis: Chalice Press, 1999).

55. It is hard to say whether the wrestling with custom and habit are the chronological concerns of the young Augustine, or the author's design for the narrative, though the Manichees were known to have criticized the morals of the patriarchs, and Augustine saw fit to write a whole treatise on Manichean customs (*De moribus ecclesiae catholicae* and *De moribus Manichaeorum*, written in 387/388). Regardless, it is interesting that Augustine first addresses ethical concerns before shifting to metaphysical concerns and then returning to the matter of chastity in particular in Book Eight.

56. *sed ex lege rectissima dei omnipotentis* (*Conf.* 3.7.13); cf. Cicero, *Resp.* III.11.18–19 and 22.33.

57. Augustine returns to the relation of parts to the whole at *Conf.* 4.11.17 with an analogy to language, recalling the insight of poetry he invokes below.

58. "Untrained minds . . . assess the customs of the entire race by the criterion of their own moral code" (*Conf.* 3.7.13); cf. Montaigne, "On Cannibals": "every man calls barbarous anything he is not accustomed to," in *The Complete Essays* (trans. M. A. Screech; London: Penguin, 1991), 231.

59. That God might treat one people differently from another and still prescribe the same justice offends an innate sense of fairness; our own instinctive embrace of radical equality makes it even more difficult to grasp Augustine's notion that justice rules differently. Equality and justice are in tension with one another, for Augustine; rendering unto each his due, while consistent with equity, is not always reducible to general principles of equality. Our outrage, Augustine suggests, may be more the surfacing of envy than a love of justice.

60. Though Augustine notes that he had not at that time applied his insights to ethics (*Conf.* 3.7.14). Augustine pursues the analogy between poetry and justice throughout his *De musica*. That beauty and fittingness occupied his intellectual energies from an early date is indicated in his account of his first book, *De pulchro et apto* (see *Conf.* 4.8.20).

61. God himself may overrule the proscriptions of an age. In the instances in which the Old Testament fathers transgress the fixed eternal law in its temporal dispen-

sation, Augustine notes, their actions are to be understood as predicting the future as revealed by God. Chadwick (p. 45 n. 30) notes: "The Manichees entirely rejected the orthodox belief that the Hebrew prophets predicted gospel events and the mission of the Church." That is, correct ethical discernment with respect to a past age requires a dual engagement of the moral imagination—conceiving of the fittingness of an action to its time, and the inappropriateness of an action with respect to its symbolic, allegorical, or prophetic valence in a future time. See also *Conf.* 3.19.17: "All the things done by your servants are done either to show what is appropriate to the present or to prefigure the future."

62. Cf. *De civitate Dei* 16.8: "For God, the Creator of all, knows where and when each thing ought to be, or to have been created, because He sees the similarities and diversities which can contribute to the beauty of the whole. But he who cannot see the whole is offended by the deformity of the part, because he is blind to that which balances it, and to which it belongs" (*The City of God* [trans. M. Dods; New York: Random House, 1950]).

63. *Conf.* 3.6.11: "How much better are the fables of the philologists and poets to these beguiling snares."

64. Augustine insists that "the acts of the Sodomites" is strictly prohibited by divine law, the law of nature, and custom. Several complementary speculations may help account for the puzzling introduction of the subject here. The Manichees may have practiced, or at least not proscribed, homosexuality. If some of Augustine's own sexual relationships were homosexual, then his treatment of the subject here is an honest, if veiled, part of his confession to God, who has an easier time reading between the lines than we do. Having justified the patriarchs' adultery on customary grounds, Augustine may be keen to emphasize that not all sexual practices are authorized. Finally, homosexuality does not fit the pattern of congruity Augustine has elucidated heretofore: sexual intercourse maintains the social bond precisely because it embraces the difference of the sexes rather than their similarity.

65. See O'Donnell's note on 3.8.16 (2:191).

66. *turpis enim omnis pars universo suo non congruens* (*Conf.* 3.8.15); Chadwick's gratuitous addition—what is *turpis* is unacceptable "to society"—unnecessarily narrows the sense to a purely social sphere.

67. The reader is left to conclude that obedience to divine command is always in keeping with the natural law, insofar as the hierarchy of authority is natural and consistent and because God alone may perceive the eternal justice of a command apparently in contradiction to the natural law. It is interesting in this context (*Conf.* 3.8.15) that when Augustine draws the analogy between human governance and divine command, he does so in the conditional subjunctive. The passage implies that obedience to kings, unlike obedience to God, is a matter of convention and not natural law.

68. *privata superbia diligitur in parte unum falsum* (*Conf.* 3.8.16); at *Conf.* 10.29.40 Augustine again compares the love of the private and love of the whole. For the metaphysical resonance of the formulation, see Plotinus, *Enn.* 1.6 and 6.9.

69. *Conf.* 3.9.17 (trans. Chadwick). The introduction of the chapter division (Chapter Nine) misleadingly separates its thematic relation to the preceding paragraphs.

70. Cf. *De doctrina christiana* 3.12.18ff.

71. *quis dubitet esse faciendum, quando ea iusta est societas hominum quae servit tibi?* (*Conf.* 3.9.17).

72. *Conf.* 3.10.18.

73. *Conf.* 3.10.18 (trans. Chadwick).

74. Psalms 143:7; 85:13. Psalm 143, in addition to the portion cited by Augustine from verse 7, speaks of the temporality of passing shadows, deliverance from

adversity, and the singing of a new song (mentioning sons in particular). Equally, Psalm 85 is a psalm of preservation and an injunction to walk in the truth. The broader themes of these psalms would certainly have echoed in Augustine's mind and perhaps in the minds of many of his readers.

75. See O'Donnell's textual note, 2:198–99, indicating that at issue was whether Monica would live in Augustine's home, not whether Augustine was prohibited from Monica's. The Donatist insistence on purity, which had begun to concern Augustine by the time of his writing *Confessions*, may also be in the background and the subject of implicit criticism.

76. Following O'Donnell, 2:197.

77. Noted by Chadwick, p. 50 n. 42.

78. See O'Donnell, 2:199.

79. At the end of the garden scene in Book Eight, as O'Donnell notes, 2:199, the phrase *regula fidei* is invoked, "a much commoner phrase in A. and one roughly equivalent to 'baptismal creed.'"

80. Not only do we take wooden rulers for granted, but we take standard measures for granted, too.

81. Much of the last three books of *Confessions* may be read as an attempt to forestall certain, especially literal, misinterpretations of Scripture. See *Conf.* 12.31.42–32.43 for how Augustine hopes he himself is interpreted.

Chapter 4: Book Four

1. The translation of Augustine's Latin, here and elsewhere, is my own, but I am indebted to the prior efforts of numerous translators, especially F. J. Sheed (*The Confessions of St. Augustine* [London and New York: Sheed & Ward, 1943]) and Henry Chadwick (*St. Augustine: Confessions* [Oxford: Oxford University Press, 1998]).

2. Manicheism is a religion that takes its name and inspiration from Mani, a religious visionary who was born in Persian-controlled Babylonia in April of 216 C.E. and executed under the reign of Bahram I in February of 277. For a concise account of Mani and the religion he inspired, see the essay by J. Kevin Coyle on "Mani, Manicheism" in *Augustine through the Ages: An Encyclopedia* (ed. Allan D. Fitzgerald, O.S.A., et al.; Grand Rapids: Eerdmans, 1999). In essence Manicheism is a religion that emphasizes the dual and irreconcilable origins of good and evil and offers knowledge as a path to redemption. Augustine tended to view Manicheism as a distorted form of Christianity, one overly pretentious in its claims to divine knowledge. For the purposes of my essay, I will be looking at Manicheism through Augustine's eyes.

3. James J. O'Donnell, *Augustine: Confessions*, vol. 2: *Commentary on Books 1–7* (Oxford: Oxford University Press, 1992), 203. O'Donnell's three-volume edition of Augustine's *Confessions*—the Latin text and two volumes of commentary—is a fabulous resource for scholars and advanced students of Augustine, but it is tough going for the Latinless. For a more accessible but still quite sophisticated commentary, I recommend Colin Starnes, *Augustine's Conversion: A Guide to the Argument of* Confessions *I–IX* (Waterloo, Ont.: Wilfrid Laurier University Press, 1990). O'Donnell and Starnes work through Augustine's text book by book, section by section (minus the last four books in Starnes). Their efforts usefully supplement the essays of this volume.

4. Starnes, *Augustine's Conversion*, 89–112.

5. Starnes seems to think so. See *Augustine's Conversion*, 106: "He has not proven that the Manichees' doctrines were wrong or that in following them he was actually going away from the truth, but he has shown how the actual misery and futil-

ity of all his actions in these years were a direct consequence of his adherence to their position."

6. My sense of Manicheism as it is represented in the *Confessions* is greatly indebted to chapter five of Peter Brown's *Augustine of Hippo: A Biography* (rev. ed.; Berkeley, Calif.: University of California Press, 2000). Brown's book remains, in my opinion, the single greatest work on Augustine in English.

7. I am not claiming that Augustine never had any interest in representing and refuting Manicheism as an abstract set of beliefs. He has a host of polemical writings that are usually grouped under the heading "Anti-Manichean treatises." My claim is that his confessional approach to the Manichees is as I have described.

8. The phrase I am invoking here to describe what moved Augustine's friend to accept baptism—"some unknown higher instinct"—actually occurs in a different section of Book Four. This is the section where Augustine describes how "a man of keen intelligence," whom he will later identify in Book Seven as the renowned physician Helvius Vindicianus, had been trying to dissuade him from looking for knowledge from astrology (4.3.5). The sticking point for the young Augustine was that many of the forecasts of astrologers seemed to come out right. Vindicianus doesn't argue the point. He simply offers Augustine the observation that in many cases of divination, whether it be the use of lots, horoscopes, or a chance reading of some passage of a book, there is a congruence between the seeker and the sign or utterance, in accord with "some unknown higher instinct" of the soul. The moral of the observation is that astrology is false not because astrologers are always wrong, but because the language of astrology is of no use for exploring the truths that astrologers sometimes divine.

The moral is a telling one as well for the case of Augustine's friend and his divination of the correctness of his baptism. Whether his baptism was a true sign of his condition would depend not only on the correctness of his intuition but on the aptness of the Catholic faith to articulate that intuition. Suppose, to be more specific, that Augustine's friend would have been right to connect his baptism to a profound feeling of personal liberation. If that is to be other than a chance divination on his part, it must be the case that Catholicism offers him the right terms for expressing and exploring the liberation.

9. For those interested in teasing out this psychology in detail, I recommend looking at these three places especially in Augustine: his account of the angelic fall in *Civ.* 12.6–8 (where he introduces the notion of a deficient cause), his account of the original human fall in *Civ.* 14.10–12 (where he makes a distinction between being seduced into sin and sinning out of pride), and finally his confession of his theft of pears in *Conf.* 2.4.9–10.18 (where he uses his own sin to suggest the way in which all sin is original).

Chapter 5: Book Five

1. J. J. O'Meara, *The Young Augustine: The Growth of St. Augustine's Mind up to His Conversion* (London: Longmans, Green, 1954) 13, 44; H. Marrou, *St. Augustin et la fin de la culture antique* (Paris: E. De Boccard, 1958), 1.

2. *Civ.*, respectively: 8.4, 5.9, 4.3 and 6.4, and 9.9. Compare *On Christian Doctrine* (trans. D. W. Robertson; New York: Liberal Arts Press, 1958), 2.6.8: "no one doubts that things are perceived more readily through similitudes and that what is sought with difficulty is discovered with more pleasure." Cf. ibid. 4.8.22. And of course, Augustine makes similar remarks in the *Confessions* about the popular and the obscure understanding of the Academics: 5.10.19 and 5.14.25.

3. *On True Religion* (trans. J. H. S. Burleigh, in *Augustine: Earlier Writings* [Philadelphia: Westminster Press, 1953]), 17.33. Compare, out of many similar

comments: "the obscurity itself of the divine and wholesome writings was a part of a kind of eloquence through which our understandings should be benefitted not only by the discovery of what lies hidden but also by exercise" (*Doctr. chr.* 4.6.9).

4. *Confessions* (trans. Maria Boulding; Hyde Park, N.Y.: New City Press, 1997), 6.5.8. Cf. similarly 3.5.9, 12.27.37. (References in the text to loci where no title is cited will be to this translation.)

5. *Conf.* 12.31.42.

6. Aquinas, *The Trinity and the Unicity of the Intellect* (trans. R. E. Brennan; St. Louis: Herder, 1946) Q. Two, art. 4.

7. This is a standard or common view. E.g., "the structural parallel between Rousseau's *Confessions* and Augustine's *Confessions* has at its center the 'conversions' recounted in Book 8 of each work. The conversion represents a radical turning point for both Augustine and Rousseau" (Ann Hartle, *The Modern Self in Rousseau's Confessions: A Reply to St. Augustine;* Notre Dame, Ind.: Notre Dame University Press, 1983), 136.

8. *Conf.* 5.1.1.

9. *Conf.* 5.8.14. Cf. 5.8.15: "You knew all along, O God, the real reason why I left to seek a different country, but you did not reveal it either to me or to my mother."

10. *Conf.* 5.13.23. The phrase succinctly expresses the paradox of God's hidden providence.

11. As he comments about the books of the Platonists, "No one there hears a voice calling, come to Me" (*Conf.* 7.21.27).

12. Cf. *On the Usefulness of Belief* (trans. J. H. S. Burleigh, in *Augustine: Earlier Writings* [Philadelphia: Westminster Press, 1953]), 16.34: "If the providence of God does not preside over human affairs, there is no need to worry about religion," and ibid. 8.20 and 13.29.

13. Cf. the opening sentence of *Conf.* 5.8.14.

14. Although he would remain publicly a member of the sect "until some preferential option presented itself" (*Conf.* 5.7.13).

15. The numbering of the paragraphs, of course, dates from the Maurist edition of 1679, but they indicate approximately the respective distances.

16. The Latin says "the Catholic Church commended to me by my parents."

17. "[P]opularly thought" is another reference to the two levels of meaning in a teaching. For a discussion by Augustine of why the Academics concealed their true theory, cf. *Acad.* 1.7.14ff.

18. He speaks later of the "keen attention I had directed toward Mani's writing," and gives examples of errors in Mani's books (*Conf.* 5.7.12–13).

19. Aristotle, *Categories* (trans. E. M. Edghill, in *Basic Works of Aristotle* [ed. R. McKeon; New York: Random House, 1941]) chap. five, 4a10.

20. *Conf.* 4.16.29. These comments of Augustine about "simple and changeless" foreshadow a problem that will dominate Book Eleven: how then can we tell a story, as Genesis does, of what God did on the successive days of creation?

21. It is interesting that there is no mention of the name Christ from the time he encounters the Manichees (*Conf.* 3.6.10) until he lands in Italy (*Conf.* 5.9.16).

22. See, for example, Cicero's presentation of the Epicurean position in *De finibus*, Book One. (For pleasure as the greatest good, 1.12.40ff.; for friendship, 1.20.65ff.) Augustine knew of Lucretius, the chief Roman expositor of Epicureanism, but cites him rarely. It seems likely that Cicero is his major source.

23. He had earlier commented that "when I wanted to think about my God I did not know how to think otherwise than in terms of bodily size, for whatever did not answer to this description seemed to me to be nothing at all. This misapprehension was the chief and almost sole cause of the error I could not avoid" (*Conf.* 5.10.19).

24. First John 2:16. Augustine refers to this triad repeatedly in the *Confessions*, e.g., "These are the chief kinds of sin, which sprout from a craving for domination, or for watching shows, or for sensory pleasure" (*Conf.* 3.8.16). Cf the similar analysis in Cicero, *Off.* 1.4.11–13.

25. Plato, *Resp.* 435ff. This tripartite division of the soul in Plato is adopted by the Platonists, e.g., Plotinus, *Enn.* 1.1.5–6.

26. In Book Ten, where he is reflecting on the three concupiscences, Augustine comments on "the temptation to win veneration and affection from others, and to want them not for the sake of some quality that merits them, but in order to make such admiration itself the cause of my joy. It is no true joy at all, but leads only to a miserable life and shameful ostentation" (*Conf.* 10.36.59).

27. For example, *Conf.* 3.1.1–3, 3.3.6; 4.2.2, 4.13.20; 5.13.23; 6.10.17, 6.15.25.

28. He describes his state at this point as "enslavement to worldly affairs," hardly a desire or concupiscence.

29. John Henry Newman, *An Essay in Aid of a Grammar of Assent* (Notre Dame, Ind.: University of Notre Dame Press, 1979), 49–92.

30. This communal end of his journey is signaled in the last lines of the last narrative book by the reference to his "fellow citizens in the eternal Jerusalem," and his request to his readers to remember his mother and father in their prayers (*Conf.* 9.13.37).

31. The order of naming: Alypius, Nebridius, and Romanianus in Book Six; Vindicianus and Firminus in Book Seven; Simplicianus, Verecundus, and Ponticianus in Book Eight; Adeodatus, Evodius, Monica, and Patricius in Book Nine.

32. *Util. cred.* 13.28 and 16.34.

Chapter 6: Book Six

1. See *Conf.* 6.11.18 and cf. 3.4.7–8.

2. The translation used here and throughout this chapter is that of Maria Boulding in pt. I/1 of *The Works of Saint Augustine: A Translation for the 21st Century* (ed. John E. Rotelle; Hyde Park, N.Y.: New City Press, 1997).

3. See *Conf.* 3.11.19–20.

4. *Conf.* 5.8.15.

5. Not Augustine's only spiritual father, since in Book Eight Simplicianus becomes his spiritual father as well.

6. See J. Patout Burns, "Ambrose Preaching to Augustine: The Shaping of Faith," in *Augustine: Second Founder of the Faith* (ed. Joseph C. Schnaubelt and Frederick van Fleteren; Collectanea Augustiniana; New York: Peter Lang, 1980), 373–86.

7. Peter Brown, *Augustine of Hippo: A Biography* (rev. ed.; Berkeley, Calif.: University of California Press, 2000), 57.

8. Pierre Courcelle, *Recherches sur les Confessions de saint Augustin* (2nd ed.; Paris: E. de Boccard, 1968), 31–32.

9. Augustine describes the thirteen books of his *Confessions* in this way in his *Retract.* 2.6.32.

10. Like the gladiatorial games, the chariot races were a blood sport, with charioteers (not to mention horses) regularly being maimed or losing their lives as their chariots collided or went too quickly around the curves.

11. *Conf.* 5.9.16; 9.13.34; 10.20.29.

12. E.g., *Conf.* 1.9.14; 8.9.21, 8.10.22.

13. *Civ.* 14.28.

14. Erich Auerbach, *Mimesis: The Representation of Reality in Western Literature* (trans. Willard R. Trask; Princeton, N.J.: Princeton University Press, 1953), 69 (modified).

15. Epictetus, *Discourses* 1.13 (trans. G. Long [modified]). For this quotation and much of the discussion of Stoicism that follows see Herschel Baker, *The Image of Man: A Study of the Idea of Human Dignity in Classical Antiquity, the Middle Ages, and the Renaissance* (New York: Harper & Brothers, 1961), 69–83 (quotation on 79).

16. Marcus Aurelius, *Meditations* 4.3 (trans. C. R. Haines), quoted in Baker, *Image of Man*, 80.

17. See Samuel Dill, *Roman Society in the Last Century of the Western Empire* (New York: Meridian Books, 1958) 55 (with references to ancient sources).

18. *Civ.* 15.5 (trans. H. Bettenson).

19. The Colosseum itself symbolized Roman civilization in a variety of ways for everyone at that time, not just Augustine. It was the tallest and most magnificent of all the monuments of Rome and one of the greatest architectural achievements of antiquity. From a sociological point of view, it brought together people of every class and status, from the emperor to the lowliest of the lowly, and unified them. True, that unification could also be described as effective crowd control, but crowd control is no mean achievement in itself, as modern European football matches have shown. Finally, the fact that the gladiators, not to mention the animals, were drawn from all corners of the empire was an advertisement for the variety of peoples and territories that Rome had conquered. Augustine takes all this symbolism for granted while subjecting it to a hermeneutics of suspicion.

20. According to Paul Tillich, "The difference [between the Stoics and Christianity] was that the Stoics did not have the concept of sin. They had the concept of foolishness, but not sin. Therefore, salvation in Stoicism is a salvation through reaching wisdom. In Christianity salvation is brought about by divine grace. These two approaches are in conflict with each other to the present day" (Paul Tillich, *A History of Christian Thought* [ed. Carl E. Braaten; London: SCM Press, 1968]), 9.

21. Quoted in *Conf.* 1.5.6.

22. Colin Starnes, *Augustine's Conversion: A Guide to the Argument of* Confessions *I–IX* (Waterloo, Ont.: Wilfrid Laurier University Press, 1990), 154–57.

23. Few of us, I think, would relish the thought of having someone else publish our *Confessions*. But we must suppose that Alypius was of one mind with Augustine in wanting to give God the praise. As Augustine once wrote, Alypius and he were one mind in two bodies (Letter 28.1.1).

24. Nebridius (6.10.17) provides a specific example of a friend and "fellow-seeker of the happy life" who shared Augustine's sense of futility and frustration at this time. I have therefore not treated his case separately from that of the other friends referred to in 6.11.18–15.25.

25. Since Miles's diagnosis is controversial, I would like to quote part of her original justification for it: "It is fashionable to smile at Augustine's adolescent behavior as normal teenage behavior. But this is to ignore his own evaluation of sex as dominating, dictating, and ordering his life. Even if he had supplied us with many more concrete details of his sexual activity, we could not make a more accurate evaluation from the vantage point of our 'objectivity' than the evaluation of Augustine himself, who found himself unfree in the pursuit of sex. Very simply, Augustine knew himself to be an addict" (Margaret Miles, "Infancy, Parenting and Nourishment in Augustine's *Confessions,*" *Journal of the American Academy of Religion* 50 [1982]: 349–64, quote 358).

Chapter 7: Book Seven

1. All translations from Greek and Latin are my own, including those from the Bible, which are usually from Augustine's Latin.

2. For a much fuller account of this mythology, which is extremely helpful in deciphering Augustine's remarks about Manicheism, see Gerald Bonner, *St. Augus-*

tine of Hippo: Life and Controversies (2nd ed.; Norwich, U.K.: Canterbury Press, 1986), chapter four.

3. Augustine uses variants of Nebridius's dilemma against the Manichees on a number of occasions, e.g., in the debate *Against Fortunatus* 1 and 7–9 and in *The Morals of the Manichaeans* 12.25.

4. Augustine, Letter 18.2. This threefold hierarchy of being is never far from Augustine's thinking, and is the first concept nonspecialists should turn to when they are puzzled by some difficult saying in the *Confessions*.

5. Our author is thinking of an inquiry into the incorporeal greatness of the soul that he pursued years earlier in his treatise *The Magnitude of the Soul*.

6. Plotinus, *Enn.* 1.6.8, quoted more fully below.

7. The verbs "rise" and "return," reminiscent of the parable of the Prodigal Son (Luke 15:18), are also for Augustine reminiscent of Plotinus, *Enn.* 1.6.8, as we shall see below.

8. See, for example, Thomas Aquinas, *Summa Theologica* I, 32.1, and Martin Luther's first sermon in *Sermons on the Gospel of John,* in the American edition of *Luther's Works,* vol. 22 (St. Louis: Concordia, 1957), 5–26. The shift from the church fathers' focus on Christ as divine Reason to later Christian theology's insistence on the incomprehensibility of the Trinity was one of the consequences of the council of Nicaea, as I argue in *Augustine's Invention of the Inner Self* (Oxford: Oxford University Press, 2000), 58–60.

9. Fragments of the *Hortensius* can be found quoted in ancient authors, most importantly in Augustine himself (*Trin.* 13.4.7, 13.5.8; 14.9.12; and 14.19.26). An attempt to reconstruct its basic structure and content has been made by Michel Ruch, *L'Hortensius de Ciceron: histoire et reconstitution* (Paris: Les belles lettres, 1958).

10. We have extensive fragments of the *Protrepticus*, collected by Ross in vol. 12 of *The Works of Aristotle* (Oxford: Clarendon Press, 1952), 27–56. Some scholars think the fragments are extensive enough to allow us to reconstruct nearly the whole of the treatise. So readers who would like to get a rough idea of the text that first turned Augustine's heart to seek God should consult Aristotle, *Protrepticus: A Reconstruction* (ed. A.-H. Chroust; Notre Dame, Ind.: University of Notre Dame Press, 1964).

11. Cf. *Civ.* 10.2, where Augustine refers to Plotinus explicitly as having the right view on participation in the divine light—almost exactly the opposite from the view of the Manichees described in *Conf.* 4.15.25. The most important thing Augustine is not telling us about the books of the Platonists is that, although Plotinus is not materialistic enough to make the soul literally part of God, there is an important sense in which for Plotinus the soul is divine. See Cary, *Augustine's Invention of the Inner Self,* 36–40.

12. Plotinus, *Enn.* 1.6.8.

13. For the pervasiveness of language from the parable of the Prodigal Son throughout the *Confessions*, see Leo C. Ferrari, "The Theme of the Prodigal Son in Augustine's *Confessions,*" *Recherches Augustiniennes* 12 (1977): 105–18. For the Plotinian meaning of the image of the prodigal, see Robert J. O'Connell, *Soundings in St. Augustine's Imagination* (New York: Fordham University Press, 1994), chap. 4, as well as 176–78.

14. Plotinus, *Enn.* 1.6.8.

15. Augustine, *Civ.* 9.17. The Plotinus passage here is different from the earlier quotation because it is translated from Augustine's Latin rather than Plotinus's Greek, and Augustine combines it with a passage from *Enn.* 1.2.3 about becoming like God. (In the latter passage Plotinus is in fact quoting a favorite passage of Plato: "the flight consists in becoming like God," *Theaet.* 176b.)

16. For the centrality of this concept of integral omnipresence in the *Confessions* and its origins in Plotinus (and particularly in *Enn.* 6.4 and 6.5), see Robert J. O'Connell, *St. Augustine's Early Theory of Man, A.D. 386–391* (Cambridge, Mass.: Harvard University Press, 1968), chap. 1.

17. Augustine, Letter 118.23.

18. I tell the story of these developing insights in *Augustine's Invention of the Inner Self*, chaps. 6–10.

19. The most famous and still very influential reading along these lines is Courcelle's interpretation of 7.10.16 and 7.17.23 as narrating "failed attempts at Plotinian ecstasy," in his *Recherches sur les Confessions de saint Augustin* (Paris: E. de Boccard, 1950), 4.3, 157–67. Contrast this with Robert J. O'Connell's case against reading them as narratives of particular experiences in his *Images of Conversion in St. Augustine's Confessions* (New York: Fordham University Press, 1996), 115–18.

20. The equation of true being with unchangeable being is fundamental to Augustine's ontology; see *Man.* 1–11, *Fid. symb.* 7, and *Nat. bon.* 1–17.

21. Giving life to the body is the fundamental function of the soul, *Conf.* 10.7.11. The relation is not symmetrical: the soul gives life to the body, but the body does not give life to the soul. This lack of symmetry is precisely why the soul is superior to the body. See Augustine, *Div. quaest. LXXXIII* 54.

22. Plato, *Resp.* 7.514a–518a (the famous "allegory of the cave"). Augustine picks up these Platonic metaphors of ascent, intellectual vision, and dazzlement at the beginning of his career as a Christian writer, quickly puts them to systematic use (see especially *Solil.* 1.6.12–7.14 and 1.13.23), and never really looks back.

23. In *Lib.* 2.3.7–15.39.

24. For the complex history of the image of swelling outward and the language of "casting out its inward parts" (at the end of 7.16.22), which combines Plotinian and biblical language, see O'Connell, *Soundings in St. Augustine's Imagination*, 255–77.

25. When Augustine is critical of Neoplatonism, he tends to link pride, polytheism, and Porphyry, as shown by J. J. O'Meara, *The Young Augustine* (London: Longmans, Green, 1954), chap. 10. The link between pride and polytheism seems to be operative in the connection between the second half of 7.9.14 and 7.9.15, where what Augustine reads in the books of the Platonists is idolatry, which is symbolically described as "Egyptian food . . . I did not eat."

26. Augustine explicitly says that pagan Platonists have (however briefly) seen God, in *Trin.* 4.15.20. See likewise *Civ.* 9.16.

27. For the contrast between Christ as mediator and Neoplatonist notions of mediation, see *Civ.* 9.15. The latter depends on some form of intermediary being (a pattern followed in the Arian view of Christ as the eternal Word acting as intermediary between the Father and the creation, in virtue of being greater than the creation but less than the Father). The former is a both/and proposition: Christ is the mediator between God and man because he is himself both fully God and fully man. But this Nicene mediatorship is made possible only because God became man, which is why Augustine, like other Nicene theologians, says he is mediator *as man*. To say he is mediator *as God* would suggest the Arian position, as if he were an intermediary God.

28. This formula, from *Civ.* 11.2, structures the whole of Augustine's soteriology, both in *Confessions* and elsewhere.

29. Here Augustine quotes Jas. 4:6 and 1 Pet. 5:5, both of which are quoting Prov. 3:34.

30. Indeed it seems likely that even in Christology Platonism helped rather than hindered Augustine's move away from Manichean habits of thought. In *Conf.* 5.10.20 Augustine describes how Manichean materialism led to christological error: he could not believe our Savior was "born in the flesh" for fear that would

mean he was "dirtied by the flesh." Platonism helps him overcome the Manichean sense that flesh dirties the soul, I have argued, because in Platonist ontology the soul is literally a different kind of being from bodies, so that flesh cannot dirty it (Cary, *Augustine's Invention of the Inner Self,* 117–20). It is ontologically impossible for material dirt to affect a nonmaterial being. The same consideration would remove the Manichean objection to the incarnation of God.

31. Notice how the story of Victorinus's baptism concludes when the congregation "all willed to snatch him into their own heart" (8.2.5). This is the power and meaning of baptism, which is an outward sign of an inward union. "Heart" is singular, because it is the heart not of diverse individuals, but of the one church, Christ's spiritual body.

32. No other view of the meaning of the *Confessions* seems able to account for its unity, as O'Connell argues in *St. Augustine's Confessions* (2nd ed.; New York: Fordham University Press, 1989), 5–22, and *Soundings in St. Augustine's Imagination*, chap. 2. If the *Confessions* is an autobiography of an individual rather than an account of the pilgrimage of the soul, then the three books of exegesis on Genesis do not belong in it.

33. *Mag.* 1.1–2.

34. Ibid. 10.33–35.

35. This phrase was prominent in the theology of Cyril of Alexandria, which triumphed at the ecumenical council of Ephesus in 431, the year after Augustine's death. See Cyril's third letter to Nestorius, especially the eleventh anathema, in J. Stevenson, ed., *Creeds, Councils, and Controversies* (London: SPCK, 1966), 280–88. Notice the oxymoron that would strike any ancient thinker in this phrase: a body that gives life to the soul!

36. For Paul, the divine light shining in our hearts gives us "the light of the knowledge of the glory of God in the face of Christ" (2 Cor. 4:6 RSV).

37. For the Eastern Orthodox, the ultimate or beatific vision of God is the same as that experienced by those who beheld the transfiguration with the eyes of both body and soul. The thought is developed most thoroughly by Gregory Palamas, *The Triads* (Mahwah, N.J.: Paulist Press, 1983), 57–92.

38. *Mag.* 11.38.

39. The possibility of seeing God with the eye of the body is something Augustine vigorously rejects for most of his career (e.g., Letter 92.3 and 147.49)—so vigorously that at one point he must apologize for speaking too harshly (Letter 148.1). He indicates a willingness to hear the opposing point of view (Letter 148.2), and evidently listened so well that he eventually changed his mind toward the end of his life (*Civ.* 22.29). One wonders what he would have said had he lived long enough to absorb the news from Ephesus.

40. Augustine builds a whole theological framework around a denial of the modern sentiment that "life is a journey, not a destination" in the first book of *Christian Instruction*. This mortal life is indeed a journey, but its whole meaning and value are defined by its destination, for we should use temporal things on the journey only for the sake of arriving at our eternal destination (*Doctr. chr.* 1.3.3.-4.4).

41. Heidegger, *Identity and Difference* (trans. J. Stambaugh; New York: Harper & Row, 1969), 72.

42. Luther's treatise, "The Sacrament of the Body and Blood of Christ—Against the Fanatics," in the American edition of *Luther's Works,* vol. 36 (Philadelphia: Muhlenberg Press, 1959), 339–42, draws heavily on Augustine's treatment of the incarnation in Letter 137.4–10, which in turn draws heavily on the notion of integral omnipresence developed by Plotinus in *Enn.* 6.4 and 6.5.

43. The first great statement of a concept of eternity that is not only immutable but altogether outside time seems to be Plotinus, *Enn.* 3.7. The concept is picked up

by Augustine (e.g., *Conf.* 1.6.10 and 11.10.12–13.16) and given a classic statement by Boethius, *Consolation of Philosophy* 5.6.

44. Dietrich Bonhoeffer, *Letters and Papers from Prison* (New York: Macmillan, 1953), 220.

45. At stake in this fierce and painful controversy were theological issues that are beginning to fade from living memory (like the term "supernatural"), but which are essential to understanding the current shape of Catholic theology. The most lucid discussion of the conceptual issues known to me is found, oddly enough, in a book on Karl Barth: Hans Urs von Balthasar, *The Theology of Karl Barth* (San Francisco: Ignatius Press, 1992), III, 2, 267–325.

46. John Paul's Augustinian anthropology, centered on the love of Truth, is especially visible in the encyclicals *The Splendor of Truth* (Boston: Pauline Books & Media, 1999) and *Faith and Reason* (Washington, D.C.: United States Catholic Conference, 1998), as well as the Apostolic Constitution on Catholic Universities, *Ex Corde Ecclesiae* (Washington, D.C.: United States Catholic Conference, 1990).

47. The key point is that "seeing the essence of God belongs to the created intellect by grace and not by nature," Thomas Aquinas, *Summa Theologica* I, 12.4.

48. This claim runs contrary to standard interpretations of Augustine, which make him out to be more Thomistic (and less Platonistic) than I think he really is. For defense of this claim, see Cary, *Augustine's Invention of the Inner Self*, 67–76.

49. For two perspectives on how this ancient philosophic spirituality plays out in an educational context, see Thomas F. Martin, "Augustine's *Confessions* as Pedagogy: Exercises in Transformation," and Phillip Cary, "Study as Love: Augustinian Vision and Catholic Education," both in *Augustine and Liberal Education* (ed. Kim Paffenroth and Kevin L. Hughes; Aldershot, U.K.: Ashgate Publishing, 2000).

Chapter 8: Book Eight

1. Augustine lived 354–430. His *Confessions* (to which such unqualified references pertain) was written 397–401. For future references to the *Confessions*, the above numbers in brackets refer to Book Two, sec. 4, par. 9 in the *Confessions*. The edition used here is that translated by Maria Boulding, O.S.B., in pt. I/1 of *The Works of Saint Augustine: A Translation for the 21st Century* (ed. John E. Rotelle; Hyde Park, N.Y.: New City Press, 1997). On the present topic of the pear theft, see also my "The Pear-Theft in Augustine's *Confessions*," *Revue des Etudes Augustiniennes* 16 (1970): 233–42. Unless otherwise accredited, all references are to my own works. For a list of all my publications on Augustine provide name and e-mail address to: ldrew@nbnet.nb.ca.

2. In *Augustinus* (Madrid) 39 (1994): 149–64.

3. This combination of science and medieval thought is particularly exemplified in my "Saint Augustine's Various Conversions: Some Insights of Modern Science," *Religious Studies and Theology* 12 (1992): 24–41.

4. Hildesheim, Germany: Georg Olms Verlag AG, and New York: Olms-Weidmann. In 1999 this was followed by the publication of the first-ever six-volume *Concordantia in XXII libros De Ciuitate Dei* (Hildesheim, Germany: Georg Olms Verlag AG, and New York: Olms-Weidmann, 1999).

5. *Beat.* 1.2 and 4, especially the last section where he links the stars which sink in the ocean with being "terrified by a childish superstition": *in errorem ducerer, labentia in Oceanum astra suspexi. Nam et superstitio quaedam puerilis me ab ipsa inquisitione terrebat.* The Latin is from W. M. Green, ed., *De beata vita*, in *Corpus Christianorum Series Latina* 29 (Turnhoult: Brepols, 1970), 66–7.

6. "On a hesité sur le sens de ces môts." From *Oeuvres de saint Augustin*, vol. 4 of *Dialogues Philosophiques* (Paris: Desclée de Brouwer, 1948), 289. As will be seen, one needs hesitate no more.

7. See my "Halley's Comet of 374 AD—New Light upon Augustine's Conversion to Manicheism," *Augustiniana* 27 (1977): 139–50. Compare with the "Chronology of the Life of Saint Augustine," in Augustine, *Confessions* (trans. Maria Boulding, O.S.B., ed. Susan B. Varenne; New York: Random House/Vintage Spiritual Classics, 1998), xxviii: "At this time . . . [of 372]," which shows a lack of acquaintance with my article of a quarter-century ago.

8. The Vintage Spiritual Classics edition's arbitrary date of 372 is therefore earlier by two years. See "Chronology," xxxiv.

9. See "Astronomy and Augustine's Break with the Manichees," *Revue des Etudes Augustiniennes* 19 (1973): 263–76.

10. See "Augustine's 'Nine Years' as a Manichee," *Augustiniana* 25 (1975): 208–15.

11. See "Augustine and Astrology," *Laval Theologique et Philosophique* 33 (1977): 241–51.

12. See "The Peculiar Appendage of Augustine's '*Enarratio in Psalmum LXI,*'" *Augustiniana* 28 (1978): 3–17, as also the previous endnote.

13. See "Augustine and Astrology" of n. 11 above.

14. See "Young Augustine: Both Catholic and Manichee," *Augustinian Studies* 26/1 (1995): 109–28.

15. "Paul at the Conversion of Augustine (*Conf.* 8.12.29–30)," *Augustinian Studies* 11 (1980): 5–20.

16. "Saint Augustine on the Road to Damascus," *Augustinian Studies* 13 (1982): 151–70.

17. Probably from his Manichean sojourn, Augustine was a great patron of the notion of the legendary mystical tree. See "The Mystical Tree in the Western Christian Tradition," *Communio Viatorum* 14 (1970): 1–12; "The Pear-Theft in Augustine's *Confessions,*" *Revue des Etudes Augustiniennes* 16 (1970): 233–42; "Symbols of Sinfulness in Book II of Augustine's *Confessions,*" *Augustinian Studies* 2 (1971): 93–104; and finally, "The Tree in the Works of Saint Augustine," *Augustiniana* 38 (1988): 37–53.

18. This mysterious voice has been shown to be symbolically the voice of the Father calling to the prodigal son to return to the house of God. See my "'Ecce audio vocem de vicina domo' (*Conf.* 8.12.29)," *Augustiniana* 33 (1983): 232–45, as well as "The Arboreal Polarisation of Augustine's *Confessions,*" of n. 22 below.

19. *Codicem . . . aperui et legi in silentio* (8.12.29).

20. Of which the pages were rolled within one another.

21. With the tree of the forbidden fruit (Gen. 3) and the "tree" of the cross (Matt. 27:32–35; Mark 15:21–28; Luke 23:33; and John 19:18).

22. "The Arboreal Polarisation of Augustine's *Confessions,*" *Revue des Etudes Augustiniennes* 25 (1979): 35–46, as well as "The Tree in the Works of Saint Augustine"(see n. 17 above).

23. See my *The Conversions of Saint Augustine* (The Saint Augustine Lecture for 1982; Villanova, Pa.: Villanova University Press, 1984), reviewed in the "Bulletin Augustinien pour 1985/86," *REA* 32 (1986): 317.

24. See "Augustine's 'Discovery' of Paul's Writings (*Conf.* 7.21.27)," *Augustinian Studies* 22 (1991): 37–61.

25. See nn. 15 and 16 above.

26. See the initial pages of my "Augustine's Conversion Scene: The End of a Modern Debate?" *Studia Patristica* 22 (1989): 235–50. For a summary of the archaeology of this ancient, protracted debate, see H.-I. Marrou, "La Querelle autour du 'Tolle, lege,'" *Revue d'histoire ecclesiastique* 53 (1958): 47–57. Unfortunately none of the participants had acquired a scientific education.

27. See Adolf von Harnack, *Augustins Konfessionen* (Giessen: J. Ricker, 1888).

28. Pierre Courcelle, *Recherches sur les Confessions de saint Augustin* (2nd ed.; Paris: E. de Boccard, 1968), 188–202.

29. Ibid., 200. See also my *The Conversions of Saint Augustine* of n. 23 above.
30. See n. 24 above.
31. See Peter Brown, *Augustine of Hippo: A Biography* (Berkeley, Calif.: University of California Press, 1967), 184, as well as n. 10 above.
32. See Brown, *Augustine of Hippo*, 74.
33. See Brown's chronological tables in *Augustine of Hippo*, 74 and 184.
34. St. Augustine, *Opera Omnia*, 2 vols. Paris (Gaume Bros., 1836). Inquiries at the Library of the Pontifical Institute of Medieval Studies (Toronto, Ontario, Canada) elicited the information that this was a respected edition, though not of the very latest quality. Still, it would quite adequately serve the purpose of my hypothesis.
35. The account of this search was published as "Saint Augustine on the Road to Damascus," *Augustinian Studies* 13 (1982): 151–70.
36. A more up-to-date edition was virtually inaccessible to me privately for use on a long-term basis for the project and in my hometown of Fredericton, as mentioned above.
37. Again, see "Chronology," xxxi.
38. Ibid.
39. As for other verses similar to Rom. 13:13–14, see my "Beyond Augustine's Conversion Scene," in *Augustine: From Rhetor to Theologian* (ed. Joanne McWilliam; Waterloo, Ont.: Wilfred Laurier University Press, 1992), 97–107.
40. Beginning at 4:15 P.M. in the Freind Room of Christ Church's Lee Building.
41. It was subsequently published as "Augustine's Conversion Scene: The End of a Modern Debate?" See n. 26 above.
42. For instance, see in his *Confessions*: 3.2.2–4; 4.1.1–3; 8.10.22–23; and 10.35.56.
43. See the conclusion to my "Reconsiderando las Confesiones de Agustín: Treinta años de descrubrimientos," *Augustinus* 42 (1997): 279–96.

Chapter 9: Book Nine

1. Colin Starnes, *Augustine's Conversion: A Guide to the Argument of* Confessions *I–IX* (Waterloo, Ont.: Wilfrid Laurier University Press, 1990), 247.
2. William Mallard, *Language and Love: Introducing Augustine's Religious Thought through the* Confessions *Story* (University Park, Pa.: Pennsylvania State University Press, 1994), 169–88, esp. 170–71.
3. James J. O'Donnell, *Augustine: Confessions* (Oxford: Oxford University Press, 1992), vol. 3, 72.
4. Robert McMahon, *Augustine's Prayerful Ascent: An Essay on the Literary Form of the* Confessions (Athens, Ga.: University of Georgia Press, 1989), 108–12.
5. Starnes, *Augustine's Conversion,* 247–66.
6. M. Miles, "Infancy, Parenting, and Nourishment in Augustine's *Confessions*," in *The Hunger of the Heart: Reflections on the* Confessions *of Augustine* (ed. Donald Capps and James E. Dittes; Society for the Scientific Study of Religion Monograph Series 8; West Lafayette, Ind.: Society for the Scientific Study of Religion, 1990), 219–35, quote 224. Cf. the same label given by Peter Brown, *Augustine of Hippo: A Biography* (Berkeley, Calif.: University of California Press, 1967), 165, citing E. R. Dodds, "Augustine's Confessions: A Study of Spiritual Maladjustment," *Hibbert Journal* 26 (1927–1928): 459–73, esp. 460.
7. Augustine, *Confessions* (trans. John K. Ryan; New York: Image Books, 1960). All quotations from *Confessions* are from this translation unless otherwise noted.
8. Pierre Courcelle, *Recherches sur les Confessions de saint Augustin* (Paris: E. de Boccard, 1950), 65: "appétit rationaliste."

9. Mallard, *Language and Love,* 171.

10. As ably shown by Leo C. Ferrari, "Symbols of Sinfulness in Book II of Augustine's *Confessions,*" *Augustinian Studies* 2 (1971): 93–104, esp. 97–101; idem., "The Theme of the Prodigal Son in Augustine's *Confessions,*" *Recherches Augustiniennes* 12 (1977): 105–18; idem., "Beyond Augustine's Conversion Scene," in *Augustine: From Rhetor to Theologian* (ed. Joanne McWilliam; Waterloo, Ont.: Wilfrid Laurier University Press, 1992), 97–107, esp. 101.

11. *Conf.* 1.18.28; 3.3.5, 3.6.11; 4.16.30; 8.3.6, 8.3.8; 10.31.45.

12. As suggested by Ferrari, "Prodigal Son in *Confessions,*" 106. Navigius is chided by Monica at *Conf.* 9.11.27.

13. Cf. A. H. Hawkins, "St. Augustine: Archetypes of Family," in *The Hunger of the Heart: Reflections on the* Confessions *of Augustine* (ed. Donald Capps and James E. Dittes; Society for the Scientific Study of Religion Monograph Series 8; West Lafayette, Ind.: Society for the Scientific Study of Religion, 1990), 237–54, esp. 248.

14. Mallard, *Language and Love,* 172–73.

15. Ibid., 173.

16. On the Platonists, see Brown, *Augustine of Hippo,* 91–100; Henry Chadwick, *Augustine* (Oxford: Oxford University Press, 1986), 8–9, 16–24.

17. On the Manichees, see Brown, *Augustine of Hippo,* 46–60; Chadwick, *Augustine,* 11–15.

18. The classic works remain P. Henry, *La vision d'Ostie, sa place dans la vie et l'oeuvre de saint Augustin* (Paris: J. Vrin, 1938); and Courcelle, *Recherches,* 222–26. Cf. the discussion of their work by Starnes, *Augustine's Conversion,* 259–61; idem., "Augustine's Conversion and the Ninth Book of the *Confessions,*" in *Augustine: From Rhetor to Theologian* (ed. Joanne McWilliam; Waterloo, Ont.: Wilfrid Laurier University Press, 1992), 51–65, esp. 57–58. On the other hand, for an analysis that makes the vision at Ostia identical (or even inferior) to the one at Milan, see J. Burnaby, *Amor Dei: A Study of the Religion of St. Augustine* (London: Hodder & Stoughton, 1938), 29–32. See also Brown, *Augustine of Hippo,* 128–31.

19. Starnes, "Augustine's Conversion," 58–59. My following discussion is based on his nine specifically Christian and anti-Platonist elements in the vision at Ostia: Starnes, *Augustine's Conversion,* 261–63; idem., "Augustine's Conversion," 59–61.

20. I here combine Starnes's second and eighth points: Starnes, *Augustine's Conversion,* 261, 263; idem., "Augustine's Conversion," 59, 61.

21. Starnes's third point: Starnes, *Augustine's Conversion,* 261–62; idem., "Augustine's Conversion," 59.

22. I here combine Starnes's fourth, sixth, and seventh points: Starnes, *Augustine's Conversion,* 262–63; idem., "Augustine's Conversion," 59–61.

23. The following discussion is based on my "The Young Augustine: Lover of Sorrow," *The Downside Review* 118 (2000): 221–30. On Augustine's critique of Stoicism, cf. Burnaby, *Amor Dei,* 45–51.

24. *City of God* (trans. H. Bettenson; New York: Penguin, 1984); all future references to *City of God* are from this translation.

25. Chadwick, *Augustine,* 9.

26. Hawkins, "Archetypes of Family," 248.

27. Much of this discussion is based on my earlier analysis in "Tears of Grief and Joy: Chronological Sequence and the Structure of *Confessions,* Book 9," *Augustinian Studies* 28 (1997): 141–54.

28. McMahon, *Augustine's Prayerful Ascent,* 109.

29. Mallard, *Language and Love,* 170.

30. Cf. the similar beginnings to Books One, Five, Six, and Eight. The beginning to Book Six, with its description of Monica, is especially similar.
31. Psalm 116:16; cf. Starnes, *Augustine's Conversion,* 247–48. "Handmaid" here could also possibly refer to the church, or both: see Mallard, *Language and Love,* 172.
32. McMahon, *Augustine's Prayerful Ascent,* 109.
33. Verecundus and Nebridius disappear completely. Adeodatus is mentioned in *Conf.* 9.12.29 and 9.12.31. On the connections with later books, cf. the similar conclusion of McMahon, *Augustine's Prayerful Ascent,* 110: "Though Adeodatus, in fact, died some time after Monica, his death is recorded before it. The prolepsis enables the author to create correspondences with the allegory on God's 'eternal sabbath' in book 13, while placing Monica's death at the climax of book 9."
34. Cf. Starnes, *Augustine's Conversion,* 254: "The last chapter before the eulogy to Monica occurred to Augustine as an afterthought at the time he was writing the *Confessions.*"
35. Two of the major points of continuity that made Augustine break with the Manichees: see Jaroslav Pelikan, *The Mystery of Continuity: Time and History, Memory and Eternity in the Thought of Saint Augustine* (Charlottesville: University Press of Virginia, 1986), 5–7.
36. Margaret Miles, *Desire and Delight: A New Reading of Augustine's* Confessions (New York: Crossroad, 1992), 85.
37. Mallard, *Language and Love,* 173–74.
38. Starnes, *Augustine's Conversion,* 257–59.
39. Starnes, "Augustine's Conversion," 52–53.
40. Cf. Brown, *Augustine of Hippo,* 29: "Yet, the balanced picture of Monica which Augustine provides in Book Nine of his *Confessions,* dissolves during most of the early books." It not so much "dissolves," as it is never formed until here.
41. Rendered as "ruthless indifference" by J. J. O'Meara, *The Young Augustine: The Growth of St. Augustine's Mind up to His Conversion* (London: Longmans, Green, 1954), 204.
42. Pelikan, *Mystery of Continuity,* 141, quoting Outler's Introduction to the *Confessions.*
43. Pelikan, *Mystery of Continuity,* 141.
44. K. Adam, *Saint Augustine: The Odyssey of His Soul* (trans. D. J. McCann; New York: Macmillan Co., 1932), 2–3, 5.
45. See, for example, Donald Capps, "Augustine as Narcissist: Of Grandiosity and Shame," in *The Hunger of the Heart: Reflections on the* Confessions *of Augustine* (ed. Donald Capps and James E. Dittes; Society for the Scientific Study of Religion Monograph Series 8; West Lafayette, Ind.: Society for the Scientific Study of Religion, 1990), 169–84; Miles, *Desire and Delight,* 81–86.
46. V. J. Bourke, *Augustine's Quest of Wisdom: Life and History of the Bishop of Hippo* (Milwaukee: Bruce Publishing, 1944), 148.
47. See my earlier "God in the Friend, or the Friend in God? The Meaning of Friendship for Augustine," *Augustinian Heritage* 38 (1992): 123–36, with bibliography. Also see Brown, *Augustine of Hippo,* 61–64.
48. Cf. the very different and negative analysis of Donald Capps, "Augustine's *Confessions*: The Scourge of Shame and the Silencing of Adeodatus," in *The Hunger of the Heart: Reflections on the* Confessions *of Augustine* (ed. Donald Capps and James E. Dittes; Society for the Scientific Study of Religion Monograph Series 8; West Lafayette, Ind.: Society for the Scientific Study of Religion, 1990), 69–92, esp. 87–92, who sees little or no affection of Augustine for his son. I am more impressed by the closeness between father and son as shown in the dialogue *Mag.,* and Augustine's quotation of Cicero as cited in Brown, *Augustine of Hippo,* 135:

"Surely what Cicero says [to his son] comes straight from the heart of all fathers, when he wrote: 'You are the only man of all men whom I would wish to surpass me in all things.'" (For the Latin, see J. P. Migne, ed., *Patrologiae Cursus Completus,* Series Latina [Paris: 1841], vol. 45, col. 1551.) Nebridius and Adeodatus both probably died in 390: see Brown, *Augustine of Hippo,* 74, 135.

49. On Cassiciacum, cf. Brown, *Augustine of Hippo,* 115–27; McMahon, *Augustine's Prayerful Ascent,* 112–13.

50. Augustine is so coy about his feelings for his son's mother that they will always invite speculation. The most simplistic is that he uniformly depicts her as a temptress, and he therefore is a neurotic misogynist: thus Miles, *Desire and Delight,* 81–87. A more complicated analysis sees Augustine as depicting *both* Monica and the mother of Adeodatus as temptress and mother, carnal and divine love: "Perhaps, too, the exaggerated emphasis in the autobiography on his affection and grief for his mother derives from a certain amount of displaced emotion—displaced from the concubine from whom he so resolutely turns. As such a displacement suggests, the archetypes of 'temptress' and 'mother' are interlocking as well as alternative figures" (Hawkins, "Archetypes of Family," 244). Even without psychological categories, the connection (if not the interpretation) of his feelings for the two women and for his son is clear: "his grief for [Monica] makes comment, by implication, on the amorphous grief felt for his dead friend and his rejected concubine. Linked to these is his touching account of his son . . . the brief account offers the final tragic note in the whole matter of the concubine and his inconclusive relation to her" (Mallard, *Language and Love,* 173).

51. Miles, *Desire and Delight,* 84.

52. Capps, "Silencing of Adeodatus," 83–92.

53. Miles, *Desire and Delight,* 81–86.

54. Starnes, *Augustine's Conversion,* 264–65.

55. O'Meara, *Young Augustine,* 204.

56. On the date, see Brown, *Augustine of Hippo,* 63–64.

57. Cf. Miles, *Desire and Delight,* 84.

58. Cf. ibid.: "At the time of Monica's death, however, he thinks that tears are theologically incorrect since Monica has died as a faithful Christian, in the hope of resurrection, so that, in fact, 'she was not altogether dead.'"

59. On Monica's weeping, see the discussion in Miles, *Desire and Delight,* 81–82. On the connection between prayer and weeping in Augustine, see J. Balogh, "Unbeachtetes in Augustins Konfessionen," *Didaskaleion* (n.s.) 4 (1926): 5–21.

60. Brown, *Augustine of Hippo,* 164.

61. Ibid.

62. The suggestion of Hawkins, "Archetypes of Family," 249.

63. Hawkins, "Archetypes of Family," 249.

64. On Augustine's more sinister expression of friendship, cf. Brown, *Augustine of Hippo,* 63: "For Augustine was an imperialist in his friendships. To be a friend of Augustine's, meant only too often becoming a part of Augustine himself."

65. Hawkins, "Archetypes of Family," 250; cf. the description in Brown, *Augustine of Hippo,* 30.

66. P. Rigby, "Augustine's *Confessions*: The Recognition of Fatherhood," in *The Hunger of the Heart: Reflections on the* Confessions *of Augustine* (ed. Donald Capps and James E. Dittes; Society for the Scientific Study of Religion Monograph Series 8; West Lafayette, Ind.: Society for the Scientific Study of Religion, 1990), 143–65, quote 152.

67. Rigby, "Recognition of Fatherhood," 152.

68. Miles, "Infancy, Parenting, and Nourishment," 233, emphasis in original.

69. Rigby, "Recognition of Fatherhood," 147.
70. Hawkins, "Archetypes of Family," 248.
71. Ibid., 254.
72. O'Donnell, *Confessions,* vol. 3, 94.
73. Though this has been influentially suggested by E. A. Clark, "Vitiated Seeds and Holy Vessels: Augustine's Manichean Past," in *Images of the Feminine in Gnosticism* (Philadelphia: Fortress Press, 1988), 367–401.
74. Pelikan, *Mystery of Continuity,* 2, emphasis in original.
75. On the rhetoric of the passage, see Miles, *Desire and Delight,* 48–51, though her comments sometimes tend toward eisegesis, as when she writes that Augustine "promises titillating scatological detail" (*Desire and Delight,* 50), unfortunately giving no indication as to what she might be referring. ("Voyeuristic" I might have been able to fathom, but "scatological"?)
76. Cf. Courcelle, *Recherches,* 68–70.
77. Hawkins, "Archetypes of Family," 254.
78. Rigby, "Recognition of Fatherhood," 147.
79. Dante, *Paradise* (trans. Mark Musa; New York: Penguin Books, 1986), IX, 103–18.
80. Cf. McMahon, *Augustine's Prayerful Ascent,* 149: "Both recapitulate—both, for Augustine, are founded in—the Christian vision of history under God's Providence. In this vision, and in the *Confessions,* sin leads to redemption, digressive wanderings become directed movements in an ascent, disorder is founded on and informed by order."
81. Pelikan, *Mystery of Continuity,* 3.
82. Pascal, *Pensées* (Brunschvicg edition; Paris: Garnier Bros., 1952), fr. 268, my translation. Though I am not a Kenny Rogers fan myself, his song *The Gambler* provides a more homespun version of this wisdom that is not without a certain appeal, and possibly a great deal more influence.
83. Augustine, *Soliloquies* (trans. K. Paffenroth; Hyde Park, N.Y.: New City Press, 2000), 2.1.1. Cf. the analysis of J. Morgan, *Psychological Teaching of St. Augustine* (London: E. Stock, 1932), 176–77.
84. Pelikan, *Mystery of Continuity,* 2–3.

Chapter 10: Book Ten

1. Translations of the text of the *Confessions* are quoted from *St. Augustine: Confessions* (trans. Henry Chadwick; Oxford: Oxford University Press, 1998).
2. Questions about the dating and the structure of the *Confessions* as a whole, and about Book Ten in particular, have generated a large body of scholarly literature. Some of the relevant studies are Pierre Courcelle, *Recherches sur les Confessions de saint Augustin* (Paris: E. de Boccard, 1950); idem., *Les "Confessions" de Saint Augustin dans la tradition littéraire, antécédents et posterité* (Paris: Études Augustiniennes, 1963); Goulven Madec, *Le Dieu d'Augustin* (Paris: Les Éditions du Cerf, 1998); Robert McMahon, *Augustine's Prayerful Ascent: An Essay on the Literary Form of the* Confessions (Athens, Ga.: University of Georgia Press, 1989); Marjorie O'Rourke Boyle, "The Prudential Augustine: The Virtuous Structure and Sense of His *Confessions,*" *Recherches Augustiniennes* 22 (1987): 129–50; James J. O'Donnell, *Augustine: Confessions,* vol. 3, *Commentary on Books 8–13* (Oxford: Oxford University Press, 1992); idem., "Augustine: *Confessions* 10.1.1–10.4.6," *Augustiniana* 29 (1979): 280–303; John J. O'Meara, *The Young Augustine: An Introduction to the Confessions of St. Augustine* (London: Longmans, Green, 1980); Michele Pellegrino, *Le "Confessioni" di Sant'Agostino Studio introduttivo* (Rome: Editrice Studium, 1956); Luigo Pizzolato, *Le "Confessioni"*

di Sant'Agostino: Da biografia a "confessio" (Milan: Università Cattolica del S. Cuore, 1968); William A. Stephany, "Thematic Structure in Augustine's *Confessions*," *Augustinian Studies* 20 (1989): 129–42; Luc Verheijen, "The *Confessions*: Two Grids of Composition and of Reading," in *Augustine: Second Founder of the Faith* (ed. Joseph C. Schnaubelt, O.S.A., and Frederick van Fleteren; Collectanea Augustiniana; New York: Peter Lang, 1990), 177–201; E. Willeger, "Der Aufbau der *Konfessionen* Augustins," *Zeitschrift für die neutestamentliche Wissenschaft* 28 (1929): 81–106.

3. *Retract.* 2.6.1.
4. Luke 15:11–32. See *Confessions* 2.10.18; 3.6.11; 4.16.30. See also Leo C. Ferrari, "The Theme of the Prodigal Son in Augustine's *Confessions*," *Recherches Augustiniennes* 12 (1977): 105–18.
5. See Chadwick, *Conf.* 10.29.40, 202, n. 27. "This passage ('You command continence, grant what you command, and command what you will') was quoted in the ears of Pelagius, the British monk, by a bishop who appeared to be condoning the number of Christians whose sexual life appeared unregenerate. The incident marked the start of the Pelagian controversy, Pelagius being the unqualified advocate of an ethical perfectionism as a requirement of the gospel and the opponent of the passivity in Augustine's understanding of grace."
6. See Mark Vessey, "Book Review, *Saint Augustine: Confessions,* by Henry Chadwick," *Augustinian Studies* 24 (1994): 163–81. In his review, Vessey has noted the varying numbers of the books (1–10 or 1–13) of the *Confessions* published in English translations between 1620 and 1887. An edition comprising just Books 1–9 was published by C. Bigg in London in 1897. Vessey quotes from the 1887 version of the *Confessions* of Books 1–10: "The remaining three books in the Latin text consist entirely of a commentary upon the early chapters of Genesis, and are seldom published with the 'Confessions'" (181).
7. See Pellegrino, *Confessioni,* 204.
8. See my study, "The Hermeneutics of Conversion," in *Handbook of Early Christian Exegesis* (ed. Charles Kannengiesser; Leiden and Boston: Brill, 2003), XI.17.
9. See McMahon, *Prayerful Ascent,* 128. McMahon suggests the following broad structure for Book Ten: sections 1–5, knowing oneself in and through God; 6–39, the ascent to the origins; 40–41, summary; 42–69, the reconciler.
10. O'Donnell, *Augustine: Confessions,* 3:150–54.
11. See Ragnar Holte, *Béatitude et Sagesse: Saint Augustin et la problème de la fin de l'homme dans la philosophie ancienne* (Paris: Études Augustiniennes, 1962). Mary T. Clark, "The Happy Life," in *Augustine of Hippo: Selected Writings* (New York: Paulist Press, 1984).
12. See my study, "Singing the Psalm: Augustine and Athanasius on the Integration of the Self," in *The Whole and Divided Self: The Bible and Theological Anthropology* (ed. John McCarthy; New York: Crossroad, 1997), 115–29.
13. *Beat.* 34.
14. *On True Religion* (trans. J. H. S. Burleigh, in *Augustine: Earlier Writings* [Philadelphia: Westminster Press, 1953]), 225.
15. O'Donnell, *Augustine: Confessions,* 3:150.
16. N. Joseph Torchia, "St. Augustine's Triadic Interpretation of Iniquity in the *Confessions*," in *Augustine: Second Founder of the Faith* (ed. Joseph C. Schnaubelt and Frederick van Fleteren; Collectanea Augustiniana; New York: Peter Lang, 1990), 159–73.
17. The topic of Christ as Mediator in the thought of Augustine has been treated extensively. The following indicate lines of argumentation on this subject: Marianne Djuth, "Fulgentius of Ruspe and the *Initium Bonae Voluntatis,*" *Augustinian Studies* 20 (1989): 39–60, esp. 41; William Harmless, "Christ the Pediatrician:

Infant Baptism and Christological Imagery in the Pelagian Controversy," *Augustinian Studies* 28 (1997): 7–34; Madec, *Le Dieu d'Augustin,* 86; Albert VerTenilghen, "Jesus Christ: Source of Christian Humility," in *Augustine and the Bible* (ed. Pamela Bright; The Bible Through the Ages; Notre Dame, Ind.: University of Notre Dame Press, 1999), 301–12.

18. Chadwick, *Confessions,* 240, n. 27; cf. Plotinus, 3.7.11.41; Phil. 3:13. See also my study, "The Hermeneutics of Conversion" (n. 8, above).

19. In Book Thirteen, toward the end of his spiritual interpretation of Gen. 1:31 (NIV), "God saw all that he had made, and it was very good," Augustine says: "A body composed of its constituent parts, all of which are beautiful, is far more beautiful as a whole than when taken separately; the whole is made of their well-ordered harmony, though individually the constituent parts are also beautiful" (13.27.43).

Chapter 11: Book Eleven

1. Unless otherwise noted, all translations of the *Confessions* are from Maria Boulding in pt. I/1 of *The Works of Saint Augustine: A Translation for the 21st Century* (ed. John E. Rotelle; Hyde Park, N.Y.: New City Press, 1997).

2. See 1.2.2: "How shall I call upon my God, my God and my Lord, when by the very act of calling upon him I would be calling him into myself? How should the God who made heaven and earth come into me?"

3. Cf. Leo Ferrari, "Reconsiderando las Confesiones de Agustín. Treinta años de descrubrimientos," *Augustinus* 42 (1997): 279–96: "Therefore the conversion scene, as indeed the entire autobiography, is to be understood *figuratively,* a mode of understanding defended by Augustine himself in the case of spiritual writings, among which his immortal *Confessions* must surely be prominently numbered" (296). These "spiritual writings" are the Scriptures themselves (see note ad loc.). I would like to thank Professor Ferrari for providing me with the English manuscript of his article, from which I have quoted.

4. Augustine gives a more complete description of his project at the end of the preceding paragraph (11.2.4): "Let me hear the voice of praise, and drink from you, and contemplate the wonders of your law from the beginning when you made heaven and earth [Books Eleven and Twelve] to that everlasting reign when we shall be with you in your holy city [Book Thirteen]."

5. James J. O'Donnell (*Augustine: Confessions* [Oxford: Oxford University Press, 1992], 3:250), along with many others, has noted that Augustine stated that the *Confessions* has two parts, Books One to Ten "about myself," and Books Eleven to Thirteen "about Scripture," in his *Retractationes* (2.6.1), written some thirty years later. However, neither O'Donnell nor anyone else, to my knowledge, adverts to the fact that Augustine was clearly aware of this structure when he wrote the last three books.

6. See the opening prayer in the second book of Augustine's *Soliloquies,* where he expresses his desire to know only two things, God and himself. Robert J. O'Connell, *St. Augustine's Early Theory of Man, A.D. 386–391* (Cambridge, Mass.: Harvard University Press, 1968) points out, "the *noverim te, noverim me*—'to know thee, to know myself'—of the *Soliloquies* is fundamentally one desideratum and not two (*Sol* II, 1; cf. I, 7)" (218).

7. Augustine seems to have come close to resolving the issue in this way in his early works. See *Ord.* 2.19.50, "Therefore, if reason is immortal, and if I who analyze and synthesize all those things am reason, then that by which I am called mortal is not mine"; and *Ver. rel.* 46.89, "our real selves are not bodies." John C. Cavadini, "Time and Ascent in *Confessions* XI," in *Augustine: presbyter factus sum* (eds.

Joseph T. Lienhard, Earl C. Muller, and Roland J. Teske; Collectanea Augustiniana; New York: Peter Lang, 1993), 171–85, comments, "We do not 'fall' into time; we 'fall' by trying to escape time into eternity, by claiming that time is more than our own remembering, attending, and expecting as historical subjects defined by that remembering, attending, and expecting" (177).

8. See Mary T. Clark, "Augustine on Immutability and Mutability," *American Catholic Philosophical Quarterly* 74:1 (2000): 7–27: "But in recognizing God as the *Omega*, and the stimulus for human restlessness, Augustine discovered the temporal nature of humanness as a distinctive perfection. In other words, human beings are naturally historical. This does not mean that they have not been created according to a divine Idea. It means that although all creatures are subject to temporal development, only human beings are responsible for discovering the purpose of their existence and progressing toward it through time" (18).

9. John M. Quinn, O.S.A., "Four Faces of Time in St. Augustine," *Recherches augustiniennes* 26 (1992): 181–231; and Roland J. Teske, S.J., *Paradoxes of Time in Saint Augustine*, The Aquinas Lecture 1996 (Milwaukee, Wis.: Marquette University Press, 1996) are two prominent examples of scholars who believe that Augustine does intend a definition of time. Contrary to this view, Gerard O'Daly, *Augustine's Philosophy of Mind* (Berkeley, Calif.: University of California Press, 1987), 153, asserts that Augustine's "famous definition of time as a *distentio animi* cannot be a definition, but is, rather, a metaphor which evokes whatever accompanies or follows upon the cognitive act of measuring time."

10. Teske, *Paradoxes of Time*, 1–2.

11. See *On Genesis against the Manicheans*, Book One, chap. 2, where Augustine takes up this question and gives the same response.

12. God is outside time, yet God is present to all times and all times are in him. See *Conf.* 1.6.10, where Augustine comments on his own creation in time and contrasts his temporal beginning with God's eternity: "You are supreme and you do not change, and in you there is no 'today' that passes. Yet in you our 'today' does pass, inasmuch as all things exist in you, and would have no means even of passing away if you did not contain them."

13. See 12.29.40. In addition to temporal priority, Augustine identifies three other ways in which something can be said to be "before" another. God precedes all things because he is the source of their being. This, like logical priority, is atemporal. Interestingly, the priority that relates to preference (Augustine's example is the flower's existing for the sake of the fruit, which is therefore of higher value) reverses temporal precedence.

14. As Jaroslav Pelikan, *The Mystery of Continuity: Time and History, Memory and Eternity in the Thought of Saint Augustine* (Charlottesville, Va.: University Press of Virginia, 1986), 30, puts it, "the world was created not *before* time nor precisely *in* time, but *with* time, and therefore there could be no time without the created world."

15. Augustine's tone is unmistakably Socratic as he begins the treatment of time: "What, then, is time? If no one asks me, I know; if I want to explain it to someone who asks me, I do not know" (11.14.17). Like Socrates, he is taking a familiar reality, of which people generally think themselves knowledgeable, and shows both that it is in fact very difficult to understand and that the customary belief that passes for knowledge is at best inaccurate and often misleading.

16. Although the meaning I give to the term "moral" should be clear from my usage, it seems advisable to point out that I am not using it evaluatively, as John Quinn does. In what follows, the word "moral" refers very broadly to intelligent agency, especially human agency but not excluding angelic. Augustine distinguishes moral evil from natural evil by putting on one side all that comes from us,

including our feelings and dispositions, and on the other all that comes from outside us, including the suffering and injustice inflicted on us by other human
beings. See William Babcock, "Augustine on Sin and Moral Agency," *Journal of
Religious Ethics* 16 (1988): 28–55; and John Rist, *Augustine: Ancient Thought Baptized* (Cambridge: Cambridge University Press, 1994), 191–99.

17. The most famous of these accusers is Bertrand Russell, *Human Knowledge: Its
Scope and Limits* (New York: Simon & Schuster, 1948), 212. Another example
is Charles Frankel, *The Pleasures of Philosophy* (New York: Norton, 1972), 197,
236, 237 (cited from John M. Quinn, "Four Faces of Time in St. Augustine,"
181).

18. O'Donnell, *Augustine: Confessions,* 3:280–81, refers the issue of truthfulness in
these chaps. 17 and 18 to Augustine's own narrative. And Augustine does indeed
allude to his own childhood's presence in his memory to illustrate his point. Nevertheless, Book Eleven is scriptural exegesis, and the truthfulness of Scripture
both accounts for the dramatic quality in Augustine's address to God specifically
as his "hope" and is more congruent with Augustine's concerns. Augustine wrote
his treatise on lying (395, just two years before he began writing the *Confessions*)
precisely to counter any suggestion that the authors of Scripture might have lied
on a matter of faith or morals. See Letter 28 (to Jerome) and the final paragraph
of Augustine's treatise *On Lying.*

19. In "Time, the Heaven of Heavens, and Memory in Augustine's *Confessions,*"
Augustinian Studies 22 (1991): 191–205, Donald L. Ross gives an ingenious
argument that Augustine held that "time really exists, but it is a dimension that
is present all at once. For Augustine it is the sequentialization of time that is due
to the human mind" (197). Ross has Augustine distinguish genuine, tenseless
time from the successiveness of time as we experience it. It seems to me that
Augustine's discussion of time would be virtually pointless were Ross's interpretation correct. For a convincing refutation of Ross's arguments, see Michael
Futch, "Augustine on the Successiveness of Time," *Augustinian Studies* 33 (2002):
17–38.

20. This idea emerges more clearly in a literal translation of the Latin of 11.28.38.
When he recites a song, Augustine says, "Before I begin, my expectation is
stretched [forward] toward the whole song, but when I have begun, as much of
the song as I will have plucked [at any stage in my recital] from that expectation,
into that much is my memory stretched [backward], and the life of this my action
[*vita huius actionis meae*] is distended [*distenditur*] into memory because of the
part I have recited and into expectation because of the part I am about to recite."
His attention (*attentio mea*) to the impression of the song in his soul is the enact-
ment of his ability to hold past and future together in the present. The mind's
attention to its own activity in stretching forward to the future and backward
toward the past is the dynamism of time.

21. See 11.26.33: "Am I not making a truthful confession to you when I praise you
for my ability to measure time?"

22. See Robert A. Markus, "Signs, Communication, and Communities in Augustine's *De doctrina christiana,*" in *De Doctrina Christiana: A Classic of Western Culture* (ed. Duane W. H. Arnold and Pamela Bright; Christianity and Judaism in
Antiquity 9; Notre Dame, Ind.: University of Notre Dame Press, 1995), 97–108:
"To seek meaning is to enact transcendence" (102).

23. See 11.27.36: "In you, my mind, I measure periods of time. Don't interrupt me
with the assertion that time exists. Don't interrupt with the confusion of your
impressions. In you, I say, I measure periods of time." This might also be an example of (rather heavy) Augustinian humor: The mind's confused impressions (*affectiones*), which come from habits formed in time, prevent it from understanding

that the ability to form temporal impressions (*affectiones*) is the basis for measuring time and, thus, evidence of the mind's transcendence of temporality.

24. Augustine's most famous statement of this theme is in Book Nineteen, chap. 26 of *The City of God* (trans. R. W. Dyson; Cambridge: Cambridge University Press, 1998), 961: "Thus, the virtues which the mind seems to possess, and by which it governs the body and the vices so that it may obtain and keep whatever it desires, are really themselves vices, and not virtues at all, if they do not have reference to God. Some, indeed, suppose that the virtues are true and honourable even when they have reference only to themselves and are sought for no other end. Then, however, they are puffed up and proud, and so are to be adjudged vices rather than virtues."

25. James Wetzel, *Augustine and the Limits of Virtue* (Cambridge: Cambridge University Press, 1992), 35.

26. The idea of having "leapt down [or "burst asunder": *dissilui*] into times whose order I do not know" seems to be evidence for the idea that Augustine's *Confessions* are the story of a soul that is seeking release from a temporal world alien to its true nature, as contended by Robert J. O'Connell, *St. Augustine's Confessions: The Odyssey of Soul* (Cambridge, Mass.: Harvard University Press, 1969), esp. 11, 142–44. However, in its context this phrase refers to the immediately preceding discussion of time, and specifically Augustine's exemplification of the tendency to find permanent significance in passing things.

27. Cf. 11.9.11, alluding to Rom. 8:24–25: "We are already saved, but in hope, and in patience we look forward to the fulfillment of your promises."

28. I am here building on the insights of Charles T. Mathewes, "The Liberation of Questioning in Augustine's *Confessions*," *Journal of the American Academy of Religion* 70 (2002): 539–60.

Chapter 12: Book Twelve

1. I have deliberately maintained the Latin in my title since the English word *confession* tends automatically to suggest a meaning that is not Augustine's primary intention with the word. *Confessio* in Latin means "acknowledgment," with a threefold "acknowledgment" under way in the *Confessions*: of praise, of faith, and of sin. Exegesis (interpreting the Scriptures) for Augustine is primarily an "acknowledgment" of praise and of faith; it flows from faith in God and leads to praise of God. Though the confession of sin is an integral part of such "acknowledgments," as is clear throughout the *Confessions*, it never supersedes the confession of praise and faith.

2. In preparing this essay I have consulted the many English translations of the *Confessions* that abound: F. J. Sheed's *The Confessions of St. Augustine* (London and New York: Sheed & Ward, 1943), Henry Chadwick's *St. Augustine: Confessions* (Oxford: Oxford University Press, 1998), and Maria Boulding's *The Confessions*, pt. I/1 of *The Works of Saint Augustine: A Translation for the 21st Century* (ed. John E. Rotelle; Hyde Park, N.Y.: New City Press, 1997) in particular. Translation is always an "act of interpretation," a way of understanding a text, and in that sense also "exegesis." I have sometimes chosen one of these translations when it says exactly what I think Augustine is saying. More often I have allowed their texts to serve as a dialogue partner for my own translations. I will place in parenthesis after a translation the author of a version if I have quoted it exactly.

3. Throughout this essay I will make reference to a number of authors who have helped convince me of the importance of Scripture not only for the narrative text of the *Confessions*, but especially for the overall purpose and intention of the work itself. However, the volume of literature dedicated to Augustine's *Confessions* is

enormous. Those interested in further study should pursue the annual Augustine bibliography published in *Revue des Études Augustiniennes*; see also Richard Severson, *The Confessions of Saint Augustine: An Annotated Bibliography of Modern Criticism, 1888–1995*, Bibliographical Indexes in Religious Studies 40 (Westport, Conn.: Greenwood Press, 1996).

4. As Augustine does so often with the Latin, he plays with the same word: *indigna* for the Scriptures, *dignitas* for Cicero.

5. At this point in ancient Christianity the Old Testament version that was most common was a Greek version of the original Hebrew called the Septuagint and usually indicated by the Roman numerals for 70, LXX. It was the source of the Latin versions of the Old Testament read by Augustine. St. Jerome championed a return to the Hebrew Old Testament and undertook a new Latin translation based upon it, a controversial move at the time which offended many people and was a source of tensions between Jerome and Augustine. Augustine laments in his *Christian Instruction* (*Doctr. chr.* 2.11.16), a work virtually contemporary with the *Confessions*, the plethora of Latin versions and the unreliability they generate.

6. Regarding the Latin of Augustine's *Confessions*, see "Le Style des Confessions," in *Les Confessions, Libres I–VII* (text from the edition of M. Skutella, introduction and notes by A. Solignac, trans. E. Tréhorel and G. Bouissou; Bibliothèque Augustinienne, Oeuvres de Saint Augustin 13, 207–33; Paris: Institut d'Études Augustiniennes, 1998); Melchior Verheijen, O.E.S.A., *Eloquentia Pedisequa: Observations sur le style des Confessions de saint Augustin* (Latinitas Christianorum Primaeva, Studia ad sermonem latinum Christianum pertinentia, Fasciculus Decimus; Nijmegen, Netherlands: Dekker & van de Vegt N.V., 1949).

7. See J. Kevin Coyle, "Mani, Manicheism," in *Augustine through the Ages: An Encyclopedia* (ed. Allan D. Fitzgerald, O.S.A., et al.; Grand Rapids: Wm. B. Eerdmans, 1999), 520–25.

8. Its presence is often overlooked by commentators, exceptions being the Boulding and John K. Ryan (*The Confessions of St. Augustine* [New York: Doubleday, 1960]) translations.

9. Matt. 7:7–8 finds allusion again at 12.12.15, 12.15.22, and 12.24.33.

10. I place "Catholic" in quotation marks to remind us that in his day this term meant "universal," the "great church," and should not be confused with later more "restrictive" uses of the term.

11. For a brief description of Donatism as well as a current bibliography, see Robert Markus, "Donatus, Donatism"; Pamela Bright, "Donatist Bishops"; and Maureen A. Tilley "*Donatistas post conlationem, Contra*," in Fitzgerald et al., eds., *Augustine through the Ages: An Encyclopedia*, 284–87, 281–84, 281.

12. In this regard, see n. 3 above.

13. See W. H. C. Frend, "The Donatist Church and St. Paul," in *Le epistole paoline nei Manichei, i Donatisti e il primo Agostino* (Rome: Instituto Patristico Augustinianum, 1989), 85–123; Maria Grazia Mara, "Le *Confessioni* di Agostino: una confluenza di raggiunte convinzioni, *Augustinianum* XXXVI/2 (1996): 495–509; Maureen A. Tilley, *The Bible in Christian North Africa: The Donatist World* (Minneapolis: Fortress Press, 1997).

14. The very word comes from the Latin *tradere*, which means to "hand over."

15. See Mara, "Le *Confessioni* di Agostino," 509.

16. *Fund.* 5. It is intended to be provocative, but must not be pushed beyond what Augustine intends. He is not setting up the Scriptures over and against the church, but simply acknowledging that the Scriptures come "out of" the church and are read "in the church." For Augustine, it is as unthinkable to consider the Scriptures without the church as it would be to consider the church without the Scriptures.

17. See Maria Grazia Mara, "Introduzione alle *Confessioni* di Agostino D'Ippona," in *La "Genesi" nelle "Confessioni"* (Atti della giornata di studio su S. Agostino, Roma, 6 dicembre 1994; Rome: Academia Latinitati Fovendae, 1996), 15.

18. *Retract.* 2.6.1. *In eum excitant humanum intellectum et affectum* are his exact words in the *Retractationes*.

19. Throughout this essay I will be following Augustine's enumeration of the Psalms, one which was based on the Greek Septuagint version of the Old Testament, rather than the Hebrew. What this means in practice is that Augustine's numbering of the Psalms will often be one behind the Hebrew version. Thus Ps. 118 for Augustine would be Ps. 119 in the Hebrew Bible.

20. Augustine and his close friend and superior, Bishop Aurelius of Carthage, are at the forefront of this "Catholic" reform movement.

21. This seems to be one area of concern that united both communities. Possidius, Augustine's biographer, recounts how both the Catholics and Donatists called upon Augustine to refute a visiting Manichean preacher who came to Hippo Regius: *Vita Augustini* 6.2.4.

22. See especially Augustine's *To Simplicianus* (*Ad Simplicianum*).

23. It is important to note that Augustine "begins" writing this work, since he will not finish it until some three decades later.

24. There is not yet total scholarly consensus regarding how long it took Augustine to compose the *Confessions*. The most common opinion extends the writing over some four years, 397–401.

25. *Quaestiones evangeliorum* (*Questions on the Gospels*), *De consensu evangelistarum* (*Harmony of the Gospels*), *De opere monachorum* (*The Work of Monks*), *Contra Faustum Manichaeum* (*Against Faustus the Manichean*), *Contra Felicem* (*Against Felix*), *De natura boni contra Manichaeos* (*The Nature of the Good*), *De catechizandis rudibus* (*Catechizing the Uninstructed*). For a chronological listing of Augustine's works with English and Latin titles see Mary T. Clark, *Augustine* (Outstanding Christian Thinkers Series; London: Geoffrey Chapman, 1994), xii–xix.

26. *On Genesis Literally Interpreted* (*De Genesi ad litteram*).

27. See the multivolume *St. Augustine: Sermons* (The Works of St. Augustine, A Translation for the 21st Century, vols. III/1–11; translation and notes, Edmund Hill, O.P.; ed. John E. Rotelle; Brooklyn, N.Y.: New City Press, 1990–).

28. Prologue 1, *Augustine: Teaching Christianity, De Doctrina Christiana* (The Works of St. Augustine, A Translation for the 21st Century, vol. I/11; introduction, translation, and notes, Edmund Hill, O.P.; ed. John E. Rotelle; Hyde Park, N.Y.: New City Press, 1996).

29. O'Donnell proposes "the Word of God" as the subject of Book Twelve, but in a specifically Trinitarian sense: James J. O'Donnell, *Augustine: Confessions* (3 vols.; Oxford: Oxford University Press, 1992), 3:300.

30. For the importance of the "dialogue" in ancient philosophy and education, see Pierre Hadot, *Philosophy as a Way of Life: Spiritual Exercises from Socrates to Foucault* (ed. Arnold I. Davidson; trans. Michael Chase; Oxford: Blackwell, 1995), 89–93.

31. See *Against the Academics* (*Contra Academicos*), *The Happy Life* (*De beata vita*), *On Order* (*De ordine*), *Soliloquies* (*Soliloquiorum libri II*).

32. Who exactly are these *contradictores*? They are not Manicheans, since they believe in an "inspired" Moses. They would seem not to be Donatists, since Augustine leaves the impression that they are "within" his own church community. Pépin suggests that they refer to some "concrete personages" but Augustine leaves us little clue regarding their specific identity. Jean Pépin, "Le Livre XII des *Confessions* ou exégèse et confession," in *"Le Confessioni" di Agostino D'Ippona*, Libri X–XIII

(Lectio Augustini 4, Settimana Agostiniana Pavese; Palermo, Italy: Edizioni "Augustinus," 1987), 73. The reader will also note the similarity of title between this essay and Pépin's. Though while we both agree on the important link between "confession" and exegesis, we both develop our theses differently.

33. That is literally what Augustine calls his "occupation" in Milan as Imperial Rhetor or Orator: *cathedra mendacii*, 9.2.4.

34. See Paul Ricoeur, *Interpretation Theory: Discourse and the Surplus of Meaning* (preface by T. Klein; Fort Worth, Tex.: Texas Christian University Press, 1976).

35. *Doctr. chr.* 1.36.

36. See 7.10.16. Augustine perhaps most dramatically affirms this intimate link between love and truth in the course of one of his sermons "against the Donatists": *Victoria veritatis est caritas*—"truth's victory is love," *s.* 358.1.

37. In this regard, see Gaetano Lettieri, "La *Genesi* nel Libro XII delle *Confessiones*: ermeneutica, creazione predestinazione," in *La "Genesi" nelle "Confessioni"* (Atti della giornata di studio su S. Agostino, Roma, 6 dicembre 1994; Rome: Academia Latinitati Fovendae, 1996), 57–79.

Chapter 13: Book Thirteen

1. The Hebrew Bible and the Vulgate do not record that God saw his second act as "good." Augustine's Old Latin Version follows the Septuagint in adding to Gen. 1:8, "And God saw that it was good." Throughout I am using Chadwick's translation of *Confessions* (Oxford: Oxford University Press, 1998), unless otherwise noted.

2. This section abbreviates pp. 38–116 in my book, *Augustine's Prayerful Ascent: An Essay on the Literary Form of the* Confessions (Athens, Ga.: University of Georgia Press, 1989).

3. Robert M. Durling, "Platonism and Poetic Form: Augustine's *Confessions*," in *Jewish Culture and the Hispanic World: Essays in Memory of Joseph H. Silverman* (ed. Samuel G. Armistead and Mishael M. Caspi, in collaboration with Murray Baumgarten; Newark, Del.: Juan de la Cuesta, 2001), 179–190, esp. 185–86. Durling showed me this work in 1982, and it has been crucial to the development of my thinking on Augustine.

4. With similar imagery, Dante places the theologians in the sphere of the sun in his *Paradiso*.

5. On the contrast between Faustus and Ambrose, see D. Romanick Baldwin, "Models of Teaching and Models of Learning in the *Confessions*," in *Augustine and Liberal Education* (ed. Kim Paffenroth and Kevin L. Hughes; Aldershot, U.K.: Ashgate Publishing, 2000), 15–23.

6. A. Solignac, "Introduction" to *Les Confessions* (Bibliothèque Augustinienne 13; Paris: Desclée de Brouwer, 1962), 23–24, my translation.

7. *Ver. rel.* 39, 72; my translation.

8. My treatment of the ascent to higher and prior categories of being abbreviates *Augustine's Prayerful Ascent*, 117–41. The analysis derives from Kenneth Burke, *The Rhetoric of Religion: Studies in Logology* (Berkeley, Calif.: University of California Press, 1970), 141–57. A different yet compatible analysis of the work's ascent to unity is R. D. Crouse, "'*Recurrens in te unum*': The Pattern of St. Augustine's *Confessions*," *Studia Patristica* 14 (Texte und Untersuchungen 117; Berlin: Akademie Verlag, 1976), 389–92.

9. *The Shepherd of Hermas*, Vision 2, 4, 1: Patrologia Graeca 2, 899. Clement of Alexandria, *Paed.* 1, 6, 27: Patrologia Graeca 8, 281. For these and other relevant texts, see the *Catechism of the Catholic Church* (Washington, D.C.: United States Catholic Conference, 1994), par. 760.

10. I am grateful to Todd Breyfogle, whose conversation led me to understand the "interior progress" of Books Eleven and Twelve.

11. See William A. Stephany, "Thematic Structure in Augustine's *Confessions,*" *Augustinian Studies* 20 (1989): 129–42. My discussion draws from pp. 131–35.

12. Frederick Van Fleteren, for instance, has published articles on the "ascent of the soul" in Augustine, yet in his entry on the *Confessiones* for *Augustine through the Ages: An Encyclopedia* (ed. Allan D. Fitzgerald, O. S. A., et al.; Grand Rapids: Eerdmans, 1999) does not describe this pattern in the work as a whole. Since this is a major entry in an important new reference work, and Van Fleteren is one of the associate editors, it seems to be scholarly consensus that such a pattern does not structure the whole *Confessions.*

13. For a summary of scholarship and the bibliography on this issue, see *Augustine's Prayerful Ascent*, xi–xii.

14. Peter Brown, *Augustine of Hippo* (Berkeley, Calif.: University of California Press, 1967), 166–67.

15. Solignac, "Introduction," 12–13, my translation.

16. G. Boissou, "Le Style," ch. 7 in Solignac's "Introduction," 223, my translation.

17. My discussion of Augustine the narrator and Augustine the author abbreviates *Augustine's Prayerful Ascent*, 1–21.

18. See William E. Mann, "The Theft of the Pears," *Apeiron* 12 (1978): 51–58.

For Further Reading

Bonner, Gerald. *St. Augustine of Hippo: Life and Controversies*. Second edition. Norwich, U.K.: Canterbury Press, 1986.
 A helpful introduction to the polemical context of much of Augustine's writing, with clear presentations on the Manichees, the Donatists, and the Pelagians.

Bourke, Vernon J. *Augustine's Quest of Wisdom: Life and History of the Bishop of Hippo*. Milwaukee, Wis.: Bruce Publishing, 1944.
 A good starting place for understanding Augustine's thought on major theological and philosophical questions.

Brown, Peter. *Augustine of Hippo: A Biography*. Revised Edition with a New Epilogue. Berkeley, Calif.: University of California Press, 2000. Original edition, 1967.
 Engagingly written and comprehensive in scope, this is by far the most frequently cited work on Augustine.

Burnaby, John. *Amor Dei: A Study of the Religion of St. Augustine*. London: Hodder & Stoughton, 1938.
 Until the appearance of Brown's biography, this was the standard introduction to his thought in English. Still valuable, and a delight to read.

Chadwick, Henry. *Augustine*. Past Masters Series. Oxford: Oxford University Press, 1986.
 Very brief and authoritative, this is the most widely available and accessible introduction to Augustine in print.

Clark, Mary T. *Augustine*. Outstanding Christian Thinkers Series. London: Geoffrey Chapman, 1994.
 A thematic introduction to Augustine's thought by a leading scholar.

Fitzgerald, Allan D., O.S.A., et al., eds. *Augustine through the Ages: An Encyclopedia*. Grand Rapids, Mich.: Wm. B. Eerdmans, 1999.
 Contains articles on virtually every topic relevant to the study of Augustine, as well as entries on all his works.

Mallard, William. *Language and Love: Introducing Augustine's Religious Thought through the* Confessions *Story*. University Park, Pa.: Pennsylvania State University Press, 1994.
 A very clearly written guide that relates the narrative of the *Confessions* to the basic themes in Augustine's thought.

Miles, Margaret. *Desire and Delight: A New Reading of Augustine's* Confessions. New York: Crossroad, 1992.
 A thought-provoking book that uses Augustine's own account of his emotional life to challenge the attitudes he expresses toward his relationships with others.

O'Connell, Robert J. *St. Augustine's Confessions: The Odyssey of Soul.* Cambridge, Mass.: Harvard University Press, 1969.
A highly influential and controversial reading of Augustine as a Neo-Platonist whose life story exemplifies the travails of soul alienated from itself in matter.

O'Donnell, James J. *Augustine.* Twayne's World Authors Series. Boston: Twayne, 1985.
An excellent short introduction to Augustine's life and thought. Available online: http://ccat.sas.upenn.edu:80/jod/augustine.html

———. *Augustine: Confessions.* 3 vols. Oxford: Oxford University Press, 1992.
Although intended for specialists, this magisterial commentary contains much helpful guidance for nonspecialists.

O'Meara, J. J. *The Young Augustine: The Growth of St. Augustine's Mind up to His Conversion.* London: Longmans, Green, 1954.
An insightful attempt to provide a more detailed account of Augustine's early life.

Pelikan, Jaroslav. *The Mystery of Continuity: Time and History, Memory and Eternity in the Thought of Saint Augustine.* Charlottesville, Va.: University Press of Virginia, 1986.
A superb theological introduction to themes central for understanding the last four books of the *Confessions*.

Rist, John. *Augustine: Ancient Thought Baptized.* Cambridge: Cambridge University Press, 1994.
Philosophically astute and theologically informed, the best general critique of Augustine's thought.

Starnes, Colin. *Augustine's Conversion: A Guide to the Argument of* Confessions *I–IX.* Waterloo, Ont.: Wilfrid Laurier University Press, 1990.
An accessible guide to the structure and content of the first nine books, with detailed notes for the specialist.

Stock, Brian. *Augustine the Reader: Meditation, Self-Knowledge, and the Ethics of Interpretation.* Cambridge, Mass.: Harvard University Press, 1996.
A very detailed analysis of some key texts, centering on the *Confessions*.

Contributors

Todd Breyfogle received his B.A. from Colorado College in Classics-History-Politics (1988). At Oxford University he earned a second B.A. in Ancient and Modern History (1990) and an M.St. in Theology (1991). He graduated from the Committee on Social Thought at the University of Chicago, where his dissertation analyzed the intellect and will in St. Augustine's political thought. He is presently Director of the University Honors Program at the University of Denver and teaches in the program. He is the editor and a contributor to *Literary Imagination, Ancient and Modern: Essays in Honor of David Grene* (Chicago: University of Chicago Press, 1999), as well as a contributor to *Augustine through the Ages: An Encyclopedia* (ed. Allan D. Fitzgerald, O.S.A., et al.; Grand Rapids, Mich.: Eerdmans, 1999), and to the *Oxford Classical Dictionary* (3rd ed.; Oxford: Oxford University Press, 1996). He has also presented numerous papers on Augustine to learned societies.

Pamela Bright is Professor of Historical Theology at Concordia University, Montreal, Quebec, Canada. She is the author of *The Book of Rules of Tyconius: Its Purpose and Inner Logic* (Notre Dame, Ind.: University of Notre Dame Press, 1988), the coeditor of *De Doctrina Christiana: A Classic of Western Civilization* (Notre Dame, Ind.: University of Notre Dame Press, 1995), and the translator of *Augustine and the Bible* (Notre Dame, Ind.: University of Notre Dame Press, 1999). Her articles on Augustine have appeared in *Studia Patristica*, and in encyclopedias such as *The Encyclopedia of Early Christianity* (ed. E. Ferguson et al.; New York: Garland Publishing, 1990), and *Augustine through the Ages: An Encyclopedia* (ed. Allan D. Fitzgerald, O.S.A., et al.; Grand Rapids, Mich.: Eerdmans, 1999).

Phillip Cary is Director of the Philosophy Program at Eastern University, where he is also Scholar in Residence at the Templeton Honors College and Associate Professor of Philosophy. He is the author of *Augustine's Invention of the Inner Self: The Legacy of a Christian Platonist* (Oxford: Oxford University Press, 2000), as well as articles on Augustine in journals such as *Augustinian Studies*, and in *Augustine through the Ages: An Encyclopedia* (ed. Allan D. Fitzgerald, O.S.A., et al.; Grand Rapids, Mich.: Eerdmans, 1999). His audio- and videotaped lectures, *Augustine: Philosopher and Saint*, have been published by the Teaching Company.

John C. Cavadini is Associate Professor of Theology at the University of Notre Dame. He is the author of *The Last Christology of the West: Adoptionism in Spain and Gaul, 785–820* (Philadelphia: University of Pennsylvania Press, 1993). He was the book review editor of *Augustinian Studies* and has also edited the volumes *Gregory the Great: A Symposium* (Notre Dame, Ind.: University of Notre Dame Press, 1995) and *Miracles in Jewish and Christian Antiquity: Imagining Truth* (Notre Dame, Ind.: University of Notre Dame Press, 1999). His articles on Augustine have appeared in *Theological Studies* and in collections such as *Augustine: presbyter factus sum* (New York: Peter Lang, 1993) and *The Limits of Ancient Christianity* (Ann Arbor, Mich.: University of Michigan Press, 1999). He is presently working on a theological commentary on *The City of God*.

Frederick J. Crosson, Cavanaugh Professor of Humanities Emeritus at the University of Notre Dame, teaches undergraduate courses in the Program of Liberal Studies, and graduate Philosophy courses. A former dean of the college and national president of Phi Beta Kappa, he has been a French Government Fellow at the Sorbonne and a Belgian-American Foundation Fellow at the University of Louvain. He has published studies of Augustine's early works *On the Teacher, The Usefulness of Believing*, and the *Confessions*, in addition to publications in areas ranging from artificial intelligence to political theory.

Leo C. Ferrari, B.S. (Sydney), L.Ph., Ph.D. (Laval), is Professor Emeritus at Saint Thomas University in Fredericton, New Brunswick, Canada. With his unusual twin background in modern science and medieval studies, he has published dozens of distinctively different studies on Augustine and his *Confessions*. Also, with the help of Prof. Rodney H. Cooper (Faculty of Computer Science, University of New Brunswick), he has produced for the first time complete concordances to Augustine's *Confessiones* and his *De Ciuitate Dei* (Georg Olms Verlag AG, Germany). Other concordances to Augustine's earlier works are in preparation.

Robert P. Kennedy is currently an Assistant Professor in the Department of Religious Studies at St. Francis Xavier University in Antigonish, Nova Scotia, Canada. He received his doctorate in moral theology from the University of Notre Dame in 1997. The title of his dissertation was "The Ethics of Language: An Augustinian Critique of Modern Approaches to the Morality of Lying." He has contributed to *Augustinian Studies* and to *Augustine through the Ages: An Encyclopedia* (ed. Allan D. Fitzgerald, O.S.A., et al.; Grand Rapids, Mich.: Eerdmans, 1999). His current projects include translating a collection of Augustine's moral and ascetical works and research on Augustine's theory of the will.

Thomas F. Martin, O.S.A., is Associate Professor of Theology/Religious Studies at Villanova University. His particular area of study involves the biblical and spiritual thought of Augustine. He has lectured on Augustine in the United States, Italy, England, the Philippines, Australia, Latin America, and Africa. He has published articles on Augustine in *Studia Patristica, Downside Review, Journal of Early Christian Studies, Vigiliae Christianae,* and *Augustinian Studies.* His monograph *Rhetoric and Exegesis in Augustine's Interpretation of Romans 7:24–25a* was recently published by Edwin Mellen Press (2001).

Charles T. Mathewes is Assistant Professor of Religious Studies at the University of Virginia, where he teaches courses in Theology, Ethics, and Culture. He is the author of *Evil and the Augustinian Tradition* (Cambridge: Cambridge University Press, 2001). His recent articles relating to Augustine have appeared in *Journal of Religious Ethics* and *Modern Theology.* He is currently working on a book manuscript attempting to develop an Augustinian approach to political and social life, provisionally entitled *During the World: Theology, Politics, Culture.*

Robert McMahon is professor of English at Louisiana State University and a scholar of medieval and Renaissance comparative literature. He is the author of *Augustine's Prayerful Ascent: An Essay on the Literary Form of the* Confessions (Athens, Ga.: University of Georgia Press, 1989), and *The Two Poets of* Paradise Lost (Baton Rouge, La.: Louisiana State University Press, 1998), as well as articles on Ezra Pound, Shakespeare, Dante, Boethius, George Herbert, and Eric Voegelin.

Kim Paffenroth is Assistant Professor of Religious Studies at Iona College. He has previously taught at Villanova University, Eastern College, the University of Notre Dame, and Southwestern Michigan College. He is the author of *Judas: Images of the Lost Disciple* (Louisville, Ky.: Westminster John Knox Press, 2001), and a coeditor and contributor to *Augustine and Liberal Education* (Aldershot, U.K.: Ashgate Publishing, 2000). He is the book review editor of *Augustinian Studies* and has also published articles on Augustine in *Downside Review, Augustinian Studies,* and *Harvard Theological Review,* as well as translations of several of his works, including *Soliloquies* (Hyde Park, N.Y.: New City Press, 2000). He is currently working on a book manuscript that will trace the development of the idea and practice of Wisdom through the Bible, Augustine, and Pascal, as well as its expression in great works of literature.

Eric Plumer has received degrees from Oxford University and the University of Notre Dame. He has contributed articles to *Augustine through the Ages: An Encyclopedia* (ed. Allan D. Fitzgerald, O.S.A., et al.; Grand Rapids, Mich.: Eerdmans, 1999), as well as presented papers on Augustine to learned societies. His book *Augustine's Commentary on Galatians* is forthcoming from Oxford University Press. He is presently an Assistant Professor of Theology at the University of Scranton.

James Wetzel is an Associate Professor of Philosophy and Religion at Colgate University. He has received degrees from Princeton University and Columbia University. He is the author of *Augustine and the Limits of Virtue* (Cambridge:

Cambridge University Press, 1992). His articles on Augustine have appeared in journals such as *Harvard Theological Review*, *Religious Studies*, and *Augustinian Studies*, and in collections such as *Augustine: From Rhetor to Theologian* (ed. Joanne McWilliam; Waterloo, Ont.: Wilfrid Laurier University Press, 1992), and *Augustine and His Critics* (ed. Robert Dodaro and George Lawless; London and New York: Routledge, 2000).

Scripture Index

Subject Index

Prepared with the assistance of Brandon Vaidyanathan